T5-CVD-886

CHICAGO PUBLIC LIBRARY
HAROLD WASHINGTON LIBRARY CENTER
R0048035984

BJ 1291 .H673 1985

Hourani, George Fadlo.

Reason and tradition in Islamic ethics

DATE			

SOCIAL SCIENCES & HISTORY DIVISION

THE CHICAGO PUBLIC LIBRARY
EDUCATION & PHILOSOPHY

© THE BAKER & TAYLOR CO.

REASON AND TRADITION IN ISLAMIC ETHICS

REASON AND TRADITION IN ISLAMIC ETHICS

GEORGE F. HOURANI

FORMERLY DISTINGUISHED PROFESSOR EMERITUS OF
ISLAMIC CULTURE AND THOUGHT,
STATE UNIVERSITY OF NEW YORK AT BUFFALO

The right of the University of Cambridge to print and sell all manner of books was granted by Henry VIII in 1534. The University has printed and published continuously since 1584.

CAMBRIDGE UNIVERSITY PRESS
CAMBRIDGE
LONDON NEW YORK NEW ROCHELLE
MELBOURNE SYDNEY

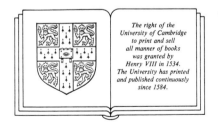

Published by the Press Syndicate of the University of Cambridge
The Pitt Building, Trumpington Street, Cambridge CB2 1RP
32 East 57th Street, New York, NY 10022, USA
10 Stamford Road, Oakleigh, Melbourne 3166, Australia

© Cambridge University Press 1985

First published 1985

Printed in Great Britain by the

University Press, Cambridge

Library of Congress catalogue card number: 85–448

British Library Cataloguing in Publication Data

Hourani, George F.
Reason and tradition in Islamic ethics
1. Islam
I. Title
297 BP161.2

ISBN 0 521 26712 9

BJ
1291
.H673
1985

480 35984

UP

TO LELLO

CONTENTS

PREFACE

This book is based on articles, published in orientalist journals during the last twenty-five years and recently revised to make a consistent book and bring it up to date in a few places.

The first acknowledgement I should like to make is to my wife for her patience and her encouragement of my writing over such a long period.

Next, I wish to thank the institutions which have financed the free time which made these studies possible: namely, the University of Michigan and the State University of New York for sabbatical leaves and various research grants, as well as the Ford Foundation and the Simon E. Guggenheim Foundation which allowed me to extend sabbaticals on two occasions.

Thirdly, I acknowledge permissions granted to republish in book form the articles held in copyright by the following publishers: Scribner and Sons for articles in the *Dictionary of the Middle Ages* (2); the SUNY Press (Albany) (2); *The Muslim World* (3); Éditions de l'Institut Supérieur de Philosophie (Louvain); *International Journal of Middle East Studies*; Bruno Cassirer (Oxford); Caravan Press (Delmar, New York); *Journal of the American Oriental Society*; *Studia Islamica* (2); and *Bulletin of the School of Oriental and African Studies* (London). Full references to the original articles are given after this Preface, showing slight variations in the titles of three articles.

Fourthly, I am grateful to several secretaries at the University of Michigan and the State University of New York at Buffalo for their work in typing these articles. Special thanks go to Mrs Judith Wagner of the Department of Philosophy, SUNY at Buffalo, who has typed most of them, as well as the difficult revised notes for the book, with superior professional skill.

Lastly, it is a pleasure to recognize the constructive thought of Jonathan Sinclair-Wilson, Philosophy Editor for Cambridge University Press, in suggesting ways to make the articles into a coherent book. Credit is due also to the meticulous work of the sub-editors and printers in producing an accurate text.

GEORGE F. HOURANI

Amherst, NY
July 1984

FOREWORD

These sixteen articles on various aspects of classical Islamic thought have an underlying unity of theme, aptly summed up in the book's title. They form a good part of their author's important contribution to the study of Islamic thought. Most of these articles have been published during the past three decades in different learned journals, in encyclopedias and books containing articles by other scholars. Their inclusion (with some revision) in one volume not only makes them more accessible, but also endows the collection with a historical perspective. The author has arranged the articles as closely as possible in the chronological order of their subjects.

The volume was already in the press when its author, George Fadlou Hourani, died of a heart ailment. It is the last gift of a scholar who had dedicated his life to research and teaching. Born in England in 1913 of Lebanese ancestry, he read philosophy and classics at Oxford, graduating in 1936. His graduate studies in the languages and history of the Near East were undertaken at Princeton University where he obtained his doctorate in 1939. His teaching career began in Jerusalem, Palestine, during the British mandate, where he taught classics, logic and the history of philosophy at the Government Arab College from 1939 until the end of the mandate in 1948. He then returned to England with his Egyptian wife, Celeste, where he spent two years in writing and research. He resumed his teaching career at the University of Michigan where he taught from 1950 until 1967 and helped build its Department of Near Eastern Studies. From 1967 until his retirement in 1983, he taught at the Department of Philosophy of the State University of New York at Buffalo, heading the department from 1976 until 1979. In 1980 he was promoted to the rank of Distinguished Professor of Islamic Thought and Civilization.

A versatile scholar, his first book published in 1959 was on ancient and medieval Arab seafaring in the Indian Ocean. As a philosopher, his special interest was ethics, for which he contributed *Ethical Theory*, published in 1956. He also contributed to classical journals and published on a variety of historical topics relating to the Middle East. The focus of much of his research, however, has been classical Islamic thought. In addition to his numerous articles in this field, he is noted for his critical edition of the Arabic text of Averroes' *Decisive Treatise*, published in 1959, his annotated translation of it, published in 1969, and his pioneer study of a highly sophisticated medieval Islamic theory of intuitive ethics, *Islamic Rationalism: The Ethics of ʿAbd al-Jabbār*, published in 1971.

A committed teacher, George Hourani guided his students with patience (and not without humour), insisting on the highest standards of scholarly objectivity and clarity of thought. He taught as he lived, guided by reason, compassion and the striving after what is just.

MICHAEL E. MARMURA

April 1985

CONVENTIONS

Capitalization of titles

(1) Books: the first noun is always capitalized, as well as names and all German nouns.
(2) Periodicals and series: all nouns and adjectives are capitalized.

Numerals

Roman small capitals are used for volume numbers of a book by a single author, e.g. Shahrastānī, *Milal*, I, 93.

Roman lower case numerals indicate 'books', sections and suras of the Qurʾān. E.g. Aristotle, Nic. Eth., i, ch. 4, 1095a 12.

'Arabic' numerals in all other cases, including volumes of periodicals and series.

'p.' and 'pp.'

Inserted for modern books in a single volume.

Omitted (1) after all numbered series, whether in books, periodicals or other series, (2) in references to sources, e.g. *Ṭabaqāt*..., 44–9.

Transcription of Arabic names and words

The principle followed is transcription of sounds, not transliteration of spelling. E.g. *ash-sharīʿa*, not *al-sharīʿa* which is misleading for pronunciation by non-Arabists.

The Arabic article is omitted in isolated words and names, e.g. Ashʿarī, not al-Ashʿarī; but inserted in the list of authors in the Select Bibliography. But articles in the middle of names and sentences cannot be omitted, e.g. Mūsā al-Aswārī.

Letters, macrons and dots follow the system of the *New Encyclopaedia of Islam*, except for *jīm* which is given as j, not dj. But macrons and dots are omitted (1) on names of modern Arab authors, which are spelled as they spell them, e.g. Madkour, not Madkūr; (2) on names which have been Anglicized by a suffix, e.g. ʿAbbasids, not ʿAbbāsids.

sh, th, and dh normally each represent a single consonant, e.g. Ibn al-Athīr (as in 'thin'). Where they represent two consonants each, they are separated by a hyphen, e.g. *aṣ-ḥāb*.

TITLES AND LOCATIONS OF THE ORIGINAL ARTICLES

Introduction: not previously published.

1. 'Islamic philosophy and theology', *Dictionary of the Middle Ages*, ed. P. Strayer (New York, 1982).
2. 'Ethics in medieval Islam: a conspectus', *Essays in Islamic philosophy and science*, ed. G. F. Hourani (Albany, 1975), pp. 128–35.
3. 'Ethical presuppositions of the Qurʾān', *The Muslim World*, 70 (1980), 1–28.
4. '*Ẓulm an-nafs* in the Qurʾān, in the light of Aristotle', *Recherches d'Islamologie: Recueil d'articles offert à Georges C. Anawati et Louis Gardet par leurs collègues et amis* (Louvain, 1978), pp. 139–48.
5. 'Two theories of value in medieval Islam', *The Muslim World*, 50 (1960), 268–78.
6. 'Islamic and non-Islamic origins of Muʿtazilite ethical rationalism', *International Journal of Middle East Studies*, 7 (1976), 59–87.
7. 'The rationalist ethics of ʿAbd al-Jabbār', *Islamic philosophy and the classical tradition, for Richard Walzer on his seventieth birthday*, ed. S.M. Stern, A. Hourani and V. Brown (Oxford, 1972), pp. 105–15.
8. 'Deliberation in Aristotle and ʿAbd al-Jabbār', *Islamic philosophy and mysticism*, ed. P. Morewedge (Delmar, NY, 1981), pp. 151–62.
9. 'Al-Ashʿarī', *Dictionary of the Middle Ages*, ed. P. Strayer (New York, 1982–).
10. 'Juwaynī's criticisms of Muʿtazilite ethics', *The Muslim World*, 65 (1975), 161–73.
11. 'Ghazālī on the ethics of action', *Journal of the American Oriental Society*, 96 (1976), 69–88.
12. 'Reason and revelation in Ibn Ḥazm's ethical thought', *Islamic philosophical theology*, ed. P. Morewedge (Albany, 1979), pp. 142–64.
13. 'The basis of authority of consensus in Sunnite Islam', *Studia Islamica*, 21 (1964), 13–60.
14. 'Ibn Sīnā's "Essay on the secret of destiny"', *Bulletin of the School of Oriental and African Studies*, 29 (1966), 27–48.
15. 'Averroes on good and evil', *Studia Islamica*, 16 (1962), 13–40.
16. 'Combinations of reason and tradition in Islamic ethics': not previously published.

INTRODUCTION

I

Islamic ethics should be of interest to Muslims and non-Muslims alike in two aspects. The first is its central place as the core of Islam, if we can include Islamic law as an integral part of ethics.[1] The Qurʾān repeatedly uses the phrase 'those who believe [in God] and do good works',[2] taking it for granted that these two attributes belong to the same group in extension, and that the first is a prerequisite of the second – but also that the first would be insincere and not true belief without the second. Following this lead, the legal profession in the first two centuries of Islam tried to make the law of the *sharīʿa* cover every ethical situation and to make the study of this law the culminating study in Islamic education. Thus, since Islamic education was the most formative element in Islamic civilization, the important rôle of ethics in this civilization becomes obvious.

The second aspect of interest lies in the theological and philosophical theories that were constructed to support normative ethics. These theories all belong to the main Western lines of rational theology and philosophy and have little relation to the theologies and philosophies of East Asia. This relation to Western intellectual history has, unfortunately, rarely been recognized in the West. As a result, Islamic thought has been generally neglected and ignored in Western histories of theology and philosophy.[3] This thought should in the future be substantially incorporated into histories of Western theology and philosophy, both for its intrinsic interest and because it constitutes a large

[1] The relation between ethics and divine law in Islam is usually stated in the reverse direction: that the whole range of ethics was absorbed into the *sharīʿa*, so that all conduct was judged as obedience or disobedience to divine law. This is true in a formal sense, that normative ethics was worked out in legal books and judgements. But we may equally observe that the purpose of this vast legal structure was ethical in a modern sense. The relation may be proved by the evidence of several legal principles, fictions and practices which broke out of the strict mould of classical theory in order to accommodate the demands of justice and public interest. An example is the Malikite principle of *istiṣlāḥ*, 'consideration of public interest', which may be used in preferring one interpretation of the *sharīʿa* to another.

[2] Qurʾān, ii, 25 and many other verses. All references to the Qurʾān are to the verse numbers of the standard Cairo edition.

[3] A recent anthology in English on ethical voluntarism was composed entirely of quotations from Western sources, without any from Islamic theology, where this theory was most fully discussed and developed. It provided the main theoretical basis for Sunnite Islamic law for roughly a thousand years (A.D. 800–1800).

part of the historical link between ancient Greek and medieval Christian thought. All this is true for ethical theory, as for the other main branches of theology and philosophy.

2

This volume consists of the author's collected articles on Islamic ethics in the formative and earlier classical periods of Islamic civilization. It is organized by schools of thought in a roughly chronological order. Most of the articles are centred around two closely related discussions: (1) an extended controversy about the ontological status of value in ethics, and (2) a simultaneous controversy about the sources of human knowledge of such value. It is the second of these themes that is indicated by the title. The two themes are seldom clearly distinguished in the classical discussions, but it will help our understanding to distinguish them from time to time.

Broadly speaking, we can discern three positions that were held on these two questions.

A. Values have an objective existence. They can be known by independent human reason or from scriptural tradition (the Qurʾān and the traditions of Muḥammad); sometimes by both. This was the position of the Muʿtazilite theologians.

B. Values are in their essence whatever God commands. Thus they can be known ultimately only from tradition, although reason can be used in subordinate ways to extend tradition. This was the position of the major school of traditionalist theologians, the Ashʿarites, and most Islamic jurists.

C. Values are objective, and they can be known *entirely* by the independent reason of wise people, including philosophers. But they are presented by a prophet to the common people in the persuasive, imaginative language of scriptural tradition. This was the position of the philosophers.

Other combinations are possible, and some were argued. We shall refer to these, but the present study will be organized primarily to illustrate the three positions outlined.

3

This brief statement can be clarified by explaining and distinguishing the main terms used. We can begin with 'Islam' and its derived adjectives, 'Islamic' and 'Muslim'. 'Islam' stands primarily for the religion itself, the religion of submission or surrender (*islām*) of man's will to the will of God, together with its direct developments in law, theology, mysticism and other branches of knowledge, and a whole set of institutions such as the caliphate and art forms such as mosque architecture. But although the spirit of Islam penetrated in different degrees every aspect of the civilization which grew up with the religion, it is strictly speaking ambiguous to refer to this civilization also as 'Islam', because a civilization is not a religion and can never be completely formed by one, to the exclusion of the many other influences which contribute to it. Rightly recognizing this distinction, Marshall Hodgson in *The Venture of Islam* coined the word 'Islamdom' to match the parallel distinction between Christianity and Christendom.[4] But 'Islamdom' is too inelegant a word to be introduced into the English language and I will not use it. I shall continue to call it 'Islam' or 'Islamic civilization' with reference to its main formative influence, but with the understanding that it includes many features not directly parts of Islam the religion.

Hodgson made a corresponding distinction between adjectives, using 'Islamic' and 'Islamicate' respectively. Here again I do not care much for his new word, and prefer to make the same distinction with the words 'Islamic' and 'Muslim'. Thus we shall have Islamic theologians but Muslim philosophers. The former based their sciences on Islam, the latter were philosophers who happened to be Muslims.

Another distinction is that between 'traditionists' and 'traditionalists'. The former term refers to the collectors of *ḥadīths*, which record the sayings and acts of the Prophet and his Companions. The latter term is much wider, referring to all those scholars who derived the Islamic sciences of law and theology entirely from the positive sources of the Qurʾān and Traditions. They are contrasted with 'rationalist' theologians, the Muʿtazilites, who gave legitimacy to a limited range of independent ethical judgements springing from a sense of equity.

The historical periods of Islamic civilization and their names are by now fairly well agreed upon by the scholarly community. There are three main periods. The first is formative, from Muḥammad in Madīna (A.D. 622–32) to about 870. The transition to the second period, the classical, is marked by the occurrence of several features which were to endure for the next millennium. The Traditions were informally canonized in the great collections of Bukhārī, Kulīnī and others; the schools of *sharīʿa* law were well established; the twelfth and last Shiʿite *imām* disappeared; the Sunnite caliphate was reduced to governing little more than Iraq; the Greek sciences and philosophy had been introduced into learned circles; the visual arts and literature were settling into steady patterns, not without constant change; the economic order was a kind of feudalism, and government almost everywhere was in the hands of secular sultans and amirs.

[4] Vol. 1 (Chicago, 1974), pp. 57–60.

This classical Islamic civilization endured for a thousand years. There are sub-periods, of which the two most important are divided at 1500, with the consolidation of the three large empires of the Ottoman Turks, the Persian Safavids and the Mughals in India. But the criterion of this division was political; Muslim society continued with little change. There was no renaissance, reformation or voyages of transoceanic discovery, therefore no transition at this time to a modern period. Thus the term 'medieval' is meaningless in relation to Islamic history. The continuity of Islamic civilization from around 870 to 1870 was expressed in a striking way by Edward Lane in his Introduction to *The Manners and Customs of the Modern Egyptians* (London, 1835). Referring to the *Thousand and One Nights*, he wrote:

> if the English reader had possessed a close translation of it with sufficient illustrative notes, I might almost have spared myself the labour of the present undertaking.[5]

This civilization is appropriately named 'classical' because it was the first actualization of Islamic concepts and ideals in a complete and durable form.

Modern Islamic civilization, the third historical period, was introduced by the overwhelming inroads of Western military power, technology, law, commerce and educational systems. Perhaps it is best symbolized by the opening of the Suez Canal to world shipping in 1869 and the consequent indebtedness of the Khedive of Egypt to the British government and French financial institutions. Whatever paths it eventually takes, Islamic civilization can never revert to its classical form because the outlook of modern Muslims has been changed irrevocably by their recent experiences, both traumatic and liberating.

4

This book is not a complete treatment of Islamic ethics, which would have required a work of larger scope.[6] It is limited in several respects. The first is the type of ethics discussed: ethical theory in the theological and philosophical modes, not normative ethics.[7] Secondly, these essays concern the mainstream of classical Sunnite thought, with the addition of a couple of philosophers.

[5] Edition of London, 1908 (reprinted, 1923), pp. xvii–xviii, n. 1. A similar illustration of the continuity of classical Islam is found in the *Description de l'Égypte* (Paris, 1809–26), compiled by the French scholars who accompanied Napoleon Bonaparte on his invasion of that country (1798–1801). This mighty work revealed to educated Europeans the existence of a still living civilization not much different from that which they knew in a vague way from the *Thousand and one nights*.

[6] See chapter 2 for a classification of types of ethics and a short review of the theories to be examined in this volume.

[7] Chapter 1 covers the whole period of Islamic theology and philosophy. Chapter 6 reaches back into pre-Islamic religions and ancient Greek philosophy. Chapter 13 touches on modern Islamic jurisprudence.

There is no attempt here to deal with the Shiʿite sect and there are only incidental references to Sufism, important as these movements are in the intellectual history of Islam. Thirdly, the time span covered is the formative period and the earlier classical period (to Ibn Rushd at the end of the twelfth century), with a few exceptions. Finally, even within the limits described there is no attempt at completeness.

In short, this is a collection of papers on such topics as I have been able to deal with over the last quarter of a century, within the bounds of my competence and the time available. All these papers present particular authors, schools or problems – sometimes of wide scope. My belief is that particular, detailed illustrations of a field of study form a more interesting and effective introduction to that field than a general survey which tries to cover the whole ground.

Certainly this is true of Islamic ethics at the present time, when the spade work has not yet extended very far. The first two articles, however, are surveys, and they are placed here to inform and orient readers with little or no previous knowledge of Islamic theology, philosophy or ethics.

These articles have undergone a few revisions, none of them major, to take account of studies more recent than themselves. Some new titles have been added to bibliographical notes. Conventions of spelling and the like have been made consistent as far as possible, as explained in 'Conventions'. But the problems of transcription from Arabic are notorious, and I beg to be excused if some inconsistencies of detail remain in the text.

1

ISLAMIC THEOLOGY AND MUSLIM PHILOSOPHY

In the early centuries of Islam theology and philosophy were regarded as two distinct disciplines, following their own assumptions and intellectual traditions. 'The science of dialectic' (*ʿilm al-kalām*) meant Islamic theology, derived only from the revealed Qurʾān and the Traditions of the prophet Muḥammad. Philosophy (*al-falsafa*) was a 'foreign' science based on natural knowledge and largely inspired by ancient Greek philosophy. As time passed theology and philosophy interacted increasingly, with varying relations in different parts of the Muslim world. But we must begin by describing them as separate, as they generally were until about the eleventh century A.D.

THEOLOGY

All teaching, discussion and writing on this subject were conducted in Arabic, the language of the Qurʾān and of other Islamic subjects such as exegesis and jurisprudence. The principal centres of theology were in Iraq and Iran.

After early discussions on conditions for salvation and the moral qualifications of caliphs the first systematic school, the Muʿtazilites, arose in Iraq in the eighth century, about a century after Muḥammad's death (632). Their self-description as 'the party of unity and justice' announced their central doctrines.

The unity of God (Allāh) was understood very strictly by them, reflecting the emphasis of the Qurʾān. Polytheism and the Christian Trinity were rejected as a matter of course. The Qurʾān could not be eternal beside God but must have been created by the one eternal being. Even the attributes of God such as His power and wisdom would raise problems if they were thought of as separate eternal entities; they had to be somehow united with an essence of God which was purely simple, since 'unity' included simplicity.

Muʿtazilite ethical theology insisted that God was just in an objective sense as understood by man. Therefore He would treat man with this intelligible justice in distributing rewards and punishments on the day of Judgement. Thus they would be punished only for sins which they had had the power to avoid. This implied that men had power to choose their own conduct, free from predestination. God has delegated to man this power to decide and even (according to the later Muʿtazilites) to 'create' his own acts.

These doctrines of God's unity and justice were worked out with much refinement and far-reaching related theories over a period of three centuries by theologians of two schools, those of Baṣra and Baghdād, with constant controversy among themselves and with opponents. They seldom enjoyed government support and were increasingly denounced. The Basran tradition culminated in the work of ʿAbd al-Jabbār (*c.* 935–1025), a Persian who wrote a long *summa* presenting the latest positions in dialectical form. After him there were few Muʿtazilites, and most of their books were destroyed by opponents or neglected in libraries.

Their method was rationalist in the sense that they started from a few principles stated or implicit in the Qurʾān, then deduced their logical consequences, without too much regard to problems of consistency presented by other assertions of the Qurʾān. Their theory of knowledge supported confidently the powers of human intellect (*ʿaql*).

The Muʿtazilites met with opposition from the beginning from a variety of viewpoints. Ibn Ḥanbal (d. 855), a famous jurist of Baghdād, disapproved of all theology on the ground that it was bound to go beyond the Qurʾān by interpreting it according to human ideas, thus distorting its messages which were perfectly expressed in the Book of God. Theology was idle speculation which had not been practised by Muḥammad and his Arab companions, the models for later Muslims to follow; it could only raise needless doubts about Islam. Nonetheless there were later Hanbalite theologians, even if their intent was negative. Ibn Taymiyya of Damascus (1263–1328) was the most influential. He made a rare attempt to refute Aristotelian logic. The Hanbalite school persists today in Saʿūdī Arabia.

Some early Shiʿite theologians of the Imāmī sect (now the majority in Iran), such as Hishām b. al-Ḥakam (d. 795/96), disagreed with the Muʿtazilites in a different way. They accepted theology, but opposed the transcendental Muʿtazilite doctrine of God and interpreted the Qurʾān more literally. God moves in space. His knowledge changes with the changes in its objects. But later Imāmī theologians absorbed many of the Muʿtazilite doctrines, such as the objective justice of God and the freedom of man.

A more formidable opposition to Muʿtazilism emerged around the ninth century from Sunnite theologians who may be called traditionalist, in the sense that they tried hard to follow closely the precise meaning of the Qurʾān. If this created apparent problems of consistency, they would interpret the text cautiously with the help of the Traditions and a careful study of the Arabic language and grammar at the time of the Prophet. Thus they were known as 'the party of tradition' (*ahl as-sunna*), who followed the guidance of transmitted sources (*naql*) rather than independent human intellect. In fact, however, they were unable to follow this programme with complete consistency since they, like the Muʿtazilites, emphasized one principle found in the Qurʾān rather than others, as will be shown.

The moderate liberalism of the traditionalist school is seen in their doctrine of God's attributes. These could not be assimilated to a single essence of God, as the Muʿtazilites proposed, because the Qurʾān mentions many attributes, often by an abstract name; e.g., God is not merely 'knowing' He also has 'knowledge'. Thus His attributes are real and distinguishable, without impairing His unity; for a single existent can have many attributes, as is commonly believed. So, too, they insisted that the Qurʾān is the eternal, uncreated Word of God, being His very thought.

The principle which the traditionalists singled out as supreme was that of God's omnipotence. This is indeed stressed greatly in the Qurʾān. Some of this school even denied natural causation in the world, because it would imply power in things other than God. In its place they constructed an 'atomic' theory of causes, by which God is the sole cause of the successive states of the world, in themselves causally unconnected with each other.

Again, respecting omnipotence they found fault with the Muʿtazilite view that there are objective standards of good and evil which God follows. Even though the Muʿtazilites had been careful to state that God follows these standards freely, their very existence was now rejected because they would be independent and prior to His thought and will. The only standard of value for God and man was the will of God; whatever He wills is good by definition. This is ethical voluntarism, which after the jurist Shāfiʿī (d. 820) became the first principle of Islamic law in most schools. By adopting it traditionalist theologians could claim that God's will suffers no ethical limits. Thus, even if He punishes sinners whose acts He has predestined He cannot be called 'unjust', for justice means nothing but obedience to divine laws, and God is not subject to any laws.

Such a position, however neat as a theory, could hardly satisfy believers in an intelligible divine justice. The Sunnite theologian Ashʿarī of Baṣra (870–935) then elaborated a subtler theory of justice, which might leave man responsible for his acts and so rightly culpable for his sins. This was the theory of 'acquisition' (*iktisāb*), suggested by the Qurʾān and already proposed by earlier traditionalists. While God creates every act of man and enables him to do it, the act is still that of the human agent, making him responsible for its consequences to himself. Ultimately, however, God predestines what act a man chooses; thus the problem is dismissed but not solved.

A solution closer to the Muʿtazilite one was worked out by Māturīdī of Samarqand (d. 944). A man really chooses how to act, then God creates for him the act that he has chosen. Man 'acquires' his act, while God 'creates' it. Thus freedom and justice are preserved, but 'creation' remains God's privilege, contrary to the later Muʿtazilite vocabulary.

The schools of Ashʿarī and Māturīdī became predominant in Sunnite Islam: the Ashʿarites in all the Arab countries and for a while in Iran, the Maturidites in Transoxania (now Uzbekistan), Turkey and India.

PHILOSOPHY

Philosophy began to be studied in the ninth century, after Syriac Christian scholars at Baghdād had made accurate Arabic translations of most of Aristotle and some later Greek commentaries on him. Plato's dialogues became known through translated summaries. Parts of the *Enneads* of Plotinus were translated and became very influential, but they were generally ascribed to Aristotle – a cause of much confusion. Major works of Greek science were also translated, such as Galen's medicine, Ptolemy's astronomy and geography, Euclid's geometry. These were regarded as the most advanced scientific books in the world, and since philosophy was not distinguished from science it shared in their prestige and came to be viewed by educated people as giving equally certain knowledge. All the philosophers were learned in one or more of the other sciences. most of them were Muslims, but philosophy was not consciously Islamic until a later period.

The first Muslim philosopher, Kindī (d. 870), an Arab of Baṣra, was a pioneer in Arabic philosophical writing. He showed some independence from the Greeks in holding that the world is not everlasting but was created in time, as the Qurʾān declares.

Fārābī (873–950) was a Turk of Transoxania who studied and wrote in Baghdād and Aleppo. He gained a high reputation as an Arabic commentator on Aristotle, but his own philosophy was more Neoplatonic. Thus he propounded the emanation of the world in successive stages from God and the higher intellectual beings. Man must strive for happiness by climbing through intellectual discipline toward a conjunction of his soul with the world's Active Intellect. The ideal community requires a political organization such as the caliphate, in which a code of divine law (*sharīʿa*) has been provided by a philosophic prophet. Prophets are distinguished by imaginative powers which enable them to teach the Law to the people in a convincing style.

Ibn Sīnā (Latin Avicenna, 980–1037) was a Persian of Bukhārā who was chief physician and minister to several princes in Iran. Besides his major medical and philosophical works in Arabic he also wrote a few in Persian, being the first to do so since Islam. His philosophy resembles that of Fārābī in being a synthesis of Aristotelian, later Greek and original views. He accepted the emanation of the world, the Aristotelian psychology of active and passive intellects and the ascent of the soul. But he was not strictly a Neoplatonist, in view of a number of differences. His cosmological argument for the existence of a First Cause is widely known. Every ordinary essence is in itself contingent, so that its existence requires an external cause. But the chain of such causes cannot be infinite. Therefore there must be one non-contingent essence which exists without a prior cause and gives existence to everything else.

The world is everlasting; 'creation' means continual emanation. The human mind is completely determined by causes, like the rest of the world. Ibn Sīnā describes a mystical path in an allegorical fable but was not himself known as a practising Ṣūfī. His philosophy is a wide-ranging and self-consistent synthesis which is central in Islamic philosophy, drawing upon his predecessors and providing the classical base for all his successors in the eastern countries. He himself thought it harmonious with Islam, but it was soon to be criticized as contrary to Islam in certain respects.

THE INTERACTION OF THEOLOGY AND PHILOSOPHY

The Ismaʿilite sect of Shiʿism had in the tenth century already incorporated into its esoteric theology a Neoplatonic cosmology of emanation. By contrast, Sunnite theologians generally ignored philosophy until well into the eleventh century. But now two brilliant theologians educated themselves in the philosophic tradition and reacted to it.

One was Ibn Ḥazm of Córdoba (995–1064), a literary author who joined the Zahirite school of law, which derived all Islamic law from a literal construction of the Qurʾān and Traditions. An imaginative writer and a learned critic of all religions other than Islam, Ibn Ḥazm applied literalism to theology in a logical and sweeping fashion which allowed no other source of religious truth than relevation. Greek logic and even metaphysical concepts could be used to explain and defend this truth but never as independent sources of religious knowledge.

The Persian Ghazālī (Latin Algazel, 1057–1111) held a somewhat similar view of philosophy, although from a more traditionalist standpoint. After studying Shafiʿite law and Ashʿarite theology under the eminent Juwaynī (d. 1085) at the college of law (*madrasa*) at Nīshāpūr, he became professor in an important *madrasa* at Baghdād. There he made a deep study of the philosophies of Fārābī and Ibn Sīnā, then wrote a devastating attack on them showing many inconsistencies and unproved conclusions. He also condemned many of their views as contrary to Islam, especially their denial of three central doctrines: creation of the world in time, God's knowledge of particulars and man's corporeal resurrection. But he appreciated Greek logic as a neutral instrument which could be used in support of Islam.

Resigning from his chair in 1095, he brought a new tone to these controversies by his personal conversion to Sufism. This Islamic mysticism had already been practised by a long line of spiritual leaders, not adhering to any one school of theology or philosophy. Ghazālī emphasized the inward and practical sides of Islam, while drawing cautiously upon Aristotelian ethics and Neoplatonic mysticism where they seemed in harmony with his religious purposes. The Qur'ān as revelation always remained for him the ultimate source of truth in religion. All these directions of Islamic thought were fused together in his greatest work, *The Revival of the sciences of religion*. Its impact has remained profound among Muslims owing to the sincerity of his thought and the force of his Arabic writing style.

ANDALUSIAN PHILOSOPHY

Philosophy was studied at Córdoba from the tenth century on. The most important work was done in the twelfth century. Ibn Bājja (Latin Avempace, d. 1139) of Saragossa wrote in the Neoplatonic tradition of intellectual mysticism, with some political interest as well. Ibn Ṭufayl (d. 1185) is chiefly known for his philosophical romance, *Ḥayy b. Yaqẓān*, showing the possibility of attaining scientific, philosophical and religious knowledge by untutored natural reason.

The foremost Andalusian philosopher was Ibn Rushd (Latin Averroes, 1126–98). Being broadly educated in Islamic law, the secular sciences and philosophy, as a young man he was commissioned by the Almohad ruler of Morocco and Andalusia to write Arabic commentaries on all the translated works of Aristotle. This huge task occupied him for the last forty years of his life. The commentaries are in three forms: summaries, middle commentaries and long commentaries – the last two kinds annotating the texts sentence by sentence. Complete sets of three have mostly not survived in Arabic, but many of the missing ones are available in medieval Latin and Hebrew translations. There is also, in Hebrew translation only, a lengthy summary and commentary of Plato's *Republic*, meant to take the place of Aristotle's *Politics* which had never been translated into Arabic.

While the Aristotelian commentaries are faithful to the thought of the master they contain a great deal of Ibn Rushd's own philosophy. Moreover, he wrote several independent works, having as their main purpose the defence of philosophy, especially that of Aristotle, against the attacks of Ghazālī and others. He did this with a variety of arguments, such as the following of general scope: that Islam allows latitude to qualified scholars to interpret the Qur⁾ān, and that philosophers are the best qualified to do so by their understanding of the truths of science, including philosophy. Revelation and science must agree, for truth is single – contrary to the medieval Christian attribution to Averroes of a theory of 'double truth'. But science and philosophy may contradict theology (*kalām*), which did not have the same authority in Islam as Catholic doctrine in the Christian West.

Ibn Rushd's philosophy is a revived Aristotelianism, purified of most of the accretions of later Greek and earlier Islamic philosophy. In ethics he upheld the objectivity of value against the Greek sophists and the Ash⁽arite theologians. He had no sympathy for Sufism. His attacks on theologians brought on him a trial for heresy in Córdoba (1195) and resulting condemnation and exile.

This event was part of a growing disapproval of philosophy in the Arab countries. But it did not fade altogether. The Aristotelian-Rushdian tradition may still be seen in Ibn Khaldūn of Tunis (1332–1406). His study of historical method led him to create a new 'science of culture' or social science, whose laws would guide the historian in judging the possibility or probability of recorded events. These ideas were set forth in his wide-ranging and penetrating Introduction (*al-Muqaddima*) to the study of history.

THE LATIN AND HEBREW TRANSLATIONS

When the Reconquista took Toledo (1085) and Saragossa (1118) from the Muslims, Christian scholars gained easy access to books of Arabic science and philosophy, which they found more advanced than their own. From 1130 on, Latin translations of parts of Avicenna's *Shifā⁾* (Latin *Sufficientia*) were being made. Toledo from 1160 to 1187 was a busy centre of translation, led by Gerard of Cremona (1114–87). The Aristotelian commentaries of Averroes followed in the early decades of the thirteenth century. Some texts of Aristotle were translated from their Arabic versions. In the same period many philosophical works were also being translated directly from ancient Greek. Thus the Latin philosophers from Albert the Great (1206–80) on had at their disposal a far richer philosophical library than their predecessors.

A parallel activity occurred as part of the Hebrew revival in Spain and southern France, including Hebrew translations of many of Averroes' commentaries. In addition, works of Jewish philosophers who had written in Arabic, such as the *Guide of the Perplexed* of Mōshe b. Maymōn (Latin Maimonides, 1135–1204) were now put into Hebrew.

LATER EASTERN PHILOSOPHY

Ghazālī had started a trend towards the coalescence of theology, philosophy and Sufism. The use of philosophical concepts and terms in elaborating an Islamic theology became bolder and more open in the works of Fakhr ad-Dīn ar-Rāzī (1149–1209), a learned and prolific commentator on the Qur'ān and Ibn Sīnā. Another commentator on Ibn Sīnā, Naṣīr ad-Dīn Ṭūsī (1201–74), is important as an encyclopedist, expounding Greek and Islamic philosophy and science mainly in Persian. His *Nasirean Ethics* in the Aristotelian mode (happiness and the virtues) is wider in scope than the earlier Arabic *Ethics* of Miskawayh (d. 1030), since it continues with domestic economy and politics.

Sufism pervaded the illuminationism of Suhrawardī the Martyr (1155–91), a philosophy or rather Wisdom which has Zoroastrian, Hermetic and Platonic roots. Reality consists of degrees of light, from the pure light of God to the most negative darkness. Unfortunately he also stated that existence was only a logical notion, prolonging a widespread misunderstanding of Ibn Sīnā who had sometimes referred to existence as an 'accident'. (Ibn Sīnā had only meant by this that the existence of any essence is contingent, not necessary.)

Ibn ʿArabī of Murcia (1165–1240) lived in many cities of western and eastern Islam, latterly in Malatya and Damascus. His comprehensive but unsystematic mystical philosophy attempted to unify all aspects of the world by relating it closely to God. The world is the manifestation of God, who perceives Himself reflected in it. Man is an image of the divine and in turn perceives God in the beauty of the world around him. In line with a common Ṣūfī outlook, Ibn ʿArabī finds the same truths expressed in all religions in their different ways. His vast writings in prose and verse are full of symbolism, making his philosophy difficult to describe but rich in poetic and religious imagination. As a Ṣūfī with personal mystical experience as well as intellectual power he became a major influence on all later Ṣūfī philosophy.

The line of mystical poets was continued in Islam most strongly in Iran. The greatest of this genre was Jalāl ad-Dīn Rūmī (1207–73), who weaves theological and philosophical ideas in endless profusion into his long Persian poem *Couplets* (*Masnavī*).

The later Persian philosophers, still writing mostly in Arabic, developed the concept of philosophy as Wisdom (*ḥikma*) or theosophy, in an unbroken chain of thought from Ibn Sīnā through Suhrawardī to the present time. The prerequisites for philosophical understanding are ethical living, following a Ṣūfī discipline and instruction by a master. As a consequence a Ṣūfī scholar may receive divine illumination, which combined with his own intellectual and spiritual efforts will bring him to understand the eternal truths of philosophy, including philosophical theology.

The leading philosopher of this school was Ṣadr ad-Dīn of Shīrāz or Mullā Ṣadrā (*c.* 1571–1640). He achieved a culminating and comprehensive metaphysics. Especially notable is his refined analysis of the meaning of existence and its relations with essence.

Mullā Ṣadrā's most important work, *The Four Journeys* (*al-Asfār al-Arbaʿa*) received a lengthy commentary from Sabzawārī (1797–1878), the foremost Persian philosopher after Mullā Ṣadrā. This combined work remains the basic text of Islamic philosophical education in Iran.

In the Arab countries the Persian philosophers are little read, and the classical Sunnite educational tradition of Ashʿarī and Ghazālī survives mainly in colleges of theology. Philosophy is making a fresh start in the universities, based on study of Western and Muslim philosophers from the ancient Greeks to contemporary thinkers.

2

ETHICS IN CLASSICAL ISLAM: A CONSPECTUS

The aim of this paper is to present a general review of one theme of Islamic ethical thought that should be of significance and interest to modern philosophers: analytical discussions of the meanings of ethical terms, together with some background information on normative ethics which provide the basis for the evolution of analytical ethics. Two other topics of contemporary interest were also discussed extensively by Muslim thinkers, the psychology of moral action and the question of moral freedom, but I shall leave these aside and concentrate on the first topic.

I shall start with a simplified classification of types of ethical writing in classical Islam, which will provide a frame of reference for the types we are interested in. Two levels of generality in ethical thinking have already been mentioned, 'normative' and 'analytical'. (I should have liked to call the latter 'philosophical', but as we shall see there is a theological theory which is consciously antiphilosophical, though just as general.) There are also two traditions of ethical thinking, which we can call 'secular' and 'religious', according to their conceptions of the proper sources of ethical knowledge. Thus we can derive a fourfold scheme of types of writing on ethics: (*A*) Normative religious ethics. (*B*) Normative secular ethics. (*C*) Ethical analysis in the religious tradition. (*D*) Ethical analysis by philosophers. I am going to review *A*, *B* and *D* rapidly, and to concentrate on *C*, where it seems to me that the most interesting thought is to be found. I shall then discuss whether one school of religiously oriented analytical thought, that of the Muʿtazilites, is not really philosophical in its method, in spite of the usual classification as theological.

A. Normative religious ethics begins in the primary sources of Islam, the Qurʾān and the Traditions, which prescribe many rules of law and morality for man. The Qurʾān also contains suggestions for answers to some more general questions of ethics, but it is not a book of philosophy or even theology, and its suggestions are not without ambiguities. If they had been, there would have been less controversy among Muslim theologians on these questions. The Traditions include the same kind of materials, more extensively but carrying less weight for Muslims. Next, we have the books on *furūʿ*, the details of

Islamic law, systematizing and classifying the prescriptions of the Qurʾān and Traditions. Another genre of moral literature in the religious tradition is the books on 'noble qualities of character' (*makārim al-akhlāq*), which are concerned not with detailed law but with religious virtues. Then we have Ṣūfī books for meditation and manuals of instruction in the path to God, which are deeply moral in a practical or normative sense. All these kinds of normative religious books provided materials for analytical ethics, without themselves analysing ethical terms.

B. Normative secular ethics is represented by 'Mirrors for princes' in the Persian tradition, giving advice to sultans and wazirs about government and politics. We may also include here wisdom literature contained in proverbs and poetry. Then there is a Greek tradition of popular Platonism, found in books like the treatises of the Sincere Brethren. The books of Miskawayh and others on character (*akhlāq*), listing the virtues and vices, should really be put here, as I shall explain when I come back to them in their customary location under philosophical ethics. All these kinds of literature provide materials for more philosophical efforts.

Of a more inward character in both lines of normative writing, *A* and *B*, there are abundant works of Ṣūfī and Platonic mysticism. These two traditions, which merged in later centuries, came close to philosophy through presenting total outlooks on life, although often not fully reasoned.

C. The study of ethical principles in the religious tradition starts with the jurists' discussions of the sources of law in the eighth and ninth centuries A.D. In these controversies we have the roots of an analytical treatment of the concepts of justice and obligation, because they take theoretical stands on how the law is known. From about the middle of the eighth century there are, roughly speaking, two parties on this issue. The party of rational opinion (*raʾy*) held that in deciding questions of Islamic law and morals judges and lawyers might make their own rational judgements independently of scripture, in cases or aspects where scripture gives no guidance. The other party, more strictly traditional, held that legal judgements can be based *only* on scripture and Traditions, or derived from them in certain approved ways, such as analogy (*qiyās*). The conflict on this question was focussed by Shāfiʿī in particular, with his systematic critique of legal methods. Shāfiʿī worked out in a very thorough way the theory of a positive law, based entirely on Islamic revelation and Traditions; and he states his primary principle in his maxim that justice is nothing but obedience to the revealed law the *sharīʿa*).

Theologians' discussions (*kalām*) of the sources of right probably arose out of the jurists' discussions, but they paid more attention to principles. The division of parties follows the same lines: the partisans of reason maintaining that man can know much of what is right and obligatory by independent thought, the traditionalists supporting revelation and Traditions as the sole source of such knowledge. This debate is part of a wider one on the sources of knowledge in religion.

In surveying the history of this debate, I shall begin with the early Muʿtazilites. They have some historical relation to Greek philosophy, Christian theology, and the partisans of opinion in law, but the details of influences on them are still rather obscure. Their rationalistic ethical theories are known only in outline from books on sects by their opponents, Ashʾarī and others, who give their bare positions with little of the arguments leading to them.

The early reactions of traditionalist theologians against rationalistic ethics were closely connected with traditionalist fears of reason in jurisprudence. Following up the line of thought started by Shāfiʿī and Ibn Ḥanbal, theologians before Ashʿarī as well as Ashʿarī himself formulated these reactions, although still in rather brief statements. The main objection they raised against rationalistic ethics was that independent human reason implies a limit on the power of God; for if man could judge what is right and wrong he could rule on what God could rightly prescribe for man, and this would be presumptuous and blasphemous. They further objected that the judgements of reason were arbitrary, based only on desires; that such judgements in fact always contradicted each other; and lastly that they arrogated the function of revelation and rendered it useless. The doctrine of this school on ethics corresponded with that of Shāfiʿī on legal justice; in brief, that right action is that which is commanded by God. In fact we can find an even closer relation than one of correspondence, for such a view merges right ethical action with legal justice. I call this view (of both jurists and theologians) 'theistic subjectivism'. It is subjectivist because it relates values to the view of a judge who *decides* them, denying anything objective in the character of acts themselves, that would make them right or wrong independently of anyone's decision or opinion. And the view is theistic because the decider of values is taken to be God. A more usual name is 'ethical voluntarism'.

Now, going on to the later developments inside *kalām*, I shall return to the rationalistic side and describe its more developed form. This was worked out by the later Muʿtazilites in defence against traditionalist attacks. By the tenth and still more the eleventh century they have been vigorously criticized. So they are alert to the objections and have to be more sophisticated in answering these and elaborating their theory. Their position is seen in its most detailed form in the later Muʿtazilite ʿAbd al-Jabbār (*c.* 935–1025), whose enormous work the *Mughnī* in about twenty volumes was recovered in the 1950s in a single Arabic manuscript in Sanʿa, Yemen, and has since been edited in Cairo by I. Madkour, G. Anawati, and others. So we have this vast material available, and it contains the most extensive discussion of ethical principles known in Islamic literature. It is not entirely ʿAbd al-Jabbār's original creation, but develops a school tradition, going back about a century earlier to Abū Hāshim (d. 932) and his father Jubbāʾī (d. 915).

It is indeed an elaborate theory of ethics. Much space is devoted to defensive arguments, showing that the power of God is not limited in any way that matters by the existence of rational human judgements of value, for God is always superior and we never have the slightest ground to criticize Him morally for what He does, thinks or commands. Moreover, our judgements of reason when properly made are not arbitrary but conform to objective principles. What these are is set forth in the detailed system of ʿAbd al-Jabbār. His principles of ethics resemble those of British intuitionism, and they are such as any rational person can know – e.g., the principle that lying is wrong, so long as it does not come into conflict with a more insistent ethical consideration. (Here we enter into a complication, which will be mentioned later.) The rationalism of ʿAbd al-Jabbār and his predecessors allows a place for revelation as an indispensable supplement to reason. It tells us some important truths on value that reason unaided could not have discovered, although reason can recognize and accept them as rational when once they have been revealed – e.g., the value of prayer in building character.

In their offensive efforts against opponents, the later Muʿtazilites argued that the commands of God are not enough to constitute right and do not by themselves, in their character as mere commands, fulfill the requirements of what we normally mean by 'right'. Moreover, we have the natural ability to know the right independently of any command or revelation, as is shown by the existence of some true moral judgements outside Islam. They also pointed out what they took to be the immoral consequences of theistic subjectivism, such as that God could then make lying right for men if He wished to do so, simply by commanding men to tell lies. And then if He wished He could punish them for not lying – or again, if He wished, for lying!

The traditionalist reactions against rationalism were sharp, and were formulated by several famous theologians, in particular Ibn Ḥazm, Ghazālī, and Shahrastānī. They renewed the insistence on the omnipotence of God: He must not be limited in any way in His power to command man. They accepted fearlessly consequences such as God's power and right to command things which seem wrong to man, such as lying, and rejected the charge of immorality in God as being meaningless or blasphemous. They attacked the rationalists' principles as inconsistent, discordant with scripture, and not really known by reason since they are not universally accepted. They objected strongly to the suggestion that revelation was supplementary, and reaffirmed that it is the primary source of ethical knowledge and provides everything that is needed. Reason is only an aid to understanding scripture, according to Ibn Ḥazm, but others allowed its use to extend the prescriptions of scripture by certain legitimate methods. To prove these positions, scripture itself was called upon regularly for quotations of texts showing approval of the traditionalist theory.

The general result of this debate in the Muslim world was that rationalism continued to be widespread in Shiᶜite countries such as Iran, where it was incorporated into Shiᶜite Islam, while the traditionalist view prevailed in Sunnite countries until modern times. But with the incursion of western rationalism, the former type of view on ethics seems to receive a favourable welcome among modern Muslim intellectuals in some countries, without any commitment to the particular Muᶜtazilite doctrines.

After this review of schools, I want to raise an important historical question of method. Is the *kalām* discussion of ethics theology or philosophy? With regard to subject matter, Islamic ethics in *kalām* is seldom far from God, and in this respect it can be classed as always theological. But with regard to method we distinguish two types of theology: revelational, based entirely on information derived from scripture (after an initial rational apologetic justifying scripture as authentic), and philosophical, based on natural knowledge and not relying on scripture for anything essential. So the question can be reworded. How much of *kalām* ethics is philosophical in method? To answer this question we have to consider the two main schools separately.

Muᶜtazilite theology as a whole starts from a few broad principles learned initially from the Qurᵓān, such as the unity and justice of God. I am not sure whether even these principles are not also justified by independent rational arguments. R. M. Frank has done significant work on the methods of *kalām*, and we may hope that he will give us further clarification of this basic question. But certainly when the Muᶜtazilites work on ethical theory it seems to me that their method is philosophical, not revelational. To judge from ᶜAbd al-Jabbār, the negative evidence is clear enough: he does not quote scripture as a decisive argument, but only in passing, if at all. The positive evidence consists in the types of argument that he uses. Two types are prominent, according to the subject matter.

First of all, there are arguments for definitions. These are asserted with reasons, then defended dialectically by answering objections. For example, an act that is *wājib*, 'obligatory', is defined in the *Mughnī* as that act whose agent deserves blame for omitting it (without deserving any praise for doing it). Such acts are called *wājib* by everyone, as can be confirmed by the authority of lexicographers. The objections which ʿAbd al-Jabbār thinks he has to answer are those of inconsistency, of discordance with linguistic usage, and of irreligion and immorality, and each one is refuted by an appropriate method. He criticizes his opponents' definitions in the same ways. For example, the definition of *wājib* as commanded by God, or that for which the omission is punished by God, implies that one cannot use *wājib* intelligently without knowing that there is a commander. This is false, because pre-Islamic peoples and pagans remote from the Islamic world have known what 'obligatory' means.

A second type of discussion concerns the specific content of the obligatory, the good and so on: ethical rules such as 'lying is always evil', 'wrongdoing is always evil'. At this level of ethical thinking, we sometimes have to weigh relevant factors against each other, so this leads to a theory of prima facie goods and evils like that of W. D. Ross. And, again as in Ross, the rules are known by rational intuitions. He answers objections in ways similar to those mentioned before. Opponents assert, for example, that if God commanded lying it would be good. He criticizes such an assertion as immoral, i.e., ultimately discordant with our ordinary conception of what is 'moral'.

The question of method in Muʿtazilite ethics needs further investigation, as does method in Muʿtazilite theology in general. Provisionally, I have to conclude that it is primarily philosophical, in a modern sense that is not essentially tied to the Greek traditions as is Muslim philosophy in the accepted sense. The Muʿtazilites have usually been classified as theologians because of their origins, their interests and, above all, the absence of explicit influences from Greek philosophy.

The method of the traditionalists accords with their first principle, that the primary source of religious knowledge is revelation. This principle is itself supported by rational apologetic arguments, such as the miracle of the Qurʾān; if it were supported by revelation the argument would be circular, as Ibn Ḥazm and others noted. But, once revelation is established as a source of truth, all knowledge of theology and ethics after that point is based on scripture or Traditions or their derivatives. Consequently, the clinching arguments of Ashʿarī, Ibn Ḥazm, and others of their tendency are quotations from the sacred texts, correctly interpreted. Quotations are not used merely to illustrate or support, as we might think at first sight; they are the main evidence, sufficient and final. So the ethics of this school is revelational, not philosophical in its method. This fact does not exclude an extensive use of dialectic to refute opponents.

This difference in primary principles and methods between the two schools often produces arguments at cross purposes. if the Muʿtazilites claim that some kind of act is immoral and therefore cannot have been approved of by a prophet, Ibn Ḥazm answers that a prophet approved of it, therefore it cannot be immoral and the Muᶜtazilite criticism of it is irreligious. This ploy follows the rules of gamesmanship in controversy, that you must whenever possible score a point that cannot be answered frankly by your opponents, in the intellectual environment of the times, for fear of ridicule, disapproval, censorship, or worse. Thus in the present instance the Muᶜtazilites could not reply that even if a genuine prophet had approved of something, such as stealing, it would still have been wrong, because it was not acceptable in classical Islam to declare that a genuine prophet was mistaken about anything, and least of all that Muḥammad was. Shahrastānī, too, is often at cross purposes with his opponents and answers arguments of rationalism made on the human level with theological considerations. Thus, when the Muᶜtazilites say that we know truths of ethics by reason, he is apt to change the subject and discuss how God knows such things or to write about the relations of obligation between God and man.

The sustained discussion on ethics in the *kalām* literature is all the more remarkable because it owes little to the Greeks except in an indirect and diffuse way. It is original in Islam, and grew quite naturally out of the early theological and juristic debates among Muslims. It appears to me as chronologically the second major occurrence in history of a profound discussion on the meanings and general content of ethical concepts, the first being that of the ancient Greek sophists and Plato. If this is a sound judgement, it gives an importance to classical Islamic ethics in the general history of philosophy that has not been realized up to now. It is to be hoped that in the future it will be more appreciated as a result of the recovery of other substantial texts in addition to those of ᶜAbd al-Jabbār.

D. I shall say little about ethics in the mainstream of islamic philosophy. What is usually known as such is the books on *akhlāq* ('character' rather than 'ethics') by Miskawayh, Naṣīr ad-dīn Ṭūsī, and Dawwānī. These works follow a settled tradition of Hellenic philosophy in Arabic, dealing with the perfection and ends of the soul, virtues as means and vices as extremes. They contain much of interest for the social history of Muslim morals, manners and society. But their philosophical framework is taken from Aristotle, the Peripatetics, and Neoplatonism, and offers little of general philosophical interest that is new. The authors do not enter into the controversy of *kalām* about the concepts of right and wrong, good and evil, so that these *akhlāq* books are not the place to look for ethical philosophy in any analytical style.

In the major philosophers, Fārābī (*c.* 870–950), Ibn Sīnā (980–1037) and Ibn Rushd (1126–98) we do find significant remarks on these concepts, in the Neoplatonic tradition but with individual developments. But they did not write much on ethics in lengthy passages or separate works, so we have to piece their views together from scattered pages. We find that Ibn Rushd, for instance, has much to say on ethics, but perhaps even in him the main interest comes just where he is reacting against Ashʿarite *kalām* and its theistic subjectivism. He compares it to the ethics of the sophists, having observed with his usual acuteness the common elements of subjectivism between the two schools, so remote from each other in time and environment. He strongly upholds the objectivism of Plato and Aristotle, with full consciousness of the great tradition he is following.

Later philosophy is predominantly mystical, a blend of Islamic Sufism and Hellenic Neoplatonism. We can look forward to finding ethical ideas of interest in the Persian works of Ṣadr ad-dīn Shīrāzī and others in this tradition, now being studied intensively by S. H. Nasr and F. Rahman.

3

ETHICAL PRESUPPOSITIONS OF THE QUR'ĀN

I

A considerable debate was carried on in classical Islam over two central and related questions of ethics.

A. A question of ontology: What is the nature of ethical value concepts such as the good and the just?

B. A question of epistemology: How can man know the presence and force of these concepts in particular situations? These are philosophical questions, and to some extent they were argued in terms of truths determinable directly by human intellect. But the debate was mainly conducted by Muslim theologians and jurists who did not always distinguish direct arguments from arguments on the corresponding questions of scriptural interpretation: what does the Qurʾān teach on the nature and knowledge of ethical value concepts? The present article attempts to answer the latter questions only, by a study of the Qurʾān in its own context.

As a framework for study it will be useful to set forth in schematic form those answers to the two questions which may be considered historically possible in the age of the Qurʾān, leaving out many modern ethical theories which do not satisfy this condition. ('Right' will be taken here as the standard concept, but we shall be dealing also with 'just', 'good', 'wrong', 'unjust', 'evil'.)

A. 1. *Objectivism. 'Right' has an objective meaning.*

By 'objective' is meant that there are real qualities or relations of acts that make them right, so that statements about the rightness of acts are true if the required qualities or relations are present and false if they are absent, independently of the opinions or desires of the person who judges them right or wrong.

This type of theory, which had been dominant in Greek philosophy, was held by all the Muʿtazilites and all Muslim philosophers.

2. *Subjectivism. 'Right' has no objective meaning. It means whatever is approved or commanded by someone or other.* This is subdivided into two theories.

(a) 'Right' means whatever is approved and commanded by the Muslim community.

This is human social subjectivism, with the validating society defined as the Muslim community, the *umma*. Such a view was attributed to Islam by Snouck Hurgronje when writing on Islamic consensus (*ijmāʿ*).[1] He thus made the Muslim community more authoritative than the Qurʾān. But it is doubtful whether any Muslim has ever held such a view and some with considerable prestige, Ghazālī in particular, have explicitly denied it.[2] There is one Tradition which may be understood as affirming it: 'Whatever the believers see as good is good with God, and whatever the Muslims see as bad is bad with God.'[3]

(b) 'Right' means whatever is approved and commanded by God.

This theory is clearly a type of subjectivism, as defined above. It may be called theistic or divine subjectivism. But it is more commonly known as ethical voluntarism, since it claims that ethical value concepts must be understood in terms of God's will. The theory is also close to legal positivism, in deriving all moral and legal rules ultimately from prescriptions enunciated by an authority – in this case, God.

It became the prevailing theory among Sunnite jurists and theologians: Shāfiʿites, Ḥanbalites, Ashʿarites and others.

B. 1. *Rationalism. What is right can be known by independent reason.*

Here 'reason' is being used in a broad sense which will cover the kinds of thinking in ethics that are defended by naturalistic as well as intuitionist theories; to distinguish these two types is irrelevant to an investigation of the Qurʾān's presuppositions, since no clear answer could be attained as to which of the two is there presupposed. Reason is called 'independent' in relation to scripture. In sum, the position is that human thinking can make correct ethical judgements by direct operations on the data of experience, without recourse to the judgements of revelation.

Rationalism in this sense can then be subdivided for our purpose into two theories.

(a) What is right can *always* be known by independent reason.

This view may be called complete rationalism. It was the major tradition of Greek philosophy, and was probably the assumption of all the Muslim

[1] See chapter 13 for a statement and criticism of Snouck Hurgronje's theory of *ijmāʿ*, with references to *Œuvres choisies – Selected works*, ed. G.-H. Bousquet and J. Schacht (Leiden: E. J. Brill, 1957).

[2] *Ibid.*, 20, 25, 33–4, and 33, n. 1.

[3] *Mā raʾāhu l-muʾminūna ḥasanan fahuwa ʿinda llāhi ḥasanun, wa mā raʾāhu l-Muslimūna qabīḥan fahuwa ʿinda llāhi qabīḥun*: from Mālik-Shaybānī, Al-Muwaṭṭā' (Lucknow, A. H. 1297 and 1306), p. 140. See chapter 13 for critical comments in the context of *ijmāʿ*.

philosophers. But, for reasons of prudence or genuine religious conviction, none of them takes an explicit stand on this doctrine. All we can say is that they never deny it, that everything they say on ethics is in accord with it, and that their general philosophical tradition would lead them to believe it.

(b) What is right can be known in some cases by reason alone, in others by revelation and derived sources alone, in others by both in agreement.

This view may be called partial rationalism. 'Derived sources' means Traditions, consensus and analogy, all of which in different ways are dependent on the Qur'ān. This was the position of the Mu'tazilites. As rationalistic theologians they found a place for both reason and revelation in ethics, complementing and never opposing each other. Variations in proportions and emphasis are easily possible within this position, which need not be elaborated here.

2. *Traditionalism. We can never know what is right by independent reason, but only by revelation and derived sources.*

This theory does not exclude plentiful use of reason in dependent ways: extracting ethical judgements by interpretation of the Qur'ān and Traditions, determining the consensus of the Community, or drawing conclusions by the method of analogy.

This was the general position of the main schools of Sunnite jurisprudence and theology, coinciding in its range with those who accepted A. 2. (b), ethical voluntarism. Their differences concerned the extent to which the dependent uses of reason were considered permissible according to Islam, understood in the voluntarist-traditionalist spirit. Here we find Shāfi'ī at one extreme and the Zahirites (fundamentalists) at the other.

2

The principal task proposed will be to determine which two of the above positions on questions A. and B. are the implicit standpoints of the Qur'ān. We cannot speak of Qur'ānic theories, because the Qur'ān by its nature and purpose is not a theoretical book of theology and therefore takes up no explicit positions on the questions being asked. But there are assumptions presupposed in the way it expresses ethical messages, and it is these that we are looking for, to bring them as far as possible into the light of day. As a preliminary to this task some brief observations on method will be in order.

The main method to be used will be the analysis of ethical terms and sentences in the Qur'ān. Account will be taken of the chronology of the suras where this is significant; but it will be found that on the whole the Qur'ān maintains a consistent position, with a certain development on question B. For chronology, Blachère's order has been followed and indicated.

The whole of the Qurʾān has been surveyed in preparation for this study. But it would have been too large an undertaking to analyse every relevant term and sentence. Nor is it necessary, since rather firm conclusions can be reached from representative samples. The many repetitions and slight variations in the text can safely be ignored, except for a few references – far from exhaustive – in the notes. But important variations that raise problems will not be ignored.

The classical Arabic commentaries will be set aside, not only because of their vast bulk, whose use would have rendered this study unmanageable, but more essentially because they belonged to schools of theology or jurisprudence which had taken up positions on the questions at issue – often for complex historical reasons arising subsequently to the Qurʾān. Interpretation of the Qurʾān was the accepted method of establishing or confirming a position reached on any grounds; therefore, the interpretations of the schools have to be distrusted. A truer understanding of the Qurʾān can be obtained by looking at it not through their eyeglasses but directly, in its own historical and philological context. For more detached interpretations of words and sentences, the translations and notes of three modern orientalists, Arberry, Blachère and Paret, have been consulted and found helpful.

The two questions, A. and B., will be separated and treated in turn. In this way the answers on ontology and epistemology can be arrived at independently of each other, and the conclusions distinguished more clearly. Finally, the combination of the Qurʾān's answers to A. and B. will be considered, and the consequences for modern Islam indicated briefly.

3

A. I. *Objectivism*. It is fair to call this the common sense understanding of ethical terms in all or most cultures and their languages. Most people who have not been much affected by philosophy or theology think that when they describe someone else as 'just', 'wicked', etc. they are describing a real quality of that person (however hard to analyse), not merely some relation of obedience or disobedience to a social group or even to God. Now we find that the Qurʾān generally uses the Arabic language in its accepted pre-Islamic usage, with a few technical inventions of its own. Therefore, the initial assumption of our discussion has to be that the Qurʾān generally uses ethical terms objectively.

These considerations lead to an appropriate method of discussion. Rather than trying to prove the more obvious conclusion, I hope to disprove the subjectivist interpretations by displaying the difficulties of understanding to which they lead. But there are one or two positive remarks in favour of objectivism that can be made at this stage.

The Qur'ān addresses a great many ethical sentences to pagans, especially in Mecca, who had not yet submitted to the *sharī'a* of Islam. It uses terms such as *ṣāliḥ, ẓulm, 'adl,* and exhorts them to be thoughtful and to reflect, to be honest in their dealings, not to be arrogant or uncharitable. The presumption is that a common ethical language is being used, understood clearly and in the same way by the speaker and the addressed parties. Such a language could not depend on their prior acceptance of the particular scripture being delivered by the speaker. It could not even depend on their acceptance of the earlier revelations of Judaism and Christianity, since the Meccans had not accepted these. Many of the terms used have definite objective meanings in Arabic as far back as we can trace, as will be illustrated in a few cases below in refutation of subjectivist interpretations.

4

A. 2. (a) *Human subjectivism*. This interpretation of the Qur'ān's ethical language can be disposed of easily. In several passages the Qur'ān mentions opposition between a divine prescription and the opinion of a human group, thus disproving decisively any claim of a human group to set the standard of right and wrong.

> When the evil [*sū'u*] of a man's deed is gilded for him so that he thinks it good (*ḥasanan*) – God leads astray whom He will and guides whom He will...[4] S. 35:8 (Bl. 88)

This verse refers to an individual as thinking good what is really evil, thus rejecting egoistic subjectivism. *Sū'u* and *ḥasanan* may here refer to moral evil and good, or simply harm and benefit to the agent.

> Fighting has been prescribed for you, although it is hateful to you. You may hate something when it is good [*khayrun*] for you, and you may like something when it is bad [*sharrun*] for you, God knows and you do not know. S. 2:216 (Bl. 93)

This verse discredits collective human disapproval and approval as standards of value. *Khayrun* and *sharrun* refer to benefit and harm to the agents, as usual

[4] Verse numbers refer to the standard Cairo edition. Translations are my own except where indicated. Blachère's chronological sura numbers are put in parentheses in the text, preceded by Bl.; in the footnotes, without this reference. Where more than one passage is quoted or referred to on the same point they are given in Blachère's order. His periods are as follows: 1–48: Early Meccan; 49–70: Middle Meccan; 71–92: Late Meccan; 93–116: Madinan. R. Blachère, *Le Coran*, II and III (Paris, 1949–51).

in the Qurʾān. All these verses are late, and we shall notice from other evidence as well an increasing tendency in the Madinan suras to assert divine and prophetic authority.

We are not yet concerned with the question whether man may sometimes *know* values without revelation. What has been proved by these verses is that values are *not the same thing* as human dislikes or preferences. And, apart from particular verses, this is what should be expected from the Qurʾān's claim to reveal a divine religion.

5

A. 2. (b) *Ethical voluntarism.* The last statement would seem to support the position that ethical value terms mean only what is approved or disapproved, commanded or forbidden by God. This in fact became the predominant theory in classical Sunnite Islam. Among the reasons for that result, some may be found in the history of Islam after the Prophet; these need not be considered here.[5] But two general features of the Qurʾān could have led to this theory. One is the sense of God's overwhelming power which is conveyed by every sura, and which led to a conclusion in ethics: that if God's commands followed objective principles of value, such as a real justice, these would be something fixed pre-eternally and beyond His control, which would thus set limits to His power and make Him less than omnipotent. The other factor is the Qurʾān's frequent theme of the necessity of God's guidance because of man's tendency to error, as illustrated in the last quotation: 'God knows and you do not know.' We shall discuss that theme in its own right under the heading B., concerning knowledge. The point to be made here is that it could easily lead to an inference: 'God alone knows what is right, therefore what He knows is His own commands', or in other words 'He alone knows what is right because He *decides* what is right'.

But these two features of the Qurʾān leading to ethical voluntarism in Islam are not inevitable interpretations of the Qurʾān. On the first point, Muslim and Christian theologians have often understood justice and other ethical concepts as both objective and attributes of God's essential nature, which are compatible with His omnipotence taken in a moderate sense. On the second point, the inference from God's knowledge to the nature of value is patently unsound, since it fails to exclude the alternative, that He knows things about an objective right that man does not know. Man's need for guidance implies nothing about what it is that the Guide knows, in its metaphysical aspect.

It must therefore be concluded up to here that nothing has been shown

[5] See chapter 5.

about the Qur'ān in general that would favour an ethical voluntarist interpretation of its ontological assumption in ethics. The test must come in textual interpretation of particular passages. I shall now try to show from a variety of texts that a voluntarist interpretation is often impossible or far-fetched.

6

We shall begin by examining texts which contain ethical terms referring to interpersonal human relations.

The verb *ẓalama*, 'to wrong', 'oppress', 'be unjust' to someone is sometimes used with a grammatical object specifying another person as wronged.

> The way [of force] is to be taken only against those who do wrong to the people [*yaẓlimūna n-nāsa*]...[6] S. 42:42 (Bl. 85)

The concept of self-inflicted *ẓulm* is frequently found.

> Whoever does that harms himself [*ẓalama nafsahu*].[7] S. 2:231 (Bl. 93)

Similarly, the verb *quasaṭa*, 'to be just', occurs, followed by the preposition *ilā* and the person treated justly.

> God does not forbid you...to be just to them [*tuqsiṭū ilayhim*]. S. 60:8 (Bl. 112)

How could these sentences possibly be interpreted in terms of obedience or disobedience to divine commands? *yaẓlimūna 'l-nāsa*: 'disobey God in regard to the people'? *tuqsiṭū ilayhim*: 'obey God in regard to them'?

Still more difficult are the passive examples of *ẓalama*.

> Except those who believe and do good deeds and mention God often, and overcome after they have been wronged [*intaṣarū ba'da mā ẓulimū*].[8] S. 26:227 (Bl. 58)

The passive can only indicate something done to a person or persons; it cannot be made to fit a relation of command and obedience between God and the wronged persons, such as 'They have been affected by an act of disobedience to God'. There is no reference to God at all in this and similar phrases affirming a wrong.

[6] Cf. S. 43:76 (63); 16:33 (75); 3:117 (99).

[7] Cf. S. 65:1 (103); 27:44 (69); 16:118 (75); 28:16 (81); 9:70 (115). There are about thirty instances of this phrase (with variations of tenses and persons). For complete references see M. F. 'Abd al-Bāqī, *Al-Mu'jam al-mufahras li-alfāẓ al-Qur'ān al-karīm* (Cairo, 1378/1958–9). See text of this article at note 11 for a brief explanation of 'harm' rather than 'wrong' in these phrases. If this is correct, the difficulty mentioned here would not arise in any of these instances, because 'harming oneself' cannot be related in its own meaning to disobeying commands.

[8] Although Blachère places the sura as middle Meccan, he thinks this final verse is a Madinan addition. Cf. S. 19:60; 21:47 (67); 16:41 (75); 2:272 (93); 4:148 (102); etc. About twenty-five instances.

All this is unnecessary, when there are fully significant objective meanings *of ẓalama* in classical Arabic, one or other of which makes good sense in every use of the verb and its derivatives in the Qurʾān. The dictionaries give the following meanings.[9]

1. (a) 'To put something in a place other than its [proper] place', i.e., 'to misplace'. E.g., *ẓalama l-arḍa*, 'he dug the ground in the wrong place'; *ẓalama ṭ-ṭarīqa*, 'he lost the track'.

(b) Intransitive, 'to go to the wrong place, go astray'. E.g., 'he who takes the wolf as a shepherd has erred (*qad ẓalama*); '*ẓalama l-wādī*, 'the torrent has overflowed, followed an unexpected course'. The Qurʾān contains an instance of this more physical sense.

Each of the two gardens yielded its produce and did not fall short of it at all [*wa lam taẓlim minhu shayʾan*].[10] S. 18:33 (Bl. 70)

In these uses, transitive and intransitive, there is no moral sense of wrongdoing.

2. (a) From 1. (a), 'to harm' someone. This is probably the sense in the Qurʾān's phrases *ẓalama nafsahu* and variants, 'he has harmed himself', etc., because there are ethical difficulties in the usual interpretation, 'he has wronged himself'.[11]

2. (b) From 1. (a) and 2. (a), 'to harm inappropriately', i.e., 'to wrong', 'be unjust' to someone. This is the common meaning in the Qurʾān, outside the context of *ẓulm al-nafs*. It is the ethical meaning, and we have now shown how this meaning arose in a natural sequence from a more physical and equally objective meaning.

This conclusion is confirmed by the careful semantic account of *ẓālim* and the related forms by T. Izutsu.[12] After remarking that 'it is one of the most important negative value words in the Qurʾān', he analyses it as follows:

The primary meaning of *ẒLM* is, in the opinion of many of the authoritative lexicographers, that of 'putting in a wrong place'. In the sphere of ethics it seems to mean primarily 'to act in such a way as to transgress the proper limit and encroach

[9] Based on E. W. Lane, *Arabic-English Lexicon*, 8 vols. (London, 1863–93, reprinted 1955–7); A. de B. Kazimirski, *Dictionnaire arabe-francais*, 2 vols. (Paris, 1846, reprinted 1960); various authors, *Al-Muʿjam al-wasīṭ*, 2 vols. (Cairo, 1960–1). All are derived from the same classical Arabic sources which make abundant use of pre-Islamic poetry. Our order for the meanings of each word is intended to show progression from the more physical to the more abstract, although any order is likely to be somewhat speculative in its details.

[10] I take *minhā* to refer to 'its produce'. Blachère has 'ne *lesèrent en rien leur maître*', taking *ẓalama* as 'harmed' and *minhu* as equivalent to an object. But *ẓalama* 'to harm', is usually followed by a direct object, and *min* cannot be explained in this way.

[11] Explained in chapter 4.

[12] *Ethico-religious concepts in the Qurʾān* (Montreal, 1966), pp. 164–72.

upon the right of some other person'. Briefly and generally speaking, *ẓulm* is to do injustice in the sense of going beyond one's own bounds and doing what one has no right to.[13]

Then, taking 'transgression' as the central notion, Izutsu shows how this can refer to two sets of bounds, those set by society for the needs of social well-being and those set by God.

Izutsu gives many examples of the former, such as usury, unjust divorce, embezzling the property of orphans. It is of particular interest to note that unbelievers, i.e., pre-Islamic Arabs, are also made to use the root *ẓulm*, referring to the destruction of their idols by Abraham (S. 21:59; Bl. 67).

Izutsu, however, remarks quite properly that in the Qurʾān it is difficult or impossible to distinguish the social from the divine bounds, 'for God in the Qurʾānic conception interferes in the minutest details of human affairs'.[14] The 'bounds of God' (*ḥudūd Allāh*) 'are destined to develop later into the Law of Islām'.[15] We should add, however, that the many references to wrongdoings in terms of transgression of divine bounds or commands do not imply that these wrongs have no objective social content and are wrong only, or even primarily, as acts of disobedience.

'Very frequently', however, 'the reason for a particular "bound" remains an unsolvable mystery to men. A "bound" is there simply because God has so decreed.' The example given is the prohibition of the fruit of the Tree to Adam and Eve – if they approach it they will be wrongdoers (*min aẓ-ẓālimīn*) (S.2:35; Bl. 93).[16] Such cases count against the view that all *ẓulm* is to be understood as objective harm or wrong. Some of the ritual and dietary prescriptions and prohibitions of the Qurʾān should probably also be understood in terms of pure decrees – in other words, as supporting ethical voluntarism. General conclusions on this issue will be stated after the rest of the particular evidence has been reviewed.

7

Next we shall consider *ʿadl*, 'justice', and the related forms. This is generally synonymous with *qisṭ*, mentioned previously, and both are opposites of *ẓulm*. If there is any difference between them in the Qurʾān, it may be one of emphasis: that *qisṭ* refers primarily to the quality of action of an agent (e.g., a judge or guardian) towards someone, *ʿadl* primarily to equitable distribution between two or more recipients of something. For instance:

[13] *Ibid.*, pp. 164–5.
[14] *Ibid.*, p. 166.
[15] *Ibid.*, p. 168.
[16] *Ibid.*, p. 167.

If you fear that you will not be just towards [*tuqsiṭū fī*] orphans, marry such women as you please – two, three, four; but if you fear that you will not be equitable [[*taʿdilū*] [between them]], then only one... S.4:3 (Bl. 102)

Both words have clear objective meanings, but we shall leave *qisṭ* aside and follow *ʿadl*.

If it [one of two quarrelling parties] yields, set things right between them with justice [*fa-aṣliḥū baynahumā bi l-ʿadli*]. S. 49:9 (Bl. 114)

What is significant here for our purpose is 'between them', because this demonstrates *ʿadl* as a certain relation between two persons, without reference to commands from a third party.

God commands justice [*ʿadl*], beneficence [*iḥsān*] and giving [*ītāʾi*] to relatives, and He forbids shameful and blameworthy acts [*al-faḥshāʾ wa l-munkar*] and insolence [*baghy*]. S. 16:90 (Bl. 75)

In this verse, a reduction of *ʿadl* to 'obedience to divine commands' would not quite make the sentence a tautology but would make it vacuous and hardly worth asserting. All the other virtues and vices mentioned (except giving to relatives) would meet the same fate. Further, if they were all reduced to obedience and disobedience, there would be no difference between the virtues or between the vices, and the vacuity of the sentence as a whole would approach a maximum. How much easier and more significant to find in each of the virtues and vices a specific, objective character! We shall shortly study what this character is in the case of *ʿadl*.

Following the procedure used above for *ẓulm*, we shall now give lexical evidence for the intelligible meaning of *ʿadl* in classical Arabic.

1. The basic meaning of the adjective *ʿadīl* is 'equal', especially in weight or bulk, and there is a noun, *ʿidl*, meaning 'an object equal to another in weight'. In a recent article,[17] C. Bailey has made a study of this root as used among the present-day bedouin of the Beersheba desert, and concluded that their image of *ʿadl* is 'flat, even or well-balanced', as seen in the proper position of the saddlebags (*khurj*) on each side of the camel or the load itself (*ḥiml*) on its hump. The opposite is *māyil*, 'listing', i.e., 'leaning to one side'.[18] Evidently this is a matter of the same practical importance to nomads with pack animals as the even loading of the cargo in a ship's hull is to mercantile

[17] 'A note on the bedouin image of 'adl as justice' *The Muslim World*, 66 (1976), pp. 133–5.

[18] The contrast of *ʿadl* and *mayl* is found in S. 4:129 (102): 'You will be unable to be equitable (*taʿdilu*) between wives, even if you desire it. Then do not follow your inclination totally (*falā tamīlu kullaʾl-mayli*) so as to leave any of them as it were in suspense.'

seamen. There are related physical meanings of *ʿadl* as 'balanced', 'symmetrical', 'well-proportioned'.

2. From 1., *ʿadl*, 'just' and *ʿadala*, 'to be just'. Hence, *ʿaddala*, 'to adjust' 'render justice', and *aʿdala*, 'to redress' an uneven balance of rights.

3. *ʿadala bayna ʾl-amrayn*, 'to hesitate' between alternatives, also derived from 1., 'to be in equilibrium' in thoughts and desires.

4. *ʿadala*, 'to turn aside', 'go astray': not clearly related to the other meanings.

The conclusion from all the evidence must be that *ʿadl* originated as an intelligible physical concept of even balance and was developed into a no less intelligible concept of the equitable, the balance of natural justice. This was commonly applied to interpersonal relations, as with corresponding concepts in all cultures, and it had primarily nothing to do with obedience to the commands of revelation. This latter interpretation developed in Islam out of another aspect of the Qurʾān which will be dealt with later: the emphasis on divine guidance as the main or sole source of knowledge of justice. It finally led to Shāfiʿī's stark definition of *ʿadl*: 'Justice is that one should act in obedience to God [*wa l-ʿadlu an yaʿmala bi-ṭāʿati ʾllāh*].'[19] This was no doubt one of the most successful stipulated definitions in history, since it provided the theoretical basis for the classical system of Sunnite law and much of theology. But it should be clear by now that it was not based on the meaning of *ʿadl* as used in the Qurʾān.

8

The adjectives *ḥasan*, 'good', and its contrary *sūʾ*, 'evil', can be analysed in a different way. They are each applied as qualities of two kinds of things, (1) experiences and (2) actions, including speech. It will be more enlightening to start by examining their meanings in the Qurʾān as applied to experiences.

The Reward of the next life is an experience often described as 'good', e.g., in S. 92:6 (Bl. 14): '...and believes in the best thing [*al-ḥusnā*]' [i.e., Reward].[20] This and similar sentences show *ḥasan* meaning 'satisfactory', 'beneficial'; it cannot possibly be interpreted as 'commanded' or 'permitted'.

When we turn to actions and speech, we do not find a sharply different meaning, connected with commands. This is well illustrated in a sentence in which the two applications of *ḥasan* are closely linked.

And it is said to those who fear God: 'What has your Lord sent down?' They say 'Good [*khayran*]. For those who have done good [*aḥsanū*] in this world there is a good

[19] *Risāla*, ed. M. Shakir (Cairo, 1358/1940), p. 25.

[20] So Arberry, Blachère, Paret; Blachère notes that this is the traditional interpretation of the classical commentators. Cf. S. 18:2 (70): 'a good Reward (*ajran ḥasanan*)'.

[*ḥasanatun*] [reward, in this life?], and certainly the House of the after-life will be better [*khayrun*], and pleasant will be [*niʿma*]the House of the godfearing.' S. 16:30 (Bl. 75)

Here *aḥsanū* is balanced by *ḥasanatun*, and the only common meaning that can pair them is 'benefit': 'done something beneficial to others' and 'received a reward beneficial to themselves'. Thus *aḥsanū* applied to actions cannot mean '*obeyed the sharīʿa*'. The argument is reinforced by the presence of *khayr* and *niʿma*, both referring to satisfying experience and being practically equated with *ḥasan*.

Equally clear is S. 55:60 (Bl. 28): 'Is the Reward of doing good [*iḥsān*] anything but doing good [*iḥsān*]?' The second *iḥsān* refers to an act of God, and so cannot possibly mean 'permitted' or 'approved by the *sharīʿa*'. This is a point to be developed later when acts of God will be studied within our context. What is pertinent to human relations which we are now studying is that if the second *iḥsān* means 'beneficence', 'benefitting others', the first must mean the same thing because of the clear parallelism; compare the English saying, 'One good turn deserves another'.

In S. 51:15–19 (Bl. 49), the doers of good (*al-muḥsinūn*) are described in specific terms as those who pray most of the night and give alms to beggars and outcasts.

In S. 16:90 (Bl. 75), 'God commands justice [*ʿadl*], beneficence [*iḥsān*]', etc. This verse has already been commented on above in connection with *ʿadl*, where it was argued that if the virtues and vices mentioned meant only 'obedience to commands' the whole sentence would be almost tautologous and certainly pointless.

S. 27:89 (Bl. 81): 'Anyone who delivers a good [deed] [*jāʾa bi l-ḥasanati*] will receive something better [*khayrun*] than it.' Here is a clear correspondence of *ḥasan* and *khayr*, both in the sense of 'beneficial', *ḥasan* referring to an act, *khayr* to an experience (a reward). *Ḥasan* cannot mean 'commanded' or 'permitted' without losing the comparison, 'good' – 'better'.

The classical dictionaries explain the main meaning of *ḥasan* and related forms in a straightforward way. The adjective *ḥasanun* means (1) 'beautiful', (2) 'good', and the primary form of the verb *ḥasuna* means (1) 'to be beautiful', (2) 'to be good'. II. '*Ḥassanaʾ* means 'to make beautiful or good', then (less common) 'to think beautiful or good', i.e., 'to approve'. IV. *Aḥsana* means (1) 'to make beautiful', and more commonly (2) 'to do good', 'to benefit someone', (3) 'to know well'. X. *Istaḥsana* means 'to find beautiful, good', i.e., 'to approve'.

Among the significant points are these two. The basic meaning is aesthetic, and beauty is not based on commands or approval. The tenth form, *istaḥsana*, would make no sense if *ḥasuna* meant 'to be commanded, permitted or approved', for then it would have to mean 'to find approved', etc. Thus it implies an objective meaning for *ḥasuna*, 'to be good'.

All this is confirmed by Izutsu in his description of *ḥasan* in the Qurʾān: 'Like *khayr*, this word has a very wide range of application. It is an adjective which may be applied to almost anything that is felt to be "pleasing", "satisfying", "beautiful" or "admirable"'.[21] There follows a series of illustrations of meanings of *ḥasan* and related forms.

It is true that one of the common specific meanings of *iḥsān* is 'fear of God' (*taqwā*), described by Izutsu as 'profound piety towards God and all human deeds that originate in it',[22] and this meaning falls within the scope of religious obedience rather than objective virtue. This gives us occasion to note an important point concerning the status of the argument between objectivists and voluntarists on the interpretation of value terms in the Qurʾān. Voluntarists maintained that these terms as applied to actions and character *never* have any objective meaning but refer only to divine commands or prohibitions, and obedience or disobedience to them. Their opponents claimed much less on the other side, simply that objective meanings *often* occur, not that every value term in the Qurʾān has such a meaning. Thus their task was easier in this respect: not to prove every instance according to their interpretation, but only to disprove voluntarist claims with regard to some cases. Actually, as we are seeing, objective uses are far more than a few, and perhaps the majority.

9

There will be no need to continue with further examples. I shall simply name some of the more common remaining ethical concepts of the Qurʾān. The contrary of *ḥasan* is generally *sūʾ*. A similar pair of contraries is *khayr* and *sharr*, 'good' and 'bad', but these two refer more often to experiences than to actions. They may also serve as nouns, so that *khayr* may mean 'goods' and even be synonymous with *māl*, 'wealth'. Then it is extended to God's benefits to man, the real goods.[23] *Birr*, 'piety', and *ithm*, 'sin', may also be regarded as a pair. *Ṣāliḥ* and *sayyiʾ*, 'good' and 'bad', refer most often to actions, as in the frequent clause, 'those who believe and do what is good (or right)' (*alladhīna āmanū wa ʿamilū ṣ-ṣāliḥāt*).

Ḥalāl and *ḥarām*, 'permitted' and 'forbidden', *ṭāʿa* and *maʿṣiya*, 'obedience' and 'disobedience', are two pairs which refer directly to divine commands and

[21] Izutsu, *Ethico-religious concepts*, p. 221.
[22] *Ibid.*, p. 224.
[23] *Ibid.*, pp. 217–21.

prohibitions and derive their values from them. Somewhat similar are *maʿrūf*, 'what is recognized', and *munkar*, 'what is rejected', as in the famous sentence 'to prescribe what is recognized and forbid what is rejected [*al-amru bi l-maʿrūfi wa n-nahyu ʿani ʾl-munkar*]' (S. 7:157 [Bl. 89], and elsewhere). *Al-maʿrūf* was originally 'what is recognized by society' (the tribe or the Arabs), hence, 'acceptable', 'appropriate', 'right'; and the corresponding sequence is found in *al-munkar*. In the Qurʾān they appear to mean simply 'right' and 'wrong', but they may have acquired fresh meanings of divine recognition and rejection.[24]

There are many other terms, all carefully explained by Izutsu, but enough has been said to illustrate how they range between clear objective meanings and meanings referring directly to divine commands and prohibitions. The general conclusion must be that there are plenty of inescapable examples of the former and, in consequence, that the voluntarist interpretation of *all* human ethical terms in the Qurʾān is untenable.

10

Many ethical attributes are predicated of God, and these are impossible to interpret in terms of obedience to His own commands, which were made for man. E.g.:

> that He may justly [*bi ʾl-qisṭi*] reward those who believe and do good deeds.
> S. 10:4 (Bl. 86)

> God is not a wrongdoer [*laysa bi ẓallāmin*] to His servants. S. 8:51 (Bl. 97)

Even more hopeless are some negative passive sentences, in which it is denied that anyone is wronged by God.

> To each one there will be degrees [of recompense] depending on what they have done, so that He may pay them in full for their deeds and they shall not be wronged [*lā yuẓlamūn*]. S. 46:19 (Bl. 90)

> Whatever you spend on the Path of God will be restored to you, and you will not be wronged [*lā tuẓlamūn*].[25] S. 80:60 (Bl. 97)

Both grammatically and theologically, fantastic contortions would have to be performed to interpret such sentences in terms of disobedience to God's

[24] *Ibid.*, pp. 213–17, an excellent analysis of these two terms.
[25] Other verses denying God's wrong to servants: S. 16:33 (75); 16:118 (75); 11:101 (77); 30:9 (76); 7:160 (89); 2:57 (93); 4:40 (102); etc.

commands, and the resulting equivalent sentences would be so absurd that they are better left unmentioned.

Similar difficulties arise with other qualities of God:

In the name of God, the Merciful, the Compassionate. S. 1:1 (Bl. 46)

The word of your Lord has been completed in truthfulness and justice [*ṣidqan wa ʿadlan*]. No one can alter his speeches, He is hearing, knowing! S. 6:115 (Bl. 91)

Faced with many examples of moral qualities ascribed to God, voluntarist theologians like al-Ashʿarī could only argue that these terms could not be understood in the same senses when applied to God, following the interpretative method of 'purification' (*tanzīh*) by which God is cleared of all human resemblances. This method might solve the immediate problem suggested above, as well as others, such as that of reconciling God's justice with predestination – God does not have to be 'just' in the human sense, but in another, transcendent sense. But the price for this manoeuvre is too great: it renders these attributes of God meaningless and unappealing to man's moral feelings and religious devotion. What loyalty does man owe to a God who is not just in the way we understand justice? All that would be left as a motive for loyalty is fear. This surely is not the whole message of the Qur'ān about man's relation to God. A general view of the Book will not support such an interpretation, for it is a book full of human ethical attitudes, and these attitudes are ascribed to God as parts of His perfection, without any suggestions that something completely different is meant. How much simpler and more effective will the notion of *ʿadl* be if it is understood in a sense intelligible by a human analogy!

II

The conclusion on the ontological status of values studied under the heading A. has now become very clear: that the Qur'ān frequently refers to objective values, which cannot be analysed completely in terms of commands and obedience. This conclusion coincides with that of the classical Muʿtazilites.

When we turn to question B., man's knowledge of right and wrong, we get a different picture, although a less decisive one. Here the emphasis is on man's need for divine guidance in ethical matters. The evidence on this question will be reviewed in the order of the theories outlined as possible in §1.

B. 1 (a). This is an extreme position: that man can *always* know what is right and wrong by the use of his natural reason, independently of revealed scriptures. A modified form of this view, though still extreme, was that the uneducated majority of people does need revelation to teach them ethical truths in ways they can understand and accept, but that there is a minority able to work out these truths for themselves in *all* situations.

It can easily be shown that even the modified view is not that of the Qurʾān. From the general tenor of the Qurʾān it can be seen as improbable that it allows a class of moral people who can do without revelation altogether. That would make revelation morally useless to some people, contrary to the Qurʾān's emphasis on the need of all mankind for it. It is true that the Qurʾān distinguishes 'those who know' and 'those who reflect' from the heedless people, but there is no reason to think that the former class can do without the help of revelation. The Qurʾān stresses the opposite, the dependence of all men and women on divine guidance as contained in scriptures, as a necessary source of moral knowledge. We may as well present at this point some of the evidence for this assertion; the entire evidence would be far too great to write down, and unnecessary since it pervades the whole of the Qurʾān.

We can begin with the concept of guidance (*hudā*) and its opposite, error (*ḍalāl*). From the earliest suras to the latest this pair is a leading theme.

He found you wandering and guided you. S. 93:7 (Bl. 4)

There have been different interpretations of *ḍāllan*, but the most natural one is 'in error' in religion, including perhaps ethical ideas.

He knows better who has wandered from His path, and He knows better who has been guided. S. 53:30 (Bl. 30)

And We made them leaders guiding by Our command. S. 21:73 (Bl. 67)

And whomever God guides, He is the rightly guided, and whomever He leads astray
You will not find patrons for them, apart from Him. S. 17:97 (Bl. 74)

Guidance is done through the Book, as will be shown, but leading astray (*iḍlāl*) is obviously not done by this means. This shows that God influences human minds in other ways, perhaps by making them disposed to ignore scripture.

And formerly We gave guidance to Moses, and bequeathed to the Israelites the Book
As guidance and a reminder to men possessed of minds [*ulī l-albāb*].
S. 40:53–4 (Bl. 80)

Here guidance and the Book are identified.

Announce the good news to my servants Who listen to the statement and follow the best of it. They are the ones whom God has guided, and they are the possessors of minds. S. 39:17–18 (Bl. 82)

This is the same triple connection: the Book, guidance, intelligence.

You did not know what the Book was nor what belief [*īmān*] was; but We made it a light by which We guide whom We will of Our servants. And you will guide along a straight path, the path of God... S. 42:52 (Bl. 85)

And they say: 'Praise to God who guided us to this! We should not have been guided rightly if God had not guided us; the messengers of our Lord came with the truth [*bi l-ḥaqqi*]. S. 7:43 (Bl. 89)

Say: 'God's guidance is the true guidance, and we are commanded to surrender [*li nuslima*] to the Lord of the worlds. S. 6:71 (Bl. 91)

The conjunction of guidance and surrender may be significant, indicating the Muslim's surrender of his personal judgement to the guidance of God.

That is the Book, in which there is no doubt, guidance to the godfearing...
S. 2:2 (Bl. 93)

Here the idea of the Book as guidance occurs at the opening of one of the most important suras of the Qur'ān.

Give good news to the patient
Who when a disaster strikes them, say: 'We belong to God and to Him return!'
Upon them are blessings and mercy from their Lord, and they are the rightly guided.
S. 2:155–7 (Bl. 93)

These verses are quoted to illustrate a frequent meaning of *hudā* and its derivatives: not so much instruction on particular duties as orientation to man's situation in the world, his belonging to God and awaiting a Judgement from Him.

It is not for any believer, man or woman, when God and His Messenger have decreed a matter, to have the choice in the affair. Whosoever disobeys God and His Messenger has gone astray into manifest error. S. 33:36 (Bl. 105) (Arberry's translation)

Here is an unusually sharp command to Muslims to surrender their moral judgements to the decisions of God and the Prophet. The Qur'ān grows more authoritarian in the later suras.[26]

12

Certain other themes are closely linked with that of guidance, reinforcing the stress on revelation as by far the most important if not the only source of guidance.

[26] For other evidence see S. 2:29 (93): 'the bounds of God (*ḥudūd allāhi*)'; 64:12 (95): 'Obey God and obey the Prophet'; 3:20 (99): 'If they surrender they will be rightly guided;' 3:164 (99): 'He the Messenger will teach them the Book and wisdom (*al-ḥikma*)'; 5:44 (116): 'Whoever does not judge according to what God has sent down, these are the unbelievers' (also verses 45–50); 5:87 (116): 'You who believe, do not prohibit the good things that God has allowed you.'

The theme of the Book of God is repeated over and over in various forms from beginning to end. It is impossible to cover this theme in its details;[27] indications will be given from a few passages showing that the Book is the prime source of religious knowledge, including moral knowledge.

The earliest sura in the Qurʾān according to both traditional and modern scholars is S. 96 (Bl. 1), and it contains this well-known emphatic message in verses 3–5:

Recite: And your Lord is the most generous
Who taught by the pen,
Taught man what he did not know.

Although these verses do not specify moral knowledge, they set a tone which was to be followed in the rest of the Qurʾān: that this Book is the source of the most important knowledge, and without it man would be ignorant of such knowledge.

What is the matter with the way you make decisions [*taḥkumūn*]?
Do you have a Book in which you study? S. 68:36–7 (Bl. 51)

Muḥammad is still in Mecca and the passage is directed to pagans. It is implied clearly enough that a scripture is indispensable for sound moral judgements.

We gave them clear evidence [*bayyināt*] of the Command. So they did not disagree until after knowledge had come to them, being insolent to each other.
S. 45:17 (Bl. 73)

This may be the first explicit description of revelation as a command. Knowledge is here equated with the message of revelation; natural knowledge is ignored.

We never punish until we have sent a Messenger. S. 17:15 (Bl. 74)

The implication is that before or beyond the reach of revelation man cannot attain the moral knowledge required to make him accountable and liable to just punishment. S. 40:53–4 (Bl. 80), already quoted above, states:

We formerly gave Moses guidance and bequeathed to the Israelites the Book
As guidance and a reminder to those possessing minds.

These two verses state neatly the idea of the Book as guidance. But the last phrase may well be interpreted in the opposite direction, because 'a reminder' (*dhikrā*) must be of something known previously, and 'to those possessing minds' suggests that either the reminder or the previous knowledge must come through the intelligence.

[27] See especially A. Jeffery, *The Qurʾan as Scripture* (New York, 1952).

An interesting sidelight is cast by the story of Adam and Eve, as narrated in S. 7:19ff. (Bl. 89) and elsewhere. The Tree is not called a tree of knowledge but a tree of life; after eating its fruit the first couple became conscious of their sexual organs. Knowledge could not be gained by eating fruit or by any other natural means, but only by a revelation, which was to be given first to Noah.

Shall I seek a judge [*ḥakaman*] other than God, when it is He who has sent down to you all the Book with clear distinctions [*mufaṣṣalan*]? S. 6:114

There were no state judges in ancient Arabia, but the English word 'judge' connotes, better than 'arbiter', the function of making moral judgements, which is well indicated in this verse.

Truly God was gracious to the believers
when He raised up among them a Messenger
from themselves, to recite to them His signs
and to purify them, and to teach them
the Book and the Wisdom, though before they were
in manifest error. S. 3:164 (Bl. 99) (Arberry's translation)

This is a concise summary of the Qurʾān's central message. 'The Wisdom' (*al-ḥikma*) probably includes moral wisdom; it is closely associated here with the teaching of the Book. 'Guidance' (*hudā*) is not mentioned here, but it can be inferred from its opposite, 'error' (*ḍalāl*).

We have sent down to you the Book with the truth [*bi l-ḥaqqi*], that you may judge between people according to what God has shown you. S. 4:105 (Bl. 102)

The verse suggests that the Book has given Muḥammad some special knowledge enabling him to make ethical and legal judgements. That, however, would be a temporary advantage due to his prior knowledge of the texts; soon they would be available equally as a guide for all Muslims.

We can safely conclude from all these passages and many others that knowledge (*ʿilm*) is closely associated with scripture as its source. Next, we may ask what it is contrasted with. The obvious answer is ignorance, and that answer can hardly be avoided in a general sense. But if we take the Arabic word *jahl* and its relatives as 'ignorance' in a purely intellectual sense we are liable to misunderstand this word in its Qurʾānic context. Here it means 'moral ignorance', 'perverseness', 'sinfulness', as in the verse S. 7:138 (Bl. 89):

And they said, 'Moses, make us a god like the gods they have!' He said, 'You are an ignorant people [*qawmun tajhalūn*]'.

In S. 33:72 (Bl. 105), *jahl* appears in an emphatic form and is almost synonymous with wrongdoing:

We offered the trust to the heavens and the earth and the mountains, but they refused to carry it and were afraid of it; and man carried it. Surely he is sinful, very foolish [*ẓalūman jahūlan*]. (Arberry's translation)

Once *jahl* is contrasted with *hudā*, 'guidance':

If God had willed, he would have gathered them to guidance, so do not be among the ignorant. S. 6:35 (Bl. 91)

Since *hudā* is closely associated with scripture, as has been seen, *jahl* must here be thought of as synonymous with *ḍalāl*, the condition of wandering in error which is characteristic of those without a scripture.

It might be thought that revealed knowledge is contrasted with natural knowledge acquired by 'reason' (*ʿaql*). But that is a later Islamic contrast, of which there is no sign in the Qurʾān. The noun *ʿaql* does not occur at all. The verb *ʿaqala*, 'to understand', is quite frequent, but it nearly always refers to people understanding 'the signs' (*āyāt*) of God. His message expressed in writing or through nature. Two phrases are common: 'Will you not understand? [*alā taʿ-qilūn*]' and 'Perhaps you will understand [*laʿallakum taʿqilūn*]'. Certainly there is no opposition towards understanding, but its proper object is regularly God-given truths, not scientific knowledge without religious relevance.

Let us come now to what is really contrasted with revelation, as a source of moral guidance: it is passion (*al-hawā*), which is an arbitrary force, 'whims and fancies', leading man to mere supposition (*ẓann*) and error (*ḍalāl*) in his practical decisions.

Your friend is not wandering nor astray
Nor does he speak from impulse (*ʿani l-hawā*).
It is nothing but a revelation revealed. S. 53:2–4 (Bl. 30)

These verses and others like them set the alternative sources of speech: either guidance by revelation or error springing from personal impulses and desires. The third source, reflection by natural reason, so highly prized by Greek philosophers, is nowhere in sight.

David, we have made you a successor on earth, so judge between people by the Truth and do not follow passion [*al-hawā*], for it will lead you astray from God's path. S. 38:26 (Bl. 61)

Then We set you on a Path [*ʿalā sharīʿatin*] of Command [*min al-amri*], so follow it and do not follow the passions of those who do not know. S. 45:18 (Bl. 73)

The contrast is very clear in these two verses: either God's path or passions.

Many lead astray by their whims, without knowledge.[28] S. 6:119 (Bl. 91)

To judge between them in accordance with what God has revealed. Do not follow their passions, away from the truth that has come to you. For each of your communities We have made a Path and a Way. S. 5:48 (Bl. 116)

Finally, it will be relevant to quote a sentence that uses quite a different metaphor but reinforces the importance of divine guidance.

And he to whom God does not provide a light, for him there is no light.
S. 24:40 (Bl. 107)

This is the concluding sentence of the famous Light verses. These verses do not refer specifically to the light of knowledge from scripture, but they may well include this kind of light which is so prominent in the Qurʾān's moral and religious teaching.

The general conclusions from the evidence sampled in this section must be that the Book itself is regarded as far the most important or the only source of moral and religious guidance for man, and that neglect of this guidance leaves open only one alternative, an immoral one: to follow passions. Thus the thesis suggested in B. 1 (a) (beginning of § 11), that man (or even some men) can *always* know moral truths by natural reason, has to be rejected as being at the opposite extreme to what the Qurʾān is saying.

13

B. 1 (b) Can man *sometimes* know right by natural reason, independent of scripture? In spite of the heavy emphasis on reliance on revelation, the use of independent reason in ethical judgements is never ruled out explicitly in the Qurʾān, and there are some considerations that favour an implicit assumption of its use.

First of all, there is a general point: that the Qurʾān and Muḥammad both display a common sense attitude, and we should not expect either of them to claim that for every ethical judgement he makes a man must consult a book or a scholar, or work out an analogy when the book or scholar give no direct answer to the problem. The *Sīra* and the Traditions confirm this view of Muḥammad, for they are full of impromptu ethical judgements by him and his Companions. We can assume that Muḥammad understood the intention and spirit of the Qurʾān, and that the Companions followed his practice.

[28] Cf. S. 6:116 and 148 (91), *aẓ-ẓann*; 4:135 (102), *al-hawā*.

Second, although the noun *ʿaql* (intellect) is not found, the Qurʾān is full of references in other expressions to people who are intelligent (*yaʿqilūn*), who think (*yatafakkarūn*), are possessed of minds (*ulī l-albāb*), are observant (*ulī l-abṣār*), etc. It is true, as stated above, that in most passages the proper object of thought is said to be the 'signs' (*āyāt*) of God in nature and history, showing His benevolence to man and His judgement of man in this life and the next, rather than the content of particular or general ethical judgements. Still, the former are considered necessary ingredients of an ethical outlook; the reflective activity in them clearly goes beyond reading scriptures; and the same intelligence would surely be capable of making ethical judgements.

Third, in the Meccan period, where the Qurʾān confronts pagans, they are condemned for moral evil although they were unacquainted with scriptures; hence, they must have been assumed to have a moral sense independent of scriptures.

'What has pushed you into Saqar?' They say: 'We were not of those who prayed, and we did not feed the needy.' S. 74:42–4 (Bl. 36)

Have We not given him two eyes,
And a tongue and two lips,
And guided him on the two Paths?
Yet he has not attacked the steep Path.
And what makes you understand what is the steep Path?
It is freeing a slave
Or giving food on a day of hunger
To an orphan relative
Or a needy man in misery.

S. 90:8–16 (Bl. 40)

In passages such as these it seems clear that the pagan is expected to know his duties by his own thought.

But in the Madinan period there is a shift of emphasis; here the Qurʾān addresses Muslims and is concerned to build up a system of ethics and law based on revelation, as well as to bolster Muḥammad's authority as an arbitrator and judge.

Say to those who have been given the Book and to those without one [*al-ummiyyīn*]: 'Have you surrendered [*a-aslamtum*]?' For if they have surrendered they are rightly guided.[29] S. 3:20 (Bl. 99)

A fourth point is that the Qurʾān urges not merely the performance of

[29] Cf. S. 2:155–7 (93); 3:164 (99); 5:44–8 (116), all quoted above, §11 and 12, in evidence of the authority of scripture.

specific kinds of acts but the cultivation of virtues – patience, gratitude, sincerity, and so forth – and it is a strained interpretation to reduce all these to obedience (*ṭāʿa*) and fear of God (*taqwā*). In other words, patience, gratitude, sincerity, etc., have their own moral content which can be understood by intelligence and cultivated by the good person.

None of these points is conclusive by itself, but taken together, and with other similar indications, they make it quite probable that the Qur'ān allows for independent ethical judgement by man. One reason why no certain conclusion can be attained is that the Qur'ān couples so closely two qualities of the good person: belief in God and doing right. The phrase 'those who believe and do right acts' is constant. Is it only those who believe who do right acts? If so, do they always do them? And when they do them, does it always follow from their belief and, more particularly, from guidance derived from revelation? Or, on the contrary, does man start with right action and proceed from there inevitably to belief? We do not know the Qur'ān's answers to these questions, because it never faces them. From its unquestioning simplicity much of its religious force is derived; but it has left many unanswered questions to stimulate theologians and historians alike. For my part, I can only given an unproved opinion based on many impressions suggested above: that the Muʿtazilites were right in their interpretation of the Qur'ān as allowing some scope for rational ethical judgements by believers and unbelievers.

14

2. The final alternative, that man can know right only through revelation, now receives an answer which is the obverse of that just given in 1 (b): that it cannot be proved incorrect, but that it is more probable that man has other paths to ethical knowledge besides revelation. The truth discovered under 1(a), however, remains a certainty: that the Qur'ān lays heavy emphasis on itself as the prime source of ethical knowledge and guidance for man.

15

The conclusions attained may now be summarized and related to each other. A. Ontology: Ethical value has an objective reality and is not reducible in essence to the commands and prohibitions of God. Too many passages in the Qur'ān would otherwise be inexplicable, as shown at length above. B. Epistemology: The chief source of ethical knowledge is revelation, particularly the Qur'ān. It is probable, but unproved, that natural reason is also capable of forming ethical judgements.

In the history of Islamic thought these two questions have not been separated, so that there has constantly been a pairing of A. 2(b), ethical voluntarism, with B. 2, traditionalism (Ashʿarism and the Sunnī law schools), and of A. 1, objectivism, with B. 1(b), partial rationalism (Muʿtazilism). In particular from traditionalism in *knowledge* voluntarism in ethical *ontology* has been inferred. We can now see that this is an illegitimate inference. It is quite possible to hold both B. 2, that *all* knowledge of ethical values comes through revelation, and A. 1, that these values are objective (however useless that fact might be to man, since their objective essences and applications would be beyond the range of natural knowledge). If we now substitute 'most' (B. 1(b)) for 'all' knowledge (B. 2), we arrive at the combination advocated here as the implicit position of the Qurʾān, which also happens to be that of the Muʿtazilites.[30]

Even Izutsu makes a mistake in inferring from traditionalism to voluntarism, where he writes:

> As we might expect, the final yardstick of justice in such cases is, according to the Qurʾānic view, furnished by God's will. Revelation, in short, is the ultimate basis of *qisṭ*. The point comes out with utmost clarity in verses like the following:
>
> Whoso judges not by what God has sent down: such are *kāfirūn*.... Whoso judges not by what God sent down: such are wrongdoers (*ẓālimūn*). (V, 48–9/44–5)[31]

The verse states that man must *judge* by revelation, but it neither says nor implies anything about the final yardstick of justice, the ultimate basis of *qisṭ*. Revelation can equally well be the *channel of knowledge* of an objective justive which is the *ultimate basis* or final yardstick.

The chief contribution we have made, therefore, has been to separate two questions that had always been merged, thus permitting much greater clarity and less confusion about what the Qurʾān's positions on ethical theory really are.

16

Does all this carry any practical messages to modern Muslims? I think it does. But before discussing them, it is necessary to say that this article has been written with no practical purpose in mind, but only to reach a true understanding of what the Qurʾān presupposes on the points at issue.

On the first issue, since there is a clear presumption of objective values, the

[30] There is no contradiction between what is ascribed to the Muʿtazilites here and the 'partial rationalism' ascribed to them above. Their general view was that most but not all ethical truth is learned from the Qurʾān. Of course there could be variations in degree concerning how much could be learned by reason and how much from the Qurʾān.

[31] Izutsu, *Ethico-religious concepts*, p. 209.

basis is laid for the possibility of the independent use of man's reason in ethics. Otherwise it would be ruled out, as the Ashʿarites and their associates realized, for the combination of ethical voluntarism with rationalism[32] is an impossible one. The domination of voluntarism in classical Islamic law and theology must have undermined the confidence of ordinary Muslims in their ability to make sound ethical judgements, since these were supposed to be entirely drawn from revelation and the *ʿulamāʾ* were the possessors of expert knowledge of revelation. The consequences were not always bad, for the *ʿulamāʾ* sometimes exercised a restraining influence on autocratic rulers like the Ottoman sultan, Selim the Grim. But it means that, in general, reform movements and revolutions had to have religious leadership, by mahdis, imams or sufi shaykhs, for they alone could legitimately claim knowledge of the good of the people, through their understanding of the divine guidance through revelation. It was only when conditions in Muslim countries became desperate, owing to the domination of European powers in the nineteenth and early twentieth centuries, that secular Muslim reformers in high positions began to take steps based on national interests without seeking scriptural authority. The extreme case was Atatürk, who thought that to make a social and political revolution he had to reject Islam itself and diminish its power in Turkey. He was probably right about the traditional Islam which he knew. But on the basis of a proper understanding of ethical objectivism in the Qurʾān it is clear that the use of ethical reason is possible for Muslims. Many modern Muslims have in fact understood this, without having proved it decisively from texts.

Meanwhile, recent philosophers in the West have mounted heavy attacks on objectivism in ethics from various points of view. This is not the place to discuss the merits of modern theories of ethics, on which there is no agreement. All we need say in the present context is that objectivism, of one type or another (especially naturalistic theories), is holding its own in the current unsettled debate, and that this is the viewpoint of the Qurʾān, which clearly rejects all types of ethical subjectivism, emotivism, prescriptivism, existentialism, etc., without being specific about the type of objectivism it accepts.

On the second issue, it has been shown as probable that some extent of exercise of human ethical judgement independent of revelation is permitted by the Qurʾān, but no precision emerges about the extent. What we can do, then, is to state the limits on both sides. On the side of latitude, I do not think it is possible to be a Muslim in the full sense while taking no ethical guidance at all from the Qurʾān, in view of the Qurʾān's heavy emphasis on the need

[32] As stated in § 1, 'rationalism' is being used in a broad sense, to include naturalist as well as intuitionist theories of ethical knowledge.

of man for such guidance and the certainty of his going astray without it. On the traditional side, it has been shown that there is no proof that the Qurʾān intended to regulate every detail of life in the ways worked out by the traditional law schools, and some indications that it permitted and perhaps encouraged independent ethical thinking. Even in classical Islamic civilization attempts to impose control of the *sharīʿa* over all spheres of life generally broke down, especially where state interests were concerned. In modern society, with its new problems, the traditional attitude to law and ethics has become considerably more difficult to work out without forced interpretations and practical gaps.

These limits as stated still leave a wide range of latitude, in which Muslims will take up different stands, as they have in the past. Thus all the theories and moods of modern Islam, except the most extreme, are accommodated in this field.

4

'INJURING ONESELF' IN THE QURʾĀN, IN THE LIGHT OF ARISTOTLE

1

The Qurʾān frequently says of sinners *anfusahum yaẓlimūn* or something similar. The usual interpretation of the expression is 'They wrong themselves', but this raises problems. Is it possible for anyone to wrong himself? If it is, are sinners likely candidates for wronging themselves? And does the Qurʾān assert or suggest that these people suffer any wrong? Although these problems have been perceived in varying degrees by medieval and modern commentators (most recently by Kāmil Ḥusayn in Egypt),[1] I believe that a sharper understanding of them is possible when once we have understood what Aristotle had to say about injustice to onself in the *Nicomachean Ethics*, Book V, chapters 9 and 11. I shall therefore begin with a short account of Aristotle's reasoning and conclusions on this question, to the extent that they can lay the ground for a fresh interpretation of the Qurʾān.[2]

2

Aristotle distinguishes two main senses of the Greek verb *adikein* (chs. 1–2). One is a general sense, 'wronging' (followed by a direct object for the person wronged, as in English 'wronging someone'). In this sense we call wrong those acts which go against the aims of the laws, which are 'to produce and preserve happiness and its components for the political society' (ch. 1, 1129b 17–19): such acts as desertion and fleeing in war, adultery, assault and slander (1129b 20–3). The other sense is more specific, 'treating (someone) unjustly', and

[1] Dr Muhammad Kamil Husayn read a paper on *ẓulm* in the Qurʾān to the Arab Academy in Cairo, 1956 or 1957. Translated with comments by K. Cragg, 'The meaning of ẓulm in the Qurʾān', *The Muslim World*, 49 (1959), 196–212. Also summarized with comments by H. Teissier, 'Le *zolm* dans le Coran d'après le docteur Kamel Hussein', *Mélanges de l'Institut Dominicain d'Études Orientales*, 4 (1957), 255–61.

[2] References to the *Nicomachean Ethics*, Book v, will be given in the text of this chapter, using the standard chapters, pages and lines; translations by W. D. Ross, *Ethica Nicomachea* (Oxford, 1925). References to the Qurʾān, also in the text, are to the verse numbers of the Cairo edition; translations by A. J. Arberry, *The Koran interpreted*, 2 vols. (London, 1955), with modifications.

this is defined in terms of distributing goods unfairly, i.e. not in proportion to merit, upsetting a fair balance and failing to compensate for the injured party's loss or suffering (chs. 2–5). Aristotle's discussion of injustice to oneself concerns mainly this specific sense, so I shall speak of 'injustice' rather than 'wronging' in this context. Most of what he says can be applied as well to the broader sense, 'wronging oneself', and thus it is relevant to the Qurʾān.

In addition to the definition of injustice now given, further conditions are necessary if one is concerned, as Aristotle is, with passing a *moral* judgement on an agent of an unjust act, i.e. deciding that he is responsible and to be blamed for his act. The conditions required for such condemnation are (a) that the unjust agent must have acted voluntarily and with knowledge, i.e. with deliberate and conscious intent, and (b) that the patient, in the technical sense as contrasted with the agent, must have been afflicted against his will (ch. 6, 1134a 17–23 and ch. 8). These conditions are important to Aristotle because he is dealing with justice and injustice in the context of his account of the virtues and vices. These are states of character, so that considerations of intention are indispensable for understanding and making moral judgements in this more inward, subjective side of ethics. He also has an eye on the judicial criteria for guilt and innocence.

Moral injustice (*adikein*) is then distinguished by Aristotle from merely doing unjust things (*adika prattein, poiein*) in an incidental manner, without intent to do wrong (ch. 9, 1136a 25–8, 1136b 31). For example, a slave who kills someone by command of his master 'does not act unjustly, though he does what is unjust' (1136b 31). His act may be called 'unjust' in an external, objective sense, but does not render him culpable.

Now, if these are the conditions for moral injustice, there must be at least two parties involved, a willing agent and an unwilling patient. So Aristotle has to conclude that it is impossible for one person to do injustice to himself, in the moral sense. This can be demonstrated by the following dilemma. When a person inflicts harm on himself, he must do so either involuntarily or voluntarily. If he does so involuntarily, for example wounding himself by a fall, the event is not strictly speaking an act, he is not an agent and so he cannot be an unjust agent.[3] If he does so voluntarily, then as a voluntary patient he does not fulfil a condition for being unjustly treated (ch. 9, 1136b, 3–8; ch. 11, 1138a 20–3). To state the case another way: a single person's mind is a unity, so that at any one time it can only be either in an involuntary state as both agent and patient or in a voluntary state as both agent and patient. But injustice requires a relation of voluntary agent to involuntary

[3] Aristotle does not discuss this alternative, perhaps thinking it obvious, but it is mentioned here to complete the argument.

patient, therefore injustice can exist only between at least two persons (ch. 11, 1138a 19–20).

All this applies to wrongdoing as well as to specific injustice. But an additional reason rules out any injustice to oneself in the specific sense of maldistribution of goods. It is impossible because there can be no distribution at all between a person and himself; for even if we imagine something being given unfairly by a person to himself, we have also to imagine the same amount being recovered *ipso facto* by the same person (ch. 11, 1138a 13–19).

All that Aristotle will admit on the subject falls within the boundaries of the principles explained here. One may suffer unjust effects (*adika paskhein*) at one's hands, but without being treated unjustly (*adikeisthai*) by any moral agent (ch. 9, 1136a 27–8). For example, one may deprive oneself unduly by excessive generosity to others (ch. 9, 1136b 16–21), but 'he suffers nothing contrary to his own wish, so that he is not unjustly treated as far as this goes, but at most only suffers harm [*blaptetai monon*]' (1136b 23–5).

This brief account of Aristotle's thought on injustice to oneself can help our study of the related topic in the Qurʾān in two ways. The first is by arousing doubt about the interpretation of *ẓulm an-nafs* as 'wronging oneself'. Aristotle firmly denies that such an act is possible, and his arguments as usual deserve serious consideration. Secondly, his treatment provides concepts and ideas which can be valuable in criticizing interpretations of the Qurʾān.

3

But we have not quite finished with Aristotle. Further help may be drawn by noticing the kind of difficulties that confront his theory. In current English we do speak of people 'not doing justice to themselves', in the following typical cases: when someone does not express himself, or defend his viewpoint or his rights, as well as we know he can do; when someone, normally sober, gets drunk and (as we also say) 'makes a fool of himself'; more widely, when anyone gives away too much and keeps less than he deserves for himself; and most strikingly, when a martyr chooses to suffer an unjust death rather than betray his convictions or his colleagues. Evidently the Greeks too used the corresponding expression, *auton hauton adikein*, otherwise Aristotle would not have seen it as a problem. How are such expressions to be explained without contradicting his theory?

Aristotle has answers for some of the difficult cases, and could probably answer others without abandoning his principles.[4] But the point to be

[4] Aristotle's solutions to the problem never abandon his principle that accepting an injustice cannot be voluntary. His firmness on this point is based on more than a purely linguistic

observed here does not require us to study his answers. it is simply that the cases just mentioned which provide evidence for the possibility of self-wronging are mostly cases of good people hurting themselves or being eminently generous to others, who therefore arouse our sympathy; whereas those whom the Qurʾān has in mind are clearly indicated as wrongdoers. This is strange company, and it leads us to ask, even if (contrary to Aristotle) there are some people who really wrong themselves, is it likely that the Qurʾān is placing sinners in this class? The Qurʾān, too, must be taken seriously, and we must hesitate before we interpret it in a sense that is at least paradoxical on the surface: that people who give too much to others are thereby wrongdoing themselves.

4

The expression *ẓulm an-nafs* in the Qurʾān raises in an acute form the main problem discussed by Aristotle. For not only does it seem to speak of people who wrong themselves voluntarily, but further: these are not people who do injustice to themselves by being over-generous, they are wrongdoers who bring on themselves the punishment of the next life. The Qurʾān leads us emphatically to think that they deserve what they get, that their punishment is just. So how can it be said that they wrong themselves? Before solutions to the problem are suggested it will be helpful to give some contextual description of *ẓulm* and *ẓulm an-nafs*.[5]

Ẓalama, *ẓulm* and other forms are very frequent in the Qurʾān. Sometimes the verb has an object, 'to wrong someone'; at other times it is used without an object, 'to do wrong'.[6] In most cases *ẓulm* means definitely 'doing wrong', not merely 'harming', 'paining', in a way that might be accidental.[7] It is thus

conviction on how we define a morally unjust act. Behind this is a deeper psychological axiom which he has taken over from Socrates and Plato: that, even if current language allows one to speak of a voluntarily accepted injustice, such a thing never happens because no one willingly accepts evil for himself, including injustice done to him without compensation.

So he answers the difficulties that occur to him by allowing for temporary ignorance or counterbalancing goods. Thus, the incontinent person harms himself because for a while he loses sight of his real good which is the object of his 'real will' (*boulēsis*) (ch. 9, 1136b 1–8 and Book vii, chs. 2–3). And the self-sacrificing person 'perhaps gets more than his share of some other good, e.g. of honour or of intrinsic nobility (*tou haplōs kalou*)', ch. 9, 1136b 21–2).

[5] For a more detailed analysis see T. Izutsu, *Ethico-religious concepts in the Qurʾān* (Montreal, 1966), pp. 164–72.

[6] Kamil Husayn says: '...when it has no stated object we take it to mean self-injury or self-wronging. And on this showing self-wronging is the most frequent significance of the term *Ẓulm* in the Qurʾān'. (Tr. Cragg, *Muslim World*, 49 (1959), 202; cf. Teissier, *MIDEO*, 4 (1957), 257). The grammatical assertion cannot be supported, hence the statistical inference from it falls as well. In any language the primary usage of words for 'wrong' has surely a social reference, so that wronging is normally understood as directed against other people even when no object is expressed.

[7] Clearest at iii, 161: *thumma tuwaffa kullu nafsin mā kasabat wa hum la yuẓlamūn*. See also vi, 131 and 169; xi, 117; xvii, 33; xxviii, 59.

a moral term, referring to wilful evildoing; it is one of several terms that give a tone of indignation to the Qurʾān, together with *kufr*, *kadhb* and others. Most of the acts and attitudes that are called *ẓulm* are related to God or His worship: such as ingratitude and unbelief (*kufr*), polytheism and idol-worship, denying the signs of God and calling Him a liar, turning away from Him after having heard the signs, preventing worship in mosques and trying to destroy them, befriending enemies of Islam. Others are primarily human offences: making vain promises (done by the *ẓālimūn* to each other), embezzling the property of orphans.[8] The wide range of *ẓulm* thus makes it equivalent to Aristotle's general sense (which, of course, includes specific 'injustice'), and it is normally accurate to translate it as 'wrong' or 'wrongdoing'.

Ẓulm an-nafs occurs twenty-nine times in various forms.[9] In at least three passages it is distinguished from other evildoing, e.g. 'Whosoever does evil, *or* wrongs himself' (iv, 110).[10] Such sentences incline us to look for a special character of acts named *ẓulm an-nafs*, but there are few examples to yield clues: e.g. transgressing the bounds of God (lxv, 1), denying His signs (vii, 117), taking the golden calf as an idol (ii, 54).

The phrase usually occurs in close connection with the punishment of the next life. The *ẓālimī anfusahum* will be losers (*min al-khāsirīn*) as a result of their misconduct. *Ẓulm an-nafs*, 'injury to oneself', is not said of the everlasting punishment itself; it is predicated of the sinful act in this life.[11] However, the injury to oneself is not anything that occurs at the time of the act; it is, rather, the fact that *the act is the cause of the later punishment.*

Finally, the phrase is contrasted in the same sentences with two other phrases, both concerning God. The most frequent thought is: God does not injure them, they injure themselves.[12] More rarely it is said: They do not injure God, they injure themselves.[13]

[8] Some quotations and references in Izutsu, *Ethico-religious concepts*.

[9]

ii, 54, 57, 231	xviii, 35
iii, 117 (twice), 135	xxvii, 44
iv, 64, 97, 110	xxviii, 16
vii, 23, 160, 177	xxix, 40
ix, 36, 70	xxx, 9
x, 44	xxxiv, 19
xi, 101	xxxv, 32
xiv, 45	xxxvii, 113
xvi, 28, 33, 118	lxv, 1

There are no less than twenty-five variant combinations of tense, number and word order, but the variations are without significance. R. Blachère, *Le Coran*, II–III (Paris, 1949–50) classifies none of these passages as early Meccan, three as middle Meccan and the remainder as late Meccan or Madinan.

[10] *wa man yaʿmal sūʾan aw yaẓlim nafsahu*. See also iii, 135; iv, 64.

[11] The distinction between *ẓulm an-nafs* and *khasr* is clear at vii, 23: 'They said, "Lord, we have injured ourselves, and if Thou dost not forgive us, and have mercy upon us, we shall surely be among the lost".'

[12] iii, 117; x, 44; xi, 101; xvi, 33, 118; xxix, 40; xxx, 9.

[13] ii, 57; vi, 160.

Up to this point, *ẓulm an-nafs* has been translated in a neutral, uncommitted way: *ẓulm* as 'injury', *nafs* as 'self'. 'Wronging oneself' has been avoided because this is just the sense that appears difficult as a result of reflecting on Aristotle's analysis. In seeking a correct interpretation of the Qurʾān's words we shall have to consider which more precise translations will avoid the Aristotelian difficulty, while not transgressing the limits set by the Arabic language and the contexts of the Qurʾānic passages.

5

I shall put forward three suggestions. The first will be rejected outright. The second will be rejected as too simple as it stands, but it will be incorporated into a third, more complex analysis which will be proposed for acceptance.

1. An obvious thought which occurs is that *an-nafs* means 'the soul', so that the evildoers wrong their souls. In this view the soul is passive and receives the wrong unwillingly, being itself a naturally pure and innocent part of the whole person. We are reminded of the Socratic/Platonic soul which is corrupted by wrongdoing. This interpretation is supported by Kāmil Ḥusayn.[14] It would solve the Aristotelian problem by providing two distinct centres of consciousness, the self as voluntary agent of wrong, the soul as involuntary patient of it. But it is hard to support such an interpretation with evidence. Usually the *nafs* is active, not passive, as in the famous saying of Joseph:

> 'Yet I claim not that my soul was innocent –
> surely the soul of man incites to evil –
> except inasmuch as my Lord had mercy' (xii, 43).[15]

And there is no clear-cut dualist psychology in the Qurʾān.

2. The next suggestion is that *ẓulm* in this phrase does not mean 'wrong', something immoral, but only 'harm', 'hurt', which are not essentially moral terms. Thus the more frequent contrast will say 'God does not harm them, they harm themselves', and the less frequent contrast will say, 'They do not harm God, they harm only themselves'. This interpretation if tenable solves the Aristotelian problem, because an agent may harm himself involuntarily through ignorance; no conscious intent to harm occurs, and so there is no

[14] Tr. Cragg, *Muslim World*, 49 (1959), 204–5; Teissier, *MIDEO*, 4 (1957), 258–9.

[15] The central line, *inna n-nafsa la-ammāratun bi s-sūʾi*, is understood by Kamil Husayn as 'Verily the soul labours under an evil bias' (trans. Cragg, *Muslim World*, 49 (1959), 205), which transforms into passivity the active force of *ammāratun*, an emphatic variant of *āmiratun*, 'commanding'. See Cragg's critical note 9. Other references for *nafs* in the Qurʾān, mostly in an active role, are given by E. E. Calverley, 'Nafs', *Shorter Encyclopaedia of Islam* (Leiden, 1953), p. 433.

moral wrongdoing to himself. Moreover, there is a sentence in the Qurʾān where *ẓalama* is used of physical things:

> 'each of the two gardens yielded its produce
> and failed naught in any wise'

(*wa lam taẓlim minhu shayʾan*) (xviii, 33). (Another interpretation is 'did not harm him'.) In any case a moral sense, 'did no wrong' or 'did not wrong him', is here impossible. Further support for 'harm' can be found in the classical dictionaries, for what they are worth.[16] Such a non-moral sense, 'harm' or 'deficiency', may be historically prior, and 'wrong' derivative.

But here again there are difficulties in application. *Ẓulm* in the Qurʾān usually means 'wrongdoing'. And although there is nothing impossible in principle in *ẓulm an-nafs* bearing a special and different meaning, there are in fact passages where it clearly means 'wronging oneself', not merely 'harming oneself', as shown in the contexts by some contrast or other relation.

> 'And of their seed some are good-doers,
> and some manifest self-wrongers' (xxxvii, 113).[17]

'Self-harmers' would not make a proper contrast with 'good-doers' (*muḥsinūn*).

> 'They said, "Lord, we have wronged ourselves",
> and if thou dost not forgive us...' (vii, 23).[18]

'Harmed ourselves' would not be an occasion for forgiveness. Thus the idea of 'wrong' cannot be shut out of *ẓulm an-nafs*.

3. What I shall suggest as most likely is that both 'harm' and 'wrong' are present in *ẓulm an-nafs* in a close association which is not made explicit but which can be inferred because it makes the best sense of the phrase in all passages.

[16] E. W. Lane, *Arabic-English Lexicon* (London, 1863–93), s.v. *ẓulm*: 'the putting a thing in a place not its own (*waḍʿu sh-shayʾa fī ghayri mawḍiʿihi*), putting it in a wrong place, misplacing it: it is by exceeding or falling short, or by deviating from the proper time and place; or the acting in whatever way a man pleases in the disposal of the property of another: transgressing the proper limit much or little: or according to some it primarily signifies *Naqṣ*, making to suffer loss or detriment: and it is said to be of three kinds, between man and God, between man and man and between man and himself, everyone of which three is really a wrongdoing to oneself'.

Since the last point is evidently a reflection of the Qurʾānic meanings and 'wrongdoing' is the traditional English translation of *ẓulm*, nothing is settled by this sentence. In the first sentence, too, 'wrong' has no moral meaning, it is merely 'unsuitable'; and this latter emerges from all the definitions as the basic common element. The explanation as *naqṣ* brings it close to 'harm'.

[17] *wa min dhurriyatihimā muḥsinun wa ẓālimun li-nafsihi mubīn.*

[18] *qālā rabbanā ẓalamnā anfusanā waʾin lam taghfir lanā*... Cf. iv, 110: *wa man yaʿmal sūʾan aw yaẓlim nafsahu thumma yastaghfiri llāha.*

Probably the older meaning of *ẓulm* is the more concrete 'harm', but since harm wrought by human agents is nearly always wrong, the meaning 'wrong' came to dominate the word almost completely. Parallels may be found in other languages, such as English 'damage' and 'damages', French *léser*, German *schaden*, Latin *nocens* and *innocens*. At the stage reached by the Arabic language of the Qurʾān, I think 'wrong' has become primary for *ẓulm*. But 'harm' is in the background and becomes significant in *ẓulm an-nafs*, in the following way. The *ẓālimī anfusahum* are in the first instance *ẓālimūn*, plain wrongdoers. But *all wrongdoers also harm themselves* as a result of their own acts. The harm comes inescapably as punishment for these acts. (Possibly they also cause immediate harm to their souls by these acts; but I suspect that this idea is too Platonic for the Qurʾān, and that soul damage only comes into Islamic thought with philosophers in the Hellenistic tradition, or perhaps earlier with Ṣūfīs touched by that tradition.)

With respect to God, it fits the message of the Qurʾān to say that He does not wrong the self-injurers. Eventually He does *harm* them with terrible punishments – sometimes even in their lives on earth – but He neither initiates their troubles nor punishes them unjustly. In the less common phrase *wa mā ẓalamūna* it is possible to understand 'They have not wronged Us', for the reason that wronging is out of the question in the acts of men towards their all-powerful Creator. On the other hand, their ingratitude and disobedience to Him might well be considered wrongful. So the alternative, 'They have not harmed Us', is preferable; it is more to the point for God to say 'They are not hurting Us by their sins, they are hurting only themselves'.

Perhaps the fluid sense of *ẓulm an-nafs* is well captured in English by 'ruining oneself', or better still 'injuring oneself', which covers nicely the two sides, wrong and harm. Thus the English word 'injury', used previously because of its ambiguity, is brought back at the end for precisely that reason. Does this mean that the Qurʾān is confused in its use of the expression? No, we should rather say that it uses the natural Arabic language of its time, but it does so in a poetic way, that is to say with semantic depth, where one meaning leads on to another by a fertile fusion of associated ideas. Such a use of language may set problems for analytical minds, but the Qurʾān must be understood not as a mere textbook of religious and ethical doctrines but more valuably as a rich and subtle stimulus to the religious imagination.[19]

[19] The view of the Muslim philosophers. See F. Rahman, *Prophecy in Islam: philosophy and orthodoxy* (London, 1958), pp. 36ff., and Part II, note 22, referring back to Proclus.

5

TWO THEORIES OF VALUE IN EARLY ISLAM*

Among the debates conducted in Islamic intellectual circles in the early ᶜAbbāsid period, one of the most significant was the debate about the nature of value. To simplify the situation a little, we may say that two main theories opposed each other. One was that of the Muᶜtazilites, that values such as justice and goodness have a real existence, independent of anyone's will, even God's: this view is classed as 'objectivism'. The other theory was that of Ashᶜarī and his like, that all values are determined by the will of God, who *decides* what shall be just and so forth: this will be called 'theistic subjectivism'. Following a struggle between the two doctrines, that of Ashᶜarī finally prevailed in most learned circles of classical Sunnite Islam, a result which had far-reaching consequences in law and other spheres of Islamic civilization. As far as the writer is aware, no one has yet examined as a separate problem the reasons why the Ashᶜarite theory of value prevailed.

* This chapter needs to be modified with regard to both the antecedents in the Qurʾān and the later history of the two theories, in light of more recent studies.

Support for an objectivist theory of value in the Qurʾān is far more definite than I had realized before writing 'Ethical presuppositions of the Qurʾān'. On the other hand the Qurʾān emphasizes itself and the Prophet as the principal sources of ethical *knowledge*, without altogether ruling out the possibility of rational knowledge.

Our perspective on the later history of Muᶜtazilism has been completely changed by the discovery and study of ᶜAbd al-Jabbār's *Mughnī*, a work of the later tenth century. It reveals a continuous flourishing of the school until that time. See chapter 7 and *Islamic rationalism*.

The turning point in the suppression of Muᶜtazilism occurred in the eleventh century with the credal proclamations of the caliph Qādir beginning in 1017, followed by Hanbalite demonstrations in Baghdād in the 1060s and the favour shown to the Ashᶜarites by the Seljūq sultans and their *wazīr* Niẓām al-Mulk. See G. Makdisi, *Ibn ᶜAqīl et la résurgence de l'Islam traditionaliste au XIe siècle* (Damascus, 1963), pp. 299–310, 327–40.

Ashᶜarism was not a powerful movement until the late eleventh century. See G. Makdisi, 'Ashᶜarī and the Ashᶜarites in Islamic religious history', *Studia Islamica*, 17 (1962), 37–80 and 18 (1963), 19–39.

Still, I believe the present chapter remains mostly valid for the conflict between the two theories in the formative period of Islamic theology, from the rise of Muᶜtazilism in the 740s to the death of Ashᶜarī in 935.

A more recent account is given by R. M. Frank, 'Moral obligation in classical Muslim theology', *Journal of Religious Ethics*, 11 (1983), 204–23.

The primary philosophical question about value can be stated broadly thus: What is the common element in all that is called 'good', 'right', etc.? This question includes the more specific ones of ethics: What constitutes a right action? and, How do we know the right action? At the outset the discussion will be carried on in terms of the broader question of value, because no less than this was made an issue among the Muslim theologians; at a later stage it will be appropriate to speak in terms of ethics. First of all it is necessary to go briefly over the meaning and history of the two broad theories that opposed each other.

By 'objectivism' we mean any theory which affirms that value has a real existence in particular things or acts, regardless of the wishes or opinions of any judge or observer as such. (Objectivism is not necessarily absolutist; in fact most objectivist theories include a certain type of relativism. To take a material example, if we say that light clothing is better in a warm climate and thick clothing in a cold one, we are saying that each kind of clothing has a real objective advantage relative to a particular climate, and not merely a conventional acceptability or a subjective attractiveness to some people.) Objectivism in one form or another has been the prevailing view of western thought before the twentieth century. Socrates affirmed it when he convinced Euthyphron that piety is loved by the gods because it is good in itself; it is not made good by the mere fact that the gods love it. This was the view developed by Plato and Aristotle into the theory of the rational good, then upheld by the Stoics and most of the Catholic philosophers in the doctrine of natural right. In modern times Kant and other intuitionists, the utilitarians and some other naturalists, have all accepted the objectivity of value while differing about everything else. It may be termed the classical tradition of Europe, although there are exceptions. In Islam objectivism was upheld both by the philosophers, who were the full inheritors of the Greek tradition, and before them by the Muʿtazilites, who came under some Greek influence. All of the Muʿtazilites asserted that there is a real good, which God wishes for the world, and a real justice which He upholds; and further that man can know what these are in specific instances by his reason.

The name 'subjectivism' applies to any theory to the effect that the value of things or acts is always determined solely by the opinions or emotional attitudes of some judge or observer. In ancient Greece, many of the sophists put forward a social or conventional subjectivism: thus, what is called 'justice' in a particular society is determined only by the opinions of the rulers, or of the majority. Similar types of theory have become fashionable in our age; they are 'sophisticated' in a sense that is not always fully understood.

In classical Islam, however, subjectivism took a form which seems remote from the view of the sophists, though there is an underlying relation which was recognized by the acute mind of Ibn Rushd.[1] This was *theistic* subjectivism, the belief that 'good', 'right' and similar terms have no other meaning than 'that which God wills': thus God makes things good or right for us by His decision that they should be so. It is denied that these words denote anything that has an objective existence; their meaning applies only to whatever God wishes, decrees or approves for the world. (This doctrine is also called 'ethical voluntarism', but 'theistic subjectivism' describes more closely the place of the theory in a logical classification of theories of value.) This was the theory of value held by Ashᶜarī and all Ashᶜarites, including Ghazālī. It is not peculiar to Islam, since it occurs in medieval Judaism and occasionally in western thought; but it was probably more prominent and widespread in Islam than in any other civilization.

The prevalence of theistic subjectivism in Islam may appear surprising, if we judge it merely on its merits as a theory of value. Objectivism of one type or another may be thought more 'natural' to man, in the sense that it has been more widespread in history and seems implied by most value language as it is used spontaneously and uninfluenced by theories. These matters cannot be argued here, but it is relevant to mention that in classical Islam, too, objectivism was not without widespread support, both implicit in the practice of early Muslims and explicit in the writings of many distinguished theologians and philosophers. Some serious objections to theistic subjectivism were voiced, such as this consequence of it: that if God had commanded theft and idolatry, it would have been *ipso facto* right for man to commit them. Ashᶜarī, Ibn Ḥazm and Ghazālī did not shrink from accepting this extreme consequence;[2] but a philosopher like Ibn Rushd could well point out how such a position would undermine faith in God and belief in ordinary morality.[3]

When, on the other hand, we look at the two theories in the context of early Islamic thought, the triumph of Ashᶜarī's theory seems almost inevitable, given the way in which Islam was generally understood in those times. The rest of this article will be devoted to explaining why this was so, in early

[1] *Jāmᶜi mā baᶜd aṭ-ṭabīᶜa*, in *Rasāʾil Ibn Rushd* (Hyderabad, 1947), 172. After criticizing the Ashᶜarite theory of value he concludes: 'All these are views like those of Protagoras.' Cf. *Avveroes' Commentary on Plato's Republic*, Hebrew ed. and Eng. trans. E. I. J. Rosenthal (Cambridge, 1956), I, xi, 3; more recently trans. R. Lerner, *Averroes on Plato's 'Republic'* (Ithaca and London, 1974).

[2] Ashᶜarī, *Kitāb al-Lumaᶜ*, in *The theology of al-Ashᶜarī*, ed. and Eng. trans. R. J. McCarthy (Beirut, 1953), sect. 171; Ibn Ḥazm, *Kitāb al-fiṣal fil-milal*, Leiden, Warner MS. 480, fol. 200a, quoted by I. Goldziher, *Die Ẓâhiriten* (Leipzig, 1884), 163–4; Ghazālī, *al-Iqtiṣād fil-iᶜtiqād* (Cairo, Tijariyya Press, 1st ed., n.d.), 81–2.

[3] *Jāmiᶜ mā baᶜd aṭ-ṭabīᶜa*. 172; *Kitāb al-Kashf ᶜan manāhij al-adilla*. ed. M. J. Müller, in *Philosophie und Theologie von Avveroes* (Munich, 1859), 113.

Sunnite Islam. Three kinds of reason may be found, which can be classified as ethical, theological and extraneous. The first will be dealt with at greatest length.

In dealing with the *ethical* reason we have to start from the history of Islamic jurisprudence before the time of Ashʿarī. Here the Muslims faced a question of practical ethics which was more immediate than any philosophical question about ethics or value in general, namely: From what sources can a judge or *muftī* find out in all circumstances what is the right action? The starting points were, of course, the Qurʾān and Traditions, and by the middle of the eighth century of the Christian era it was agreed that duties explicitly laid down in them were known from those sources. The question that remained, then, was how duties and right actions were to be determined when they were not mentioned in the Qurʾān or Traditions. We may classify the answers into two main types, omitting many variations and details which need not concern us here.

(1) On one side were lawyers who practised and allowed *ijtihād ar-raʾy*, the exercise of independent personal judgement in cases where the revealed sources did not contain explicit guidance. This was common practice in the ancient law schools of Madīna and ʿIrāq, which left their influence particularly on the classical schools of the two imāms Mālik and Abū Ḥanīfa. 'When it [*raʾy*] reflects the personal choice of the lawyer, guided by his idea of appropriateness, it is called *istiḥsān* or *istiḥbāb*, "*preference*". The term *istiḥsān* therefore came to signify a breach of strict analogy for reasons of public interest, convenience or similar considerations.'[4]

The ethical basis which might justify such a practice may have remained unarticulated in the law schools; but Muʿtazilite theologians supplied a theory of ethics which could support *ijtihād ar-raʾy*, if lawyers wished to avail themselves of it. This was the theory that there is an objective good, including a real public interest and a real justice, and that these could be recognized by human reason, *ʿaql*. The process of recognition involved can be termed 'moral judgement', to distinguish it from other types of personal judgement. *Raʾy*, therefore, might have been restricted to moral judgement as described, and justified on that basis.

It might be supposed that all lawyers would have welcomed the latitude allowed them by a system in which judgements of public interest and equity would have been given an authorized position. But it appears that the attitude of legal theorists was in general dominated by fears that this latitude would

[4] J. Schacht, *The origins of Muhammadan jurisprudence* (Oxford, 1950), pp. 98–9.

be misused. Two dangers might be anticipated. One was that *raʾy* would be employed arbitrarily by caliphs, governors and other administrative officials exercising judicial powers. Very significant in this context is the rejection, in the early years of the ʿAbbasids, of Ibn al-Muqaffaʿ's theory that the caliph alone has the right to exercise *raʾy*, and that he may use it to modify and codify Islamic law.[5] Acceptance of this proposition would have opened a valuable way to evolution of that law to cope with changing conditions. But from the lawyers' viewpoint ibn al-Muqaffaʿ was offering the worst of two worlds, for he was both withdrawing *raʾy* from themselves and allowing it to the chief executive. Thus they rejected it; probably they felt that a law based squarely on the Qurʾān and Traditions alone would serve a more vital purpose, by acting as a constitutional check on rulers and preserving Islamic standards in public life.

The other danger came from the side of Shiʿism. If *raʾy* were allowed, the opinions of ordinary lawers were fallible. This would make more attractive the idea of a living authority, such as a Shiʿite *imām*, who could give an infallible opinion. We know that much later, around 1100, Ghazālī was acutely aware of this possibility as a threat to the Sunnite community, and his answer rings out clear in refutations of the Batinites: there is no need for a living *imām*; the *imām* of the Muslims is Muḥammad, and all ethical and legal questions can be answered from the Qurʾān and Traditions.[6] Now Ghazālī was a Shafiʿite, and his Shafiʿite ideas on law were perfect for answering Shiʿites.[7] Whether this purpose was in the mind of Shāfiʿī three centuries before is another question, which could only be answered by discovering reactions of Shāfiʿī to Shiʿism.[8]

Quite apart from its lack of adoption by the legal profession, the Muʿtazilite

[5] See S. D. Goitein, 'A turning-point in the history of the Muslim state', *Islamic Culture*, 23 (1949), 120–35.

[6] *Al-Mustaẓhirī – Faḍāʾiḥ al-Bāṭiniyya*, extracts and summary in I. Goldziher, *Streitschrift des Gazālī gegen die Batinijja-Sekte* (Leiden, 1916); *al-Qisṭās al-mustaqīm*, in *al-Jawāhir al-ghawālī* (Cairo, 1934), 156ff.; and especially *al-Munqidh min aḍ-ḍalāl*, ed. J. Saliba and K. Ayyad, 3rd ed. (Damascus, 1939), 111ff.

[7] The passage in *Munqidh* referred to in note 6 follows closely the arguments of Shāfiʿī's *Risāla* justifying *ijtihād al-qiyās*. See below on Shāfiʿī.

[8] We can trace the opposition between Tradition and the call for an *imām* as far back as Khayyāṭ in the early tenth century. The following passage is worth quoting: 'The doctrine that unbroken Tradition (*al-khabar al-mutawātir*) is true and that it compels knowledge destroys most of the proof of the Rafidites in affirming the imamate. That is because one of their chief proofs (in their own eyes) that people must have an infallible imam, pure within and without, uniting all the sciences of religion, is that all the rest of the Community besides him is liable to carelessness...': *Kitāb al-Intiṣār*, ed. H. S. Nyberg and French trans. A. N. Nader (Beirut, 1957), sect. 103. Conversely, the Ismāʿīlī qadi Nuʿmān in the tenth century was denying the efficacy of *qiyās* because he knew that without it the Sunnite ('Traditional') theory of law would break down: *Daʿāʾim al-Islām*, ed. A. A. A. Fyzee (Cairo, 1951), I, 103ff., quoted in B. Dodge, 'The Fatimid legal code', *The Muslim World*, 50 (1960), 30–8.

theory of ethics had a weakness of its own. An objectivist ethical philosophy ought to be able to show how moral judgement operates and to indicate the possibility of its being reasonable, if not scientific. But here the Muʿtazilites failed, and their failure was almost inevitable at the stage in the history of religion and philosophy at which they lived. Aristotle had suggested that practical reason is directed by an end, the real good for man, but in the *Nicomachean Ethics* he had disappointingly not made clear what this right end is for a society, except for a few individuals who might find their fulfillment in the life of the intellect or the spirit. (His *Politics* was unfortunately not available to Muslims.) For Muslims, an end *was* indicated which applied to everyone, namely eternal happiness, *al-saʿādatal-ukhrāwīya*. This suggests that the Muʿtazilites might have developed a utilitarian type of ethics along the following lines: the end or interest (*maṣlaḥa*) of the Muslim community consists in the happiness of as many as possible in the next life; right action is that which promotes this end. But here they would have faced a theoretical gap between means and end which does not disturb a more worldly utilitarianism. It is possible to some extent to discover by empirical reason what produces happiness in an earthly society, and to see the causal relation between the means and the end. But where the goal is happiness in an after-life, given as a *reward* for a certain way of life on earth, the utilitarian formula throws no light on the practical means, the particulars of right conduct, for there is no intelligible relation between the cause (certain kinds of action) and the effect (the reward of bliss in the next life).

Moreover, even apart from its relation to the effect, the cause in itself could not be understood as having a single objective character. This was because the *sharīʿa*, or scripture regarded as a code of law, gave no unifying ethical principle to explain what is common to fasting, almsgiving, dealing just weight, etc., other than the fact of being commanded by God. Consequently a Muslim seeking guidance for an Islamic life on issues where the commands are not explicit or appear to conflict would find no rational method to follow, except the method of analogy with what is commanded, and this is exactly that *qiyās* which was recommended by the opponents of *raʾy*.[9]

Lastly we may ask whether the sacred texts of Islam themselves gave any encouragement to an objectivist theory of value. This is a question which really requires a separate investigation; only a few general remarks may be made here. Certainly the Qurʾān often refers to values, such as *al-iṣlāḥ*, 'doing

[9] Christian ethics follows a different course, because it is not a detailed set of laws but principles based primarily on the injunction to love God and to love one's neighbour, as expressed, for example, in Luke, x, 27. These principles provide a method of judgement which can be applied in any moral situation. Thus analogies from the life and sayings of Jesus do not have the same place in Christianity as *qiyās* in classical Islamic law.

good', which may easily be understood in an objective sense. It also urges man to think for himself, and such thought could be taken to include independent moral judgement. Then there are Traditions like the much-quoted answer of Muʿādh Ibn Jabal to the Prophet's question as to how he would decide cases in the absence of a text from God or the Prophet: 'Then I shall use my own judgement [*ajtahidu raʾyī*].' Unfortunately for the theory under discussion, no text gave unequivocal support to it; even *ijtihād* in the Tradition quoted was interpreted by Shāfiʿī as *ijtihād al-qiyās*, not involving independent moral opinion.[10] Meanwhile the quotations on the other side were more clear-cut, as will be shown.

(2) The legal opponents of independent judgement were those who insisted that every decision must be justified by texts from the Qurʾān or the Traditions or by the implications of such texts as determined by *qiyās*, 'reasoning by analogy'. On this side we must count the Shafiʿites and the Ẓāhirites:[11] these two groups differed on the legitimate methods, but they were at one on the fundamental principle of not allowing independent judgement. Now, corresponding to each weakness shown above in the position of the supporters of *raʾy*, we find a point of strength on the side of the partisans of textual authority (*naṣṣ*).

From the viewpoint of legal practice it looked like an advantage to be able to construct a complete positive law, which would provide for every judgement the solid authority of texts and their implications. The original Divine Law of the scriptures was like a regional map, with the roads well marked within the limits of the region. As jurisprudence is a science which aims to be precise and does not mind being slow, the ideal of most lawyers of early Islam was to construct a series of such maps, to cover the entire world of possible action.

In the field of ethical theory, the Shafiʿites and allied legal schools had a neat position: that right action could always be known from revelation or by legitimate extensions of it. Beyond that they did not need to go, though there are hints of a theory of value in some statements by Shāfiʿī and early theologians.[12]

In the Qurʾān Shāfiʿī found many quotations to support a theory of positive law: for instance, references to the Book as *hudā*, guidance, and passages associating the guidance of the *sunna* of the Prophet and the judgements of

[10] *Kitāb al-umm* (Bulāq, 1321–5 h./1903–7), VII, 273.

[11] The founder of the Zahirite school, Dāwūd b. Khalaf, was at first a Shafiʿite. His doctrine carried the main theoretical tendency of Shāfiʿī to an extreme, by ruling out even *qiyās* as a source of legal knowledge. See Goldziher, *Ẓâhiriten*, pp. 27ff.

[12] Shāfiʿī, *ar-Risāla*, ed. A. M. Shakir (Cairo, 1940), 25: 'Justice is obedience to God'; 33, quotes Qurʾān, xxi, 23: 'He shall not be questioned as to what He does.' Ashʿarī, *Maqālāt al-Islāmiyyīn*, ed. H. Ritter (Istanbul, 1929), 191: Jaʿfar b. Ḥarb taught that God has willed that unbelief should be evil.

the Book, or associating obedience to the Prophet with obedience to God. He attached key importance to the sentence, 'Does man reckon that he shall be left to roam at random [*yutraka sudan*]?', taking it to refer to man's moral situation.[13] But far more potent than explicit statements was the example of the Book's own practice. The Qurʾān contains a number of injunctions that are clearly of legislative force and are stated as divine commands, prohibitions, permissions and so on. But these injunctions cover only a fraction of the spheres of conduct, whereas ʿ*al-Islām*ʾ means surrender of the human will to God's guidance in *all* spheres. Therefore, it was thought, God could not have left man without guidance in the remaining spheres – and this guidance can be expected to take the same form in principle as the explicit guidance of the Qurʾānic legislation. This last step was fatally easy, especially in view of the failure of reason as a guide. In short, the prestige of the Qurʾān led to the search for other positive sources to extend the scope of the *sharīʿa*.[14]

Having these advantages, the Shafiʿite principles prevailed in the classical theory of Islamic law which became consolidated in the course of the ninth century of the Christian era. The victory was qualified by one or two major concessions to opposing views; but it was none the less a victory, as we may see from the classical procedure of *qiyās* which is designed to exclude as far as possible any element of independent judgement.

Now we must notice that the Shafiʿite theory of scriptural authority as the basis for all legal and ethical *knowledge* would naturally support a theory of value like theistic subjectivism, which claims that right and wrong have no *meaning* but the will of God. The theory of value is not quite a logical implication of the theory of knowledge, for it is theoretically possible to hold that an objective right exists but that we can know its practical applications only through scripture. However, it is doubtful whether anyone held such a view. Certainly the Shafiʿites would be delighted to dispose of objective values, for this would cut the ground completely from under the feet of their adversaries, and leave the supposed 'independent moral judgement' as nothing but idle fancy, as *ẓann* based on *ahwāʾ*'. And since law and theology were so closely connected in the education of the ʿ*ulamāʾ*, the prevalence of

[13] Qurʾān, lxxv, 36, quoted by Shāfiʿī, *Risāla*, 25 and *Kitāb al-umm*, VII, 271. In the latter passage Shāfiʿī claims the support of all authorities in understanding '*sudan*' as 'what is neither commanded nor forbidden'. This interpretation seems to read too much into the text, since the context concerns only the inevitability of the gathering of all mankind at the resurrection. More impressive is Qurʾān, v, 41–50, with its refrain 'So judge between them according to what God has sent down.'

[14] The same development took place in the history of Judaism, in which the oral law of the rabbis and later the Talmud grew up to supplement the limited commands of the Torah. We must not attribute the similarity directly to any inherited 'Semitic mind'; it is rather a seemingly logical outcome of the character of a Semitic scripture.

Shafiᶜite ideas of law prepared the way thoroughly for the later spread of the Ashᶜarite theory of value. It is not accidental that three of the greatest Ashᶜarite theologians, Ashᶜarī, Juwaynī and Ghazālī, were all Shafiᶜites[15] and that Ibn Ḥazm was a Ẓāhirite.

The *theological* reasons for the triumph of Ashᶜarite subjectivism can be stated quite briefly. All of them are implications of God's omnipotence. The overwhelming power of God is greatly emphasized in the Qurʾān, so that it became the primary fact of religion for one broad school of thought, the self-styled *ahl as-sunna* who were the opponents of the Muᶜtazilites and the forerunners of Ashᶜarism. For them theistic subjectivism served three invaluable ends, and solved problems that might otherwise have arisen from the divine omnipotence.

(1) Man seems powerful and clever when compared with the rest of visible creation. But the vast superiority of God can best be shown by contrast with man's real feebleness. As one aspect of the contrast, theologians of this school were disposed to stress, negatively that man is ignorant of any principles of ethics, and positively that God's will is the source that defines the right for man. Such doctrines would bring out man's utter dependence on God's help, through the *sharīᶜa*.

(2) In relation to God, objective values appeared as a limiting factor to His power to do as He wills. The Muᶜtazilites discussed whether He could do evil if He chose. Naẓẓām said He could not, because justice is of the essence of His acts: this was logical for a Muᶜtazilite, but it seemed to limit God's power. Others said God could do evil, but He would never do it, because of what He is – an answer which did not avoid contradiction, as Khayyāṭ pointed out.[16] Ashᶜari got rid of the whole embarrassing problem by denying the existence of objective values which might act as a standard for God's action. By defining 'justice' as obedience to the commands of a law, he set God free from the ethical limits that confine man, for 'the Lord of the worlds...is not under a *sharīᶜa*'.[17]

(3) The same answer conveniently solved the awkward problem of evil. There was an evident contradiction between the assertion that God is absolutely omnipotent, predestining man's good and evil acts and then punishing them for the evil ones, and the assertion that God is just in the sense

[15] See Ibn ᶜAsākir, *Tabyīn kadhib al-muftarī*, ed. H. Qudsī (Damascus, 1928–9), 140, Eng. trans. R. J. McCarthy, *The theology of al-Ashᶜarī*, pp. 167–8: 'The Shāfiᶜites followed the doctrine of al-Ashᶜarī and composed works agreeing with it.'

[16] *Intiṣār*, sect. 10: 'When Ibn ar-Rāwandī was asked, "Do you deny that He actually does what you have described Him as capable of doing?", he answered, "That is impossible and absurd".'

[17] *al-Ibāmna ᶜan uṣūl ad-diyāna*, in *ar-Rasāʾil as-sabᶜa fil-ᶜaqāʾid* (Hyderabad, 1948), 54.

we normally understand. Ashᶜarī and his school preferred to stand by omnipotence and throw out justice in the ordinary sense. This could be done if human justice were defined in terms of law, since again 'the Lord of the worlds...is not under a *sharīᶜa*' – therefore 'He is not foolish' when He wills folly in man.[18]

Lastly, it is necessary to mention a chain of *extraneous events* having no particular connection with theories of value, namely the general defeat of the Muᶜtazilites in the ninth century. The main issue on which they met their downfall was the question of the creation of the Qurᵓān. But their defeat on this point need not have involved a general decline if they themselves had not unwisely brought politics into theology a generation earlier. By accepting the official backing of the Caliph Maᵓmūn and encouraging the persecution of their opponents as 'unorthodox', they gambled with the risk of a reversal of the persecution, and this came to pass at the hands of Mutawakkil. Their opponents were too numerous and too steadfast, and, led by Aḥmad b. Ḥanbal, they held out until the tide turned. The persecution of the Muᶜtazilites in their turn was part of a conservative movement in Islam, perhaps a 'failure of nerve',[19] led by the Caliph himself who was having trouble with his Turkish guards and tried to appeal beyond them to the broad support of the *ahl as-sunna*. Thus the check to Muᶜtazilite ideas on value was to some extent just part of their misfortunes as a whole, but this did not reduce the seriousness of the consequences in the controversy about values. Henceforward any objections to their value theory would strike all the more sharply because they were now a minority sect under the disapproval of the ᶜAbbasid state.

In explaining within a limited space the dominance of one theory, this article has unavoidably been one-sided in dwelling more upon the weaknesses of one party and the strength of the other. It has been the writer's intention to show that the result was due to powerful forces in classical Sunnite Islam, but not to show that it was a necessary product of Islam itself. For modern Muslims, what has been written has a certain relevance because they face essentially the same problem about value as their classical predecessors. But the interest of the classical solution lies less in any immediate acceptance that it may receive today than in its resemblances and contrasts with what Muslims of our time are likely to think. It is doubtful that many of them will return to a pure Ashᶜarite theory of value, but it is hoped that a detached study of the origins of that theory will assist some Muslims and some non-Muslims to clarify their thoughts on value in its relation to Islam.

[18] *Ibid.*

[19] G. Murray, *Five stages of Greek religion* (London, 1935), ch. 4, referring to later Greek religion.

6

ISLAMIC AND NON-ISLAMIC ORIGINS OF MUʿTAZILITE ETHICAL RATIONALISM[1]

I

The ethical theory of the Muʿtazilites is properly called 'rationalism', because it held that the values of human and divine actions are knowable in principle by natural human reason. Since this doctrine and related parts of the theory (mentioned in the next section) were the prevailing ethical theories in the major pre-Islamic religious cultures of Iran and Byzantium, the question easily arises, to what extent were the Muʿtazilites as the first systematic theologians in Islam indebted to these cultures for their ethics?

This question is part of a wider one, that of the origins of systematic theology in Islam (*kalām*) as a whole. In order to provide a context for my inquiry into the origins of the ethical system, it will be useful to begin with a brief review of the conclusions of scholars on the origins of *kalām*.

Perhaps it was Maimonides who, more than anyone else, set the tone for early modern views in a famous passage of his *Guide of the perplexed*:

> Know also that all the statements that the men of Islam – both the Muʿtazila and the Ashʿariyya – have made concerning these notions are all of them opinions founded upon premises that are taken over from the books of the Greeks and the Syrians who wished to disagree with the opinions of the philosophers and to reject their statements [after those two nations became Christian]...
>
> When thereupon the community of Islam arrived and the books of the philosophers were transmitted to it, then were also transmitted to it those refutations composed against the books of the philosophers. Thus they found the kalām of John Philoponus, of Ibn ʿAdī, and of others [and used them for their own purposes].[2]

The importance of John Philoponus as a source for Islamic *kalām* has been demonstrated by Herbert Davidson.[3] But Maimonides is undoubtedly

[1] G. E. Von Grunebaum published two articles of characteristic breadth and richness on topics related to our problem: 'The concept and function of reason in Islamic ethics', *Oriens*, 15 (1962), pp. 1–17, and 'The sources of Islamic civilization', *Der Islam*, 66 (1970), 1–54, also in *The Cambridge History of Islam* (Cambridge, 1970), II, 469–510.

[2] *Dalālat al-ḥaʾirīn*, ed. S. Munk and I. Joel (Jerusalem, 1930/31), i, 71 at p. 122; as translated by S. Pines, *Moses Maimonides: The Guide of the Perplexed* (Chicago, 1963), pp. 177–8.

[3] 'John Philoponus as a source of medieval Islamic and Jewish proofs of creation', *Journal of the American Oriental Society*, 89 (1969), 357–91.

exaggerating when he claims that all *kalām* arguments are derived from the pre-Islamic sources mentioned. The weight of his authority is reduced considerably when we realize that he had a strong aversion to the *mutakallimūn*, shown throughout the *Guide*; that he was writing more than four centuries after the beginning of *kalām*, when rather less was known about it than we know today; and that he made a chronological blunder in the passage quoted when he put this beginning of *kalām* later than the translations from Greek philosophy and even than the lifetime of Yaḥyā ibn ᶜAdī (d. 974).

Many of the older scholars of the twentieth century, while not going as far as Maimonides, emphasized the influence of Greek philosophy and Christian theology on early *kalām*. Michel Allard, in a valuable survey of orientalists' opinions on this question, suggested that their motives for seeking these connections may have been a desire to explain obscure Arabic texts in the light of more coherent predecessors, and to see what changes Muslim theologians brought about.[4] However that may be (and it is always risky to attribute motives), Allard was on sure ground in pointing out some difficulties in these views, and he summed up their major weakness by saying that 'their authors do not explain adequately the concrete conditions in which these influences were exercised'.[5] He then surveyed the more cautious approach of recent scholars, such as W. M. Watt and O. Pretzl, leading to more reserved conclusions about non-Islamic influences, and found similar conclusions being drawn independently about other fields of early Islamic learning, such as law and grammar.

The study of Muᶜtazilite origins has until now been incidental or fragmentary, amounting to a few pages at most out of a treatment of some larger subject. It deserves a monograph, in which the possible influences on each topic of theology would be carefully estimated on the basis of all available evidence, and some general conclusions would be drawn from comparison of the results on the separate topics. What is attempted here is a beginning on one topic: a study of origins concerning Muᶜtazilite ethics only. It is undertaken in full awareness of limits of my specialized knowledge in some of the cultures involved, the scarcity of evidence, and the absence of cumulative indications that a study of all the topics of theology together would provide. But it is hoped that others will make studies of the same kind on other topics of Muᶜtazilite theology, until finally a solid basis will have been laid for broad conclusions.

[4] *Le problème des attributs divins dans la doctrine d'al-Asᶜarî et de ses premiers grands disciples* (Beirut, 1965), pp. 156ff.

[5] *Ibid.*, p. 161.

2

Muʿtazilite theories of ethics naturally varied in detail between one author and another. Nonetheless it is possible to state five main points which were constant in the school, and which provide a manageable starting place for our inquiry.

1. Values are objective. Good and evil, just and unjust are descriptive characters of reality which are no less 'there' in things than their other qualities such as shape and size or mental qualities.[6]

2. There is one God, the only divine Creator. He knows all good and evil. He wishes and commands only good for men, but He allows them to do evil and to disobey His commands.

3. The value of many things and acts are known rationally by men. This knowledge does not come through sense perception alone but through the intellect, after we are informed of the relevant facts. A consequence of this rationalism is that people without a revelation are able to make sound ethical judgements to a certain extent.

4. Man has power to act as well as to know values, and so he is responsible for his just and unjust acts.

5. God rewards the just and punishes the unjust in an everlasting afterlife, and He does so justly because of man's full responsibility as mentioned in points 3 and 4.

Did these ideas come to the minds of the first school of theology in Islam from within the intellectual resources of early Islam, that is to say, from less explicit ideas suggested in the Qurʾān, the Traditions, and/or the earliest Muslim individual thinkers such as Ḥasan of Baṣra? Or did they come directly from one or more of the older religious or philosophical cultures without any previous Islamic filter? Such a formulation of questions already achieves a certain progress in defining as 'Islamic' anything that is mediated through the earliest sources of Islam, regardless of whether these had originally drawn upon non-Islamic sources. But two problems call for brief discussion.

The first is in regard to this definition. It may seem arbitrary to call 'Islamic' any idea that comes through an early Muslim before the Muʿtazilites, for Ḥasan and even his predecessors may already have been receiving non-Islamic ideas. But at about this point, as we look back into past time, the sources recede into an inarticulate, almost indiscernible past, and in order to pose answerable questions we must set this conventional rule: Whatever a Muʿtazilite took

[6] For the present purpose we can leave aside the Muʿtazilite definitions of value terms, e.g. of 'evil' as blameworthy, etc. These were probably constructed later. For the developed theory see G. F. Hourani, *Islamic rationalism: the ethics of ʿAbd al-Jabbār* (Oxford, 1971).

directly from another Muslim or whatever he thought out for himself is Islamic, at that stage.

The second problem arises from the oversimplified formulation of the questions at the beginning of this section. They are defective in demanding yes/no answers which cannot contain the complexity of historical reality. To move one step away from simplicity, some of the five points may be Islamic in origin, others non-Islamic. Then to move another step, some of the five may be more Islamic, others less Islamic, for within each one there may be combinations of sources resulting from several influences playing on one or more minds, and the receiving minds may – almost must – themselves change what they receive. We have to think in terms of transmissions with multiple termini at both ends; that is, with several donors and several recipients; and of transformation by recipients through more or less conscious fusion with ideas from other sources, including their own creative thoughts and those of contemporary associates and adversaries.

Our questions should therefore be refined thus: to what extent did the earliest Muʿtazilites derive their ethical system from Islamic and non-Islamic sources, and how much of the main points did they derive from each source? This is about as precise as we should be, and even with an amount of deliberate vagueness in the questions we must not expect more than probable answers because of the deficiency of historical evidence.

3

At first glance, a non-Islamic origin for Muʿtazilite ethics appears to be favoured by the fact that the main opposing view is so strongly Islamic in its claims and tone.[7] This is the traditional ethics that soon became dominant among Sunnite jurists and theologians, from Mālik to Shāfiʿī, Ibn Ḥanbal, Ashʿarī, and all their disciples. It agrees with the Muʿtazilites only on the unity of God; apart from that, the theory differs sharply from theirs on all five points.

1. Values are not objective in a sense that is prior to God; they are created by His will.

[7] This argument was used by C. H. Becker, 'Christliche Polemik und Islamische Dogmenbildung', first published in 1911 and reprinted in his *Islamstudien* (Leipzig, 1924), I, 432–49. Supporting a Christian origin for the Muʿtazilite view of human *qadar*, he wrote: 'Certainly the opponents on both sides could later prove their opinions with Qurʾān quotations, but the contest over the whole question is yet in the first place *imported* into Islam; for John of Damascus [who has been shown to have been well informed about early Islam] indicates determinism as absolutely the Islamic doctrine, with which he contrasts free will [*to autoexousion*] as the specifically Christian doctrine' (p. 439, my translation). Allard (*Problème*, pp. 160–1) notes the weakness of this argument. But Becker gives other evidence; see below, §8, on Christian theology.

2. God can wish good or evil for men, according to His unrestricted will and power.

3. Man can know values only by revelation directly, or by reasoning dependent on the data of revelation, but never by any process of reason independent of revelation.

4. God has power over all man's choices and acts, and ultimately predestines their direction by giving or withholding His grace.

5. Whatever God decides is just, because He decides it as the Lord and not because it conforms with standards of 'justice' thought out by human reason.

This theory arose from strong currents in primitive Islam. But to conclude that its Muʿtazilite opponents were therefore deviators from Islam in their own times would be to judge them from a false perspective of later history; and to go further and infer a non-Islamic origin of their doctrines would be unwarranted on the basis of their minority status alone.

To find more solid arguments for a non-Islamic origin we shall have to look for features of Muʿtazilite thought in the religious and philosophical systems of the preceding and surrounding non-Muslim cultures. But general resemblances will not be enough. Before proceeding to particulars it will be useful to reflect briefly on methods and criteria for establishing historical truth in matters of intellectual transmission.

To reach an adequate proof of affiliation of ideas, an intellectual historian needs one or both of two kinds of evidence: (i) external evidence of affiliation; for example, a report of a biographer that one scholar was taught by another or was favourably impressed by his works; (ii) detailed resemblances so close that they could not be accidental; for example, exact correspondence of sentences, or numerous correspondences in technical terms. No precise rules can be set. Combinations of external evidence with several general resemblances may give conclusions of various degrees of probability.

But it may happen that there is little external evidence and only general resemblances. This is the case with Muʿtazilite origins. The background of the school before Wāṣil's foundation of it is almost prehistoric, in the proper sense of being unrecorded in writing, and we know little enough of him and his contemporaries. From the nature of the situation, they would not express any intellectual debt they owed to non-Muslim sources. Consequently we have to rely heavily on circumstantial evidence, and this will produce probable hypotheses at most.

In considering possible non-Islamic sources of influence we can quickly eliminate two bodies of thought. One is Arabian paganism. Most of the Muʿtazilites were not Arabians, so they would have learned nothing of the Arabian tradition through their families. Any influence it had on them must have been filtered through the Qurʾān and Traditions, so that it is not to be counted as non-Islamic, according to the criterion set up previously. The other possible source is Judaism. This was a developed system of religious thought, which may have had some influence on the origins of other Islamic sciences such as grammar and history, but of which no traces have yet been found in early Islamic theology, so far as I know.

This leaves four systems with which Muslims had substantial contacts: Zoroastrianism, Manichaeism, Christianity and Greek philosophy. These four will be examined in turn. Finally, the background of Muʿtazilism within Islam itself will be considered, and some general conclusions will be drawn.

4

To provide a context for the case of Zoroastrianism, it will be useful to give here a broad survey of the historical encounter of Zoroastrians and Muslims in the first three centuries of Islam. To begin with their political and social relations, it should be remembered that the Zoroastrian religion in its straight dualist form, with its supreme gods Ohrmazd and Ahrimān,[8] had been the orthodox faith of Sassanid Iran, supported by the Shah, and consequently by the civil service, army, and *dihqāns* (landlords). Its priests, the *mōbeds*, had been almost an arm of the government and had shown little independence or intellectual vitality under that régime. Its flocks were large, containing the mass of Iranian townsmen and peasants, who no doubt accepted the religion with more or less enthusiasm in proportion to their appreciation of its wholesome and positive teaching and their pride in the power and glory of their national empire. There was no missionary activity because this was a national religion that was exclusive of non-Iranians.

In spite of its long survival, such a religion rested largely on the precarious foundation of support by the state, which could lead it to collapse in face of one of the more vigorous new world religions, endowed with believers ready to proselytize and if necessary to accept martyrdom. The Manichaeans in the Sassanid empire had been held down by persecution; the Christians too, at times, yet the Nestorian church had gained numerous adherents, especially in Aramaic-speaking ʿIraq. But the Arab Muslims came in with an army as well as a faith and destroyed the Sassanid state. The *dihqāns* were then mostly won over to Islam by economic policies which allowed them to retain their

[8] Distinguished thus from the Zurvān heresy, with its more ultimate source of the two gods – Zurvān or Infinite Time. See R. C. Zaehner, *The Dawn and twilight of Zoroastrianism* (London, 1961), ch. 8.

lands and tax-collecting privileges on condition of conversion.[9] This double loss of political and economic support left the *mōbeds* and the people to struggle as best they could for the continuation of their old religion. In the circumstances they were fighting a losing contest.

But it took several centuries before Zoroastrianism became negligible in Iran. The first emigration of Zoroastrians to Gujerat and Bombay occurred in 717.[10] Islamic heresies with roots in one or another branch of Zoroastrianism appeared in the form of popular revolts in Iran under the earlier ʿAbbasid caliphs, such as those led by al-Muqannaʿ and Bābak. Māziyār in the ninth century and Mardāvīj in the tenth attempted without success to recreate Zoroastrian states in Tabaristan. Quite large Zoroastrian populations held out in the mountain areas of northern and western Iran, as well as in Fārs, Yazd, and Kirmān, into the ninth century[11] and even the tenth.[12]

It should not be thought, however, that the struggle between Muslims and Zoroastrians was conducted entirely on the political level. There were also intellectual encounters, and it is these that concern our subject more directly.

Most of the surviving sources of our knowledge of Zoroastrianism date from the Islamic period: the *Dēnkart* and other Pahlavī books, and the Arabic writings on heresies.[13] But it is certain that the doctrines found in them had been formulated under the Sassanid dynasty. The first Muslims who came into ʿIraq and Iran therefore faced a pre-existing developed religion. And this religion, although by now less vital than it had been, presented an intellectual challenge to them because it was new to them in a sense that Christianity and Judaism were not. For the Qurʾān itself had prepared some answers and attitudes to the Christians and Jews but had barely mentioned the religions of Iran.[14] It was thus a task for the first Muslim theologians to take up this challenge, and particularly to refute the prevailing dualist position of the

[9] B. Spuler, *Die Chalifenzeit* (Leiden, 1952), Eng. tr. F. C. Bagley, *The Muslim world: a historical survey*, I, *The age of the caliphs* (Leiden, 1960), p. 28, and *Iran in Früh-Islamischer Zeit* (Wiesbaden, 1952), pp. 134–6.

[10] Spuler, *The age of the caliphs*, p. 54.

[11] *Ibid.*, pp. 54–5; T. W. Arnold, *The Preaching of Islam*, 2nd ed. (London, 1913; reprinted Lahore, 1965), pp. 212–13.

[12] Mardān Farrukh, *Škand-Gumânîk Vičar: la solution décisive des doutes*, ed. and French tr. P. J. de Menasce (Freiburg, Switzerland, 1945), p. 130; Arnold, *Preaching*, pp. 212–13.

[13] For bibliography of Arabic and Persian writings on the Iranian religions under Islam see G. Monnot, 'Les écrits musulmans sur les religions non-bibliques', *Mélanges de l'Institut Dominicain d'Études Orientales*, 11 (1972), 5–48. G. Monnot, *Penseurs musulmans et religions iraniennes: ʿAbd al-Jabbār et ses devanciers* (Paris and Cairo, 1974) contains translations of texts of ʿAbd al-Jabbār and other Muslim authors against the Zoroastrians and Manichaeans. P. J. de Menasce, *Le Troisième livre du Dēnkart*, French trans. (Paris, 1972).

[14] Qurʿān, xxii, 17 mentions the Magians (*al-Majūs*), without clarifying the attitude to be taken by Muslims towards them. *Al-Majūs* in Arabic texts refers to the Zoroastrians (Magians). The Manichaeans are called *ath-thānawiyya* (dualists).

Zoroastrians. The Muʿtazilites were the predominant early theologians, and nearly all of them were born and lived in ʿIraq or Iran; many were *mawālī*, converts or sons of converts.[15] They did not ignore the challenge, and there is evidence of early debates. For instance, Abū al-Hudhayl (*c.* 751–849), who received a large stipend from the ʿAbbasid government, debated with Zoroastrians, Manichaeans, and others, and is said to have converted more than 3,000 men to Islam.[16] Mūsā al-Aswārī (d. *c.* 816) taught Qurʾān interpretation (probably in Baṣra) and 'used to set the Arabs on one side and the *mawālī* on the other, and explain to each group in their own language'.[17]

5

To estimate the probable influence of Zoroastrian on Muʿtazilite ethics in this historical situation, we have next to compare the two systems. This may be done most effectively for our purpose by setting them side by side in their barest elements.

	Zoroastrian ethics[18]	*Muʿtazilite ethics*
1.	Objective values	Objective values
2.	Ohrmazd and Ahrimān, sources of good and evil	Allāh, source of good alone
3.	Rational knowledge of values	Rational knowledge of values
4.	Man's power	Man's power, source of evil
5.	Everlasting rewards, purgative punishments	Everlasting rewards and punishments

[15] Individual origins of Muʿtazilites in A. Nader, *Le système philosophique des Muʿtazila* (Beirut, 1956), pp. 16–46, and in biographies in the *Encyclopaedia of Islam*, New Edition (*EI*²) (Leiden, 1960–). A historical problem that deserves attention is why the former Byzantine provinces of Syria and Egypt ceased to be active centres of intellectual life after the Islamic conquest and were so soon overtaken by Iraq and Iran, both of which under the Sassanids had been undistinguished on the world scene of the sciences. Did the Islamic caliphs do something to deaden eastern Mediterranean culture and to bring Iraq and Iran to new life? The answer is clear for the ʿAbbasids, founders of Baghdād, but the change started under the Umayyads whose capital was Damascus. Whatever the explanations, the fact is undeniable and applies to law, literature, historiography, theology and even the secular sciences with their strongly Hellenistic bases and traditions.

[16] Ibn al-Murtaḍā, *Ṭabaqāt al-Muʿtazila: Die Klassen der Muʿtaziliten*, ed. S. Diwald-Wilzer (Wiesbaden, 1961), 44–9.

[17] *Ibid.*, 60. The second language must have been either Aramaic or Persian. If the latter, then we are witnessing here an aspect of the origin of modern Persian (Fārsī), since a Muslim theologian must have injected an extensive Arabic religious vocabulary into any Middle Persian (Pahlavī) lectures. A short argument between 'Amr b. 'Ubayd (699–761) and a Zoroastrian is also recorded in a late source, Taftazānī, *Sharḥ ʿala l-ʿaqāʾid an-Nasafiyya* (Cairo, 1939), 99, Eng. trans. E. E. Elder, *A Commentary on the creed of Islam* (New York, 1950), pp. 83–4.

[18] Drawn from the Dēnkart and other Pahlavī works, Eng. trans. R. W. West, in *Sacred books of the East*, ed. M. Müller (Oxford, 1880 sqq.), vols. 5, 18, 24, 27, *Pahlavī texts* (Delhi, 1965), parts 1–4; and Mardān Farrukh, *Škand*, French trans. de Menasce.

The resemblances between these two systems are impressive at first sight, and combined with the eastern origins and environment of most of the Muʿtazilites they may lead to a spontaneous conclusion that these Muslim theologians took over most of their ethical theory from their Zoroastrian predecessors. Such a conclusion was indeed drawn by opponents at a very early stage, before the Muʿtazilites had systematized their doctrine but when their first leaders or even their predecessors were known for their doctrine of *qadar*, human power to act. The accusation found its way into a Tradition, in which the Prophet is reported to have declared, 'The Qadarites are the Mazdeans of this people'.[19] But such accusations were commonly used to discredit opponents: the same one is found later in use against the Shiʿites,[20] and the Muʿtazilites were sometimes charged with taking doctrines from the Christians.[21] Thus such statements cannot be assigned any weight as historical evidence. For a Zoroastrian–Muʿtazilite influence there is, in fact, no direct evidence, either external or philological, known to me at present. It will therefore be necessary to fall back on estimates of the total situation.

Let us return, then, to the comparison of the two theories. With all their resemblances, the dominant fact in the minds of the adherents of both systems at the time of their encounter was the unbridgeable gap between their positions on the second point. The Muʿtazilites held to the basic doctrine of Islam, the unity of God, and could not admit the infringement on His divinity that would be constituted by a co-eternal being, original cause of the evils of the world, and not to be subdued by God's efforts until the final days. In spite of holding less extreme views on God's omnipotence than their traditionalist Muslim opponents, Muʿtazilite theologians emphasized His unity and uniqueness to the extent that *tawḥīd* was one of their watchwords. And we must not lose the full significance of this word by relating it only to inner disputes of Islam; in those days the Muʿtazilites were missionaries of Islam against the eastern religions,[22] and *tawḥīd* was their battle-cry against every form of dualism and polytheism.

There was also disagreement with the dualists on the fourth point, following from the disagreement on the second: for Zoroastrians could relate evil in man (sin) to Ahrimān in a causal manner, whereas the Muʿtazilites refused to do that for the relation of man to God with respect to human sin. On the fifth point, it would have been convenient for Muʿtazilite ethics to have

[19] See J. Van Ess, 'Kadariyya', *EI*², IV, 371. Quoted by Ashʿarī, *al-Ibāna ʿan uṣūl ad-diyāna* (Cairo, 1348 h./1930), 7–8, 57; Eng. trans. W. C. Klein (New Haven, Conn., 1940), pp. 47–8, 113. But Ashʿarī interprets cautiously in terms of resemblance, not influence.

[20] Mentioned by A. Bausani in the *Cambridge History of Iran* (Cambridge, 1970), V, 286, with reference to an anonymous *Baʿd faḍāʾiḥ ar-Rawāfiḍ*.

[21] See below, note 31.

[22] See, for example, Ibn al-Murtaḍā, *Ṭabaqāt al-Muʿtazila*, 44, 49, 50–9, 60.

argued for the temporary limits of punishments in the afterlife, but they were prevented from doing so by explicit teaching of the Qurʾān that the punishment of wrongdoers is everlasting. Thus they had to find other arguments than purgatory to support their theodicy. On top of these differences, there were others beyond ethics which need not be mentioned. At the basis of all, and making any compromise with Zoroastrian doctrines impossible, was the fundamental divergence about the source of religious authority, between the followers of the Avesta and those of the Qurʾān.

The central disagreement, on the cause of moral evil, may be illustrated briefly from two controversial writings which survive. On the Zoroastrian side we have a Pahlavī book of the mid-ninth century by Mardān Farrukh, the *Škand Gumānīk Vičār*,[23] which includes arguments against the Muʿtazilites as well as against traditionalist Islam. On the Muʿtazilite side, late in the tenth century ʿAbd al-Jabbār wrote the fifth part of his *Mughnī*, dealing with non-Islamic sects.[24] These two theologians do not address each other directly, but they are familiar enough with the positions of their adversaries to enable us to draw from them the main elements of the disagreement between the two groups on the problem of evil.

The Zoroastrian knows that the Muʿtazilites would not accept to make God the cause of moral evil in man or allow Him to be defective in any way. He therefore has to attack the Muʿtazilite view that man alone, not Ahrimān, is the cause of such evil. His argument is that if the devil is excluded as a cause, man's doing evil is impossible to explain without imputing a defect to God. For either God would be ignorant or impotent to prevent the evil, which makes Him defective in knowledge or power, or else He would be wise and able to prevent it but unwilling, in which case He would be lacking in goodness and mercy. But if one believes with orthodox Zoroastrians that there is a devil who is uncreated, independent of God in his actions and evil by essence, then it is impossible for God to prevent him from showing ill will and doing evil, and he is the prime cause of human evildoing. God's omnipotence does not extend to the impossible, so no defect is now imputed to Him. Nevertheless He will control the devil at the end.

The Muʿtazilite on his side argues that an uncreated devil is impossible, because if he were uncreated the whole world might equally be so, and then both God and the devil would be unnecessary as causes of what exists. But if the devil is a creature of God, as Islam holds, the Zoroastrian argument collapses because, once it is admitted that God has created this most evil being

[23] Ed. and French trans. de Menasce, ch. 11.

[24] Abu l-Ḥasan ʿAbd al-Jabbār al-Asadābādī, *al-Mughnī fi abwāḥ at-tawḥīd wa l-ʿadl, V: al-firaq ghayr al-Islāmiyya wa l-kalām fi l-asmāʾ wa ṣ-ṣifāt*, ed. M. Khudayri (Cairo, 1958), 71–9.

without a defect in Himself, it can equally be admitted that He has directly created other beings who do evil, without a need for the devil as an intermediate creator. Thus the devil is not a necessary part of the world; he exists as a contingent fact, and he does not have the attributes and rôle ascribed to him by the Zoroastrians. Man chooses evil; he is tempted by the devil, but the devil is not a cause of his evil acts in the proper sense of 'cause', as when we refer to natural causes.

There are similar arguments concerning the punishments of the just in the next life. The Zoroastrian is at an advantage in his theodicy in being able to hold that all punishments of men in the afterlife are purgatorial and all men will end up in paradise. But there is no need to go further. The tone of debate between Zoroastrians and Muᶜtazilites is mild, compared with the far more severe opposition of Mardān to traditionalist Islam, or the severity of Muᶜtazilite authors against the Manichaeans. Still, the Muᶜtazilites were nowhere near being close to the Zoroastrians. They were of two different religions engaged in a life-struggle, and nothing could bring them into alliance or sympathy. For ᶜAbd al-Jabbār the Zoroastrian myths of creation were nonsensical tales (*khurāfāt*) which hardly deserved refutation.

Does all this mean that the resemblances between Muᶜtazilite and Zoroastrian ethics are mere coincidences? No, there is probably influence; but the relation is less definite than a take-over of specific doctrine from specific texts. Islam as a system of beliefs was still fluid, capable of being interpreted in different ways by different parties. Traditionalist Islam, with its voluntaristic and predestinarian ethics, was not yet an orthodoxy and was in sharp contrast with the prevailing ethical beliefs of the eastern regions with their masses of Zoroastrian and recently converted subjects. It was natural that there would be another Muslim party that would take account of these beliefs, to the extent that they were not excluded by the evident meaning of the Qurʾān. This party would then make a stronger appeal for conversion to surviving Zoroastrians and have a more attractive Islam with which to hold and indoctrinate converts. Thus the influence of Zoroastrianism would take the form of a pervasive pressure for accommodation to large numbers of people, both educated and illiterate, who formed an important part of the intellectual environment of the Muᶜtazilites at the period when they were constructing their theology. This explanation is a hypothesis; perhaps we shall never have texts to prove it, because the nature of the influence does not admit confinement to any specific texts. But the hypothesis will be strengthened by the accumulation of similar ones in relation to other sects to be examined.

6

The Manichaeans had never had an established church in Iran or ᶜIraq, and their numbers were always far fewer than those of the Zoroastrians. On the other hand they were missionaries for a new world religion, the last before Islam, and they seem to have penetrated intellectual circles in the cities of ᶜIraq. There was an upsurge of Manichaean propaganda in Arabic before and after the ᶜAbbasid revolution, led by ᶜAbdallāh ibn al-Muqaffaᶜ, ᶜAbd al-Karīm ibn Abī al-ᶜAwjā, and other prominent authors, according to later Arabic sources.[25] We cannot be sure about individuals, but at any rate enough alarm was aroused in Muslim circles by these *zindīqs*[26] to stimulate the caliph al-Mahdī and some successors to combat them with official persecution, and to provoke refutations by Muᶜtazilite theologians.

The Manichaean position on ethics resembled that of the Zoroastrians in its general dualistic lines, but differed from it in important respects. The source of good was eternal Light, the source of evil eternal Darkness; and the good and evil acts of men were caused in them by these two natural forces. These doctrines aroused sharper opposition from the Muᶜtazilites than Zoroastrianism had. Light and darkness were physical forces, thus making the Manichaeans ultimately materialists, however much they might disguise their doctrine in myths. As physical forces they could not be eternal and must be created, hence in need of a Creator above them, Himself eternal. There was no correspondence of light with good, of darkness with evil, for there are common situations in which light is harmful (for example, in helping criminals to find their victims) and others in which darkness is beneficial (for example, concealing the innocent from aggressors). Finally, the attribution of the good and evil acts of one man to the forces of light and darkness, working respectively in him, denies both the unity of the person – that it is the same person who does both good and evil – and his freedom, since he has the power to act by choice, not by the compulsions of nature. These and other Muᶜtazilite objections are gone over in detail in the two longest surviving refutations of Manichaeism in Arabic, by Qāsim ibn Ibrāhīm[27] in the ninth century and ᶜAbd al-Jabbār[28] in

[25] For an account of the leading figures, real or supposed, see G. Vajda, 'Les zindîqs en pays d'Islam au débuts de la période abbaside', *Rivista degli Studi Orientali*, 17 (1937), 173–229. For a bibliography of Arabic and Persian writings on the Manichaeans see Monnot, 'Les écrits musulmans'.

[26] The name was applied in Sassanid Iran and early Islam to apostates from Zoroastrianism, principally Manichaeans and Mazdakites, but later more widely to followers of nonbiblical religions. See L. Massignon, 'Zindîq', *Shorter Encyclopaedia of Islam* (Leiden,, 1954). Bīrūnī, *Taḥqīq mā li l-Hind*, Eng. trans. E. C. Sachau, *Alberuni's India* (London, 1888, reprinted Delhi, 1964), I, 264. The Manichaeans at this period won converts by presenting Mānī in an attractive way.

[27] *ar-Radd ᶜala z-zindîq al-laᶜîn Ibn al-Muqaffaᶜ: La lotta tra l'Islam e il Manicheismo*, ed. and Ital. trans. M. Guidi (Rome, 1927).

[28] *Mughnī*, v: *al-firaq*, 9–15, 22–70.

the tenth. Qāsim reacts more passionately to Manichaean attacks on the Qurʾān and Muḥammad; ʿAbd al-Jabbār's criticisms are more profound.

From the hostility of the Muʿtazilites to the Manichaeans we can conclude that they took nothing from Manichaean ethics, except probably some terms.[29] It is also unlikely that they made any effort to accommodate their doctrines to attract Manichaeans, who as mentioned were not numerous. The main effort was directed to rescuing wavering minds from the temptations of this infidel religion.

7

The situation of the Christians in the new empire of Islam differed from that of the Zoroastrians in several respects, most of which placed them in a stronger position in face of Islam than the Zoroastrians enjoyed. They were by far the majority of subjects in Syria and Egypt, and remained so for more centuries than the adherents of the eastern religions in ʿIraq and Iran. They maintained a presence in ʿIraq which was more important intellectually than their smaller population there would suggest. It is true that the Christians were divided into sects, Chalcedonian (Orthodox), Monophysite and Nestorian, and this division weakened them politically, but in the areas of controversy their division was on the issue of the nature of Christ, which had no bearing on the ethical questions that are being considered here.

Two other political factors are more relevant. One is the survival of the Byzantine empire, in contrast with the Sassanid empire. Close to the Christian provinces of the caliphate, just across the Mediterranean Sea and the Taurus Mountains, was the everlasting Christian state, heir to Rome, with its glorious capital the new Rome on the Bosporus. Christ had for a while cut off his servants in the East because of their sins and divisions, but He had not abandoned His larger flock in the West, and they would return to restore His reign when penance had been done. The proximity of Byzantium, and the hopes it aroused, certainly brought dangers from the inevitable reactions of Muslims, but on balance these factors gave confidence to the Christians under the Umayyad and early ʿAbbasid governments. So long as they exercised tact in their dealings with their new rulers they would have the benefit of the protection and tolerance prescribed for peoples of the Book, which applied to them more clearly than to Zoroastrians. They were subject to social and economic discrimination which would in time bleed their communities, but such pressures would have their least effects on the clergy who conducted religious discussions with Muslims.

The other political factor that favoured the Christians more than the

[29] See Allard, *Le problème des attributs*, p. 163, referring to O. Pretzel, *Die frühislamische Attributenslehre* (Munich, 1940), p. 8.

Zoroastrians was that the Orthodox church had not been quite so heavily dependent on the state, and the Monophysite and Nestorian churches had had to maintain themselves against the state. Thus they were less liable to collapse when left to rely on themselves under Muslim rulers.

In the sphere of polemics, both sides in the Christian–Muslim controversy were more confident in their intellectual stances than the parties in the dualist–Muslim controversies. Confidence on the Christian side was supported by the factors mentioned above and, on the theological level, by the high degree of sophistication that their leading preachers and authors had attained after so many centuries of debate with pagan Greek philosophers and other Christian theologians. If we can judge from early dialogues, which have survived only in Christian records, Christians were able to rebut their more simple-minded adversaries by questions that they could not answer.[30] Muslims on their side were more confident in facing Christians because the Qurʾān had already given them a few guidelines for debating with them. Their criticisms were directed mainly against the divinity of Christ and problems of the Trinity.

8

Before we attempt to answer our specific problem, the influence of Christian ethics on Muʿtazilite ethics, it is necessary to review at some length the more general question of influences of Christian theology on Muʿtazilite theology. Marked resemblances have long been noticed in several areas of theology: divine attributes, ethical principles, structure of treatises, methods of interpretation of scripture and so on. Contemporary Muslim opponents of the Muʿtazilites were the first to draw the inference of Christian influence, which in their eyes amounted to an accusation of heresy. This accusation was made early enough to get into the accepted collections of Traditions of the Prophet, in these sentences: 'Perhaps you will live long enough after me to meet people who will deny the power of God and ascribe sins to His servants. They [will] have drawn this argument of theirs from the Christians.'[31] This Tradition contains an unmistakable reference to the early Qadarites, who probably go back to a time before the first Muʿtazilites but held the same beliefs on free

[30] See F. Nau, 'Lettre de Mar Jean, patriarche, au sujet d'un colloque qu'il eut avec l'emir des Agaréniens', *Journal Asiatique*, 11th series, 5 (1915), 225–67; with corrections by H. Lammens, 'Un colloque entre le patriarche jacobite Jean I et ʿAmrou Ibn al-Âsî?', *Journal Asiatique* (1919), 97ff., reprinted in his *Études sur le siècle des Omayyades* (Beirut, 1930), pp. 13–25. John of Damascus, 'Dialogue between a Christian and a Saracen', *Patrologia Graeca* (*PG*), ed. J. G. Migne (Paris, 1857 sqq.), 94, cols. 1585–96 and 96, cols. 1336–48; Eng. trans. D. J. Sahas in *John of Damascus on Islam: the heresy of the Ishmaelites* (Leiden, 1972).

[31] Quoted by Becker, 'Christliche Polemik', p. 441, referring to ʿAlāʾ ad-Dīn al-Muttaqī al-Hindī, *Kanz al-ʿummāl* (Hyderabad?, 1894), 1, 35, no. 652; cf. 36, no. 668.

will and human responsibility. The saying is, of course, without value as historical evidence of Christian influence; all it shows is that such an assertion was thought by some early traditional Muslim to be plausible and was expected to discredit the Qadarites among many Muslims. Thereafter, the sophistries of guilt by association were not unknown to the *mutakallimūn* and were applied freely in associating opponents with non-Muslim doctrines.[32]

But if these medieval assertions prove nothing about causal connections, we must take more seriously the conclusions of many modern scholars relating the Muʿtazilites to Christian theology. No doubt von Kremer was the first to do so,[33] and he was followed by de Boer, Macdonald, Goldziher, Arnold and most thoroughly by Becker in his influential article 'Christliche Polemik'.[34] Becker's first argument on the question of *qadar* has already been mentioned: that because John of Damascus treated predestination as the characteristic doctrine of Islam, its Muslim opponents must have drawn their doctrine of *qadar* from a non-Muslim source.[35] He then goes on to point out some similarities of the Christian and Qadarite positions, which are not very striking. Next he quotes the Tradition given above, which proves nothing. On the question of creation of the Qurʾān, he is able to show how the doctrine of the uncreated Qurʾān would arise naturally from dialogues with Christians about Christ as the Word. A similar argument follows, on the question of anthropomorphic attributes of God and the incarnation of Christ. Then some emphatic statements on the Christian origin of the methods of *kalām*, an argument that has been viewed more recently with scepticism by Gardet and Anawati in their classic study of Islamic theology.[36]

The cumulative weight of so many resemblances should not be disregarded,

32 Some references in Allard, *Problème*, pp. 153–6 (not limited to Muʿtazilites and Christians). Other examples: Ashʿarī, *Ibāna*, 22 (Klein, p. 68) and 37 (p. 188), on Jahmites and Christians.

33 *Kulturgeschichtliche Streifzüge auf dem Gebiete des Islams* (Leipzig, 1873), pp. 2ff.

34 References to predecessors on p. 432. Also Arnold, *Preaching of Islam*, pp. 74–5.

35 See note 7.

36 Although they do not refer to Becker on this point, it will be instructive to quote the two passages side by side in translation:

Becker, 'Christliche Polemik', p. 445: 'It is known that the whole method of *kalām* springs from Christianity. Whoever reads Islamic dogmatic writers and Christian patristics in turn is so convinced of the connection that he has no further need of detailed proof. They form a single world of thought.'

L. Gardet and G. Anawati, *Introduction à la théologie musulmane: Essai de théologie comparée* (Paris, 1948), p. 206: 'Again we reserve our opinion on the question of possible sources, and we in no way believe that a very general correspondence in plans must necessarily lead to a conclusion of direct influence. In any case, the only common points are related to the order: (1) God in Himself (and His attributes); (2) God and his acts ad extra; (3) the economy of salvation (in one case Christology, in the other prophetology); and the outline thus traced is so normal for monotheistic theologies which have reached a certain level of elaboration, that it is no doubt as hard to prove a direct influence of [St. John] the Damascene on the problematics of Abū l-Hudhayl as it seems to us idle, in spite of Asín, to see in the plan of the *Iqtiṣād* [of Ghazālī] the prime origin of the plan of the later *Summas*.'

and it must be held a reasonable hypothesis that Christian theology had some influence on Islamic theology. But no decisive proof can be expected unless more precise answers can be obtained to the questions, How, when and where? Prompted by awareness of this need, attempts have been made to answer such questions. They have generally focused on St John of Damascus (*c.* 675–750),[37] so the arguments for his being the main link between the two systems will next be discussed.

9

At first sight, John seems to combine sufficient elements to constitute a probable influence on the early Muᶜtazilites. There are many points of resemblance between his theology and theirs. He was educated in Damascus, the Umayyad capital and lived there until around 730, in close contact with Muslim ruling circles. He knew Arabic and wrote something in it. He was familiar with the Qurʾān and Islam and wrote a short manual in Greek for use by Christians in discussing religion with Muslims, the *Dialogue between a Christian and a Saracen*, as well as a sharp criticism of Islam in a chapter of his *Heresies*.[38] Finally, he was a contemporary of the first two Muᶜtazilites, Wāṣil ibn ᶜAṭāʾ (699–748) and ᶜAmr ibn ᶜUbayd (699–761) and a predecessor of Dirār ibn ᶜAmr (*c.* 728–815)[39] and Abū al-Hudhayl (*c.* 751–849), the founder of a more systematic Muᶜtazilite theology.

The argument has some weaknesses in its geography and chronology. Damascus was the political capital but not an important centre of Islamic learning. Wāṣil and ᶜAmr lived in ᶜIraq. So did Ḍirār, Abū al-Hudhayl and the other Muᶜtazilites of the first ᶜAbbasid century; and they had no reason to visit Damascus after the ᶜAbbasids opened Baghdād as their capital (762). How would John's writings have reached them? For Wāṣil and ᶜAmr it is next to impossible, for reasons of chronology and language. John's main work, the

[37] E.g. Becker, 'Christliche Polemik'; Gardet and Anawati, *Introduction*, pp. 200–7; A. Abel, 'La polémique damascénienne et son influence sur les origines de la théologie musulmane', *L'Élaboration de l'Islam* (Paris, 1961), pp. 61–85.

[38] *De Haeresibus*, ch. 101, in Migne, *PG*, 94, cols. 764–73; trans. F. H. Chase, *St. John of Damascus: Writings*, in *Fathers of the Church*, 37 (New York, 1958), 153–60. The authenticity of this chapter was attacked by A. Abel, 'La polémique', p. 65, and 'Le chapitre CI du livre des Hérésies de Jean Damascène: son inauthenticité', *Studia Islamica*, 19 (1963), 5–25, but Abel's thesis has not found general support. See replies by A.-T. Khoury, *Les théologiens byzantins et l'Islam: Textes et auteurs* (*VIIIe–XIIIe s.*) (Louvain and Paris, 1969), pp. 49–55; and D. J. Sahas, *John of Damascus on Islam*, pp. 60–6.

[39] Ḍirār has not usually been counted a Muᶜtazilite, but he is mentioned here because of a recent reconsideration of his place in the history of *kalām* by J. Van Ess, 'Ḍirār b. ʿAmr und die Čahmīya', *Der Islam*, 43 (1967), 241–79 and 44 (1968), 1–70, esp. 7–14. Van Ess regards Ḍirār as a link between Wāṣil and Abū l-Hudhayl, who was not excluded from being viewed as a Muᶜtazilite merely because of his divergence from the rest of them on the question of *qadar*.

Fountain of knowledge, was completed in or after 743 and not in Damascus but at the monastery of Mār Sāba, to the southeast of Jerusalem. Since it was written in Greek, it would have had to be translated into Arabic and brought to the attention of Wāṣil and ᶜAmr within a maximum period of seven years, even if we suppose that their Muᶜtazilite position was not formed until the very end of their lives. The known Arabic writings of John are insufficient as a basis for Muᶜtazilite theology.

A use of John's works by Ḍirār is chronologically possible because of the sixty-five years' interval between the dates of their deaths; and for Abū al-Hudhayl the interval is a century. Still, the language barrier remains. The *Fountain of knowledge* is not known to have been available in Arabic before the latter part of the ninth century,[40] and they would not have read it in Greek, nor in Syriac (if there was a Syriac translation). There are also doubts related to these two theologians individually. Ḍirār's doctrine of predestination removes him further from the likelihood of influence by John than other Muᶜtazilites. Abū al-Hudhayl's life-span is rather late to make a predominant influence by John probable, in the light of the extent of theological development already found in his most direct Muslim predecessors, Wāṣil, ᶜAmr and Ḍirār. It would be different if we could point to any evidence for verbal copying or even a close resemblance in reasoning in a specific passage, but we cannot.

Thus a link between John of Damascus and the early Muᶜtazilites remains not only unproved but without grounds to support any degree of probability. All that can be said is that it is not impossible for the generations that followed Wāṣil and ᶜAmr.

10

The foregoing discussion of John of Damascus brings out the fault in method of efforts to link individuals to individuals, in the absence of specific evidence of the kinds required. But this does not rule out influences of undetermined Christian theologians on undetermined early Muᶜtazilites inferred from resemblances in doctrine. What needs to be sought is a broader relation, to be supported by a broader consideration of the history of the two religions in the centuries before and after their contact. This is attempted first with reference to theology as a whole and afterward with reference to ethics in particular.

John of Damascus' *Fountain of knowledge* is a *summa* that distills the essence of centuries of preceding Christian theology in the tradition of the Greek fathers. In the direct line of his predecessors the main figures are Origen, the

[40] F. Peters, *Aristotle and the Arabs: the Aristotelian tradition in Islam* (New York and London, 1968), p. 19.

Cappadocians Basil and the two Gregories, then Nemesius of Emesa, Pseudo-Dionysius the Areopagite and Maximus Confessor. Platonic and Neoplatonic ideas and Aristotelian logic are absorbed in the accumulated product of this tradition.[41] Now some works of each of these writers except Maximus had been translated into Syriac before Islam,[42] and were therefore accessible to the Nestorian and Monophysite scholars of ʿIraq. Thus to a large extent these ʿIrāqī Christians shared a common heritage with John. They too, like John, must have known Arabic well by the beginning of the eighth century at the latest. The Muʿtazilites of ʿIraq were much closer to them than to him and communication with them is more likely.

What form communication took is hard to discover. There may have been conversations and dialogues. Some of the Muʿtazilites, being converts, may have read Syriac theological literature before or after conversion. Or they may have read Arabic works after Christians had begun to write in Arabic. The most notable and pertinent Christian Arabic theologian was Theodore Abū Qurra (*c.* 750–820 or 825), an Orthodox Christian schooled in the tradition of John, who lived at Edessa, Ḥarrān where he was bishop, Jerusalem and perhaps Mār Sāba and made missionary journeys to Egypt, ʿIraq and Armenia. Abū Qurra's Syriac works are lost, but several in Greek and Arabic have survived. They show a bold and active apologist, although the Arabic works are said to be more cautious than the Greek.[43] It seems rather probable that his Muslim contemporaries, Ḍirār and Abū al-Hudhayl, were acquainted with his thought through personal contact, reading his Arabic treatises, or both. How formative such contacts would be, however, is debatable in view of these Muslims' well-advanced intellectual evolution.[44]

This survey is not meant to exclude John of Damascus, but only to put him in his place as one of several sources of influence, and probably not the most important. The total of resemblances and contacts makes it difficult to deny

[41] *Ibid.*, pp. 20–1; Gardet and Anawati, *Introduction*, pp. 202–3, and generally on Greek Christian Platonism before St John, I. P. Sheldon in *The Cambridge History of later Greek and Early Medieval Philosophy* (Cambridge, 1967), chs. 28–32.

[42] Origen: A. Baumstark, *Geschichte der syrischen Literatur* (Bonn, 1922, reprinted Berlin, 1968), p. 164; Gardet and Anawati, *Introduction*, pp. 196, 213. Basil: Baumstark, pp. 78–9. Gregory of Nyssa: Baumstark, pp. 79–80; R. Walzer, *Greek into Arabic: essays on Islamic philosophy* (Oxford, 1962), p. 81, with a reference to H. Langerbock in *Gnomon*, 22 (1950), 377. Gregory of Nazianzen: Baumstark, pp. 77–8, 260. Pseudo-Dionysius: Baumstark, pp. 168, 260.

[43] See Khoury, *Théologiens byzantins*, pp. 83–92; G. Graf, *Geschichte der christlichen arabischen Literatur*, II (Vatican, 1947), 15–25.

[44] For the same reason, and more strongly, later Christian Arabic works and translations from Greek are of little relevance. Translations from the ninth century include Nemesius of Emesa, *On the nature of man* (not Gregory of Nyssa's *Peri kataskeuēs anthrōpou*), Gregory of Nyssa, *al-Abwāb ʿalā raʾy al-ḥukamāʾ wa l-falāsifa* (a doxographical collection) and John of Damascus, *De fide orthodoxa*. See Peters, *Aristotle and the Arabs*, pp. 19, 122–3; C. Brockelmann, *Geschichte der arabischen Literatur* (Leiden, 1937–49), Suppl. vol. I, 369.

that there was an influence of Christian on Muʿtazilite theology, but the forms it took are elusive to the historian and will probably remain so. The reasons for this lie in the reticence of medieval Muslim theologians to acknowledge any studies beyond Islam, except for the purpose of refutation, and in the sheer multiplicity of channels. Historians have expressed this elusive but real relation of the two cultures in a variety of ways: the common thought-world (Becker), osmosis (Gardet and Anawati), taking spoils (Van Ess).[45] Another symbol of the process may be found in the Corinthian capitals found on columns in early mosques, taken from unknown older buildings but all harmonized in the new Islamic art of the mosque. This image also reminds us that we must not overestimate the extent of influences. The sharp differences between Christian and Islamic theology, even at their closest convergence, have been pointed out by Catholic scholars in particular.[46] In different ages, each one has taken from the other what it has found useful and adapted what it took to its own structure and needs.

The quest for Christian influences on Muʿtazilite theology is further hampered by the extent of common doctrines between Christian and dualistic theologies. Since the same early Muʿtazilites had access to Christian, Zoroastrian and Manichaean theologies, it is sometimes impossible to decide whether they took ideas on a particular topic from one of these sources rather than another. An example is the doctrine of human free will. If a Muʿtazilite looked outside Islam for suggestions on this question, he would find the same affirmation of free will in all three preceding religions. Meanwhile he would also be thinking for himself within the circle of Islamic discussion.

II

Within the historical and theological framework outlined we can now consider the influence of Christian ethics on Muʿtazilite ethics. It has become clear that John of Damascus is rather late to have been a dominant influence on the earliest Muʿtazilites. It will be helpful to go back to a much earlier thinker, whose ideas would certainly have had time to enter the bloodstream of Orthodox and Eastern Christianity before the first Muslim theologians were at work. To some extent it is arbitrary who is to be considered, since we cannot

[45] Becker, 'Christliche Polemik', p. 445; Gardet and Anawati, *Introduction*, p. 213; Van Ess, 'Ḍirār', p. 268. A judgement by R. M. Frank is also pertinent, from 'The divine attributes according to the teaching of Abū al-Hudhayl al-ʿAllāf', *Le Muséon*, 82 (1969), 451–506. After drawing attention to 'strikingly near' parallels between Abu l-Hudhayl and Origen he writes (pp. 458–9): 'Very little is known concerning Abū al-Hudhayl's theological background, and to seek sources by grasping at the straws of too easily paralleled formulae is fruitless.'

[46] Gardet and Anawati, *Introduction*, *passim*, esp. p. 207, last paragraph; Allard, *Problème*, pp. 165–9.

easily trace direct links between any earlier Christian theologian and the Muʿtazilites. We should look for someone with similar ideas on ethics. We could find notable resemblances between Origen and the Muʿtazilites, and he is worth mentioning as a founder of Christian rationalistic theology. But perhaps this would take us too far back (A.D. third century) to be relevant. We shall do better to attend to Gregory of Nyssa (335–394), a central mind in Christian theology who expressed an ethical doctrine steeped in Neoplatonism which can be regarded as 'classical', in the sense of setting the main lines for most of medieval Christian ethics in both east and west. His thought on ethics can be gathered from his *Oratio catechetica magna*,[47] and is set out briefly under the five headings used before.[48]

1. *Objective values*. The Logos is good and chooses good in everything. It made the world good (v, 2).

2. *God, source of good alone*. He had to share His light and pour out His love, so He made man able to participate in the divine goodness (v, 3–4). He cannot be the creator of evil, which is not in Him (v, 11).

3. *Rational knowledge of values*. Man had to be provided with reason and wisdom, so that he might desire to know the divine and have a relation with it (v, 6).

4. *Man's power, source of evil*. Man must also have been given freedom, so that he could practice virtue and be rewarded for it (v, 9–10). But this implies the possibility of choosing evil, which is vice (v, 11; viii, 18–19; vii, 3). This is lack of good, without actuality (v, 11; vii, 3). Its causes lie in man, with professional help from the Devil (vi, 1–11; viii, 6, 18–19).

5. *Everlasting rewards and purgative punishments* (viii, 11).

All five headings of Gregory's ethics coincide with those of the Muʿtazilites, except for Gregory's belief in a purgatory which will be temporary for all sinners until the final purification of souls at the time of Judgement (viii, 11). But the details differ in many respects, above all in Gregory's doctrine of the negative character of evil and other Neoplatonic elements, none of which are found in Muʿtazilite ethics. Both purgatory and negative evil give Gregory more complete solutions to the problem of evil and its special form, the problem of theodicy, than the Muʿtazilites could achieve.

With all the variations, however, the agreement on the main positions between Gregory and the Muʿtazilites is notable. Could the latter have had any direct knowledge of Gregory's writings? Many of these were translated into Syriac, including the *Oratio*.[49] The possibilities for Muʿtazilite knowledge

[47] Text in *Works*, ed. W. Jaeger et al. (Leiden, 1952–), IX. German trans. J. Barbel, *Gregor von Nyssa: Die grosse Katechetische Rede* (Stuttgart, 1971).

[48] See above, § 3.

[49] See note 42.

of Syriac learning have been discussed above (section 10). There is no known translation of Gregory into Arabic before the nineteenth century.[50] Thus there is no definite evidence linking Gregory with early Muslim theologians.

A similar situation is true in regard to Pseudo-Dionysius, who may be considered because he is probably later than Gregory (most likely of the later fifth century). The same positions on ethics are found in his work *On the Divine Names* whose chapter 4, 'On good and evil', is heavily dependent on Proclus.[51] His works were translated into Syriac in the early sixth century by Sarjīs of Rīshᶜayna.[52] There are several in Arabic translations, but none known to be of early date.[53]

Maximus Confessor, of the same school of Christian Neoplatonists, would have been still more promising on chronological grounds since his life (*c.* 580–662) coincides with the origin and first expansion of Islam. But there is no evidence that he was known to medieval Muslims except as a mere name, listed among commentators on Aristotle.[54]

So we return to John of Damascus, this time as an ethical thinker. We find in his treatise *On the Orthodox faith* all five of the Muᶜtazilite propositions, coinciding also with those of Gregory of Nyssa except for a tacit abandonment of universal purgatory for sinners.[55] It would be tedious to repeat these headings or go into details. John's way of thinking is less Neoplatonic and more Aristotelian than Gregory's, and his style of writing is more in the manner of a systematic textbook, but his intellectual affiliation is clearly with the Cappadocians and Maximus. The broad resemblance to the Muᶜtazilites on ethics is just as marked, making allowance for the differences between Christianity and Islam, especially in Christology. But here an affiliation cannot be assumed, for reasons of time and place mentioned previously. The decisive point is that some of the Muᶜtazilite positions on ethics are already found in Islamic sources before the thought of John could have been known to Muslim theologians. This point needs to be supported by some details of the chronology of early Islamic ethics. Approximate dates are given for the earliest recorded assertions under the five headings of Muᶜtazilite ethics.

50 See note 44.

51 Migne, *PG*, 3, ch. 4, cols. 693–736; Fr. trans. M. de Gandillac, *Oeuvres complètes du pseudo-Denys l'Aréopagite* (Paris, 1943), pp. 94–127. Gandillac (Introduction, pp. 17, 37–8), says it is all taken from Proclus, *De malorum subsistentia*, referring to studies of H. Koch. See also E. R. Dodds, ed. of Proclus, *The Elements of theology*, 2nd ed. (Oxford, 1963), pp. xxvii–xxviii.

52 Baumstark, pp. 168, 260.

53 Graf, I, 370–1, giving no dates of translations.

54 Nadīm, *Fihrist*, ch. 7, sect. 1 (Cairo, 1930), 357; Eng. trans. B. Dodge, *The Fihrist of al-Nadīm* (New York, 1970), II, 614. (Ibn) al-Qifṭī, *Taʾrīkh al-ḥukamāʾ*, ed. J. Lippert (Leipzig, 1903), 321, following Nadīm. No mention of Syriac translations in Baumstark. Later Arabic translations, Graf, I, 372.

55 *De Fide orthodoxa*, in Migne, *PG*, 94; Eng. trans. Chase, *John of Damascus: Writings*, pp. 165–406.

1. *Objective values.* Wāṣil (d. 748) in discussing *qadar*: God is 'Wise and Just', man 'is the agent of good and evil'.[56] Objectivity seems implicit in these statements, in the context of what we know of Wāṣil's thought. Probably the earliest explicit statement is by Abū al-Hudhayl (*c.* 751–849): Man prior to revelation 'must know the goodness of what is good and the evilness of what is evil'.[57]

2. *God is the source of good alone.* Ḥasan of Baṣra (d. 728): 'Everything is by the decree and determination of God except sins.'[58] Then Wāṣil on *qadar*: 'Evil and injustice cannot be attributed to God.'[59] These are negative statements, but the positive side, that God is and does good, can be taken for granted in Islamic thought from the Qurʾān onward.

3. *Rational knowledge of values.* The earliest statement seems to be one by Abū al-Hudhayl, that obligation is prior to revelation: A man ought to know God by proof (*ad-dalīl*), and he should know as well the good and evil qualities of human acts.[60] Thus the theory of ethical knowledge starts relatively late, as would be expected.

4. *Man's power is the source of moral evil.* This is the position of the Qadarites, forerunners of the Muʿtazilites. The problem of *qadar* arose early in Islam. The first to discuss it was Maʿbad al-Juhanī (d. 699) at Bạsra.[61] Maʿbad is said to have talked with and learned from an ʿIrāqī Christian named Sūsan.[62] The statement of Ḥasan quoted above under point 2 implies that man is responsible for sins. Wāṣil says it plainly: 'It is the servant [man] who is the agent of good and evil, belief and unbelief, obedience and disobedience.'[63]

5. *Everlasting rewards and punishments.* The doctrine hardly needs to be documented in early Islam, but it is well known that the Muʿtazilites from the beginning insisted on it as a consequence of their belief in God's justice. Wāṣil says that man is requited for his acts; Abū al-Hudhayl that a man who is morally ignorant is subject to everlasting punishment.[64]

Thus it appears, based on the limited evidence, that points 2, 4 and 5 are

[56] Shahrastānī, *al-Milal wa n-niḥal*, ed. M. F. Badran (Cairo, 1375 h./1956), I, 51.

[57] *Ibid.*, I, 55.

[58] Ibn al-Murtaḍā, *Ṭabaqāt al-Muʿtazila*, 19. Cf. a similar statement associated with Ghaylān ad-Dimashqī (d. before 743), in Ashʿarī, *Maqālāt al-Islāmiyyīn*, ed. H. Ritter (Istanbul, 1929), 513, quoted by W. M. Watt, *Freewill and predestination in early Islam* (London, 1948), p. 41 and n. 36.

[59] Shahrastānī, *Milal*, I, 51.

[60] *Ibid.*, I, 55.

[61] A. J. Wensinck, *The Muslim creed* (Leiden, 1932), p. 53, quoting the opening sentence of Muslim's *Ṣaḥīḥ*.

[62] Wensinck, *ibid.*, quoting Ibn Ḥajar al-ʿAsqalānī, *Tahdhīb at-tahdhīb* (Hyderabad, 1325–7 h.), X, 225ff. Ibn ʿAsākir, *Taʾrīkh madīnat Dimashq*, makes the connection more definite: 'The first to discuss *Qadar* was an ʿIrāqī called Sūsan, a Christian who became Muslim, then returned to Christianity; Maʿbad al-Juhanī derived from him, and Ghailān from Maʿbad': Watt, *Freewill*, pp. 59–60, quoting from H. Ritter, 'Ḥasan al-Baṣrī', *Der Islam*, 21 (1933), 58ff.

[63] Shahrastānī, *Milal*, I, 51.

[64] *Ibid.*, I, 51 and 55.

prior in Islamic theology to John of Damascus, point 1 is roughly contemporary, and only point 3 is later. On this basis no strong case can be made for an influence of John on Muʿtazilite ethics in its formative age.

The latest Christian theologian who could be considered as having had an influence is Theodore Abū Qurra. As mentioned, his contacts with the Muslim intellectual world were close. What is known of his ethical views seems to follow the doctrines of his predecessor John. But by his time (*c.* 750 to 820 or 825) the Muʿtazilite theory was formed in its main lines, since his contemporary was Abū al-Hudhayl who was the real founder of this rationalism as a system.

From this whole account, what connections can be seen between Christian and Muʿtazilite ethics? In every instance of a Christian theologian, taken alone, the conclusion seemed to be negative: no influence of this particular theologian on the Muʿtazilites could be proved. yet a survey of the field as a whole has given a different view. From the fourth to the eighth centuries there is a definite coincidence of doctrines on five major headings of ethics between a long line of Christian thinkers and all or most of the Muʿtazilites. If we cannot point to this or that Christian as an influence, there was plenty of time and adequate opportunity for some Christian or other to have been influential. Whether or not any one or several had such an influence must remain obscure in the absence of sufficient evidence. But the probabilities will be affected by our answer to questions still to be asked concerning the internal development of early Islamic thought: to what extent is there a necessary logic leading from the Qurʾān and Traditions to Muʿtazilism as one side of an Islamic dialectic? And what evidence is there that this position was actually worked out among Muslims debating with one another?

12

The three non-Islamic religions studied up to this point in their relations to the Muʿtazilites had adherents, in greater or less numbers, whose opposition or conversion to Islam was an important consideration always present to the minds of Muslims. The situation of Greek philosophy in the Islamic world was completely different. It was represented by a handful of disciples of the ancient philosophical tradition, working in Syriac or Arabic. They were not to be feared as a popular challenge to the solidarity of the Muslim community. Yet in another way Greek philosophy could be very powerful. Precisely because it was not a living threat, educated Muslims could respect its intellectual appeal all the more. Some of them did so intensely, in the small circles that cultivated the secular sciences and philosophy, from the days of Hārūn al-Rashīd (reigned 786–809) and thereafter for several centuries; and these circles adopted Greek thought in form and content, with no attempt at concealment and with varying efforts to harmonize their theories with Islam.

As a preliminary step to estimating the influence of this philosophy on Muʿtazilite ethics, it will be helpful to review the main stages by which it became familiar to Muslims and, parallel to these stages, the knowledge of Greek philosophy attributed to leading early Muʿtazilites.

No trace of Hellenism is to be detected in the founders of Muʿtazilism, Wāṣil and ʿAmr, and this is to be expected in the light of the general ignorance of Greek thought in Islam at their period. But a surprising discovery has recently been made about a Muslim theologian contemporary with them, Jahm ibn Ṣafwān (d. 746). Richard Frank has shown the Neoplatonic structure of his thought, to a degree that can hardly be accidental.[65] Jahm is not counted among the Muʿtazilites, but he was close to them, so his Neoplatonism opens the possibility of Greek influence on the earliest of them. Yet there is no evidence of this.

In the reign of Hārūn the first translations of Greek philosophy were made; meanwhile Abū al-Hudhayl (*c.* 751–849) was working out the first detailed Muʿtazilite system. It is reported that 'he studied something of the philosophers' books',[66] but as he had a long life it is impossible to give any precision to the period of his study. Another Muʿtazilite, Naẓẓām (d. 845), showed impressive knowledge of Aristotle in the presence of Hārūn's vizier Jaʿfar ibn Yaḥyā al-Barmakī.[67]

In the reigns of Maʾmūn (reigned 813–33) and Muʿtaṣim (reigned 833–42) Islamic philosophy came to birth, evidently with some encouragement from the Muʿtazilite movement. Maʾmūn was an enthusiastic patron of both the Muʿtazilite doctrines, which he exalted to an official orthodoxy, and the intensive translation of the major writings of Greek philosophy. This double patronage was continued by Muʿtaṣim, although with less interest. The first philosopher in Islam, Yaʿqūb ibn Isḥāq al-Kindī (d. *c.* 866), was close to the Muʿtazilites in his theological views.[68]

The final stage in the adoption of philosophy in Islam was the physical homecoming of the philosophers to Baghdād. Max Meyerhof in a celebrated article described how the small remnant of the school of Alexandria emigrated from there to Antioch in the reign of ʿUmar II (reigned 717–20), from Antioch to Ḥarrān under Mutawakkil (reigned 847–61), and finally to Baghdād under

[65] R. M. Frank, 'The Neoplatonism of Ğahm ibn Ṣafwān', *Le Muséon*, 68 (1965), 395–424.
[66] Ibn al-Murtaḍā, *Ṭabaqāt*, 44.
[67] *Ibid.*, 50.
[68] Walzer, 'New studies on al-Kindī', *Greek into Arabic*, pp. 175–205.

Muʿtaḍid (reigned 892–902).[69] At the period of this last move, Jubbāʾī (d. 915) was working out at Baghdād and Baṣra the classical Muʿtazilism of the Baṣra school in its more or less complete and enduring form.

This sketch shows that there was contact, through books or persons, between the Muʿtazilites and Greek philosophy at several times in the period under consideration; and it is probable that there was much more contact than is known from the haphazard evidence. Without going into the general question of the extent of affinity between the two schools, we may ask with regard to ethics: what were the points of agreement and difference? Such a question can only be answered here in a broad way, leaving out the many variations in the positions of individuals of both schools.

1. The objectivity of good and evil was accepted unanimously on both sides. The Muʿtazilites had to assert it and argue it emphatically against their voluntarist opponents in Islam; the Greeks could almost take it for granted, since to them the eternal 'laws' of the universe had always been supreme over gods and men alike. Even the hymn to Zeus of the Stoic Cleanthes is only a personalized paean to the immanent law or logos that governs the world. But the later Greek conceptions, from Aristotle to Plotinus, of good as actuality and evil as privation, are absent from Muʿtazilite thought. And this absence continues down to ʿAbd al-Jabbār (*c.* 935–1025), although the Greek theory was well known in his lifetime through the works of the Muslim philosophers and the *Ikhwān as-Ṣafā*. This suggests that the absence is due not to ignorance but to rejection, and although the Muʿtazilite writings are generally silent about this theory a few critical remarks on it are made by ʿAbd al-Jabbār.[70]

2. Although in both systems 'good' is not defined by a relation to God, equally in both God is a source of actual good in the world, and of good alone, never of evil. But there is a difference in the manner of His causation of good: simply stated, to the Greeks it flows from His nature, to the Muʿtazilites He creates it by His will.

3. Both groups held that man can know good and evil, obligatory and wrong acts by his reason. But the Muʿtazilites accepted in addition a second source of ethical knowledge, the commands of God given in revelation. A legend reported in the *Fihrist* attributes the Muʿtazilite view to Aristotle. It is said there that one of the reasons why books on philosophy became abundant was a dream of Maʾmūn, in which he saw Aristotle and questioned him as follows:

[69] M. Meyerhof, 'Von Alexandrien nach Baghdad', *Sitzungsberichte der Akademie der Wissenschaften* (Berlin), 23 (1930), 389–429.

[70] *Mughnī*, VI.i, 80; Hourani, *Islamic rationalism*, pp. 65–6.

Q. 'What is the good?'
A. 'Whatever is good by reason.'
Q. 'What next?'
A. 'Whatever is good by the Law [*ash-sharīʿa*].'
Q. 'What next?'
A. 'Whatever is good according to the public.'
Q. 'What next?'
A. 'Nothing next.'[71]

4. In the ethical writings of Plato and Aristotle, as in those of the Muʿtazilites, man has power to do evil. But in all of them the possibility and actuality of this moral evil did not create much of a problem in relation to God; He is simply not responsible for human sins. For the Stoics with their stronger sense of divine omnipotence and providence it created a problem of harmonization, somewhat akin to that of traditional Islam (even though their solution was different from that of Ashʿarī).

5. Rewards and punishments in an afterlife are not taken very seriously in Greek philosophy, as they have to be in any theology based on the Qurʾān. Plato writes of them in myths at the end of some dialogues, thus making clear their speculative status. Consequently problems of theodicy are also not prominent among the Greeks, whereas the Muʿtazilites devote much attention to them in controversy with their traditional Muslim opponents.

Aside from the differences mentioned under the five headings, Muʿtazilite ethics as known fully from ʿAbd al-Jabbār is developed in quite another way from Aristotle's ethics which became the basis for philosophical ethics in Islam; for example, in Miskawayh's *Tahdhīb al-Akhlāq*. Among the notable omissions by the Muʿtazilites are any use of Aristotelian technical language and the whole theory of virtue, including habit, the mean, the life of happiness, the methods of practical reason, and so on.

The conclusions from this account are fairly clear. Muʿtazilite theologians from Abū al-Hudhayl onward either knew something of Greek philosophy or had it available if they wished to study it. Since they did not make use of it in their ethics, this must have been a deliberate choice. The main lines of their ethical thought were already laid down prior to Abū al-Hudhayl, determined by their Islamic background and whatever influences had come in from Christianity or elsewhere. They then developed it according to the demands of their controversies with Muslim traditionalists and with opponents in other religions.

[71] Nadīm, *Fihrist* (Cairo, 1930); trans. Dodge, II, 583.

13

We must now try to see how Muʿtazilite ethics could have grown to its finished form as a result of stimuli occurring within the sphere of Islam. As a methodological device all outside influences will be excluded at this stage, with a view to estimating how far we can explain the system of thought on a purely Islamic basis.

Discussion on ethics in Islam was carried on within the framework of two fixed points, the unshakable beliefs of all parties with regard to point 2, 'God is one, the Creator and entirely good', and point 5, 'He rewards and punishes men justly in an afterlife'. The first problem that arose was that of theodicy, when a strict predestinarian interpretation of point 2 led to the doctrine of *jabr*, that God creates all the acts of everyone: thus there was no room under point 4 for human freedom and responsibility. The roots of such an interpretation lie in many passages of the Qurʾān, but the Qurʾān also contains roots for an opposite interpretation, so the Book as a whole did not settle the question. The Traditions are generally more predestinarian, perhaps reflecting ancient Arabian beliefs, as Watt suggested.[72] John of Damascus shows predestinarianism as the prevailing belief of Muslims in his time.[73]

Such a position raised the obvious theodical conflict between 2 and 4 as thus interpreted and 5: 'If God compels the evil acts of men, He cannot be just in punishing them for these acts.' The Qadarites took up the challenge of this conflict and solved it in a simple way by reinterpreting 2 and 4. God was the all-powerful Creator but had given men the power to determine their own acts. Thus the punishments of God for a man's sins would be just. This position was taken up by the Muʿtazilites, who called themselves the party of justice (*ahl al-ʿadl*) as against their Muslim opponents of predestinarian views. Thereafter both parties refined their positions as a result of their mutual tensions.

The remaining two headings, 1, ontology of value and 3, theory of ethical knowledge, were the products of a more advanced stage of thought on each side. They were not logically dependent on the first three but rather were derived from the same attitudes to God and scripture which had produced those three.[74]

The traditional party (*ahl as-sunna*) were those who insisted on two principles: the overwhelming power of God and the obligation on man to

[72] *Freewill*, pp. 17–30.
[73] *Dispute of a Saracen and a Christian*, *PG*, 96, cols. 1335–48.
[74] See ch. 3, 'Ethical presuppositions of the Qurʾān' for an account of what the Qurʾān might reasonably have suggested to each party on ethical value and knowledge of it.

follow the teaching of revelation as the sole source of religious knowledge. From the latter principle point 3 follows directly: revelation is the sole source of ethical knowledge. Point 1 follows from both principles: values must be derived from God's will and could not be independent objects knowable by human reason. In other words, objectivity of values would set a limit to God's power and would threaten the monopoly of revelation as the source of religious knowledge.

The Muʿtazilites sought above all a reasonable and morally convincing religion which they believed could also be justified by the text of scripture. If God is just, man must be responsible for his acts, and responsibility implies the possibility of sufficient moral knowledge even when a scripture is not available, as for many non-Muslims. This leads to 3, the power of human reason to know right and wrong in actions. And from this point 1 follows directly, since reason must have real objects for its knowledge.

This is a bare outline of positions, which could be enriched almost infinitely from the history of the two theological schools in detail, as well as by a study of parallel movements in jurisprudence and by considerations of political history. But the intention has been only to show how the intellectual constructions of both schools could have arisen out of a purely Islamic background, and this could be shown more clearly by presenting the essential structures of their thought without distractions of detail.

14

The conclusion that may seem to emerge from these investigations is that there are no non-Islamic sources for Muʿtazilite ethics, since none can be pinned down to definite evidence, and that the whole theory grew out of controversies among Muslims. But that is too simple a statement. For although there is no definite evidence linking a Muʿtazilite with a non-Muslim theologian, the accumulation of circumstantial evidence on the historical relations between early Muslims and their non-Muslim neighbours and rivals cannot be ignored. A more accurate conclusion may be expressed as follows.

Within the context of early Islam, two main ethical positions were easily possible, of which one would be more acceptable to former Zoroastrians, Manichaeans and Christians, while the other might appear more purely Islamic to Muslims untouched by such circles or reacting against them. The Muʿtazilites were the party who took the first position, because they were missionaries on the frontiers of Islam, who felt the weight of the large populations and powerful intellectual traditions that they were called upon to combat. The pressures in the sphere of ethics may be illustrated with a few quotations showing non-Muslim demands for theodicy.

On the Christian side we may go back to Origen, who lived long before Islam but was one of the formative founders of Christian theology.

We say that God is unable to do evil, because a God who would be able to do so would not really be God. For if God does anything evil He is not God.[75]

John of Damascus takes up this theme against his traditional Muslim opponents.

CHRISTIAN: But how do you say that good and evil things are from God? God according to you will then be unjust, which He is not.[76]

In the Zoroastrian tradition, Mardān Farrukh attacks the contradiction in any religion which affirms that evils can come from a perfect God.

If they could, that would mean that He would not be perfect; and if He is not perfect, it is not right to praise Him for divinity and perfect goodness.[77]

There is no need to gather more quotations. The idea of theodicy was deeply embedded in the two religions. It may even be called a 'natural' human idea, and it was one that would inevitably have been demanded by many Muslims even if they had not found it in their own scriptures and the teachings of other religions. The Muslim community would have been insensitive if it had not produced a response to this demand which came from all sides. The Muʿtazilites were those who tried hardest to respond to it.

15

Beyond the particular sphere of ethics, rationalistic methods are normal in interreligious controversy, because if the adversaries are to be able to discuss religion at all they must find common ground and not presume the truth of their own faith. This is an idea that recurs constantly in the history of religion. Theodore Abū Qurra says he will argue with Muslims not on the basis of scripture but 'from common, agreed notions' (*ek koinōn kai homologoumenōn ennoiōn*).[78] On the Muslim side, a certain Hāshimī of the time of Maʾmūn expresses the rational spirit of the age in a letter inviting a Christian, Kindī, to embrace Islam:

[75] *Contra Celsum*, v, 23.
[76] *Dispute*, *PG*, 96, col. 1337.
[77] Ch. 8, sect. 110.
[78] *Opuscula*, in *PG*, 97, col. 1551; quoted by Becker, 'Christliche Polemik', p. 445. Cf. also Khoury, *Théologiens byzantins*, p. 90.

Therefore bring forward all the arguments you wish and say whatever you please and speak your mind freely. Now that you are safe and free to say whatever you please, appoint some arbitrator who will impartially judge between us and lean only towards the truth and be free from the empery of passion: and that arbitrator shall be reason, whereby God makes us responsible for our own rewards and punishments. Hereby I have dealt justly with you and have given you full security and am ready to accept whatever decision reason may give for me or against me. For 'there is no compulsion in religion' and I have only invited you to accept our faith willingly and of your own accord.[79]

St Paul practiced the same method without formulating it when he preached to pagan Greeks near the Areopagus in Athens: he presented his argument for Christianity in rational terms which might persuade Stoic and Epicurean philosophers.[80] Before long this became a firm policy of early Christian apologists, when the problem had to be faced on a larger scale, as Werner Jaeger explained so clearly in his *Early Christianity and Greek Paideia*:

Thus there came into existence, about the middle of the second century, a large body of literature through which Christians spoke to the pagan majority of the population in self-defence. It is obvious that this polyphonic chorus could not in their apology take for granted what they were going to defend. That is what distinguished their situation from earlier Christian literature. These new advocates of their religion had to find some common ground with the people they addressed if they wanted to reach an understanding. That compelled them to take a more rational approach to their own cause, in order to make it possible for others to join them in a real discussion.[81]

Finally, Thomas Aquinas gave classic expression to this necessity in announcing his intentions in the *Summa contra Gentiles*:

...some of them, such as the Mohammedans and the pagans, do not agree with us in accepting the authority of any Scripture, by which they may be convinced of their error. Thus, against the Jews we are able to argue by means of the Old Testament, while against heretics we are able to argue by means of the New Testament. But the Mohammedans and the pagans accept neither the one nor the other. We must, therefore, have recourse to natural reason, to which all men are forced to give their assent. However, it is true, in divine matters the natural reason has its failings.[82]

So this is what the Muʿtazilites were doing, only without the reservation stated in the last sentence quoted from Thomas. As time passed and Islam

[79] *Risālat ʿAbdallāh...al-Hāshimī ilā...al-Kindī* (London, 1885), as translated by Arnold, *Preaching of Islam* (Lahore, 1965), pp. 433–40.

[80] Acts of the Apostles, xvii, 15–34; see W. Jaeger, *Early Christianity and Greek Paideia* (Cambridge, Mass., 1961), p. 11.

[81] *Ibid.*, pp. 26–7.

[82] I, ii, sect. 3, as trans. by A. C. Pegis, *On the truth of the Catholic faith* (New York, 1955), I, 62.

became ever more secure and dominant, these pioneer apologists were reproached for having deviated from the true religion, now seen by Sunnites more and more in a traditionalist, predestinarian and voluntarist light. Such reproaches were defective in historical understanding of the original context and rôle of the Muᶜtazilite movement. For the Muᶜtazilites always chose whatever doctrines suited their position inside Islam and were never overwhelmed by any non-Muslim system, however impressive it might be on an intellectual level. That is proved by their cool reception of Greek philosophy, which they passed by almost unnoticed, although it was certainly known to them.

Von Grunebaum stressed the independence of early Islamic culture, taking it back to the cocoon stage in Arabia.

> Even when every allowance is made for the contingent character of historical developments it still remains safe to state that on their exodus from the Peninsula the Arab Muslims had made the 'governing decisions' in regard to what they considered their physical and spiritual ancestry; hence they had so to speak predetermined what, on being exposed to a large spectrum of cultural possibilities, was to fit in with their sense of cultural affiliation, and thus, too, the sources on which they might draw to solve problems and fill gaps of which as yet they were, for the most part, unaware.[83]

Perhaps von Grunebaum went too far. If we try to apply his generalization to the Muᶜtazilites, we have to remember that they were ᶜIrāqīs or Persians, whose cultural background was Babylonian or Persian, Christian, Zoroastrian, or Manichaean. It was not likely that they had so quickly assimilated themselves to the Arabs as to accept Arabian attitudes not considered essential to Islam. But certainly their outlook on life was already firmly bound within the new *Weltanschauung* created by the Arabic Qurʾān. No ancient culture, however rich, could withstand the tremendous power of the Book.

[83] G. E. Von Grunebaum, 'The sources of Islamic civilization', *Der Islam*, 46 (1970), 14–15; also in *Cambridge History of Islam*, II, 479–80.

7

THE RATIONALIST ETHICS OF ᶜABD AL-JABBĀR

I

Rationalism has been vigorous in modern western ethics, from British moralists of the eighteenth century to Kant and his disciples, then to more recent intuitionists such as Moore and Ross. The common elements have been the beliefs that the values of acts and intentions to which we refer by words such as 'good' and 'obligation' are objective or factual, but in some sense 'non-natural', and that they are recognizable by intellectual acts which are different in kind from those by which we recognize characters of sense data or our own mental states. From this brief description we can see that modern rationalism has followed roughly the tradition of Aristotelian ethics. No doubt one could trace its lineage through medieval Christian theories of natural law.

In classical Islam also the existence of rationalist ethics has long been familiar to scholars in the Muᶜtazilite theology, with its insistence on the objective nature of good and evil, justice and injustice. Here it was not opposed to naturalistic ethics, as in the modern West, but to the voluntaristic theory developed by the Ashᶜarites out of Shafiᶜite jurisprudence: the definition of value in action as obedience to divine commands, and the consequent impossibility of knowing right and wrong except from revelation or something dependent on it in one way or another – Traditions, analogy, consensus of the *ᶜulamā*ʾ.[1] Ashᶜarite ethics have always been well known through the works of Ghazālī, Shahrastānī and others. Muᶜtazilite ethics, on the other hand, have usually been studied from the summary accounts of their opponents, the heresiographs Ashᶜarī, Baghdādī and Shahrastānī. Until recently it was assumed all too easily that their theories could not be found in surviving writings of their own: an assumption that has been false for many years now, since several works of later Muᶜtazilism have in fact long been available.[2]

[1] For surveys of the earlier phase of this controversy see ch. 5, 'Two theories of value in early Islam', and recently R. M. Frank, 'Moral obligation in classical Muslim theology', *The Journal of Religious Ethics*, 11 (1983), 204–23.

[2] The following works may be cited as accessible for the past 50 years at least:

Sharḥ al-uṣūl al-khamsa, in catalogued manuscripts in Milan (Ambrosiana) (2 MSS.), Vatican, Vienna, Istanbul. See Addendum, below.

Yūsuf b. Ibrāhīm al-Baṣīr, Kitāb al-Muḥtawī, Arabic ed. and Hungarian trans. M. Klein and

480 35984

But whatever reason there may have been for not studying the thought of the Muᶜtazilites in their own writings was finally overturned after 1951. In that year Dr Fuᵓad Sayyid, curator of Arabic manuscripts of the Egyptian National Library, rediscovered in Sanᶜa most of the huge treatise of ᶜAbd al-Jabbār, *al-Mughnī fī abwāb at-tawḥīd wa l-ᶜadl* ('Summa on the topics of unity and justice'), in twenty long books.[3] The excitement aroused by the discovery of the *Mughnī* stimulated the publication of another important work the *Sharḥ al-uṣūl al-khamsa* ('Exposition of the five principles'), a compendium of Muᶜtazilite theology which is by no means a short book but is more systematic than the dialectical and rambling *Mughnī*.[4] Another work is *al-Majmūᶜ fi l-muḥīṭ bit-taklīf* ('Comprehensive collection on obligation'), which in spite of its title is of lesser value for ᶜAbd al-Jabbār's ethics, being the composition of a disciple.[5]

These three books, and some others by him not mentioned here, constitute a detailed source for the theology of a late Muᶜtazilite master, a product of two centuries of development in the school. Arab and western scholars have quickly appreciated the interest of ᶜAbd al-Jabbār, and several are at work on various aspects of his thought. My book on his theory of ethics (see note 11) is the first detailed account of an Islamic theory of this type, i.e. a rationalist theory centred on the analysis of ethical terms and problems of ethical knowledge, as in modern ethics. (In the classical books of *akhlāq*, 'ethics', by Miskawayh, Nāṣir ad-Dīn Ṭūsī and others, another interest is foremost, the classification and description of virtues and vices according to the Aristotelian doctrine of the mean.) The present essay is a short account of the theory in some of its main features. But before it is described it will be useful to place the author in the intellectual context of Iran and ᶜIraq in his time.

E. Morgenstern (Budapest, 1913). Yūsuf (Joseph ben Abraham) was a Karaite, a 'Jewish Muᶜtazilite', contemporary with ᶜAbd al-Jabbār in Iraq and Iran in the early eleventh century. His theory of ethics is similar to ᶜAbd al-Jabbār's: See I. Husik, *History of medieval Jewish philosophy* (New York, 1916), pp. 48–55.

Abū Rashīd of Nīshapūr (a student of ᶜAbd al-Jabbār), *Masāᵓil al-khilāf*, German trans. M. Horten, *Die Philosophie des abū Raschīd* (Bonn, 1910), pp. 211–17. 'Das Gute und Bose'.

Ḥasan b. al-Muṭahhar al-Hillī, *al-Bāb al ḥādī ᶜashar*, English trans. W. M. Miller (London, 1928), Section 4, 'on God's justice'. Ḥillī was a fourteenth century Shiᶜite, with distinctly Muᶜtazilite views on ethics.

We may also recall Zamakhsharī's (1075–1143) Muᶜtazilite commentary on the Qurᵓān, *Kashshāf ᶜan ḥaqāᵓiq ghawāmiḍ aṭ-ṭanzīl*.

3 Ed. I. Madkour, G. Anawati et al. (Cairo, 1962–70). For an account of the discovery and a table of contents see G. Anawati et al. in *Mélanges de l'Institut Dominicain d'Études Orientales (MIDEO)*, 4 (1957), 281–316 and 5, 417–24.

4 Ed. ᶜAbd al-Karīm ᶜUthman (Cairo, 1384 g./1965). The editor gives a list of ᶜAbd al-Jabbār's work, Introduction, pp. 13–36 and an index of sources for his life, pp. 817–20. See *MIDEO*, 8 (1964–6), 281–91 for a table of contents of *Sharḥ*. See Addendum below, on authorship.

5 Vol. I, ed. O. Azmy, revised A. F. el-Ahwany (Cairo, 1965); also vol. I, ed. J. J. Houben (Beirut, 1965) and vol. II, ed. J. J. Houben and D. Gimaret (Beirut, 1981). The disciple was Ḥasan b. Mattawayh.

His lifetime, the later tenth and earlier eleventh centuries, was probably the most vital period for learning in eastern Islam. In theology, the Muʿtazilite doctrine, continued to develop, as will be mentioned. Side by side with it, the Ashʿarite school grew to maturity in the works of Bāquillānī (d. 1013) and ʿAbd al-Qādir al-Baghdādī (d. 1037). Neoplatonism in its Islamic form was getting into the main stream of education through the encyclopaedia of the Sincere Brethren (mid-tenth century), and the climax of this philosophy was achieved in the consummate synthesis of Ibn Sīnā (980–1037). In sciences, this was the age of Bīrūnī (d. 1051 or 1052), Miskawayh (*c.* 940–1030), Ibn Nadīm the author of the *Fihrist* (988) and many other distinguished scholars.

ʿAbd al-Jabbār (*c.* A.D. 935–1025) was known as 'al-Hamadhānī al-Asadābādī', names which indicate his family origins in two cities of Iran. His earlier Muʿtazilite education took place in Iraq, where he studied under Abū Isḥāq b. ʿAyyāsh of Baṣra and Abū ʿAbdallāh al-Ḥusayn b. ʿAlī, another Basran who taught in Baghdad. These scholars had been students of 'the two shaykhs', Abū ʿAlī al-Jubbāʾī (d. 917) and his son Abū Hāshim (d. 932). ʿAbd al-Jabbār often refers to their doctrines and generally regards them as his masters, although he sometimes diverges from one or both of them. From 978 until his death he lived in Rayy, which was for most of this time the capital of the Buwayhid state of Jibāl; and for some time he was the chief qāḍī of the city and its province. Thus he enjoyed the patronage of Shiʿite princes such as Fakhr ad-Dawla and viziers such as Ibn ʿAbbād, who favoured the Muʿtazilite theology.[6]

In the light of recent studies of the Buwayhids and the later Muʿtazilites, we must now revise the older view of this school as one which flourished principally in the ninth century and breathed its last gasp in Jubbāʾī and his son. For it not only received political tolerance – a necessary condition of survival – from various rulers much later than the caliphs Maʾmūn and Muʿtaṣim. More important for its permanent merit, the school continued its internal evolution, in reaction to the Ashʿarite challenge arising in the tenth century. Thus we find in the works of ʿAbd al-Jabbār not a late 'decadent' summary of an earlier school, but the culmination of the school's intellectual life, which had profited from the thought of the earlier masters and opponents to present the most elaborate defence of Muʿtazilism that was ever composed. It included an extensive and sophisticated treatment of ethics.

[6] See 'Abd al-Jabbār b. Aḥmad, 'Buwayhids or Buyids' and 'Fakhr ad-Dawla' in *EI*²; and R. Caspar, 'Le renouveau du mo'tazilisme', *MIDEO*, 4 (1957), 141–201.

	Evil (*qabīḥ*): Doer deserves blame	Not obligatory (*ghayr wājib*): Omitter does not deserve blame
Good (*ḥasan*): Doer does not deserve blame	Permissible (*mubāḥ*): Doer and omitter do not deserve blame or praise	
	Act of grace (*tafaḍḍul*) or Recommended (*nadb*): Doer deserves praise Omitter does not deserve blame	
	Obligatory (*wājib*); Omitter deserves blame	

2

The ethical thought of this Muslim theologian moved constantly between two levels, human and divine. The human ethics is developed to a large extent in the service of the theodicy. But it is always made clear which level he is speaking of, so that it is possible to reconstruct the human ethics accurately by itself; and this has been my main aim. In any case, in a Muʿtazilite theory the concepts of value are predicable of God's acts in the same sense as of man's. I have reconstructed the system from many passages of the *Mughnī* and the *Sharḥ*, and found it on the whole consistent.

The theory can be outlined most clearly by going through in order the different types of propositions in ethics that men can know, with explanations of how they know each type, according to the author, and a few other points of interest connected with each.

(1) The frame of the system is a network of *definitions* of the principal value terms, all rather well articulated and related to each other. The accompanying chart will show the system.

The most noticeable feature of these definitions is that the predicates all consist of some relation of desert to praise or blame. Thus they are of the same type as in A. C. Ewing's older theory,[7] in which he defines 'good' as 'fitting

[7] *The definition of good* (New York, 1947), ch. 5.

object of a pro attitude' and 'bad' as 'fitting object of an anti attitude'. This is one of many parallels between the ethics of ᶜAbd al-Jabbār and those of modern British ethical intuitionists. Both definitions, ᶜAbd al-Jabbār's and Ewing's, are exposed to a criticism on grounds of circularity. In the formula of ᶜAbd al-Jabbār, it is the concept of 'desert' which gives trouble in this way, for it seems to contain in itself a concept of value, thus:

Definition of 'evil': An act is evil when the doer *deserves* blame for it.

Definition of 'desert': Deserving blame means that it is right or *obligatory* to blame it.

Definition of 'obligatory': An act is obligatory when the one who omits it *deserves* blame for that.

Definition of 'desert':...

'Abd al-Jabbār was challenged on this point (*Mughnī*, XIII, 346) and attempted to answer it by analysing 'desert' in terms of relations of 'correspondence' between evil acts and blame, beneficent acts and praise:

It is established by reason that it is characteristic of blame to be corresponding to evil and doing mischief, so as to be requital for it, and it is characteristic of praise to be corresponding to beneficence in the same manner... (*ibid.*)

The concept of 'correspondence' is supposed to be factual in a sense that is free of value. But if we ask, what kind of correspondence? it is hard to avoid answering in terms of fittingness. Thus it is doubtful whether it is possible to find an analysis of 'desert' that does not ultimately employ a value concept in it. The conclusion then would be that the main terms of value such as 'evil' and 'obligatory' are logically prior to 'desert', so that 'desert' cannot be used in defining them.

Another notable feature of the definitions as displayed in the chart is that evil comes first. This reflects ᶜAbd al-Jabbār's usual order of treatment, which is not arbitrary but based on the fact that the definition of evil has a positive subject, the doer (not the omitter) and an affirmative predicate. The qāḍī explicitly rejects the Neoplatonic definition of evil in terms of negation. He also has more to say about evil than about any other concept, so altogether we are justified in regarding it as the key concept in his ethics.

He says little that I have discovered about how definitions can be known. But from his own procedure in discussing them it seems that he is concerned mainly with real, i.e. lexical, definitions and that the method is one of testing ordinary language to find the definition which corresponds most closely with the way we speak.

(2) The next type of propositions with which ᶜAbd al-Jabbār is concerned

in ethics is *general truths*, other than definitions, i.e. statements about what classes of acts satisfy the definitions. He is conscious of a logical difference between a definition and a general statement of non-linguistic fact, e.g. between '"Evil" means "whatever is deserving of blame"' and 'Wrongdoing (*ẓulm*) is always evil'. Although he does not make the later European distinctions of 'analytic' and 'synthetic' propositions, he knows that in the first proposition the subject and the predicate refer to the same essence, while in the second wrongdoing is not the essence of evil but one of the *grounds* which make an act evil.

'What makes the object have the attribute [evilness] may vary....lying is evil because it is lying, wrongdoing because it is wrongdoing,' etc. (*Mughnī*, VI.i, 61).[8]

There are two sub-classes of such general truths, according to his theory.

(a) Absolute general propositions, which are always true in fact in their simple form. The example given above is of this class: wrongdoing is *always* evil, regardless of the circumstances, the state of mind of the agent, the moral code of his society, even (hypothetically) the commands of revelation. There are a few other absolute grounds of evil, such as: lying, useless acts, a will for evil. (But more will be said below on lying.)

Such truths have the status of axioms of reason, which every sane man can know immediately. These are primarily what give the Muʿtazilite ethics the character of intuitionism – quite in line with the Aristotelian tradition, although the historical affiliation is hard to trace. To a modern critic, they raise the Kantian problem of knowledge: how can we know *a priori* the truth of any synthetic proposition? No one in Islam expressed the problem in this way; yet it may well have been the unformulated doubt behind the criticisms by the opponents of Muʿtazilism, that its ethical axioms were arbitrary, not supported by reason as was claimed but only by fanciful whims (*ahwā'*). To these criticisms ʿAbd al-Jabbār replies with somewhat dogmatic assertions about what the rational man knows and the insincerity of those who say they don't know such evident truths.

(b) But, apart from the few kinds of act which are good or evil whenever they occur, in the majority of cases we have to consider together various *aspects* (*wajh*) of the act before we can determine its value as a whole. The first step in the process of judgement is to know the value of each aspect when

[8] It may be thought that ʿAbd al-Jabbār is guilty of another piece of circularity here, if 'wrongdoing' is a concept which already contains that of 'evil'. But this accusation can perhaps be answered by considering his definitions in more detail. He defines 'wrongdoing' as 'any injury without benefit exceeding it or repulsion of harm greater than it, which is not deserved and not thought to have any of these aspects' (*Mughnī*, XIII, 298). If the concepts 'injury', 'benefit', etc. can be understood in terms of non-value facts, the circularity can be avoided. But I prefer not to go further into this question, since he does not do so.

taken in isolation. For example, pain is evil in itself, i.e. when it is simply useless suffering, not a necessary step to future benefits and not a just punishment for wrongdoing. In other words, pain is a 'prima facie evil', to use the term proposed by W. D. Ross in his notable expositions of intuitionist ethics.[9]

The usual manner of knowing such prima facie truths according to ʿAbd al-Jabbār appears to be also by immediate intuition, to judge from the small evidence I have come across; and this is what we should expect, for the knowledge acquired is of much the same kind as that of general truths of ethics, described above under (a).

ʿAbd al-Jabbār shows some hesitation about lying, whether it belongs to absolute or prima facie evils. In principle he holds it an absolute evil, but he has to face hard cases raised by his Ashʿarite opponents. Would it be evil to tell a lie to save the life of a Muslim, for example by saying he is not at home to someone coming to his house with evident intent to murder him? ʿAbd al-Jabbār says one can always escape from such a dilemma by insinuations or silence, and never needs to tell a direct lie (*Mughnī*, VI.ii, 342). In spite of his principles, he refuses to say outright that it is wrong to tell a lie even when it is the only way to save a life. This attitude is damaging to the consistency of his theory, but surely speaks highly for the honesty of his moral judgements, a prominent feature in his thinking as in that of Ross.

A special group of acts falling under class (b) consists of those known as good by revelation alone. These are the acts of worship, such as prayer and pilgrimage and fasting. Human reason unaided (*ʿaql*) would have declared them useless and inconvenient. It is only by revelation that we can know them as beneficial to man, other things being equal – i.e. as prima facie good. (Their inclusion in this class of goods is implied by the *sharīʿa* principle of *ḍarūra*, that in cases of overriding hardship these normal religious duties may be omitted, as the Qurʾān itself recognized.)

ʿAbd al-Jabbār is careful to make it clear that God does not *make* religious obligations good by decree, he only *reveals* their genuine goodness to us.

> Revelation only uncovers about the character of these acts aspects whose evilness or goodness we should recognize if we knew them by reason; for if we had known by reason that prayer is of great benefit to us, leading us to choose our duty and to earn Reward thereby, we should have known its obligatory character [also] by reason. Therefore we say that revelation does not necessitate [*lā yūjib*] the evilness or goodness of anything, it only uncovers the character of the act by way of indication, just as reason does, and distinguishes between the command of the Exalted and that of another being by His wisdom, Who never commands what it is evil to command. (*Mughnī*, VI.i, 64.)

[9] First in *The Right and the good* (Oxford, 1930), pp. 19–20.

A statement like this (and there are many similar ones) safeguards several principles important to Muʿtazilite theology.

(i) It gives a useful function to revelation in ethical guidance to man.

(ii) That function is a rational one, in the same sense as that of human reason and directed to the same kind of objects.

(iii) Therefore it harmonizes the conclusions of revelation with those of reason.

(iv) At the same time it attributes to God's reason superior wisdom to human reason.

(v) It affirms the objective value of whatever God commands to man, even when man by his own power cannot see wherein the value consists. Thus God's commands are not arbitrary but always directed to man's benefit.

(vi) It affirms the goodness of God in an intelligible sense, that His purpose is always to bring about the maximum objective good.

To this last point objection was made by Ashʾarite opponents that it limits God's omnipotence by claiming superior eternal standards to which He conforms. ʿAbd al-Jabbār's position in answer to this well-known challenge is an interesting one. He does not admit that God has to conform to those standards, that it is impossible (*lā yumkin*) for Him to do less than the best. Nor on the other hand is he content to say only that God in fact always does what is best. He wants to take a middle position, that although it is logically possible (*yumkin*) it is not admissible to think (*lā yajūz*) that God does less than the best. As a free agent He has the power to do evil, but having no need of it He has no conceivable motive to do so, hence there is no reason to think He does it. (*Mughnī*, VI.i, 177 ff.)

How are the ethical propositions of revelation known by us to be true? The answer, of course, lies in our faith in revelation, and the Muʿtazilites like other Muslim theologians rested their case on apologetic reasoning, which can be stated at its briefest in a syllogism:

Whatever is spoken by a prophet is true
These words are spoken by a prophet
Therefore these words are true.

Each premise naturally has to be substantiated, and ʿAbd al-Jabbār goes into all this at length.

(3) The last type of ethical proposition is the *particular proposition*, i.e. the assertion that an individual act, done at a certain time and place by a person in certain circumstances, is right, or wrong, or obligatory, etc. It is this type of proposition that is most important practically, since all our practical decisions are particular ones, in the sense defined.

The methods of judgement follow logically from the sub-classes given under

(2), according to the nature of the sub-class that the particular proposition falls under. thus they can be explained quite easily.

(a) If the particular act in question is one of those which fall under absolute rules, all we need is a single syllogism, e.g.

Wrongdoing is always evil
This act is wrong
Therefore this act is evil.

(b) If the act is one which falls under no absolute rule, we have to weigh together its various prima facie aspects and decide which predominates. For instance, this act would bring much immediate pain to someone and the pain would be undeserved, but it would bring great ultimate benefits to many other people. As for how we are to measure such disparate factors as pain and desert, ʿAbd al-Jabbār leaves us in the dark, so far as I have discovered. The problem is a difficult one, and not only for intuitionists.

If the act is one of the specific kinds prescribed in revelation, we begin by consulting the *sharīʿa* to find out that fact. This still presumably gives us only a prima facie value, as has been said; for we always have to consider the other prima facie aspects of the act, according to the doctrine of *ḍarūra* by which even scriptural obligations may be suspended in cases of undue hardship or injury. Thus in cases of this kind the particular decision is again made by weighing all the prima facie factors, including the command of revelation. This last will prevail in normal circumstances.

A Muʿtazilite jurisprudence must have been formulated by ʿAbd al-Jabbār within the bounds of these principles, and it would be interesting to state it in detail; but I have not yet done so to my satisfaction. The *Mughnī* has a whole book (XVI) on *sharʿiyyāt*, principles of law.

3

This brief description has concentrated on the constructive side of ʿAbd al-Jabbār's ethics and attempted to show its general character. Many interesting features have had to be left out, and nothing has been said of the controversial side of his work, in which he attacks Ashʿarite voluntarism especially – with considerable force on a number of points.

The theory is significant not only in itself, as by far the most detailed of its type known from classical Islam, but also for the light it throws backwards and forwards on the history of ethics in Islam. With regard to predecessors, the *Mughnī* is full of quotations and paraphrases, mostly from the two shaykhs of a century before. Since the works of Jubbāʾī and Abū Hāshim have perished in any first-hand form, we shall now be able for the first time to reconstruct their individual systems in a substantial way, not only in ethics but in theology and other topics. In relation to successors, ʿAbd al-Jabbār shows us a more immediate and richer background than had been known for the later Ashʿarite opponents of Muʿtazilism, such as Juwaynī, Ghazālī and Shahrastānī. It is naïve to think of them as reacting against old Abū l-Hudhayl and his contemporaries – although Naẓẓām long remained a good horse to flog. Their most formidable target was undoubtedly the developed Muʿtazilite doctrine of the two shaykhs and their school, which came to full maturity in the writings of ʿAbd al-Jabbār. In ethics, his rationalism seems to be just what Shahrastānī was answering in his *Nihāyat al-iqdām*, although this impression needs to be confirmed by further study.

In relation to modern thought, the work of the qāḍī is significant in two directions. It will be of interest to western philosophers because of its many anticipations of modern intuitionist ethics, and should lead to a new perspective on the history of ethics, in which Islamic ethics would at last receive its proper place as a branch of western thought. And it will certainly affect the view of historical Islamic theology by modern Muslims. Instead of appearing as an early error which was abandoned as soon as Muslims had fully understood their religion, the Muʿtazilite school will be seen as a steady movement that produced serious thinkers in a long line during the most vigorous centuries of classical Islam.[10] Such a new view will encourage the strong tendencies already present in modern Islam towards rationalism in a broad sense, without necessarily reviving the particular teachings of the Muʿtazilites.[11]

Addendum

Since the writing of this article and *Islamic rationalism*, D. Gimaret has proved convincingly that the so-called *Sharḥ al-uṣūl al-khamsa* is in fact a supercommentary by a Zaydite disciple of ʿAbd al-Jabbār, named Mānkdīm or Māngdīm (d. 1034), on ʿAbd al-Jabbār's commentary on his own short creed *al-Uṣūl al-khamsa* ('the five principles'). 'Abd al-Jabbār's commentary is lost. The work of Mānkdīm is correctly entitled *Taʿlīq sharḥ al-uṣūl al-ḳhamsa li qāḍī l-quḍāt ʿAbd al-Jabbār*...etc. This is the work edited by A. K. Uthman. It contains the text of the original *al-Uṣūl al-khamsa* and many quotations from the qāḍī's lost commentary. All this is demonstrated clearly by Gimaret in an

[10] This was, of course, their own view and that of later sympathizers. See especially the historical account of a Zaydī *imām*, Ibn al-Murtaḍā (1363–1437), *Ṭabaqāt al-Muʿtazila*, ed. S. Diwald-Wilzer (Beirut, 1961) – derived in part from an earlier work with the same title by ʿAbd al-Jabbār.

[11] See G. F. Hourani, *Islamic rationalism: the ethics of ʿAbd al-Jabbār* (Oxford, 1971).

important piece of research, 'Les *uṣūl al-hamsa* du qāḍī ᶜAbd al-Jabbār et leurs commentaires', *Annales Islamologiques*, 15 (1979), 47–96, including a new critical text of the Uṣūl (79–96).

In spite of the new attribution of the so-called *Sharḥ*, I do not believe much damage has been done to my reconstruction of ᶜAbd al-Jabbār's ethical theory with the help of this work, since it evidently follows his thought to a large extent; but Gimaret gives reason to believe that Mānkdīm developed his master's doctrine (56–7).

A valuable bibliography of recent editions of texts and scholarly works on the Muᶜtazilites is given by M. Bernand, *Le Problème de la connaissance d'après le Mugnī du cadi ᶜAbd al-Ğabbār* (Algiers, 1982), Introduction.

8

DELIBERATION IN ARISTOTLE AND ᶜABD AL-JABBĀR

I

The subject of deliberation leads us to the core of ethics, because it concerns a method of reaching practical decisions, and to understand this method requires an understanding of how value concepts can be recognized and estimated in practical situations, and this understanding in turn must be based on understanding what value concepts are. In this paper I shall compare the theories of deliberation of two rationalists of different traditions, Aristotle in ancient Greece and ᶜAbd al-Jabbār in classical Islam. Any historical link of affiliation between them is either very indirect or nonexistent, and the interest of comparing them does not reside in a search for origins. It consists rather in illustrating two ways in which deliberation has been thought of in the past, and how each way arose out of its own intellectual tradition and environment.

The choice of Aristotle for this study hardly needs explanation, since he alone of the Greeks gave a detailed discussion of deliberation, in his systematic yet probing manner. On the side of Islam the Muᶜtazilite school represents the rationalist tradition in theology, and among them only the works of ᶜAbd al-Jabbār survive in substantial length. A Persian who lived in Iran and Iraq in the tenth and eleventh centuries (*c.* 935–1025 A.D.), this theologian wrote his many volumes of the *Mughnī* and other books in Arabic, as was usual at that time. So far as I have discovered, he nowhere discussed deliberation as a distinct topic, as Aristotle did, but from his many scattered discussions of ethical knowledge we can compose an adequate account of his thought about it.

I shall treat the question topically, under three headings: the limits of objects of deliberation; the objects of deliberation, what we deliberate about; and the methods of thinking. Under each heading I shall give an account of the two authors in turn, making some comparisons.

2

There is little to say about the first topic. Aristotle sets the limits of what we deliberate about firmly and clearly. Since the purpose of deliberation is to determine our choice in action, it must be limited to making judgements on things we can hope to affect by our action or, as he puts it, 'about things that are in our power and can be done' (*Nic. Eth.* iii. 3, 1112a 30–1). This excludes not only eternal, invariable parts of the universe, but also the changing physical world that moves naturally, as well as human affairs beyond our control (iii. 3, 1112a 22–9), events in the past (vi. 2, 1139b 5–11), and things known to be impossible to achieve (implied at iii. 2, 1111b 20 ff.). All this is obvious, for a reason that Aristotle does not mention, that these limits are rendered analytically true by the definition of 'deliberation' (*bouleusis*) as thought directed to action, since all action by rational persons aims solely at affecting something which the agent thinks he is capable of affecting.

Although ʿAbd al-Jabbār does not discuss this question explicitly, there is every reason to assume that he accepts Aristotle's limits implicitly, since the Muʿtazilite theologians worked within a framework of similar concepts of man's freedom and responsibility, both of which they emphasized very much.

3

Concerning the object of deliberation, the primary point that Aristotle makes is that it is always about means, never about ends. This is because we deliberate with a view to making a choice between alternatives; but if two supposed 'ends' were presented to us as alternatives, we could compare their merits only by regarding them as alternative means to a higher end. Expressing this in another way, we may say that when anything is considered as a true end it is thereby regarded as a given goal, with no question of alternatives to choose between – a doctor does not deliberate whether he shall heal – nor does anyone else deliberate about this end. They assume the end and consider how and by what means it is to be attained (iii. 3, 1112b 12–16). At the most general level there is only one supreme end, *eudaimonia* (which I shall translate as 'the happy life', without being able to give reasons here for that translation). Here there is no choice; everyone aims at it, by a psychological necessity unquestioned since the ethical philosophy of Socrates at least. Thus no one deliberates on whether to seek a happy life (iii. 2, 1111b 27–9), but everyone rational deliberates on how to seek it; in Aristotle's terms, on the 'means' to it, although we should correct his language by pointing out that what comes immediately under the most general and vague 'happy life' is a consideration of its constituents – activities of virtue, being honoured, enjoying wealth, pleasure, health, etc. These are not strictly means to a distinct experience of 'happiness' beyond themselves. Still, they share with means the characteristic of being alternatives for choice, therefore Aristotle can rightly consider them proper objects of deliberation, alongside of true means. Thus 'it is thought to be the mark of a man of practical wisdom to be able to deliberate well...about what sorts of thing conduce to the good life in general' (vi. 5, 1140a 26–8).

Thus it may be concluded that Aristotle's conception of deliberation is tied to teleological systems of ends and acts.[1]

Aristotle thinks that we can deliberate with a view to either our own good or that of society. More frequently he refers to the former. The man of practical wisdom (the *phronimos*) is he who deliberates prudently about what is good and expedient for himself (vi. 5, 1140a 26–7; vi. 9, 1142b 27); philosophers are said to lack *phronesis* because they are 'ignorant of what is to their own advantage' (vi. 7, 1141b 5–6). But a statesman deliberates about the means to the public ends of law and order (iii. 3, 1112b 14)15). Both kinds of ends, personal and public, are combined in statesmen who have *phronesis*, 'because they can see what is good for themselves and what is good for men in general' (vi. 5, 1140b 7–11).

We can deliberate at any level of generality: at one extreme, about the general means to a good life, the supreme *eudaimonia* (vi. 5, 1140a 27–8; vi. 9, 1142b 28–9), at the other extreme about the act to be done on a particular occasion (vi. 9, 1142b 30–1).

4

When we turn to the thought of ᶜAbd al-Jabbār we find a different focus of concern, different objects of deliberative thinking. He is not so much concerned with finding the means to the ends of man or men, conceived in terms of interest or the happy life; he is writing about what is obligatory (*wājib*) and what is evil (*qabīh*). These words are defined respectively as that for whose omission one deserves blame (*Sharḥ*, 39) and that for whose commission one deserves blame (*Mughnī*, VI.i, 26). We are here definitely in the realm of moral concepts. That is in contrast with Aristotle's discussion of deliberation, which reflects indifference as to whether the practical thinking being analysed is

[1] I should not want to say outright that for Aristotle all acts have only instrumental value. In several passages he speaks of acts as noble (*kalon*) or to be done for their own sakes (e.g. *Nic. Eth.* vi. 12. 1144a, lines 14–20. As these passages are apparently inconsistent with the main trend of teleology, they raise a major problem about Aristotle's ethics, which is too large to enter into here.

prudential or moral, and indeed takes most of its examples from prudential thinking.

Another question worth mentioning in passing is a historical one: when and how did the transition occur in ethics from the ancient Greek focus on good ends to the medieval Islamic focus on obligation? No doubt the trail leads through Stoic philosophy, Christian theology, and the Qurʾān; but the question is a vast one, involving not only far-flung investigations of sources but also a deep understanding of the concept of obligation and its equivalent expressions in Greek, Latin and Arabic. I could not attempt an answer here.

Another difference also emerges between Aristotelian and Muʿtazilite ethics: the difference between a purely teleological and a partly deontological theory. ʿAbd al-Jabbār insists that some types of acts are obligatory or evil 'in themselves', such as wrongdoing or injustice (*ẓulm*) and lying. Other types are obligatory because of benefits they produce, so his theory is partly teleological (as every objective theory has to be; by a 'deontological theory', we have to understand one which regards *some* acts as obligatory, evil, etc. in themselves). Deontology is not a necessary characteristic of any theory of obligation; a Utilitarian type of theory, for example, attempts to explain obligation teleologically. But deontology is in fact a characteristic of the Muʿtazilite theory, and I shall explain it in more detail shortly.

The main thrust of ʿAbd al-Jabbār's ethics, however, has not yet been mentioned. That is its rigorous and insistent objectivism. The issue of objectivism *vs.* subjectivism had arisen in Islamic theology as the main ethical issue between the Muʿtazilites and their traditionalist opponents, who were voluntarists of the most extreme kind. Ethical voluntarism is a form of subjectivism, since it relates all ethical concepts to divine commands and prohibitions, approval and disapproval. ʿAbd al-Jabbār, therefore, is not content with the mere definitions of 'obligatory' as deserving blame for omission and of 'evil' as deserving blame for doing – objective as these are. He also insists that there are reasons why some acts deserve blame for omitting or doing, consisting in further objective characteristics or grounds[2] belonging to certain types of acts.

Know that, although a single definition embraces evils as we have explained, the respects in which they are evil differ...So if this is true, lying is evil because it is lying, wrongdoing because it is wrongdoing, etc. (*M*.VI. i, 61).

So it is necessary to show for what reasons evil things are evil, good things good and obligations obligatory (*M*.VI. i, 58).

[2] A 'ground' is *maʿnā*, *ʿilla* or *wajh*. See Hourani, *Islamic rationalism*, pp. 18 and 63. References are to the *Mughnī* (*M*) and *Sharḥ al-uṣūl al-khamsa*. Concerning the authorship of *Sharḥ* see Addendum to ch. 7.

In the examples just given lying is considered by ᶜAbd al-Jabbār as an unqualified and simple ground, whose presence always makes an act evil.[3] Wrongdoing, on the other hand, while equally unqualified, is complex. This means that it is made up of various aspects (*wajh*);

> The essential nature of wrong is any injury without benefit exceeding it or repulsion of harm greater than it, which is not deserved and not thought to have any of these [good] aspects (*M.*XIII., 298).

These aspects are what W. D. Ross called prima facie factors of rightness and wrongness. The process of estimating them in particular cases must be reviewed under the heading of methods.

5

Aristotle's treatment of the method of deliberation is on the whole explicit and clear-cut, so only a reminder of it is needed. Deliberation starts from ends already given, as previously stated. There is no need here to describe the prior processes by which ends are to be determined – mainly induction from particular experiences of value, with elements of rational intuition (*nous*). Taking a single given end, then, we deliberate by deduction of the best means to it, by practical syllogisms. Alternative means are considered, impracticable ones are rejected, the best one is accepted: then this determines choice; desire for the end must be present or aroused; action follows. All this is familiar. I just want now to make a comment on it which will help to bring out a contrast with ᶜAbd al-Jabbār.

I shall draw attention to a serious oversimplification in Aristotle's account of deliberation (quite apart from the points that John Dewey made in his justly celebrated criticisms).[4] That is that, in his examples of how we decide upon a means, Aristotle so far as I know does not consider the occurrence of elements of conflicting value within a single means of the following kind: within a means X, element A contributes to the end Y, but element B detracts from Y. Thus, it should be argued, drinking wine will give some pleasure and as such is good, but beyond a certain point it will bring headaches and other health problems which outweigh the advantages of the pleasure.

Now this example recalls the analysis of incontinence in *Nicomachean Ethics*, Book vii, chs. 2–3, where he does consider conflicts within a single process of choice. But there he considers them in a rather peculiar way, as conflicts

[3] There is an apparent inconsistency on this point, but see Hourani, *ibid.*, pp. 76–81 for a discussion, concluding that ᶜAbd al-Jabbār's predominant position is that lying is a simple ground.

[4] J. Dewey, *Theory of valuation.*

between alternative means. He thinks that in the quest for *eudaimonia*, by a person who is normally prudent, there can occur a substitution of the ultimate 'means' (constituents), when pleasure temporarily replaces prudent or 'virtuous' behaviour as the supposed 'means' (cf. vi. 5, 1140b 16–19). Then it becomes for the time being the apparent proximate end for action, and a spurious practical syllogism follows, in a kind of mock deliberation towards this end; we now reason, 'Wine is sweet and pleasant', etc. Here is a conflict, but Aristotle does not consider it as a conflict of elements within a single means, as I think he should have done in order to throw a clearer light on conflicts in deliberation.

6

ʿAbd al-Jabbār writes on the methods of practical reasoning in a number of passages, and from them we can compose an account of his ideas on the subject. They are shaped by the direction of his interest in obligation and evil as the main objects of ethical inquiry, as well as by his general theory of knowledge, which is rationalistic.

The starting point for ethical judgements according to him is the most general ethical truths, which, as mentioned, are either grounds in themselves ('Lying is always evil') or prima facie aspects ('Pain is prima facie evil'). Most of such truths are known immediately by intuitive reason, and they can be known by every rational person. This does not mean that they are knowable as general principles temporally prior to any experience, but that they are recognized as true on a particular occasion, then transferred to all like cases (*M*.XII, 66 and XIII, 351).[5]

Such knowledge is attainable independently of any divine revelation, so it is accessible to unbelievers. That doctrine naturally raised a question in the minds of Muslims: of what use then is revelation? ʿAbd al-Jabbār gives it an important, though essentially supplementary, function. Revelation first informs us of the instrumental value of some of the more specific types of act, such as the value of prayer in moral education; and it even prescribes the precise institutions best fitted for our well-being, as we should never have discovered them by unaided natural reason. Thus,

> the teaching of the messengers is nothing but a detailed specification of what is determined in its generality by reason (*Sharḥ*, 565).

[5] 'For the evil of a certain lie is established immediately, and it is known by an indication of reason that it is evil only on account of its being a lie; then we transfer the judgement to all other lies' (*Mughnī*, XIII, 351). This is what C. D. Broad called 'the Milder Form of Intuitionism about Ethical Universal Judgements', *Five types of ethical theory* (London, 1934), pp. 271–2. See Hourani, *ibid.*, pp. 21–2.

We are still at the stage of prima facie principles and rules, because the particular application has always to be determined in the light of all the circumstances. Even the institutions laid down in the Qurʾān were acknowledged as subject to override in conditions of hardship – e.g., not everyone is in a position to fast or make the pilgrimage. This is the excuse of *darūra*, 'due necessity', which the Qurʾān itself encourages.

But such a position given to revelation by the Muʿtazilite at once poses a threat in the opposite direction: does it not break down rationalism by providing another source of ethical knowledge independent of reason? ʿAbd al-Jabbār gives his answer in brief in a phrase quoted above, that revelation specifies 'what is determined in its generality by reason'. But this is explained more fully in another passage, which rejects subjectivism decisively and puts all the ethical truths of revelation under the banner of truths knowable in principle by reason.

> Revelation only uncovers about the character of these acts aspects whose evil or goodness we should recognize if we knew them by reason. For if we had known by reason that prayer is of great benefit to us, leading us to choose our duty and to earn Reward thereby, we should have known its obligatoriness by reason. Therefore we say that revelation does not necessitate the evil or goodness of anything, it only uncovers the character of the act by way of indication, just as reason does, and distinguishes between the command of the Exalted and that of another being by His wisdom, who never commands what it is evil to command (*M*.VI.i, 64).

In the continuation of a short passage quoted previously he gives an analogy between doctors and prophets.

> The case is analogous to that of doctors, when they tell us that this herb is beneficial and that harmful, when we already know in advance that repulsion of harm from the self is obligatory, and drawing benefit to the self is good. Just as, in view of the situation we have stated, they could not have taught anything at variance with reason, the same is the case of these messengers (*Sharḥ*, 565).

The sum of this doctrine is thus that the specific prescriptions of revelation are always justified by being subsumed under one or more of the general principles knowable by reason. Finally it should be noticed that according to this theory there is never a conflict between the prescriptions of reason and revelation. That follows from the rationalistic theology of the Muʿtazilite, based on a primary principle that God is perfectly good, in an objective sense not determined by a mere act of will on His part.

We now have an array of principles which can serve as major premises for particular ethical judgements. What is needed next is to find which one or ones are applicable to the particular act under consideration. This is done by understanding the values instantiated in it. In the case of a simple ground this is easy enough: 'This is a case of lying', and it leads directly to an ethical conclusion, 'therefore it is evil'. In the case of a complex ground such as 'wrong', we have to review all the aspects relevant to it.

The final stage in the complex case is then to weigh together these aspects. This process presents no problem when they all tend in the same direction. For instance,

> ...an injury with no benefit and no repulsion of injury greater than it, which is not deserved or thought to be deserved, when a free and capable person performs them (*M*.VI.i, 18)

is known immediately to be wrong and therefore evil. Where there are conflicting aspects of benefit and injury the process requires measurement, but this too is not difficult in principle, if benefit and injury are thought of (as they are by ʿAbd al-Jabbār) as terms on a common scale of pleasure–pain, sorrow–joy.

> In cases where the act leads to benefit and injury, comparison of them is necessary. If the injury is greater, it is as if the act does not lead to benefit...If the benefit is greater, it is as if the injury does not exist...If the proportion between them is doubtful, the proper method is to use personal judgement and estimation, as we know that intelligent people do when they are pushed into such situations, and it is necessary in making the judgement of benefit to consider both how much suffering is involved in the act and how much injury in its consequences; and if the benefit exceeds them together, the judgement is made in its favour (*M*.XIV, 26–7).

A more difficult case, however, is when we have to balance more disparate aspects, such as benefit or injury against desert, and here ʿAbd al-Jabbār's answer is less clear. He writes,

> Know that in matters of desert there is no need to show the amount of what is deserved and that it is greater than the injury, for in this sphere [desert] no consideration is given to greater or less... (*M*.XIII, 347).

This is explained further:

> When injury is good because it is deserved, it is self-evident that it is not changed from being good to being evil by the loss of benefits... (*M*.XIII, 365).

This is still not very clear, for it surely cannot mean that the amount of loss of benefits directly involved in the severity of a punishment is irrelevant to the justice (desert) of the punishment. There must be a reference here to some loss extraneous to the punishment.

The relation of benefit and desert, or utility and justice, in ethical judgements is a difficult problem that is still with us. I shall not pursue any further the speculation on ᶜAbd al-Jabbār's solution. I shall merely draw attention to two differences between Aristotle and ᶜAbd al-Jabbār that have been brought out in these accounts of their methods of deliberation. It will be seen, firstly, that Aristotle is closer to the teleological problems of Utilitarians, while ᶜAbd al-Jabbār takes us into the world of Deontological Intuitionism, with remarkable anticipations of W. D. Ross in particular. The difference is, of course, that Aristotle does not have to make his peace with any revelation, whereas ᶜAbd al-Jabbār does. I do not mean to hint at the least insincerity in the Muslim theologian, who was after all the chief *qāḍī* (judge) of Rayy for many years. What he shows is a harmonious blend of Islam with rationalism, which had been worked out in the course of two centuries or more of vigorous study and controversy by his Muᶜtazilite predecessors.

Yet with all their differences in time and outlook Aristotle and ᶜAbd al-Jabbār come rather close to each other when seen within the total range of ethical thinkers of the past and present. They are similar in intellectual style: in their prosaic, down-to-earth search for truth about practical life, at the expense, if need be, of a neat simplicity of theory. Both believe firmly in the objective reality of values – Aristotle with little argument because his work had been done by Plato against the sophists, ᶜAbd al-Jabbār in sharp combat with voluntarist theologians. Both teach reason as the method of deliberation, in the varying ways described. Their 'reason' includes a number of mental processes, and it is invoked confidently by both because the challenges of modern empiricism had not yet arisen in epistemology. But ᶜAbd al-Jabbār's confidence in reason gives out a more shrill note, because he faced the challenge of an antirationalistic theology that regarded the claims of independent human reason to knowledge of good and evil as having no sound basis, leading to erratic and arbitrary judgements based on inclinations and rejecting arrogantly man's utter dependence on the scripture of God (with certain permissible extensions) for all knowledge of practical values. The qāḍī had sober answers to these accusations, but they were shouted down by the new orthodoxy of Sunnite theologians and governments, and his books were lost for centuries, until their recovery in Yemen in modern times.

9

ASHᶜARĪ

Al-Ashᶜarī, Abu l-Ḥasan ᶜAlī b. Ismāᶜīl (approximately 873–935), a leading conservative theologian in Sunnite Islam, after whom an enduring school of theology is named.

Born in Baṣra, he received the usual Islamic education in the Qurʾān, Traditions, Arabic philology and *sharīᶜa* law, then studied theology (*kalām*) under the foremost Muᶜtazilite theologian of the Baṣra school, Jubbāʾī (d. 915). He gained a reputation as an excellent debater on theology in the mosques and wrote works in the rationalist tradition of his master, which have not survived. At the age of forty, however, he changed his doctrinal position to a more traditionalist one and became a strong opponent of the Muᶜtazilites. This event is reported as resulting from three dreams, in the first two of which Muḥammad commanded him to defend a more traditional Islam, while in the third he insisted that he should not abandon the dialectical method of *kalām* but should use it to combat Muᶜtazilite rationalism.[1] Then for the rest of his life Ashᶜarī championed traditional Islamic theology, moving at some time from Baṣra to Baghdād where he died. Among his few surviving works from this later period are two that present in dialectical form his doctrinal positions and arguments, the *Ibāna* and the *Lumᶜa*, as well as a valuable survey of the sects of Islam, *Maqālāt al-Islāmiyyīn*.[2]

The most distinctive and influential feature of Ashᶜarī's new 'conservative' theology is its method. This is foreshadowed in the dreams, but can be understood better as a synthesis between the positions of two groups prevalent in his time. On one side, the Muᶜtazilites had taken as first principles a few dominant ideas in the Qurʾān, especially the unity and justice of God, and made far-reaching deductions from their principles even at the cost of ignoring or distorting other ideas in the Qurʾān. This had led to serious

[1] Ibn ᶜAsākir, *Tabyīn kadhib al-muftarī*..., ed. H. al-Qudsī (Damascus, 1928/29), p. 110, as translated by McCarthy, *Theology*, pp. 152–3 (see note 2 below).

[2] *al-Ibāna ᶜan uṣūl ad-diyāna* (Cairo, 1348 h., = 1930; transl. W. C. Klein (New Haven, Conn., 1940). American Oriental Series, vol. 19. *Kitāb al-Lumᶜa*, text and translation by R. J. McCarthy, *The Theology of al-Ashᶜarī* (Beirut, 1953). References are to McCarthy's paragraphs. *Maqālāt al-Islāmiyyīn*, ed. M. M. ᶜAbd al-Hamid, 2 vols. (Cairo, 1950). (Also ed. H. Ritter, 3 vols. (Istanbul, 1929–30).)

problems and to growing accusations that Muʿtazilism was not true Islam, but a speculative construction by theologians. In reaction against this system, which he had learned from the inside, Ashʿarī conceived his task as the working out and defence of a theology based more faithfully on the meaning of the Qurʾān and Traditions. 'The Qurʾān is to be understood in its apparent meaning. It is not permissible to understand it in any other way, except by proof.'[3] This ruling called for an accurate and wide knowledge of the Arabic language of the Qurʾān; and Ashʿarī was generally able to maintain a high standard of textual interpretation. There were texts for which he sensibly abandoned a literal interpretation, such as anthropomorphic assertions about God. On other points there appeared to be real contradictions in the Qurʾān, for example on predestination and free will.[4] In such cases he seems to have used another principle of interpretation: to follow the predominant intention of scripture as a whole. This was in fact the method used by the Muʿtazilites, but the selection was different, for Ashʿarī emphasized divine omnipotence as the dominant teaching of the Qurʾān. As will be shown, he tried hard to reconcile all the tests, but not without strain.

Much of the theology worked out by Ashʿarī was based on doctrines of his traditionalist predecessors. But most of these had taken a different stand against the Muʿtazilites by refusing to discuss theology at all. Their foremost leader, the great jurist Aḥmad b. Ḥanbal (d. 855), had argued that the Qurʾān had not authorized *kalām* and the early Muslims had not practised it, and that it was therefore a heretical innovation. Good Muslims should settle theoretical problems as far as possible by quotations from the Qurʾān and Traditions, and beyond that maintain silence. Now Ashʿarī, while claiming to be a follower of Aḥmad, broke with the method of his school and used the full technique of argument that he had acquired in his Muʿtazilite education to do combat with his former associates. Only occasionally did he fall back on the Hanbalite answer, 'No explaining "How"', in face of unfathomable obscurities in the divine message.

The existence of God is briefly affirmed on the basis of statements in the Qurʾān that because man is unable to produce or to retard his own growth there must be another maker and governor above him.[5] There is an assumption here which runs throughout Ashʿarite thought: that physical causes alone are insufficient to produce change; only a living being can be an ultimate cause. The unity of God is similarly supported by a brief Qurʾanic argument: that if there were two or more gods at least one could not be

[3] *Ibāna*, p. 14; Klein, p. 57.
[4] See W. M. Watt, *Freewill and predestination in early Islam* (London, 1948), ch. 6.
[5] *Lumʿa*, 3–6.

omnipotent.[6] These two principles of theology were accepted by all Muslims.

Concerning the eternal attributes of God, such as knowledge, power and the many others mentioned in the Qurʾān, Ashʿarī took issue with the Muʿtazilite position that God is knowing, powerful, etc. but does not have 'knowledge', 'power', etc. because these would be eternal beings besides God. He explains that 'having knowledge' means the same as 'being knowing', so that the problem is dissolved as one of mere grammar.[7] God has attributes, which belong to Him without being Himself and without being other individuals.

The Qurʾān is uncreated, contrary to the Muʿtazilite doctrine. This question is discussed following the attributes, because Ashʿarī understands the Qurʾān as meaning the speech of God (*kalām Allāh*), primarily in the sense of His power of speaking. This power is eternal and uncreated. The inference from here to the eternity of the product of the power, the spoken or written Qurʾān, is drawn from an unacknowledged ambiguity in the word *kalām*: 'speaking' or 'that which is spoken'. Another argument is derived from the Qurʾān's assertion that God creates things by His command, 'Be'; since this word is used in all creation, it, at least, must be uncreated.[8]

The anthropomorphic qualities of God mentioned in the Qurʾān, such as his hands and eyes, are dealt with in the Hanbalite manner: they are real, not metaphorical, but we do not know in what sense. More importantly, God will be seen by the blessed in the future life, in some literal sense not to be understood as 'known by the intellect', as the Muʿtazilites claimed. The basis of Ashʿarī's argument is his principle of literal interpretation, except where that would lead to an impossible meaning. Now scripture promises the vision of God, and there is nothing impossible in this. Moreover, it is a logical corollary of His perfection. Therefore, the vision is true. It is neither intellectual nor physical, but somehow He will be seen.[9]

The problem of human action was formulated in Islamic thought not in terms of free will but of the power to act. On this question the Muʿtazilites and their opponents agreed on one point: that God creates man and consequently creates in him any power that he has. But beyond that basis they differed.

According to the Muʿtazilites, two persons cannot have power over the same act. All power is ultimately derived from God, but in creating man he has delegated real power to him to make choices and then to act on them. Further, He gives sufficient grace to everyone, believers and unbelievers, to know what is right and to choose it if they wish. Thus the rewards and punishments of

6 *Ibid.*, 8.
7 *Ibid.*, 19.
8 *Ibid.*, 27–30.
9 *Ibāna*, pp. 13–20; Klein, pp. 56–65.

the next life could easily be justified. Support for this straightforward view could be found in many verses of the Qurʾān. But there are many other verses which assert predestination of all man's acts by God, and the Muʿtazilites had to attempt a reconciliation by interpretations that were sometimes forced.

The earliest opponents of this view, such as Jahm B. Ṣafwān (d. 746), had proposed a hard predestination, by which God was the sole cause of every human act, and any 'power' that a man has is to 'choose' and do the particular act which God has decided upon for him. But this doctrine was too extreme for most Muslims to accept, in face of the Qurʾān as a whole and the problem of divine justice which it fails to solve.

Another theologian of the eighth century had proposed an intermediate view which was to provide the nucleus of Ashʿarī's doctrine: 'The ground of the separation of Ḍirār b. 'Amr from the Muʿtazilites was his view that the acts of the servants [men] are created, and that a single act has two agents: one of whom creates it, namely God, while the other acquires it, namely the servant' (*Maqālāt*, I, 313).

Ashʿarī took up this view because it suggested the possibility of allowing man's responsibility for his acts and reconciling all the statements of the Qurʾān. His achievement was to formulate an elaborate and subtle exposition which satisfied many Muslims on some crucial and interconnected issues. To begin with, he had to defend the principle that one act can have two agents. Two Bible stories (also narrated in the Qurʾān) were used to illustrate this possibility. In one, Cain was the direct agent of his brother's murder but Abel was also an agent in a more passive sense, for having allowed Cain to do it rather than retaliate. Similarly, the Egyptian governor imprisoned Joseph, but Joseph had chosen this alternative rather than be seduced by the governor's wife. So God and man can both be agents of the same act (although their relations to it are very different from those in the human examples).[10]

What then are the precise relations of God and man to a human act? Every time a man acts God creates in him the power to choose and the power to carry out his act effectively. Thus man has 'created power', existing only for the moment when he uses it. 'No one can do a thing before he does it.'[11] Still, with this created power man carries out the essential act of choosing one act rather than another, and this choice would seem to make him responsible for his acts. Ashʿarī observes that we know intuitively the difference between God's direct causation of events in nature, including our involuntary transformations like digestion and sickness, and His 'leaving us free' to go and come, to commit sins and all other voluntary acts.[12] He uses the language

[10] *Ibāna*, pp. 49–50; Klein, pp. 104–5.
[11] 'Two creeds', arts. 16 and 17 in McCarthy, p. 239.
[12] *Lumʿa*, 92.

of 'acquisition' to describe the latter class of acts, defining it thus: 'The true meaning of acquisition is that the thing proceeds from its acquirer in virtue of a created power.[13] Thus, because everyone acquires his own voluntary acts he is sufficiently responsible for them to deserve the rewards and punishments of the next life.

Up to this point, Ashʿarī appears to leave man a free agent by his doctrine of acquisition; 'acquiring' the act involves choosing it. But then he takes away the essential feature of choice by denying that we ever have 'power' over two alternative and contrary acts, because 'it is a condition of created power that its existence includes the existence of the object of the power'.[14] This conclusion permits a fully predestinarian doctrine of divine grace. God has guided the righteous and made them believers, and He could have done the same for unbelievers. However, He has willed not to make unbelievers righteous and not to favour them so that they will be believers, and has rather willed [*arāda*, 'decided'] that they be unbelievers, as He foreknew, and He abandons them and leads them astray and sets a seal on their hearts.[15] Thus, in spite of his effort to unify everything stated in the Qurʾān into a single doctrine, Ashʿarī seems to end in a real contradiction. But this is not admitted by his followers.[16]

His explicit theory of predestined grace faced the problem of theodicy: how can God be just in punishing for sins which He has predestined? He had an answer to this question, which depends on a theory of ethical voluntarism, i.e. that the will of God alone *determines* what is good or evil, just or unjust. This theory had already become prevalent in Sunnite jurisprudence, which aimed to base all judgements of law and ethics on revealed sources, i.e. on God's approval or disapproval as expressed in the Qurʾān and Traditions, and correspondingly to exclude direct human judgements of right and wrong as authorized sources of Islamic law, except in case of unanimous agreement among jurists. Ashʿarī expresses this theory of value clearly in a definition: 'A thing is evil on our part only because we transgress the limit and boundary set for us and do what we have no right to do.'[17] Therefore, when a person commits a sin, he is a sinner only because the act is forbidden by a law (*sharīʿa*) of someone in authority over him. But God is not subject to any *sharīʿa*; therefore when He wills a man to commit a sin such as unbelief, it does not follow that God is a sinner and is to be accused of injustice, since obedience and disobedience to law are inapplicable to Him.

[13] *Ibid.*

[14] *Ibid.*, 126.

[15] *Maqālāt*, creed, art. 18, in McCarthy, p. 240.

[16] See R. M. Frank, 'The structure of created causality according to al-Asʿarī', *Studia Islamica*, 25 (1966), pp. 13–75, for a detailed analysis of Ashʿarī's thought on this question.

[17] *Lumʿa*, 170.

This theory had two advantages for Ashᶜarī as a champion of traditionalist Islam. It does not limit the omnipotence of God by setting up objective standards of value to which as God He must conform. (The Muᶜtazilites were criticized on this score.) And it provided an answer to the problem of theodicy, because whatever God does to a man, such as withholding grace then punishing him for his sins, cannot be questioned by any standard. Ashᶜarī does not shrink from the extreme consequence of such a position, with which his Muᶜtazilite opponents challenged him: that lying and other conduct generally considered wicked would have been good acts if God had declared them so and obligatory if He had commanded them.[18]

Ashᶜarī was not at first succeeded by well-known disciples. Only in the eleventh century was his doctrine developed by distinguished successors such as Bāqillānī (d. 1013) and ᶜAbd al-Qāhir al-Baghdādī (d. 1037), both of whom systematized a theory of knowledge and an occasionalist theory of causation supporting God's omnipotence. The influence of the school was greatly increased when the Seljuq vizier Niẓām al-Mulk founded colleges of law and theology (*madrasas*) in Nīshāpūr and Baghdād and installed two outstanding Ashᶜarite scholars in their chairs: Juwaynī (d. 1085) in the former and Ghazālī (d. 1111) in the latter.[19] Thereafter this theology gradually became predominant in the Mediterranean countries of Islam, but other schools prevailed further east, such as that of Ashᶜarī's contemporary Māturīdī (d. 944) in Transoxania, Ibn Ḥanbal in Arabia and Shiᶜism in Iran. Ashᶜarism is still taught at the Azhar in Cairo and other colleges of Islamic theology. The thought of Ashᶜarī has had an enduring appeal to Muslims owing to the founder's conservative theology based on revelation and its systematization by some notable successors.

[18] *Ibid.*, 171.

[19] See G. Makdisi, 'Ashᶜarī and the Ashᶜarites in Islamic religious history', *Studia Islamica*, 17 (1962), pp. 37–80 and 18 (1963), pp. 19–39.

10

JUWAYNĪ'S CRITICISMS OF MUᶜTAZILITE ETHICS[1]

I

Classical Muslim and modern historians of Islam have generally recognized the Imām al-Ḥaramayn Abu l-Maᶜālī al-Juwaynī (A.D. 1028–85) as an important transitional theologian between the older Ashᶜarite *kalām* and the *via moderna* of Ghazālī and his successors. The Arabic texts of his main surviving works have been published, as well as translations of some into western languages. Careful attention has been given to him in modern studies of *kalām* such as those of L. Gardet, G. Anawati and M. Allard,[2] although no one has yet written an exclusive monograph of book size on him, as he deserves. This article is devoted to one aspect of his ethical thought, which has escaped treatment until now.

The aspect to be dealt with here is the fundamental question of the nature of value in its application to action. In classical Islam the main issue was whether value terms such as 'good', 'evil', 'obligatory' are definable only by relation to the commands and prohibitions of God, or whether they have objective meanings of their own, which can be applied even to God's actions. This question was much discussed, sometimes as one of the later topics of theology, after the unity and other attributes of God, and sometimes as a foundation for jurisprudence, since the nature of these concepts is basic for understanding how the jurist must describe the sources of Islamic law and how he must construct his theory of legal knowledge.

2

This aspect of ethics is discussed in the *Irshād*, chapter 12, 'On Justice and Injustice', and chapter 13, 'On Advantage and the Most Advantageous'.[3] Out

[1] This article is based on a paper given at the 29th International Congress of Orientalists, Paris, July, 1973.

[2] L. Gardet and G. Anawati, *Introduction à la théologie musulmane* (Paris, 1948), *passim*. M. Allard, *Le problème des attributs divins dans la doctrine d'al-Ašᶜarī et de ses premiers grands disciples* (Beirut, 1965), pp. 372–404.

[3] *Kitāb al-Irshād ilā qawāṭiᶜ al-adilla fī uṣūl al-iᶜtiqād*, ed. M. Y. Musa and ᶜA. ᶜA. ᶜAbd al-Hamid (Cairo, 1369 h./1950). The pages of this edition will be referred to in the text of this article.

of the forty-four pages covered by these chapters in the Arabic edition less than two pages are allotted by Juwaynī to expounding his own general theory of ethical value. This brevity is possible because the elements of his theory can be stated very simply. It is the voluntarist theory, which relates the value of acts directly and entirely to attitudes of God as expressed in revelation. Juwaynī gives its essence in one sentence, where he defines *al-ḥasan* and *al-qabīḥ* as they refer to acts. 'Thus the meaning of "good" is that for which scripture reveals praise for its agent, and the intention of "evil" is that for which scripture reveals blame for its agent' (p. 258). Any further discussion at this point must have appeared to the author inappropriate to its context. For it would either have led straight into the science of jurisprudence, the study of the legitimate methods of deriving normative judgements from revelation, or it would have led back to the basic question of apologetics, the proofs of authenticity of the revelation from which these judgements are derived. However, as far as the first is concerned, the *Irshād* is a treatise on theology not on jurisprudence; a discussion of the question of apologetics, on the other hand, would have anticipated the following chapter, 'On the Confirmation of Prophecies'.

The main task at the present stage, then, was to refute rival theories of ethics that might challenge voluntarism seriously. Here we might have expected Juwaynī to combat the Ḥanbalites, who were the most formidable opponents of the Ashʿarites in western Asia in the middle decades of the eleventh century, as has been shown in great detail by G. Makdisi in his book on Ibn ʿAqīl.[4] But Juwaynī does not refer to them at all in this context. The reason is evidently that his theory of ethics agreed with theirs in its basic principles, that the source of value is God and that it is known to man through revelation. Where they diverged was on two major points. One is the theory of jurisprudence, which is not treated in the *Irshād*. The other is the proper Islamic method of dealing with heretical doctrines, whether by kalām or by scriptural citations alone. Juwaynī has already argued the justification of kalām in chapter 1, and does not need to recur to it in the ethical chapters.

He also ignores the prevalent philosophic ethics, the Neoplatonic theory of the good as plenitude, as held by Ibn Sīnā, Miskawayh and other philosophers

Ch. 12, 'al-qawl fi t-taʿdīl wa t-tajwīr', pp. 257–86; ch. 13, 'al-qawl fi ṣ-ṣalāḥ wa l-aṣlaḥ', pp. 287–301. Also ed. and partial French trans. J. D. Luciani (Paris, 1938).

Only Part 1 of Juwaynī's larger work on theology, *Kitāb ash-Shāmil fī uṣūl ad-dīn*, has been published, ed. A. S. Nashshar, F. Budayr ʿUn and S. M. Mukhtar (Alexandria, 1969). A special question is treated here, whether it is obligatory to know God by study and inference, pp. 115ff., but the answer to the broader claim of the Muʿtazilites that several obligations are known prior to scripture is deferred to the chapter on 'Justice and Injustice', which is not available. The present study will therefore be limited to the *Irshād*.

4 G. Makdisi, *Ibn ʿAqīl et la résurgence de l'Islam traditionaliste au XIe siècle* (Damascus, 1963).

of the tenth and eleventh centuries. His silence here cannot be due to agreement. Nor is he ignorant of philosophic movements. The reason is probably that he considers the philosophers to be outside the milieu of Islamic scholars for whom he is writing, and not sharing the common Islamic assumptions and methods.

What remained, then, was to combat the rationalistic objectivism of the Muʿtazilites, with which he disagreed strongly and which fell within the sphere of Islamic theology, even if it was heretical. His criticisms of this position cover thirty-six pages and so constitute the bulk of what he has to say about ethics. Why does he devote so much attention to the Muʿtazilites, who had ceased to be a powerful school at the time when Juwaynī was writing the *Irshād*, in the 1070s? Perhaps the main reason is that, although Muʿtazilism had few living advocates and no political backing in the Sunnite state of the Seljūqs, its ethical theory still had intellectual stature, as the only rival theory in kalām that could challenge voluntarism. And Juwaynī's mind was of a serene cast that led him to deal with theoretical positions for their own interest rather than fight with living adversaries on hot contemporary issues.[5] Besides, there was nothing unusual in a time lag of a generation, a century, or longer in a medieval controversy; and on that time scale ʿAbd al-Jabbār (d. 1025) and even Abū Hāshim (d. 933) and his father Jubbāʾī (d. 915/16) were not viewed as antiquated thinkers but as the authors of influential books still being read by Muslims in the later eleventh century – or at any rate as thinkers whose theories were still widely known at secondhand. Finally, the refutation of Muʿtazilite ethical rationalism was bound to take considerable space because the theory as we now know it fully from ʿAbd al-Jabbār[6] was an elaborate one, which demanded an answer in some detail.

3

Juwaynī attacks Muʿtazilite ethics in two spheres, epistemology and ontology. He starts with epistemology.

The Muʿtazilite theory of ethical knowledge claimed (a) that any rational person can know some judgements of good and evil as true necessarily (*ʿala ḍ-ḍarūra*) or 'immediately', by intellectual intuition: e.g., 'Irreligion [*kufr*] is evil'; and (b) that other true judgements can be inferred from these primary ones through rational study (*bi n-naẓar al-ʿaqlī*) (p. 259).

Juwaynī challenges the first proposition, that there are intuitions of necessary truth accepted by all rational beings, by pointing to the existence

[5] See Allard, *Problème*, pp. 381–2.
[6] See G. F. Hourani, *Islamic rationalism: the ethics of ʿAbd al-Jabbār* (Oxford, 1971).

of ethical disagreements over the whole range of supposed intuitions. There are various kinds of disagreements.

In the first place, the Muᶜtazilites dispute among themselves about the list of primary ethical principles said to be known intuitively; so they cannot be necessary truths. Therefore, since all the rest of ethical knowledge is said to be derived from these principles, the entire theory collapses (p. 260). This argument is presented by Juwaynī very briefly, without examples; but it is evidently meant as a decisive refutation.

Secondly, the Muᶜtazilites disagree with most people outside their own small group.[7] In fact, their Muslim opponents are so numerous that they exceed the number required for *tawātur*, the establishment of a truth by a multitude of witnesses. But the Muᶜtazilite Kaᶜbī (d. 932) and his followers in the Baghdād school admit that *mutawātir* knowledge is demonstrative and immediate (pp. 260–1); so they should say that if anyone has intuitive knowledge in ethics it is their opponents. Here Juwaynī has introduced an inappropriate concept, that of *tawātur*, which is a criterion for historical not ethical judgements. He has done so to make a dialectical point, based on an admission of some of his adversaries.

Next, Juwaynī takes the argument to a deeper issue, by bringing up a distinction which had been ignored in the above refutations, and which allows the Muᶜtazilites to object to them. There are two kinds of disagreements in ethics. The primary kind is in normative judgements themselves, the ordinary disagreements that people have about what acts or classes of acts are good or bad, obligatory or condemned. It is at this level that the Muᶜtazilites claim that we have intuitions (e.g., that *kufr* is evil, lying is wrong) and that there is unanimous agreement. But Juwaynī's refutations have not shown disagreement occurring at this level, but at another one: that of theoretical disagreements about the methods of knowledge in normative judgements. These are disagreements of second order, which arise between intellectuals discussing the foundations of ethics. The Muᶜtazilites never claimed that the truth at this level could be known intuitively, and they admit that there are disagreements here. Thus, the refutations do not touch their position.

Juwaynī's answer to this objection is an interesting one, which displays how far apart the two schools, voluntarists and objectivists, were in classical Islam. He says that there is really no distinction between two levels of statement in ethics, because whenever we make a normative judgement we are at the same

[7] Cf. Ghazālī, *Tahāfut al-falāsifa*, ed. M. Bouyges (Beirut, 1927), pp. 29–31, and Ibn Rushd, *Tahāfut at-tahāfut*, ed. M. Bouyges (Beirut, 1930), pp. 13–16, for a discussion of necessary knowledge claimed by the philosophers concerning God's will and its effects; Ghazālī answers that the Ashᶜarites do not share that 'knowledge'.

time making a judgement about the method of knowledge. In asserting that an act is obligatory, for instance, we are at the same time asserting that this character is derived from a certain authoritative source, revelation. There are no attributes of good or evil belonging to an act over and above their being commanded or forbidden by God, so we cannot separate a factual content, the value of what is commanded or forbidden, from the method of knowledge (p. 261). The point of this answer is, presumably, that if all normative judgements are theoretical judgements, then also all theoretical judgements are normative judgements; and so the previous arguments about disagreement apply to theoretical judgements equally, and consequently do not fail to destroy the Muᶜtazilite claim that there are ethical judgements that are intuitive and therefore agreed universally.

There are two elementary logical fallacies here. (a) From 'All normative judgements are theoretical' we cannot conclude, with Juwaynī, 'All theoretical judgements are normative'. (b) And even if it were proved that all those judgements on which the Muᶜtazilites admit disagreement are normative, that would still leave other judgements as possible candidates for being intuitive and universal. The Muᶜtazilite claim was only that some, not all, ethical judgements are intuitive and universal. Juwaynī has swum out of his depth in trying to refute Muᶜtazilite arguments on the basis of his own voluntarist assumption that there is no distinction between normative and theoretical judgements.

But further, the assumption itself is surely invalid even for voluntarists. For even on a voluntarist theory it is possible to distinguish between the content of the Law, the act that is commanded, and the fact that it is made obligatory by being commanded; indeed the Ashᶜarites from Ashᶜarī onwards argued their theoretical position on the basis of such a distinction. And if this is admitted, it is possible after all for the Muᶜtazilites to argue: our belief that stealing is wrong in itself has the same practical or normative *content* as your belief that stealing is wrong by scriptural prohibition; therefore, all men do agree about *what* is wrong, in at least some cases, and this points to a rational, intuitive knowledge.

Juwaynī then retreats to a more cautious line of argument, which implicitly accepts the Muᶜtazilite distinction of levels of disagreement, and then asserts that there are some really normative disagreements, on matters where the Muᶜtazilites had proclaimed rational truths. Here he takes up a dialectically strong position, by choosing a disagreement between the supposed rational ethics and that of Islam itself, as revealed in scripture. According to rational ethics, it is always evil to inflict pain that is undeserved and will not be compensated, and it would be evil even if it were done by God (although in fact it is inadmissible that He would do such a thing). But according to Islam as understood by an Ash'arite it is admissible (*jā'iz*) that God might do it (although He does not), but if He were to do it, His act would be good just because He does it (pp. 261–2).

The Ashʿarite position was hard to answer publicly in the intellectual environment of Islam of the eleventh century, for it took courage to say that an act of God might be evil, however carefully one qualified such an assertion. Yet, Juwaynī is really begging the central question at issue between the parties: Does 'evil' when applied to acts of God have no meaning or does it have the same as 'evil' applied to human acts? The answer goes back to the question of definitions, which is the fundamental dividing line between the Muʿtazilites and their opponents. But this question is not pursued by Juwaynī.

So far the discussion has been conducted within the bounds of the Muslim community. This has given a quiet advantage to the Ashʿarite position, for it could always be claimed that everyone's ethical judgements are really drawn from knowledge of Islamic revelation, whether they admit it or not. But the Muʿtazilites had a stronger card to play, by going outside Islam and finding some sound ethical judgements made by people who had never read or heard of the Qurʾān. For this purpose it was necessary to pass over the Christians and Jews, who after all were educated in Abrahamic scriptures. The standard models chosen were the Brahmins of India. They were asserted to have some true knowledge of good and evil, and this must have been acquired by natural reason, since they had not had the benefit of Allāh's books and messengers.

Juwaynī's tactic in countering this argument is to say that it begs the question in dispute. Do the Brahmins have sound ethical knowledge? Their own conviction that they have it proves nothing. In fact they do not have it; they believe, for example, that slaughtering animals and inflicting hardship on them is evil, but this belief is moral ignorance (*jahl*), not knowledge (*ʿilm*) (pp. 262–3). (Islam allows slaughter of animals for food or protection or in religious sacrifices.)

Here again the imām has demonstrated ethical disagreement and so invalidated intuition. But once more his argument is irrelevant, because the Muʿtazilites had never claimed that *all* Brahmin judgements of ethics were sound, and they did not have to maintain that the Brahmin prohibition of animal slaughter was a genuine intuition.

Next, Juwaynī tries to refute an example of an ethical intuition which the Muʿtazilites regarded as decisive: the supposed fact that a rational man will always prefer telling the truth to lying, when both are equally effective as means to his ends. This is held to prove that truthspeaking is known as good rationally (*ʿaqlan*) (p. 263).

Juwaynī answers with four arguments,[8] but the first of these is unimportant and the second and third are based on misunderstandings, so we may pass to the fourth. When the Muʿtazilites claim that the rational man without a scripture chooses truthspeaking, other things being equal in his interest, that is true only when this man believes that lying deserves blame rationally, i.e., when he has accepted a Muʿtazilite principle of ethics; but, if he does not have this belief, a rational man finds no preference between truthspeaking and lying, when they are equally effective in his interest (pp. 264–5). Here Juwaynī has started upon a profound question of ethical philosophy: Is there any sense in which morality can be called 'more rational' than immorality, apart from the sense of being a more effective means to personal ends? But he does not carry this discussion further.

Another Muʿtazilite argument is that a rational understanding of the concepts of 'good' and 'evil' is necessary prior to our understanding these terms when they occur in scripture. Juwaynī answers this point easily by showing that it begs the question. What *do* those concepts mean in scripture? If they mean what the traditionalists say, 'commanded' and 'forbidden', these are then the concepts that we must understand prior to scripture; and we can do so without difficulty. Similarly, we can understand how a miracle would confirm the authenticity of a prophet before he performs one (p. 265).

After two more short arguments of lesser importance, Juwaynī concludes the discussion on the theory of knowledge by explaining why he has dealt with the errors of heretics before expounding the truths of religion at length, contrary to the usual proper order. He says he has done so to anticipate their objections to the voluntarist position, based on their claim to intuitive knowledge of good and evil. Juwaynī's explanation here seems to reflect a belief that the Muʿtazilites are still a living force in his lifetime, whose objections are to be anticipated in a serious spirit.

4

After dealing with Muʿtazilite ethical epistemology Juwaynī proceeds to attack their ethical ontology, the theory of objective ethical attributes, 'good', 'evil',

[8] The first three arguments are as follows, with brief critical remarks: (1) The Muʿtazilites contradict themselves by looking for an *argument* to support an assertion which they all regard as self-evident. (It is not an argument, it is put forward as a more specific case known by intuition.) (2) They contradict themselves also in asserting that lying is evil in itself, in contrast to truthspeaking, while at the same time imagining the equality of truthspeaking and lying and the equivalence of their aims. (There is no self-contradiction. The equality is in effectiveness as means to the same ends, the difference is in moral qualities.) (3) If the rational man *must* choose truthspeaking rather than lying, the sanctions of Reward and Punishment would not apply to him because he would be under compulsion and so not responsible. (Acting according to one's own reason is not a case of compulsion.)

etc. This is the more fundamental part of their ethics, for it could be held even by one who abandoned the claim to intuitive knowledge (*man inḥaṭṭa 'an da'wa ḍ-ḍarūra*, p. 266). An objectivist could assert the existence of such attributes as constituents of the world of objects, while not maintaining that we can have knowledge of them to the extent of intuitive certainty. Juwaynī is aware of two variants of this ethical objectivism, and he attempts to refute each in turn.

(a) The first variant, and the cruder one, is the view that certain kinds of acts, e.g., killing, are evil in their essence, so that all acts belonging to the class are evil regardless of circumstances. This is ethical absolutism, which was held by Kaʿbī according to ʿAbd al-Jabbār.[9] In Juwaynī's technical language, the evilness of the act on this view is due to the act itself, i.e., to its essential attribute (*ṣifa nafsiyya*) of being an act of killing. His rebuttal is simple: there is no difference in the act as such between killing wrongly, in murder, and killing with justification, in capital punishment. As acts of killing, both consist essentially of putting an end to a life by violent means. Yet we consider murder as evil and capital punishment as good. So their ethical values cannot be explained by their essential characters as this kind of act. Another example is given: the same act which is evil from an adult is not evil from a boy who is not yet responsible (pp. 266–7).

(b) The other type of objectivism abandons absolutism, with its obvious difficulties and adopts a relativistic form which gives a more complex explanation of good and evil. This is the position of ʿAbd al-Jabbār and his predecessors of the school of Baṣra, and I shall explain it in his version, since Juwaynī does not explain it adequately enough for a modern reader to understand his refutation.

ʿAbd al-Jabbār denies absolutism in these words: 'It is not true that what makes a thing evil is its species [*jins*]...'[10] 'Species' means a class (of act) that is defined in natural terms without reference to value, such as the class of killing mentioned previously. To enter someone else's house is good with the owner's permission, evil without it; but the act of entering is of the same species in both cases. To bow in prayer to God is good, to Satan evil; but bowing is the same.[11] Inflicting pain may be good if the pain is deserved or productive of greater benefits, but it is evil without such aspects.[12]

The correct ethical judgement according to ʿAbd al-Jabbār is reached by considering the bare class of act – killing, inflicting pain, etc. – in each

[9] See Hourani, *Islamic rationalism*, p. 64.
[10] *al-Mughnī fī abwāb at-tawḥīd wa l-ʿadl*, ed. A. F. Ahwani and I. Madkour (Cairo, 1962), p. 59.
[11] *Sharḥ al-uṣūl al-khamsa*, ed. A. K. ʿUthmān (Cairo, 1965), p. 310. See chapter 7, Addendum, on the attribution of this work.
[12] *Mughnī*, VI.i, 77; XIII, ed. I. Madkour and A. A. ʿAfifi (Cairo, 1962), pp. 270–92.

occurrence relatively to its context, and judging it by various kinds of relations between the agent and the patient, and between the causes and their effects: relations such as deserved, excess of benefit, promise-keeping, gratitude, and their opposites. These are the grounds or aspects (*wajh*, *maʿnā*, *ʿilla*) of value, which in balance with each other make the act good or evil.

Know that, although a single definition embraces evils as we have explained ['that for which the agent deserves blame'], the respects [*wujūh*] in which they are evil differ. The first statement [a single definition embraces evils] is not disputed, because that in which there must be unity is the realities of the attributes [i.e., the essence of the class 'evil'], but what makes the object have the attribute [*ṣifa*] [evilness] may vary, as we have shown in the Book on attributes. So, if this is true, lying is evil because it is lying, wrongdoing [*ẓulm*] because it is wrongdoing, etc.[13]

Thus there are three concepts: (i) the most general concepts of value, such as good and evil, definable in terms of deserving blame or praise, (ii) the natural species of acts, such as killing, inflicting pain, (iii) the grounds attaching to particular acts in their contexts, such as being undeserved, bringing pain with no benefit, etc. To show the value of a particular act, we have to determine the grounds applicable to it, then weigh them together. ʿAbd al-Jabbār elaborates this theory of grounds in a manner that reminds us of W. D. Ross's theory of prima facie rightness.

Juwaynī answers a view of this type, without naming ʿAbd al-Jabbār. But his comments are too brief and require interpretation. In translating his words I shall insert some interpretive explanations.

...or else it is argued [by the Muʿtazilites]: 'A thing is evil only by something other than scripture and other than evil [itself].'[14] Then if they say that, one answers them: if the thing is not evil by itself [as in absolutism], and its evilness is not related to its connection with prohibition [as in voluntarism], then it is impossible that an attribute should be evil because of another attribute [its ground], when that [first] attribute is not an attribute for evil either in its essence or as a qualifying attribute [*ṣifa maʿnawiyya*] (p. 267).

The statement is difficult, but the general intent becomes clear through

[13] *Mughnī*, VI.i, 61. ʿAbd al-Jabbār is inconsistent about lying. In this passage he regards it as a ground, a component of value, but in other passages as a class of natural acts. See Hourani, *Islamic rationalism*, pp. 79–81.

[14] *ghayri l-qabīḥi*. This phrase can be understood in terms of (i) above, the defining concept of evil, 'blameworthy'; so 'something other than evil' is the ground which ʿAbd al-Jabbār says must exist as the cause of the act's satisfying the definition of 'evil'.

In view of Juwaynī's contrast of this position with the absolutist position (a), we might have expected rather (ii), 'other than the act of killing' (*ghayri l-qatli*), which act in absolutism was offered as the cause of being evil. However, both (i) and (ii) are correct, for (iii), the ground, is other than both of them.

comparison of Juwaynī and ʿAbd al-Jabbār. Juwaynī denies the theory of grounds, by saying that one attribute (the natural species, being an act of killing) cannot be made evil by another attribute attached to it (the wajh, ground of value). He does not explain why this is impossible; he merely asserts it. His discussion is therefore disappointing at this crucial point in the entire debate on ethics, for his answer to his opponents' carefully worked out doctrine is brief, obscure and dogmatic.

5

In section 2 of chapter 12 Juwaynī proceeds to the concept of the obligatory (*al-wājib*); the section heading reads, 'that there is nothing obligatory by reason for the servant or for God' (p. 268). Concerning men, the same general arguments are applied as in the case of good and evil. There follows a discussion of one class of acts, the supposed rational obligation of gratitude to a benefactor (pp. 268–71). Concerning God, Juwaynī argues that there is no acceptable meaning for 'obligation' on God. Three possible meanings are rejected: (1) issuance of commands to Him. This is impossible because He is the Commander. (2) His expectation of harm from omitting an act. This is impossible because God cannot be benefitted or harmed. (3) The goodness of the act and evilness of its omission, as attributes of His act. This suggestion has already been answered: there are no such attributes (pp. 271–2). This triple answer is comprehensive and final enough, but Juwaynī continues with a brief dialectical refutation of the supposed obligation on God to reward His servants for fulfilling their obligations. He claims that this would not be obligatory even on rationalist assumptions (p. 272).

Section 3 deals with a problem of theodicy, the justification of pains inflicted by God on men and animals. Juwaynī's position is stated simply at the beginning. He says there is no need to justify such pains as requital for sins or as suffering to be compensated. It is enough to know that they are created by God, and everything created by God is good for that reason alone (p. 273). He then reviews the errors of various sects, the Dualists, Bakrites, Rafidites and Muʿtazilites, and answers each one in turn, the Muʿtazilites at greatest length (pp. 282–6). Here he goes over four grounds that they give to justify God-given pains, and in each case he answers them by showing that they make a false analogy between man and God. An example will illustrate the line of argument briefly. One of the grounds given to justify God's causing pain to man is that He does so in some cases to prevent a greater injury. This is easily answered: God never needs to employ pain for such a purpose.

Chapter 13 discusses a particular obligation that the Muʿtazilites claimed as falling on God: to do what is most advantageous (*al-aṣlaḥ*) for men. Two positions were held. The Baghdād school thought this applied to all spheres of man's life (p. 287). Juwaynī has little esteem for this view, and answers it with the point that if God's benevolence to man were entirely obligatory on Him there would be no room for His supererogatory favours or for man's gratitude (pp. 289–95). This is a dialectical answer, for it concedes the opponent's assumption that there can be obligations on God. The other position is that of the Baṣra school: that God is obliged to do the best for man only insofar as His benefits affect man's chances for salvation (because this is the sphere where man is threatened with penalties for failure) (pp. 288–9). This position is treated with more respect by Juwaynī. He goes back to the general objection that there can be no obligations on God, then gives some dialectical answers (pp. 295–300). The chapter closes with a short section on grace (*luṭf*), concerning two long-disputed problems, what *luṭf* means and whether God could use it to make unbelievers believers (pp. 300–1).

6

A general critical opinion on Juwaynī's attacks on Muʿtazilite ethics is that he seems to be slightly stronger in his arguments against their intuitionist theory of ethical knowledge, which is probably the weaker half of their ethics. On their ontology, the assertion of the existence of real ethical attributes and the analysis of what these are, Juwaynī gives no sufficient answer to their sophisticated and elaborate theory, as we now possess it in the works of ʿAbd al-Jabbār. There are places where he misunderstands their positions or begs the question at issue.

Degeneration in standards of argument is apt to occur when a live opposition is absent or feeble, so that no retort is expected. Such a situation could partly explain Juwaynī's faults. By the 1060s the pronouncements of the caliphs against the Muʿtazilites had taken their toll and the surviving head of the school in Baghdād, Ibn al-Walīd, was confined to teaching at his home.[15] The *Irshād* is presumed to date from the following decade, being a summary of the longer *Shāmil*.

Still, in spite of some defects Juwaynī's criticisms of the Muʿtazilite ethics are of considerable interest, both because there is probably nothing of such length on the subject by any earlier Ashʿarite theologian[16] and because of the importance of Juwaynī in the development of Ashʿarite doctrine.

[15] Makdisi, *Ibn ʿAqīl*, pp. 332–40.

[16] C. Bāqillānī, *Kitāb at-Tamhīd*, ed. R. J. McCarthy (Beirut, 1957), pp. 121–31, part of a chapter against the Brahmins.

11

GHAZĀLĪ ON THE ETHICS OF ACTION

I

With all the breadth of his interests as a theologian, jurist, logician, educator, Ṣūfī, critic of philosophy and foe of Ismaʿilism, Ghazālī's central concern throughout his life (A.D. 1058–1111) may fairly be described as an ethical one: right conduct and the purification of the soul by the individual, as means to a harmonious relation with God and the attainment of everlasting joy. This is of course a religious view of ethics, and one believed to have been learned from God through prophetic revelation and associated divine sources accepted in classical Islam.

The present study will not attempt to treat the entire system of his ethics in its prolific details. We shall be concerned with some of its general aspects. We shall also limit the study to the sphere of conduct, and not deal with the sphere of character and improvement of the soul, important as that subject is in Ghazālī's total ethics.[1]

In order to explain more precisely the object of study and its place in the system as a whole, it will be useful to begin with a summary account of three relevant religious sciences as Ghazālī conceived them: theology (*ʿilm al-kalām*), 'law' (*ʿilm al-fiqh*) and ethics of character (*ʿilm al-akhlāq*).

Kalām is defined by Ghazālī simply as the study of God, and it has four principal topics: the existence and fundamental nature of God, His attributes, His actions, and His prophets and revelation.[2] Our concern will be mainly with the third of these topics, God's actions. We shall deal with *kalām* first because it is the most general and architectonic religious science, which determines the sphere of each of the more specialized religious sciences.[3] It sets up their cosmological framework, the definitions of their value terms such as *wājib*, *ḥasan* and *qabiḥ*, and the authority of their revealed sources through its proofs of God and of the authenticity of the Prophet's mission.

[1] See M. A. Sherif, *Ghazālī's theory of virtue* (Albany, 1974), and M. Abul Quasem, *The Ethics of al-Ghazālī: a composite ethics in Islam* (Delmar, N. Y., 1978).

[2] *al-Iqtiṣād fī l-iʿtiqād*, ed. I. A. Çubukçu and H. Atay (Ankara, 1962), 43 = Spanish trans. M. Asín Palacios, *El justo medio en la creencia* (Madrid, 1929), p. 28.

[3] *al-Mustaṣfā min ʿilm al-uṣūl* (Cairo, 1937), I, 4–5.

Fiqh is concerned with human conduct. It is 'the science of scriptural rules established for the acts of people under obligation [*al-mukallafīn*]'.[4] Rules (*ḥukm*, plural *aḥkām*) are stated or implied in the scriptural sources for every class of act, determining whether the act is commanded, recommended, permitted, disapproved or forbidden by God. Thus *fiqh* in its details (*furūʿ*) is the normative religious science, theoretically able to discover the divine judgement on every class of human act. But *fiqh* has also a more fundamental part, the science of legal principles (*uṣūl al-fiqh*) or jurisprudence, which investigates in a general way the proofs of the rules of *fiqh*: the conditions of validity of the sources, Qurʾān and others (and here it overlaps with *kalām*), and of the methods of interpreting and extending the sources. We shall deal with this part of *fiqh*, since it is an inquiry into the principles of normative ethical judgements on external human acts.

The other science of human ethics is that which Muslim philosophers named 'the science of character' (*ʿilm al-akhlāq*). Ghazālī accepts this science on his own terms; in fact he regards it as more important than *fiqh*, corresponding to the superiority of character to action. But he prefers other names for it, more in line with Islamic and especially Ṣūfī terminology: 'the science of states of the heart' (*ʿilm aḥwāl al-qalb*) or 'the science of conduct' (*ʿilm al-muʿāmala*) understood as a study of the right dispositions (virtues) that underlie the acts prescribed by the Law.[5] In other words it is a study of the inward side of ethics, the cultivation of the personal soul.

Thus the scope of this article may be described as a review of the more philosophical aspects of Ghazālī's ethics of action – 'philosophical' being used here in a broad modern sense of 'concerned with fundamental questions', not necessarily connected with the Greek philosophical tradition which Ghazālī repudiated as a whole.[6] The first two of the three sciences just described will be dealt with in turn, within the limits mentioned.

But before we proceed to the content of Ghazālī's thought it will be advisable to settle a question of method. Already in the twelfth century Andalusian philosophers observed a chameleon-like quality in Ghazālī's thought; Ibn Rushd accused him of being 'an Ashʿarite with the Ashʿarites, a Ṣūfī with the Ṣūfīs and a philosopher with the philosophers', the last of which is patently unfair about a man who openly attacked the philosophers.[7] Modern

[4] *Mustaṣfā*, I, 3.

[5] *Iḥyāʾ ʿulūm ad-dīn*, Iraqi edition (Cairo, Istiqama Press, no date), I, 20–1.

[6] It is tempting to substitute 'theological' for 'philosophical' here, since Ghazālī's ethics is so emphatically based on revealed sources. But 'theology' is too closely associated with *kalām*, whereas Ghazālī's treatment of ethics goes well beyond the sphere of *kalām*.

[7] *Faṣl al-maqāl*, ed. G. F. Hourani (Leiden, 1959), margin page 18 (Müller edition), Eng. trans. G. F. Hourani, *Averroes on the harmony of religion and philosophy* (London, 1961), p. 61; see note 145 in the latter for further references and comments. Other Andalusian critics: Ibn

scholars such as W. M. Watt have drawn attention to the problem of consistency posed by the variety in Ghazālī's viewpoints and opinions and have suggested more sympathetic solutions, relying on the evolution of his thought, described by himself in *al-Munqidh min aḍ-ḍalāl*,[8] as well as on his consciousness of the need for different approaches to different audiences.

Now it may turn out that in the end certain apparent inconsistencies can only be explained in one of these ways. But such explanations will have to be well supported by evidence or strong implications; otherwise they are liable to be a lazy man's solution, resorted to because one has not sought hard enough for a real consistency behind the appearances. At any rate, we are likely to penetrate further by starting from a methodological assumption of basic unity in a thinker's views, allowing for the continuous development that is normal in anyone's thought.

It may be doubted that Ghazālī's development was normal, since it was broken by two sharp crises. But if we look at these crises closely we can see no reason why they should have resulted in sharp changes in his beliefs. The first was a sceptical crisis of youth, overcome probably before he had written any surviving books.[9] The second, culminating in 1095 at the age of thirty-seven, resulted in a change of religious orientation and values but not necessarily any intellectual change in beliefs.[10] These remained much the same, but there are new interests and a more earnest religious outlook. So let us attempt a unified account of his ethical system and see how far we can go before we meet with insoluble inconsistencies. At the end we shall be better able to estimate their extent.

2

In his main treatise on *kalām*, *al-Iqtiṣād fi al-iʿtiqād*, Ghazālī devotes the third part to God's action towards the world. He opens his part with a short statement of the dogmas of Islam on God's unbounded freedom in relation to the world and man. But before these dogmas can be demonstrated, he says, we must understand the correct definitions of the terms of value that are applied to action and character:

All these assertions are based on investigation of the meaning of 'necessary' [*wājib*], 'good' [*ḥasan*] and 'evil' [*qabīḥ*]. People have delved into the subject and engaged in

Ṭufayl and Ibn Sabʿīn. See also Sherif, *Ghazālī's theory of virtue*, pp. 19–22; and H. Lazarus-Yafeh, *Studies in al-Ghazālī* (Jerusalem, 1975), ch. 3, suggesting a method of rejecting spurious works that eliminates many of the supposed inconsistencies.

[8] Ed. J. Saliba and K. Ayyad, 3rd printing (Damascus, 1939). Eng. trans. R. J. McCarthy. *Freedom and fulfillment* (Boston, 1980), based on M. S. Šehid Ali Paşa (Istanbul), No. 1712, completed five years after Ghazali's death.

[9] *Munqidh*, 67–77; McCarthy, sects. 6–17.

[10] *Munqidh*, 122–39; McCarthy, sects. 80–90.

protracted discussions on whether intellect can make things good, evil or necessary, but confusion has only increased because they have not grasped the meaning of these expressions and the differences in their technical senses.[11]

He then proceeds to give his own definitions of these terms, and subsequently to elaborate the dogmas in a way that depends on these definitions.

Wājib is said to have two generic meanings, one of which is subdivided into two species.

(1) 'Logically necessary', predicable of anything whose non-existence leads to an impossibility. In this sense we describe as *wājib* the pre-eternal Being, or the existence of an object of knowledge where there is knowledge. This meaning does not concern ethics.[12]

(2) 'Prudentially necessary.' *Wājib* in this sense is predicable of an act, when from the standpoint of self-interest its performance is preferable to its omission in a decisive way, i.e., when severe and certain harm to the agent is to be expected from omission of the act. Thus an act is *wājib* when it is necessary for the agent to do it if he is to avoid such harm.[13] The translation given here, 'prudentially necessary', does not correspond to any two words of Ghazālī, but it is used because it is the best expression to bring out the main features of what Ghazālī means by his definition, as understood from his explanations. 'Necessary' links *wājib* in this sense to the first sense; it is a hypothetical necessity, just as in 'If there is knowledge there must be an object of knowledge'. 'Prudential' (used in its technical philosophical sense) brings out the essential condition attributed to practical necessity: the service of the act to the interest of the agent. More will be said of this feature shortly. Because of its unusual character it will be advisable not to translate Ghazālī's *wājib* (2) as 'obligatory', which has other connotations.

This second meaning of *wājib* is subdivided according to the location in which harm is to be expected, in this life or the next. (a) Expected harm in this life may be recognized by intellect. Thus a non-believer may call it 'necessary' for a person dying of hunger to eat; 'and we mean by "the necessity of eating" the preferability of action to omission on account of the harm connected with omission'. (The use of such a technical meaning (*istilāḥ*) is not precluded by the Law; 'the only prohibition comes from language, when

[11] *Iqtisād*, 160 = Asín, pp. 245–6. 'Make things good, evil or necessary' gives Ghazālī's interpretation of *yuḥassin*, *yuqabbiḥ* and *yūjib*, whereas the Muʿtazilites understood these words as 'find things good', etc.

[12] *Iqtisād*, 161–2 = Asín, pp. 246, 248. *Iḥyāʾ*, I, 111; also in separate ed. as *ar-Risāla al-Qudsiyya* (= *Iḥyāʾ*, Book ii, ch. 3), ed. and Eng. trans. A. L. Tibawi, *Al-Ghazali's tract on dogmatic theology* (London, 1965), pp. 25 and 48.

[13] *Iqtiṣād*, 161–2 = Asín, p. 248. *Iqtiṣād*, 195 = Asín, p. 192. *Iḥyāʾ*, I, 111 = Tibawi, pp. 25 and 48. *Iḥyāʾ*, I, 113 = Tibawi, pp. 27 and 53. *Mustaṣfā*, I, 40.

such a meaning is not in accord with the acknowledged convention'.)[14] (b) Expected harm in the next life is known by revelation,[15] 'as when it is said, "it is necessary for the servant to obey God so that He will not punish him with fire in the next life"'.[16] This is the more important subdivision of *wājib* (2), the sense in which it is used in religious contexts. We should examine the ethical character of this concept in Ghazālī's theory.

Two features of it call for attention. One is its place in the range of objective–subjective concepts, explained as follows. An objective concept is one whose true predication is determined by facts of the world other than the opinion of some judge or observer about it. The Muʿtazilite definition of *wājib* applied to an act is 'that, for whose omission the agent deserves blame'.[17] This is objective: 'deserves' introduces a fact which is truly or falsely predicated regardless of anyone's opinions.[18] A subjective concept is one whose true predication is determined by the opinion of some judge or observer. Such is the case of justice according to the theory of some ancient Greek sophists, that the just is determined by the laws of each state: not merely known through the laws, but determined solely by them, meaning nothing else but 'whatever the laws ordain'. There are similar modern theories which make custom or current 'values' (i.e., prevalent valuations) the determinants of what is right in any society. These theories may be described as social subjectivism. In classical Islam ethical subjectivism took a theistic form, by which *wājib* as applicable to human acts was defined as simply whatever is commanded by God, with the backing of divine sanctions by Rewards and Punishments. This was the doctrine most firmly held by the Sunnite law schools of Shāfiʿī and Ibn Ḥanbal and the theological school of Ashʿarī, as well as Ibn Ḥazm in his thoroughgoing application of Zahirite fundamentalism to theology. Its proponents explicitly denied the Muʿtazilite doctrine that *wājib* was an attribute of certain types of act in themselves, which were then commanded by God for man to perform; on the contrary, no such attribute could be discerned, and God's commanding certain types of act was itself the essential characteristic that made them *wājib*.

Now Ghazālī's position would be expected to conform to that of his Shafiʿite and Ashʿarite masters, and while it does so in a general way it introduces an element of objectivity which gives his definition a tinge of originality. This is because the hypothetical imperative by which *wājib* is interpreted. 'If you

[14] *Iqtiṣād*, 162 = Asín, pp. 247–8. Cf. *Iḥyāʾ*, I, 111; Tibawi, pp. 25 and 48.
[15] *Iqtiṣād*, 162 = Asín, p. 247.
[16] *Iḥyāʾ*, I, 111 = Tibawi, pp. 25 and 48.
[17] See G. F. Hourani, *Islamic rationalism: the ethics of ʿAbd al-Jabbar* (Oxford, 1971), p. 39, 116.
[18] This is so, irrespective of any particular set of criteria for desert. The concept causes difficulties for the Mu'tazilite and some other theories of ethics. See Hourani, *ibid.*, pp. 44–7.

want x, it is necessary to do y', expresses a causal relation which, in the world as it is constituted, is a true fact independent of any opinion. This is at any rate a formal characteristic of Ghazālī's definition. But if we go deeper and look at the conditions controlling what is *wājib* in the actual world, we learn that this world is constituted entirely by the will of God, that He creates the nature of man and his natural ends, that He decides and commands what acts it is necessary for man to do to achieve these ends, and finally that He imposes the sanctions which make such acts necessary for man. Thus Ghazālī's position is ultimately subjectivist in the sense defined, only a little less so than that of his predecessors.[19] He agrees with them that there is no attribute that makes acts necessary for man to do in his own interest, other than that they are commanded by God. The difference between his predecessors and him is a subtle one: for them, *wājib* means commanded by God, for him it means necessary because commanded by God.[20]

The second noteworthy feature of Ghazālī's concept of *wājib* is that it is related in an essential way to the interest of the agent himself. Obedience to God's commands is *wājib* in that it is necessary for serving one's own long-term interest. This doctrine is made explicit in the course of a rebuttal of a Muʿtazilite assertion that certain acts of God are *wājib* for Him because of the benefit they confer on His creatures. Ghazālī retorts: '– but that which contains benefit to others is not necessary for Him, since there is no benefit to Him in benefitting others'.[21] A parallel view is that of David Hume, who wrote in *An Enquiry concerning the principles of morals*:

> having explained the moral *approbation* attending merit or virtue, there remains nothing but briefly to consider our interested *obligation* to it, and to inquire whether every man, who has any regard to his own happiness and welfare, will not best find his account in the practice of every moral duty.[22]

[19] In one place, *Mustaṣfā*, I, 39, Ghazālī states as his own the Ashʿarite definition: '... *wājib* has no meaning (*maʿnā*) but what God the Exalted has made necessary (*awjaba*) and commanded, with threat of punishment for omission; so if there is no revelation what is the meaning of *wājib*?' This statement cannot be explained as a later development of his thought since he reverts to his usual definition on 40 were he says that *wājib* means only the preferability of action over omission. Perhaps 39 should be understood as a loose expression, in which *maʿnā* is used not for the formal essence but for the content in extension of *wājib*, so that Ghazālī is saying merely that there is nothing necessary (*wājib*) in fact but what God has made so by his command and threat.

[20] While I am unable to trace Ghazālī's position to a previous source, a suggestion towards it can be found in a passage of Juwaynī's *Irshād*, ed. M. Yusuf Musa and ʿA. ʿA. ʿAbd al-Hamid (Cairo, 1950), 271–2. Juwaynī discusses what could be meant by *wujūb* in speaking of God. and considers as one alternative God's expectation of harm from omitting an act; this is then ruled out, it is impossible for God to be benefitted or harmed.

[21] *Iqtiṣād*, 175–6 = Asín, pp. 265–6.

[22] Hume's *Enquiries*, ed. L. A. Selby-Bigge, 2nd ed. (Oxford, 1936), 278.

Ghazālī's definition of practical *wājib*, like Hume's of 'interested obligation', is in sharp contrast with obligation as understood by most modern philosophers who, while disagreeing widely in other respects, commonly connect obligation essentially with the interests of others, in relations of justice such as gratitude, repayment of debt, fulfilment of contract and so forth. Such a view is now so prevalent that it has become a question whether one can ever have an obligation to oneself. And any theory in which obligation is related entirely to the interest of the agent is regarded as analysing obligation in a prudential sense which is not ethical; or, to put it more bluntly, as not analysing obligation at all but substituting another concept for it.

3

For the definition of *ḥasan* there are two accounts, in *Iqtiṣād* and *al-mustaṣfā min ʿilm al-uṣūl*, with slight inconsistencies between them and even within each one.[23] The complications raised by attempting to explain the variations in accurate detail would not be worth the effort to the writer and readers, and a unified account of Ghazālī's position, which is clear in general, will suffice. He gives two general meanings, and the first has three technical subdivisions.

(1) *Ḥasan* in general usually means agreeable or fitting to an end; it may be translated as 'good', which corresponds to this main meaning and all the others to be mentioned. The end may be that of the agent, as in the commonest usage, or that of other persons, or of the agent in one respect or one time but not others. Thus *ḥasan* is relative (*iḍāfī*) to the end specified, and what is good for Zayd may not be so for ʿAmr, or even for one of them in different respects or times. Ghazālī does not distinguish between relations to ends actually sought and relations to opinions, and he gives some examples of the latter, e.g., an irreligious person may call adultery 'good' because he approves of it.[24] Also under the heading of 'good' he gives examples of aesthetic preferences – for colours, complexions, voices – which vary with the tastes and feelings of different people.[25]

(a) The first technical meaning of *ḥasan* is whatever is fitting for any end in this life.[26]

[23] *Iqtiṣād*, 163–74 = Asín, pp. 248–52. *Mustaṣfā*, I, 36. The account in *Iqtiṣād* is more elaborate and will be drawn on to a greater extent.

[24] *Iqtiṣād*, 164 = Asín, p. 250.

[25] *Mustaṣfā*, I, 36.

[26] *Iqtiṣād*, 165 = Asín, p. 251. *Mustaṣfā*, I, 36. In both passages this meaning is submerged in the general meaning (1), but it needs to be made distinct for the sake of completeness. The distinction corresponds to *wājib* (2) (a) above and conforms with Ghazālī's regular scheme of classification.

(b) More important is what is fitting only for the ends of the next life. This is the meaning adopted by *ahl as-sunna*, orthodox Muslims. It is what scripture urges us to seek. Ghazālī does not emphasize relativity here, presumably because the ends and the means are assigned to everyone by scripture, not by individually chosen ends. And here he seems to be referring primarily to the ends of the agent, for this is what concerns most people in regard to the future life (an exception might be made for preachers and teachers, but Ghazālī does not go into this question).[27]

(c) *Ḥasan* can be extended to cover anything that agents are permitted to do.[28]

(2) In a different usage, all God's acts are called *ḥasan*, although they have no personal end. *Ḥasan* is applied to His acts in the sense that they have no effect on Him and that they are not subject to blame, and that He is the unique Agent in His kingdom.[29]

Qabīḥ (evil) does not receive separate analysis, but in the course of the account of good it is described as the opposite of good in its various meanings. Thus, for (1), general evil is whatever is repugnant or inappropriate to an end, and so on, with mentions of its relative character. (Presumably there is no meaning (2) applicable to God.)

These definitions of good and evil resemble that of *wājib*, at a less stringent level. Instead of referring to what is indispensable for life or salvation, like *wājib*, *ḥasan* refers simply to what is serviceable to an end, *qabīḥ* to what hinders attainment of an end.

The Muʿtazilites had already objected that the meaning of good in common usage is not restricted to what promotes an end, nor the meaning of evil to what hinders attainment of an end. For people perform some acts as good on their intrinsic merits, when they cannot possibly foresee any advantage to themselves, and likewise they avoid other acts as evil even when they can see no disadvantage to themselves. As an instance of intrinsic good sought, someone gives help and comfort to a dying person with no expectation of reward; he does it simply because it is good in itself to help others in distress. As an instance of intrinsic evil avoided, a man without belief in religion, and thus in no fear of afterworld punishment, refuses to break a contract, even under threat of execution for his refusal; such a man regards breaking a contract as evil not merely in relation to ends, and avoids it as evil in itself.

Ghazālī seeks to rebut these instances by finding other explanations for them than a rational desire for good and a rational avoidance of evil. He

[27] *Iqtiṣād*, 165 = Asín, p. 231. *Mustaṣfā*, I, 36.

[28] *Mustaṣfā*, I, 36. Cf. the Muʿtazilite definition of *ḥasan*, in Hourani, *Islamic rationalism*, pp. 39 and 103.

[29] *Iqtiṣād*, 165 = Asín, pp. 251–2.

explains the first instance by instinctive sympathy between human beings, or by love of praise, or by association of ideas which leads one to do in an abnormal situation what would serve an end in a normal one – in this case, where the patient would be expected to live and show gratitude. He explains the second instance by the agent's love of praise for honesty, or by association of ideas – breaking a contract is normally followed by harmful consequences. What Ghazālī is looking for in these explanations is self-interested or emotional causes for the acts mentioned, in order to avoid admitting attributes of good and evil intrinsic to the acts themselves and acceptable or rejectable to the rational mind regardless of personal ends.[30]

It is strange to see the protagonist of religion strenuously denying intrinsic goodness to acts. But it is not accidental: his whole view of ethics is based on extrinsic relations of acts to good and evil. That is to say, an act is good when it promotes our ends; moreover, it does so not by direct instrumental causation but because God has decided upon rewards for certain acts and punishment for others. Such a view is coherent with the occasionalist theory of God's relation to the world, an Ashᶜarite doctrine which Ghazālī had learned from the books of Bāqillānī, Juwaynī and Ashᶜarī himself.

After the explanation of these concepts we shall be better able to follow Ghazālī's doctrines on the roles of God and man in turn in the ethical scheme of the world.

4

According to Ghazālī God has no ends,[31] He is too Exalted and Holy for that.[32] Or rather, more accurately, He has no needs, but He did create the world for the ends of revealing His power and realizing His will.[33] But these ends are not 'interests' or 'benefits' for Him. Consequently 'good' cannot be applied to any of His acts in the usual sense, as explained above.

'Evil' is entirely relative to (interested) ends and cannot be applied to God's acts in any sense, even though He is the creator of things that are evil in relation to human ends.[34] Equally, He cannot do wrong; for wrongdoing (*ẓulm*) consists in dealing unjustly with the property of others, but He is the Lord and master who owns everything, no one else has any property for Him to deal unjustly with.[35]

God is not under any prudential necessity (*wujūb*). This follows from the

[30] *Iqtiṣād*, 170–4 = Asín, pp. 257–63. Cf. *Mustaṣfā*, I, 37.
[31] *Iqtiṣād*, 179 = Asín, p. 271.
[32] *Mustaṣfā*, I, 39.
[33] *Iḥyāʾ*, I, 91.
[34] *Iḥyāʾ*, I, 112; Tibawi, pp. 26 and 51.
[35] *Iqtiṣād*, 184 = Asín, pp. 276–7. *Iḥyāʾ*, I, 91 and 112 = Tibawi, pp. 25–6 and 49–50.

fact that He has no needs. It is illustrated by Ghazālī in several directions, as the opening passage of *Iqtiṣād*, Part 3, shows:

The totality of acts of the Exalted is admissible [*jā'iza*] and none of them is describable as 'necessary'. We assert seven things in this part.
We assert [1] that it is admissible for God the Exalted not to impose obligations [*yukallifu*] on His servants, as well as [2] to impose on them unachievable obligations, [3] to cause pain to His servants without compensation and without [preceding] offence [by them]; [4] that it is not necessary for Him to heed what is most advantageous for them, or [5] to reward obedience or punish disobedience...and [7] that it is not necessary for God the Exalted to send prophets, and if He does send them it is not evil or absurd, but He is able to show their truthfulness by a miracle. All these assertions are based on investigation of the meaning of *wājib*, *ḥasan* and *qabīḥ*.[36]

After the investigation of these concepts (as explained above, §§2–3) Ghazālī proceeds to justify each of the seven propositions in order, with dialectic against Muʿtazilite objections.

(1) Ghazālī: God has no necessity to create creatures or, if He has done so, to impose obligations on them. The truth of this assertion follows from the definitions of *wājib* as that whose omission brings harm to the agent, or that whose contradictory is impossible. God does not expect harm from not creating; and there is no impossibility in His not creating, so long as we do not make the (needless) assumption that God has eternal knowledge and an eternal will for creation, in which case of course He cannot not create.[37]

Muʿtazilite objection: these acts of God are obligatory on Him because they bring benefit to the creatures.

Ghazālī: Benefits to others do not imply necessity in any of the senses given. (Here I have translated *wajaba* and its forms with two words, 'obligatory' and 'necessity', to bring out the disconnection between the arguments of the Muʿtazilites and Ghazālī, based on different definitions.)[38]

Ghazālī goes on: In any case it is not obvious that creatures are benefitted by the present creation, still less by the burden of their obligations (*taklīf*).

The Muʿtazilites: Our obligations benefit us by making our Reward deserved and so more agreeable.

Ghazālī: Gratuitous aid from God, without previous burdens, would have been still more agreeable. In any case, any deserts that we have are entirely due to the gift of God.[39]

[36] *Iqtiṣād*, 160 = Asín, p. 245. The sixth proposition concerns man's knowledge of God and how it becomes *wājib* on man. Therefore it will be more appropriately discussed in a later section.

[37] *Iqtiṣād*, 174–5 = Asín, pp. 264–5. Cf. *Iḥyā'*, I, 111.

[38] *Iqtiṣād*, 176–7 = Asín, p. 265. Cf. *Iḥyā'*, I, 111 = Tibawi, pp. 25 and 48.

[39] *Iqtiṣād*, 176–7 = Asín, pp. 266–7.

(2) God is able to impose obligations beyond the capacity of His servants to fulfil. This is so because the essence of *taklīf* is speech of a commander to an intelligent obligatee (*mukallaf*). There is no contradiction between this act and commanding the impossible. Nor is there any moral repugnance (*istiqbāḥ*) to accepting the possibility that God would do that, because *qabīḥ* only applies to acts with personal ends and God is free of these.[40] Finally, there are recorded cases of impossible obligations, such as the obligation to become a believer, when God knew that the person would not and could not become one.[41]

(3) God can make harmless animals, children and insane persons suffer and not compensate them. He certainly can do so, because he does it all the time. And He is under no necessity not to, because necessity as defined does not apply to Him. Nor is such action opposed to His wisdom, understood as His knowledge of the harmony of the world. Nor is He a wrongdoer in doing it, because wrongdoing is wholly inapplicable to Him, as He is not dealing with another's property and not under any Law or command.[42]

(4) God does not have to do what is most advantageous (*al-aṣlaḥ*) for His servants. This is demonstrated by repeating a well-known dialogue between Ashʿarī and the Muʿtazilite Jubbāʾī, concerning three children in the next world who discuss their fates with God; Ashʿarī proved that it was impossible that all three of them could have received the most advantageous treatment.[43]

(5) God is not under necessity to reward the obedient or punish sinners – except when He has promised to do so, for God cannot lie.[44]

(7) Sending prophets to the human race is possible for God; it is neither impossible nor necessary. The Muʿtazilite claim that it is necessary has been disproved already (under (1) and (4)), derived from the definition of prudential *wājib* and its inapplicability to God's acts.[45] Its possibility for God is proved by analysis of the constituent acts. A 'Brahmin' argument that it is impossible is refuted, then the rest of the section is taken up by apologetic arguments for the authenticity of the Prophet, against various rationalist objections.

From this account of *Iqtiṣād* the negative aspect of God's ethical relation to the world stands out: He is under no necessity to create His servants or to do any good to or for them (in the sense of *ḥasan* (1), serving their ends). In *Iḥyāʾ* we see a more positive view. God does good without necessity, and

[40] *Iqtiṣād*, 178–9 = Asín, pp. 270–1. At 179, line 8, I read *al-istiqbāḥ*, following Asín, instead of *al-istilāḥāt* or *al-istiḥsān* as in the MSS. and Çubukçu edition. *al-istiqbāḥ* is used before and afterwards in the same context.

[41] *Iqtiṣād*, 181 = Asín, p. 273.

[42] *Iqtiṣād*, 182–4 = Asín, pp. 275–7.

[43] *Iqtiṣād*, 182–4 = Asín, pp. 278–9. Also in *Iḥyāʾ*, I, 112 = Tibawi, pp. 26 and 50. For the dialogue see M. Fakhry, *A history of Islamic philosophy* (New York, 1970), pp. 229–30, with reference to Ibn Khalliqān, *Wafayāt al-aʿyān* (Cairo, 1949), III, 398.

[44] *Iqtiṣād*, 185–9 = Asín, pp. 280–4.

[45] *Iqtiṣād*, 195 = Asín, p. 293.

rewards believers for obedience by generosity, not by their deserts or any necessity.[46] He has created man and imposed obligations (*taklīf*) on him by His favour (*mutafaḍḍil*),[47] and He has poured out the bounties of nature for man's benefit, as the Qurʾān often reminds us. Still more has He favoured His community the followers of truth with the guidance of prophecy.[48]

How God causes good for men is described in a passage of *Tahāfut al-falāsifa*, in the seventeenth discussion, 'On natural causes'. Here Ghazālī wants to show that even on a theory of natural causation such as that of the philosophers, a primary cause will be needed, which is God. He argues: let us concede to the philosophers that things have natures, so that when, for example, two similar pieces of cotton come into contact with fire both pieces alike must burn. Still, these natures may change, and God can invest a piece of matter with different properties, so that it will behave in the way we call a prophetic miracle, such as recalling a dead man to life or changing a rod into a snake.

If it is said [by the philosopher]: 'Does this event proceed from the soul of the prophet or [rather] from another principle at the suggestion of the prophet?' we answer: Likewise, do those events which *you* admit may happen by the force of the prophet's soul, such as a downpour of rain or a thunderbolt or an earthquake, arise from the prophet or [rather] from another principle?

So what we say about this case is the same as what you say about the other case, and it is more fitting for both us and you to relate the event to God, either without a medium or by mediation of the angels. But the due time for its occurrence is when the prophet turns his attention to it and when the order of the good [*niẓām al-khayr*] is determined [*taʿayyun*] in the event's appearance, to the end that the order of the divine Law may endure; all this gives a preponderance in favour of [its] existence. The thing in itself is possible, the Principle of it is bountiful and generous, but it issues from Him only when the need for its existence preponderates and the good becomes determined [*mutaʿayyinan*] in it; and the good becomes determined in it only when the prophet needs it for confirmation of his prophecy in order to disseminate the good.[49]

[46] *Iḥyāʾ*, I, 91.

[47] *Iḥyāʾ*, I, 110 = Tibawi, pp. 25 and 48.

[48] *Iḥyāʾ*, I, 105 = Tibawi, pp. 16 and 32–3, with quotations from Qurʾān, lxxviii, 6–16; ii, 164; lxxi, 15–18; lvi, 58–73.

[49] *Tahāfut al-falāsifa*, ed. M. Bouyges (Beirut, 1927), 289; Eng. trans. S. A. Kamali (Lahore, 1963), pp. 191–2. Quoted by Ibn Rushd, *Tahāfut at-tahāfut*, ed. M. Bouyges (Beirut, 1930), 534; Eng. trans. S. Van den Bergh (London, 1954), I, 327. 'Good' here is *khayr*, not *ḥasan*. *Khayr* is more metaphysical and more appropriate to the good of the universe; it is the word used by the philosophers, see *Tahāfut al-falāsifa*, 159, *Tahāfut at-tahāfut*, 308.

Van den Bergh understood *taʿayyana* and *mutaʿayyinan* as active, and so translates, 'the order of the good determines its appearance' and 'the good only determines it'. But *taʿayyana* cannot be active in this sense, being a reflexive fifth form, and *tuʿayyinu* (second form, imperfect active, 3rd person fem.) will not work because *niẓām* is masculine. Moreover, Van den Bergh

In this imaginary dialogue, even while moving over towards the philosophers' theory of natural causation for the sake of an *ad hominem* argument, Ghazālī states the causation of good in a way that accommodates the Muslim theologians' view of God, with a subtle difference from that of the philosophers. For the latter, following the Platonic and Neoplatonic tradition, the good 'determines the acts of God, who finally (if not implicitly already in Plato) becomes a part of the determined order of the universe. For Ghazālī God remains a person, the only completely free one, and He is the decider of every event. If He decides to do good for man, the good 'is determined', 'particularized', 'instantiated' in the world on those occasions when it is most useful, but always by His gracious will.

The problem of predestination is suggested here but it will not be pursued. It is sufficient to note that, while Ghazālī supports predestination like any other Ashʿarite theologian, he does not see it as incompatible with human choice and 'acquisition' of acts in a certain sense. With this attitude he feels able to assume the freedom and responsibility of man in all contexts that concern human decisions.[50]

5

Within a study of this scope it is impossible to present Ghazālī's thought on the ends of man and the means to their attainment in all its richness and breadth.[51] We shall content ourselves with a short general account of some formal elements that give structure to this thought.

The end of man as an individual is the attainment of happiness, and happiness is to be found overwhelmingly in the next life. This is known from the Qurʾān, which also gives descriptions of this happiness; but the descriptions are to be understood variously according to each person's capacity for understanding, ranging from literal to mystical.

The primary means to the end are of two kinds: external acts of obedience to the rules of conduct, revealed in scripture (with certain permitted

thus transformed Ghazālī into a Neoplatonist philosopher for whom the good determines what occurs in the world. But for Ghazālī God always remains the sole determiner, and this is allowed in my translation of this passage. (Kamali's translation here is more like a paraphrase and also makes the determinant other than God.) *taʿayyana* here means that the abstract *khayr* is particularized in a temporal occurrence.

I am indebted to Michael E. Marmura for valuable suggestions on the interpretation of this passage, as well as for other comments on the present chapter.

50 See L. Gardet, *Dieu et la destinée de l'homme* (Paris, 1967), pp. 74–7, for a discriminating analysis of Ghazālī's position on this problem.

51 A brave attempt at this vast undertaking has been made by A. I. Othman, *The concept of man in Islam in the writings of al-Ghazālī* (Cairo, 1960). Much ground is also covered in a systematic way by Sherif, *Ghazālī's theory of virtue*, and M. Abul Quasem, *Ethics of al-Ghazālī*. The *Iḥyāʾ* is an almost inexhaustible mine for research on the content of Ghazālī's ethical thought.

extensions), and internal cultivation of the virtues of the soul. External acts are helpful both because obedience is rewarded directly for its sake and because these acts contribute towards the acquisition of virtues. But the inner state of the heart is more important than any external acts in the eyes of God and more conducive to Reward. The virtues form a scale with levels, and at the highest point of the mystical virtues a few people can enjoy in this life a foretaste of the happiness of the hereafter.[52]

None of the relations just described is causal. Acts do not cause virtues, as they do in Aristotle's doctrine of habituation. Acts do not cause rewards in the next life. And even virtues do not cause rewards, as they do in Hindu *karma* or Ibn Sīnā's eschatology. In all cases the rewards or the moral progress are bestowed by God through His grace. Here once again, God is the only cause and He is under no necessity. Religious enlightenment consists largely in understanding these truths.

The secondary means are those which are necessary for the effectiveness of the primary means to happiness. These are principally knowledge and motivation. The mission of the prophets is designed to provide these aids, for scripture gives both guidance and inspiration, both to acts of obedience and to the virtues. Finally, the Muslim community when it is working properly sustains the individual in various ways through its organization and leaders.[53]

Corresponding to the two human means to happiness are two practical sciences mentioned previously: *fiqh*, the ethics of action, and *akhlāq*, the ethics of character. Because of their fruits they are the most important kinds of knowledge for men below mystical knowledge, and it is necessary for everyone to study them. Their more advanced portions, however, the study of their principles, is not for everyone but for scholars in religion. The following sections give an account of the principles of the ethics of action, with special attention to their sources of knowledge.

6

Ghazālī's theory of the ethics of action is a modified form of the theory of ethical voluntarism (or theistic subjectivism) which had already had a long history of powerful support in earlier Islam. The core of that theory was, on the negative side, that the value terms applied to action, such as *wājib*, *ḥasan* and *qabiḥ* have no meanings in themselves, hence their application to action cannot be known by natural human intellect. The positive side was that these

[52] See Sherif, *ibid.*, chs. 2–4.

[53] A full account of Ghazālī's political theory is given by H. Laoust, *La politique de Gazālī* (Paris, 1970).

terms have meanings related to the commands and prohibitions of the divine Law (*sharʿ*), so that their application can be learned exclusively by studying that Law. The opponents whose position is denied were, of course, the Muʿtazilites with their ethical objectivism and rationalism; voluntarism had been developed in reaction against them by all the more conservative spokesmen of Islam, who referred to themselves as 'the people of tradition and the Community' (*ahl as-sunna wa l-jamāʿa*).

From an early time Muslims who understood the overwhelming power of God as the chief message of the Qurʾān could not admit that man could ever work out by his own intellect, without aid from scripture, what was right and what was wrong in the world, still less what was obligatory for God to do or not to do with His creation. The Traditionalists naturally felt this way since the Muʿtazilite claim undermined the utility of their collections. More weightily, the schools of law inclined in this direction increasingly, until voluntarism as a theory of jurisprudence was worked out with the most thoroughgoing logic by Shāfiʿī (d. 820). Ghazālī's Shafi'ism is apparent in many details of his ethics of action. On the side of theology, voluntarism found a champion in Ashʿarī (873–935) and his successors, but we do not find extensive argument in the surviving works of the school before Juwaynī (1028–85), who disputes the Muʿtazilite theory at some length.[54] Ghazālī develops the position of his master Juwaynī on this question, enriching it with his broader viewpoint on Islam and his more lively style of exposition.

Ghazālī in this sphere of ethics is still reacting chiefly against Muʿtazilite rationalism. This is surprising since the Muʿtazilites were no longer a living, fighting school in his lifetime in Baghdād or the cities of Iran and Syria where he studied and wrote.[55] The main reason is probably that the Muʿtazilite theory was the only articulate theory that could be set in contrast to the prevailing trend of Islamic thought on ethics in theological and juristic circles. It raised primary issues, which could not have been addressed through less fundamental discussions with the other schools of law or theology. As for the philosophers, whose position was objectivist and rationalist from a somewhat different viewpoint from that of the Muʿtazilites, Ghazālī ignores them, choosing to concentrate on their metaphysics in *Tahāfut al-falāsifa*. It is possible that he did not find in the writings of Fārābī and Ibn Sīnā any considerable passages on the points at issue in ethical philosophy, on which he could focus an attack. Moreover, in his principal writings on the ethics

[54] *Irshād*, 257–301. See G. F. Hourani, 'Juwayni's criticisms of Mu'tazilite ethics', *The Muslim World*, 65 (1975), 161–73.

[55] See G. Maqdisi, *Ibn ʿAqīl et la résurgence de l'Islam traditionaliste au XIe siècle* (Damascus, 1963), on the decline of the Mu'tazalites in Baghdad under Hanbalite and caliphal pressure.

of action he was addressing a milieu of theologians and lawyers who were little interested in philosophy.

Ghazālī's longest discussions of the subject occur in three books which constitute his major contributions to the three sciences mentioned previously: *Iqtiṣād* on *kalām*, *Mustaṣfā* on the principles of *fiqh* and *Iḥyā*ʾ on *akhlāq*. These books were written over a period of fourteen eventful years in the author's life. *Iqtiṣād* was written in 1095, probably in the first half of the year, before Ghazālī entered the acute stage of his personal crisis which led to his conversion to Sufism and departure from Baghdād.[56] The second book of *Iḥya*ʾ, on the articles of religion, where he discusses this side of ethics, dates from his residences in Jerusalem and Damascus, 1096–7.[57] The *Mustaṣfā* can be dated exactly: it was completed on August 5, 1109.[58] In spite of the intervals of years between these books, no differences in their views on the ethics of action are noticeable, and differences in presentation and range of topics can easily be explained by the varying purposes of the books. Several of the arguments are found in two or all three of them, in more or less similar forms. It will therefore be permissible and instructive to conflate the materials from the three accounts into a single systematic account. A few points can be added from *Miʿyār al-ʿilm* and *Munqidh*.

7

It is time now to turn our attention to Ghazālī's theory of ethical knowledge, which shall be our central subject. How should the individual acquire knowledge of the *wājib* for him, of his good and his evil? Bearing in mind the definitions of these terms and the ends and means of man as explained, we can see that these are questions about a man's knowledge of his true interests, i.e., of what he should do and become to attain happiness in the life of the next world. Such questions can be posed either with regard to a particular choice, how to act in the situation that confronts one immediately, or with regard to a long-range policy for life.

The form of ethical question that Ghazālī seems to consider in this context may be presented as follows. We want to bring each act and attitude under a general rule (*ḥukm*), a judgement of normative value for a type of act or attitude, so that we may have for our guidance a steady system of such rules

[56] M. Bouyges and M. Allard, *Essai de chronologie des œuvres de al-Ghazali* (*Algazel*) (Beirut, 1959), pp. 33–4; G. F. Hourani, 'A revised chronology of Ghazali's writings', *Journal of the American Oriental Society* (forthcoming); A. Badawi, *Muʾallafāt al-Ghazālī* (Cairo, 1961), pp. 87–8.

[57] Bouyges and Allard, *ibid.*, pp. 41–3. Hourani, *ibid.*, *Journal of the American Oriental Society*.

[58] Bouyges and Allard, *ibid.*, pp. 73–5. Hourani, *ibid.*, *Journal of the American Oriental Society* (forthcoming); Badawi, pp. 216–18.

to cover all occasions. The main question for an ethical theory of knowledge is, therefore, What are the sources of knowledge of rules?

He discusses this question in terms of a choice between two large sources, which between them cover all alternatives: independent reason and revelation. By 'independent' reason we mean precisely any reasoning that proceeds without any help from revelation. That is what is often called simply *ʿaql*, 'reason', in the well understood convention of the Islamic sciences. It is contrasted with *naql*, 'tradition', which covers revelation in its direct and derivative forms, also with *sharʿ*, scriptural texts and Traditions viewed as sources for *aḥkām*. But reason also has dependent uses, when it serves to draw out implications from *sharʿ* in certain ways to be specified below.

Now the main drive of Ghazālī's ethical theory of knowledge can be stated in two short sentences: Ethical knowledge is not derivable from independent reason; it is derivable entirely from revelation. The negative side will be elaborated in §§ 8–11, the affirmative in § 12.

8

The denial that ethical rules can be known by independent reason is made repeatedly by Ghazālī. Although his entire contemporary milieu of Sunnite intellectual society agreed with him on this point, he insists on it against the arguments of past Muʿtazilite scholars. Evidently his strong feelings on this question arose from the threat of rationalism to the position of the Qurʾān and Traditions as the unique and indispensable sources of all ethical knowledge. Ghazālī's entire loyalty was to these sources and their supreme Source. Even if there were almost no living Muʿtazilites within the central lands of Islam, their books survived and expressed the principal direct opposing view to what had now become orthodoxy on this question. But before we come to a discussion of his arguments against them it will be well to dispose of another opposing view, that of the philosophers.

Objectivist theories of ethics are nowadays commonly divided into teleological and deontological, and the theories of the Islamic philosophers and the Muʿtazilites fall respectively into these two divisions. In a teleological theory the value of acts is considered to be determined by their efficacy in promoting ends. Ancient Greek philosophers from Socrates onwards took as their starting point the ends of the individual and concentrated on his good, with little attention to obligation. They assumed that there is a natural comprehensive end for everyone, which is happiness, and attempted to show how all less comprehensive ends were either constituents of happiness or means to it. The main thrust of their arguments was that virtuous living is the key to happiness: but not because of any direct external rewards it gives – experience shows the contrary – but because constant activity of this sort purifies the soul and makes it delight in such activity more and more. So much is common to Socrates, Plato, Aristotle and the Stoics. But Plato went further, and in the more speculative form of his 'myths' suggested that purity of soul is carried over to a future immortal life where it brings to its owner everlasting bliss. Through the combined influences of Plato, Neoplatonism and Islam this last doctrine was inevitably taken up by Muslim philosophers. Ibn Sīnā, for instance, worked out in clinical fashion just how purity of soul would cause happiness and impurity misery in the future life.[59]

Now Ghazālī does not refute this theory, so far as I know. He is silent about it, perhaps because in his one book against the philosophers, *Tahāfut al-falāsifa*, he concentrates on their metaphysics and physical philosophy, attacking twenty of their doctrines in these spheres. He is not entirely averse to ethical philosophy, which he considers to have been taken from the Ṣūfīs, some of whom must have existed in every age;[60] but the philosophers have muddled their pure sources and their ethics presents dangers to undiscriminating readers.[61] He himself makes use of Platonic and Aristotelian schemes of the virtues, with Islamic adaptations of his own.[62] He, too, shares with the philosophers a common point of some generality, in holding a teleological theory of ethics. We have seen how his theory is based on his definitions of *wājib*, *ḥasan* and *qabīḥ* as related to ends, principally the ends of the agent.

Yet, in spite of all these points, it is certain that he was opposed to their teleological ethics. And, in spite of his silence in answering them, it will be instructive to see why he must have opposed them. The opposition turns around two points, their different metaphysics of causality and the prominence of the after-life in Islamic theology.

The core of Greek ethics is an attempt to demonstrate causal relations, showing how certain ways of life directly cause certain changes in the subject (as well as in other people through education or corruption); and such explanations are extended, with some hesitation, to the states of souls in the next life. The entire construction is based on the assumption of natural causality which was shared by all the Greek and Muslim philosophers. But Ghazālī rejects natural causality and, as stated above (§ 5), he applies this

[59] *Najāt*, ed. M. S. Kurdi (Cairo, 1938), 291–8; Eng. trans. A. J. Arberry, *Avicenna on theology* (London, 1951), pp. 64–76.

[60] *Munqidh*, 100.

[61] *Munqidh*, 100–7.

[62] See Sherif, *Ghazālī's theory of virtue*, ch. 2, and Ghazālī's *Mīzān al-ʿamal*.

rejection to every stage in the chain of 'means'[63] and ends. Let us make these assertions specific in connection with ethical knowledge. Firstly, we do not know how acts operate on the character of the subject; this is a mystery, and *ʿilm al-akhlāq* had better be expounded in terms of divine assistance. Secondly, we have no clue to how virtuous acts lead to rewards in the next life; we only know through revelation that they do so in fact, owing to divine mercy, and it is presumptuous to think like Ibn Sīnā that they must do so as an effect of the merits of human acts. And thirdly, we likewise do not understand how virtuous character leads to rewards, for similar reasons.

Further, because causal connections are absent or hidden, we do not even know by any process of independent teleological reasoning *which* acts improve character, *which* acts bring rewards and *which* dispositions of character bring rewards. All we know about these facts is known from scripture.

9

A teleological ethics different from that of the philosophers would have been possible for the Muʿtazilites along the following lines. The end of man is happiness, and this results from the rewards of God at the Judgement. Since justice is an attribute of God, His rewards follow His known character; and, although it is theoretically within His power to reward evildoers, it is inconceivable that He would do so. Thus, since man also knows rationally which acts are good and which evil, he can attain practical certainty about the means to his end. Here is the closest thing to causality, although it is not natural but mediated through God's will which is known from revelation.

However, the Muʿtazilites chose to define the main terms of ethics in ways which avoid teleology. Muʿtazilite ethics is deontological, because it explains *wājib*, *ḥasan* and *qabīḥ* not entirely by relations to ends, but sometimes at least as characters of acts themselves. *Wājib* as an attribute of acts is defined as 'that for the omission of which the agent deserves blame', *qabīḥ* as 'that for doing which the agent deserves blame', and so on. The blame can be known by the intelligence of any rational person, often – as in the cases of lying and injustice – without reference to consequences.

Thus the Muʿtazilites developed an ethical theory that was original in relation to that of Greek philosophy. In the paucity of knowledge about the beginnings of Muʿtazilite theology we may speculate why their ethics took this

[63] It may be questioned whether we should speak of 'means' at all in discussing an occasionalist theory. But I shall continue to do so for convenience, with the understanding that these 'means' are not strictly causes but only occasions for God's favour or disfavour.

sharp turn from teleology to deontology. Probably the deepest reason lies in the new prominence of obligation in Islamic ethical thinking, as compared with Greek. This prominence is due to the relations of God and man as the Qurʾān establishes them: relations of contract, in which God imposes burdens and promises rewards, relations of law in which God legislates and man obeys, relations of justice in which every man is to receive what he deserves. In such relations obligation in the proper sense occupies a central role. The Muʿtazilites took it seriously. This is not the place to estimate their success in analysing it, but we may say this much in their favour: that at least they did not try to dissolve it by explaining *wājib* in terms of the interest of the subject. In discussing *wājib* they were discussing 'obligatory', and continued to do so until their school faded away.

Their central position on ethics is that man can know some of his obligations, his good and evil too, by the independent use of his reason, before and without the aid of scripture. The basic ontological assertion that makes these value attributes accessible to human reason is their objectivity: they are real attributes belonging to individual acts and classes of acts. In the developed Muʿtazilite ethics as found in ʿAbd al-Jabbār (*c.* 935–1025), objectivity is worked into a complex and flexible theory. *Prima facie* values of different aspects of an act should first be judged separately, then these aspects should be weighed against each other to produce an overall judgement. This process will lead to varying conclusions in varying situations. But the process is not possible in all cases, for there are certain classes of act which have invariable value characters, regardless of other aspects. For example, all acts of *ẓulm* (wrongdoing, injustice, oppression), useless acts, ungrateful acts and (probably) all lies are evil, and are known to be such by all rational persons. These are universal rules, and they give an absolutist dimension to a part of the objective facts of ethical value.[64]

Now Ghazālī does not argue directly with the feature of objectivity as such in the Muʿtazilite ethical concepts, apart from occasional sweeping denials that these concepts have any objective meanings. His attack is concentrated against the partial and inessential feature of absoluteness in some of the rules, and the main thrust of his attack is that there are no universal ethical rules (*aḥkām*) knowable by independent reason. Thus he makes the issue one of relativism versus absolutism, rather than (as it should have been) of subjectivism versus objectivism. This formulation becomes clearest in a passage of *Mustaṣfā*. After he has given his own relativistic definitions of *ḥasan*, he states the Muʿtazilite objection: we do not deny these meanings, but

[64] For details see Hourani, *Islamic rationalism*, especially pp. 29–33, 62–81.

there are also some acts good or evil by essence, agreed on by all intelligent people without regard to relative conditions, e.g., wrongdoing, lying, unbelief and ignorance.[65]

Ghazālī's refutations of rational universal rules occur in various places in his works and take different forms, with some overlap of arguments between different works. In the following account I shall attempt a systematic exposition of his arguments according to their forms, bringing together under each one what he says in different places.

According to Ghazālī, the claim of rational universal rules fails several tests that it should meet if it is to be accepted.

(1) All proposed rational rules fail in universality. 'Killing is evil' is not universal, for the Muʿtazilites themselves immediately qualify the judgement with exceptions: killing is not evil when it is punishment for crime, or when the victim is to be compensated in the next life.[66] (This is an unfair argument because the Muʿtazilites did not claim that killing is universally evil. All Ghazālī can show is that their rule about it is complicated.) 'Lying is evil' is not universal, because it is permitted and even required to lie to save a prophet's life.[67] 'Spreading peace is good' is not universal; it is untrue in circumstances of dire necessity.[68] These and similar propositions are only generally true: they are thus not fit to be major premises in demonstrative practical syllogisms, but are suitable only for conjectural use in legal arguments.[69]

(2) The supposed universal ethical truths fail to pass the subjective test of indubitable certainty which is required for all intuited first principles of the intellect. Here Ghazālī draws upon a typical Avicennan argument: if you were to come into existence fully rational but without experience of society or instruction, having only sense experience and images, you would be able to doubt such premises as 'Killing a man is evil', or at least to hesitate about them, but you could not doubt 'Negation and affirmation cannot be true of the same state of a thing' or '2 is greater than 1'.[70]

These judgements are such, that if one were to confine himself to his pure reason, his faculties of estimation and sense, the mind (with the aid of reason and sense alone) would never arrive at any of them. Rather, the mind makes these judgements only as the result of accidental causes that confirm and fix them in the soul.[71]

[65] *Mustaṣfā*, I, 36.

[66] *Mustaṣfā*, I, 36–7.

[67] *Mustaṣfā*, I, 37. *Miʿyār al-ʿilm* (Cairo: Kurdistan Press, 1329 h./1911), 113.

[68] *Miʿyār*, 113.

[69] *Miʿyār*, 111, 114. See M. E. Marmura, 'Ghazālī on ethical premises', *The Philosophical Forum* (New Series), I (1969), 393–403, a translation and analysis of the relevant passage of *Miʿyār*.

[70] *Miʿyār*, 114; taken from Ibn Sīnā, *al-Ishārāt wa t-tanbīhāt*, ed. S. Dunya (Cairo, 1953), I, 400–1.

[71] *Miʿyār*, 112. Quotations from *Miʿyār* are as translated by Marmura.

What these accidental causes are, in Ghazālī's opinion, will be described in the next section.

(3) Any proposition that is intuited immediately or necessarily (*bi ḍ-ḍarūra*) must command unanimous agreement. But the suggested rational truths of ethics fail to do so, for important Islamic schools disagree with them. The Muᶜtazilites retort that the disagreement is on the theory of ethical knowledge (such as the question here at issue), but not on first order normative propositions, which are what they consider rational. But this is untrue, says Ghazālī, there are also disagreements in normative knowledge, for example on the wrongness of causing pain to animals: this is claimed by the Muᶜtazilites as known by reason, but God in scripture has revealed approval for it, in animal sacrifices.[72]

(4) But even unanimity is only a necessary not a sufficient condition for proof of immediate knowledge. For instance, belief in the existence of God is almost universal, but even if it were completely so it would still not be immediate.[73] The reason (not mentioned here) is that it needs to be demonstrated, it is 'acquired' (*muktasab*) not 'immediate' (*ḍarūrī*).

(5) If *wājib* is understood in the 'correct' Ghazalian sense of 'necessary to produce benefits', it is impossible for reason to demonstrate this kind of *wujūb* for any of the Muᶜtazilite rules. Ghazālī expounds his refutation lucidly in *Mustaṣfā*, proceeding by a definition and a series of dilemmas.

Gratitude to a benefactor is not necessary by reason, contrary to the Muᶜtazilite. The proof of this is that 'necessary' (*al-wājib*) has no meaning but what God the Exalted has made necessary (*awjabahu*) and commanded with threat of punishment for omission; so if there is no revelation what is the meaning of 'necessity'? This argument is confirmed as follows:

'Reason should make gratitude necessary either for some benefit or for none. It is impossible that reason necessitates it for no benefit, for that would be useless and foolish. If it is for a benefit, it must either be for the One served, but that is impossible since He is too Exalted and Holy to have ends, or for the servant. The servant's benefit must either be in this world or in the next. But there is no benefit to him in this world, rather he is [only] wearied by study and thought, knowledge and gratitude, and deprived by them of desires and pleasures. And there is no benefit [known by reason] in the next world, for Reward is bestowed as a favour from God, and is known by His promise and His announcement; and if He did not announce it how would it be known that there is to be Reward?'[74]

[72] *Mustaṣfā*, I, 37. Cf. Juwaynī, *Irshād*, 261. In answering the same objection Juwaynī denies the distinction between two levels of knowledge, but falls into fallacies in his answer. Ghazālī composes a more direct reply by pointing to normative disagreements.

[73] *Mustaṣfā*, I, 37.

[74] *Mustaṣfā*, I, 39. Cf. *Iḥyāʾ*, I, 113 = Tibawi, pp. 26–7 and 51–2; *Iqtiṣād*, 186–91 = Asín, pp. 285–8.

Ghazālī's refutation is unconvincing to a detached observer, for it assumes his own definition of *wājib*, as stated, and his own theodicy in which Reward for human desert cannot be inferred from the divine nature. But on their own definition of *wājib* in the sense of 'obligatory' the Muᶜtazilites would not have to prove that reason sees the *benefit* of acts to agents, but only their *obligatoriness*, a concept that Ghazālī does not seem to grasp at any stage (and we must admit after the struggles of modern ethical philosophy that it is a puzzling concept). But even if the Muᶜtazilites were required to prove a rational knowledge of the otherworldly *benefits* of fulfilling obligations, they could do so on their own theodicy by inferring rewards for human desert from the justice of God in His acts, a justice that sprang from His nature and was to be understood in the same sense as human justice.

What all this shows is that Ghazālī should have gone deeper into a discussion of the divergent assumptions of the Muᶜtazilites and himself. Perhaps he did so elsewhere in his extensive writings, but he did not bring any such discussions to bear on this particular argument. The absence of living challengers was taking its toll on the level of argument of Sunnite theologians, as it had done already on that of Ghazālī's predecessor Juwaynī. We are far from the laborious and seemingly interminable dialectic of ᶜAbd al-Jabbār a century earlier, with its painstaking efforts to answer every criticism spoken, written or imaginable.

10

Ghazālī is not content to combat intellectually the error of ethical absolutism. He also shows a great interest in explaining its causes,[75] intellectual and emotional, and suggests a number of them. He addresses himself to this question in three passages in *Miᶜyār*, *Iqtiṣād* and *Mustaṣfā*. There is naturally some overlap between these passages. I shall take *Miᶜyār* as the primary account, since it is the earliest and the most elaborate, but some important points from the other two texts will be added.

In *Miᶜyār* Ghazālī gives a long list of examples of ethical rules 'commonly believed' (*mash-hūrāt*) to be universal:

These are exemplified by our judging it good to spread peace, feed others, bestow largesse on kinsfolk, adhere to truthfulness in speech, observe justice in legal suits and

[75] It may be wondered how Ghazālī as an occasionalist can speak of 'causes' other than God, as he does here and frequently elsewhere in his writings. Presumably if challenged he would have said that he was using the conventional language, and that the true relation between two events that we call 'cause' and 'effect' is always a constant conjunction caused by God, according to the doctrine of *ᶜāda* (God's 'habit').

judgements; and by our judging it bad that one should harm humans, kill animals, disseminate slander – that husbands should acquiesce in the licentiousness of their wives, that benevolence should be repaid with ingratitude and oppression.[76]

After denying that these are rational judgements he claims that they are due to 'accidental causes' and lists five.

(1) Tenderness of heart, a quality of innate disposition. This explains the belief that slaughtering animals is evil according to reason. Only scripture has turned most people away from this belief by recommending animal sacrifice.[77]

(2) Pride, another inborn quality of temperament. This explains most husbands' jealousy of their wives' intimacy with other men, although the husbands believe their disapproval is an immediate rational judgement. But husbands in some societies, and adulterers everywhere, regard such conduct as good. So neither of these contradictory judgements can be a rational intuition, since they fail the test of unanimity.[78]

(3) Love of conciliation and cooperation. This explains belief in the absolute goodness of spreading peace and the absolute badness of ingratitude. But others incline towards conflict and regard it as better than peace. Without any feelings one way or the other, 'their minds in their natural state [*fiṭra*] would make no judgements about these things in terms of goodness and badness'.[79]

(4) Religious instruction, from childhood on. Beliefs gained from repeated instruction become so ingrained that they come to appear rational, e.g., the beliefs that kneeling and prostration in prayer, of animal sacrifice, are good. Intellect alone would make no judgement.[80]

By his choice of examples here Ghazālī shows that he is quite indifferent to any need for rational justification of such beliefs; he is confident in the sufficiency of their scriptural justification.

(5) 'The induction [*istiqrāʾ*] of numerous particulars; for, when a thing is found in many of its circumstances conjoined with another thing, it is thought that it is conjoined with it absolutely.' For example, spreading peace is good in most situations, so that one forgets that it is bad in cases of dire necessity. Likewise truthfulness is nearly always good, so one forgets that it is evil to disclose truthfully the location of a prophet hiding from enemies seeking to

[76] *Miʿyār*, 118.

[77] *Ibid.* Ghazālī digresses here to a discussion of how the Muʿtazilites try to justify the scriptural ruling rationally and how their attempts fail. There is no need to present this discussion here. Cf. *Iqtiṣād*, 182–4 = Asín, pp. 275–7; and *Iḥyā'*, I, 112 for other discussions of harm to animals.

[78] *Miʿyār*, 113. Cf. *Iqtiṣād*, 164 = Asín, p. 250.

[79] *Miʿyār*. 113.

[80] *Ibid.* Cf. *Iqtiṣād*, 167 = Asín, pp. 253–4, on the effects of education and repetition in this context.

slay him. There are conditions for the goodness of truthfulness; the error of absolutism arises from ignoring them.[81]

Two further causes of error are mentioned in other books.

(6) Inability to accept the interests of others as valid grounds for relative goodness. This leads us to describe as absolutely evil what may be good for the ends of another.[82] This is the typical fault of egoists: they call evil absolutely and essentially whatever does not suit their own purposes.[83]

(7) Imaginative associations of ideas, leading us to react in uniform ways to what is associated with something regarded as usually good or evil – as when a person with a horror of snakes shrinks from a twisting rope of mottled colour.[84] Such associations explain the prejudices of Muʿtazilite and Ashʿarite theologians, their repulsion against theories which they recognize as coming from the other camp.[85]

All these causes of error may be resumed under two heads. One is incomplete induction, leading us to universalize what is only generally the case. The other is emotion, distorting our rational judgements. These two are not exclusive of each other but interact. There is much of interest in Ghazālī's remarks on this subject. But attempts to psychoanalyse one's opponents are laden with dangers of misunderstanding except in the hands of an unusually sympathetic critic, which Ghazālī was not in regard to the Muʿtazilites.

II

There remains for consideration one argument for rational obligation which the Muʿtazilites considered a trump card, and which Ghazālī is at pains to refute. This is the argument that there must be at least one obligation known by reason prior to revelation: the obligation to inquire into (*an-naẓar fī*) the authenticity of the prophet as shown by the evidence of his miracles. This obligation is the starting point for accepting scripture as authentic, and therefore for accepting all obligations derived from scripture. But the obligation to accept scripture and its obligations obviously cannot be derived from scripture prior to its acceptance as scripture.

[81] *Miʿyār*, 113–14. Cf. *Iqtiṣād*, 167 = Asín, pp. 253–4; *Mustaṣfā*, I, 37. When Muḥammad and Abu Bakr were hiding in a cave in the course of their emigration from Mecca to Madīna, Abu Bakr's daughter Asma denied knowledge of their whereabouts to Abū Jahl and other men of Quraysh who were searching for them: Ibn Isḥāq, *Sīra*, ed. F. Wüstenfeld, *Das Leben Muhammed's* (Göttingen, 1858–60), I, 329–31; Eng. trans. A. Guillaume, *The Life of Muḥammad* (London, 1955), pp. 224–5.

[82] *Mustaṣfā*, I, 37.

[83] *Iqtiṣād*, 166 = Asín, p. 253.

[84] *Mustaṣfā*, I, 38.

[85] *Iqtiṣād*, 167–9 = Asín, pp. 254–7. Cf. 171–2 = Asín, pp. 258–62.

Ghazālī's answer to this challenge[86] starts from his own definition of *wujūb* as strong preferability; the *wājib* is anything the neglect of which is seriously harmful to one's real interest. Now since God has set the conditions for salvation and made them known through scripture, it is objectively to everyone's interest to inquire into scripture, and therefore to take the first step by inquiring whether the prophet's miracles are a proof of his mission being authentic and his message of divine origin. Somewhat in the spirit of Pascal's wager, Ghazālī says it only needs ordinary prudence for anyone to take this step. It is as stupid to omit it by asking to be convinced of a 'necessity' in advance of inquiry, as for a man, warned of a lion at his back, to answer 'I shall not look behind unless I am first convinced of your truthfulness in warning me',[87] or for an invalid offered medicine to tell the doctor 'I shall not take it unless I know whether it is necessary by reason or by your word'.[88] In fact God has provided all we need to lead us to an intelligent decision: a prophet to warn us, miracles to back his authority, our intellect to understand the warnings and grasp the significance of the miracle, and our natural inclination to motivate us to avoid harm and seek reward.

> The true formulation is to say that necessity [*al-wujūb*] is preferability [*ar-rajḥān*], the necessitator [*al-mūjib*] is God the Exalted, the informer is the Messenger, while that which instructs us on what is prohibited and the truthfulness of the Messenger is reason. What urges us to follow the way of salvation is nature.[89]

Ghazālī adds that if the Muᶜtazilite circular argument were valid it would apply equally if intellect were the necessitating force: 'if one does not inquire he does not know the rational necessity to inquire, and if he does not know the necessity to inquire he does not inquire'.[90]

It may be objected that Ghazālī has based his reply to the Muᶜtazilites on his own definition of *wājib*, which is not theirs and is false anyway. However, his reply points to a valid reply even if *wājib* is understood as 'obligatory': that there is no need for anyone to prove that inquiry into miracles and scripture is obligatory before embarking on such an inquiry. All one needs is a natural concern for our own interest. Thus the circle of 'an obligation to learn about obligation' is broken by denying the Muᶜtazilite assumption of an initial obligation.

[86] *Iqtiṣād*, 191–5 = Asín, pp. 288–92. *Mustaṣfā*, I, 40. Less fully in *Iḥyāʾ*, I, 113 = Tibawi, pp. 27 and 52–3.
[87] *Iḥyaʾ*, I, 113 = Tibawi, pp. 27 and 52. *Mustaṣfā*, I, 40.
[88] *Iqtiṣād*, 193 = Asín, p. 290.
[89] *Iqtiṣād*, 195 = Asín, p. 292. *Mustaṣfā*, I, 40. Further points in Ghazali's exposition: (1) God gives man the possibility of knowledge; He does not need to give actual knowledge (*Mustaṣfā*, I, 40). (2) Reason by itself does not motivate, inclinations are necessary for this (*Iqtiṣād*, 194 = Asín, p. 291. *Mustaṣfā*, I, 40). ᶜAbd al-Jabbār defined motives entirely as intellectual states (Hourani, *Islamic rationalism*, pp. 82–4).
[90] *Mustaṣfā*, I, 40.

12

The affirmative side of Ghazālī's theory of knowledge of the rules of action will now be considered.

The bare fact that the rules for action are all derived from revelation or authorized extensions of it is one of Ghazālī's most basic principles, and is stated by him in many places.[91] But the theory of the sources and methods of knowledge of rules is the subject of the science of *uṣūl al-fiqh*, consequently the details are dealt with principally in *Mustaṣfā*. The theory follows the classical lines of the Shafiʿite school, and the book is less notable for originality than for lucid and attractive exposition, a quality that has kept it in the curriculum of Islamic law studies to the present time. There will be no need to enter into much detail, but only to note a few salient features.

The rules of action are produced in the first place by three kinds of 'proofs' (sing. *dalīl*, pl. *adilla*); those found in the Qurʾān, the *sunna* and consensus.[92] Concerning the authority of the Qurʾān no question ever arose.[93] Previous scriptures are disallowed as sources of proofs.[94] The *sunna* is limited to the acts, words and silences of the Prophet Muḥammad.[95] Following the Shafiʿite tradition, the *sunna* of the Companions is not accepted, for they disagreed and were not infallible.[96] Consensus (*ijmāʿ*), while not being a textual source like the first two, is accepted as a source of proof on the authority of the Qurʾān and *sunna*, especially of the *sunna*, which is clearer on this matter.[97] Consensus is to be defined as that of competent scholars, not of the public at large.[98]

The fourth 'root' (*aṣl*) of the Law is analogy (*qiyās*), but this is not a 'proof' or 'source' (*madrak*) in the sense in which the first three are: it is rather a method of drawing out the meaning to be understood (*al-maʿqūl*) in the sacred texts or the statement of consensus.[99] So here Ghazālī is moving into the sphere of reason. As expected in the Shafiʿite tradition, the use of reason in law is carefully restricted with a view to making it entirely derivative or dependent on the revealed sources, never independent by having its own sources in natural experience and intuition. Compared with the *muqallid* who merely follows authorities, the *mujtahid* is the scholar who is competent to exercise

[91] E.g., *Iqtiṣād*, 160 = Asín, p. 245; 192 = Asín, p. 289. *Iḥyāʾ*, I, 91; 113 = Tibawi, pp. 26–7 and 51–3. *Mustaṣfā*, I, 35–6.

[92] *Mustaṣfā*, I, 5 and 64–127.

[93] *Ibid.*, I, 64–83.

[94] *Ibid.*, I, 131–5.

[95] *Ibid.*, I, 83–110.

[96] *Ibid.*, I, 135–7.

[97] *Ibid.*, I, 110–27. See ch. 13.

[98] *Mustaṣfā*, I, 115.

[99] *Mustaṣfā*, I, 144–5 and II, 54–101. See R. Brunschvig, 'Valeur et fondement du raisonnement juridique par analogie d'après al-Ġazālī', *Studia Islamica*, 34 (1971), 57–88. This valuable article uses other juristic works of Ghazālī besides *Mustaṣfā: al-Mankhūl fī uṣūl al-fiqh* (Damascus, 1970), *Shifāʾ al-ghalīl fī bayān masālik at-taʿlīl* (Baghdad, 1971), 'Asās al-qiyās', MS. Beşir Ağa (Suleimaniye), 650, fols. 178–201.

his own judgement. But he has no choice in deciding the rules of action, they are all given in revelation; his function is merely to infer them where they are not obvious.[100]

The method most proper to *ijtihād* is analogy based on revelation (*qiyās sharᶜī*). The starting point must be a rule (*ḥukm*) known exclusively from scripture, and this must not be distorted by enunciation of a divine reason (*ᶜilla sharᶜiyya*) at this stage. The *ᶜilla* is to be inferred from the original rule, through understanding this rule in its context; then the final operation of *qiyās* consists in applying the *ᶜilla* to give a rule for cases analogous to the original case in respects relevant to action. An *ᶜilla* is not indispensable for every rule, since God can issue rules without reasons; but when it is present the human race is allowed to discover it and use it to extend its knowledge of the divine rules.[101]

There is, however, another method of reasoning which falls partly outside analogy: consideration of social interests (*istiṣlāḥ*). Because it is on the frontiers of the permissible use of reason, it will be illuminating to examine how Ghazālī deals with it and to see how far, or how little, he is willing to stretch those frontiers.

Ghazālī begins his examination of *istiṣlāḥ* in *Mustaṣfā* by distinguishing three possible relations of human interest (*maṣlaḥa*) to the Law, with a view to isolating where the real problem lies:

(a) Where the Law provides evidence for a *maṣlaḥa* being used in revelation as an *ᶜilla*, it is legitimate to draw analogies from it. Ghazālī gives a familiar example. The prohibition of wine leads by analogy to the prohibition of all other intoxicating drinks,

> because they are forbidden in order to preserve the intellect which is the pivot of imposed obligation (*taklīf*), and the Law's prohibition of wine is the proof for observing this interest.[102]

Here the preservation of uninterrupted mental sanity in man, so that he may always understand his obligations, is the *ᶜilla* or divine reason for the prohibition of wine, as is made clear in the text of scripture; so it may be used as a basis for analogy to apply the prohibition to drinks which similarly impair sanity. And the *ᶜilla* is a purpose of God to safeguard a *maṣlaḥa* of man. In such cases, then, *Istiṣlāḥ* is absorbed into the method of normal *qiyās*, and no special problem arises about it.

(b) Where the Law provides evidence for rejection of a *maṣlaḥa*, it must be rejected. Here too no problem arises.[103]

[100] *Mustaṣfā*, I, 144–5.
[101] See Brunschvig, 'Valeur et fondement', pp. 75–6, 83–4.
[102] *Mustaṣfā*, I, 139.
[103] *Ibid.*

(c) Where the Law provides no evidence for or against a *maṣlaḥa*, there is a problem whether this *maṣlaḥa* should be a consideration in determining the rule, and if so by what authority it is a valid consideration in Islamic law. This had become the classic problem of *istiṣlāḥ* by Ghazālī's time, and he devotes attention to a solution. It was a problem because lawyers had in earlier times based decisions rather freely on judgements of social interest based on their own sense of equity and the public good, and while these decisions may have been practically and ethically sound they could in no way be justified as Islamic in the strict sense required by jurisprudence; the interests in question therefore came to be known as *maṣāliḥ mursala*, 'interests cut loose' from any link with *sharʿ*. The theoretically easy way to deal with them was to reject them entirely. But while this might be done lightly by academic jurists like Ibn Ḥazm, practising lawyers could not brush aside the public interest. There is no need here to recount the ways in which *istiṣlāḥ* was dealt with in classical Islam, but only to attend to Ghazālī's treatment.

He approaches the problem in typical fashion by offering a definition of *maṣlaḥa*. The original meaning of the word is 'deriving benefit or repelling harm', but this is not what is meant by it in law because 'benefits' and 'harm' are normally understood as human interests and the ends of human purposes.

> We mean by *maṣlaḥa* preserving the purpose of the Law, and the purpose of the Law for man is fivefold: the preservation for them of their religion, soul, intellect, offspring and property. Whatever includes the preservation of these five elements is a *maṣlaḥa*, and whatever dispels these elements is a cause of damage (*mafsada*) whose repulsion is a *maṣlaḥa*.[104]

Such a sweeping generalization about the purposes of God is a bold move by Ghazālī, running contrary to the predominant aversion of Sunnite jurists to any ethical statements going beyond the piecemeal evidence of the *sharʿ*. The five purposes look like rational deductions from God's justice and providence, such as the Muʿtazilites might have made, but of course they are nothing of the sort. They are known by induction, 'through numerous proofs that cannot be limited, from the Book and the *sunna* and their contexts'.[105] There is no question of any objective good or evil in the rationalist sense that Ghazālī rejected; all that is stated is the purposes that God has willed for the human race, as known from scripture.

Can the five purposes of the Law be used as *ʿilal*, divine reasons from which specific commands and prohibitions can be inferred? This is a delicate question because these purposes are not stated in a particular text (*naṣṣ muʿayyan*) in scripture, so it would seem repugnant to the very 'positive' spirit

[104] *Ibid.*, I, 140.

[105] *Ibid.*, I, 144.

of Islamic law to use them as bases for judging rules. But Ghazālī does accept them, under strict limits. The rule deduced must be for something necessary (*ḍarūrī*) for preserving one of the five vital interests, something of universal concern (*kullī*), and something beyond doubt (*qaṭʿī*). The classic example, given by Ghazālī among others, is the rule permitting a Muslim army to shoot at Muslim prisoners being used as a screen by an attacking infidel army, when the entire Muslim people is being imperilled by such an attack. He thinks the intention of the Law is certain in such cases and a few others, even without a particular text.

The method of decision here is essentially the same as in analogy, but he prefers to call it *maṣlaḥa mursala*, not *qiyās*, because of the difference in the kind of *ʿilla* – understood from scripture in general not from a particular text. And, although he is willing to call this method *istiṣlāh*, he rejects *istiṣlāh* in weaker cases where the purpose is need (*ḥāja*) at the ordinary level or mere improvement and doing good (*taḥsīn*). In such cases the use of *maṣlaḥa* as a basis for decision is a usurpation of the function of the Legislator, on the same forbidden level as using personal judgement on what is best (*istiḥsān*).[106]

We may conclude this account of Ghazālī's theory of ethical knowledge, applied to action, by contrasting it with Aristotle's theory of deliberation as expounded in the *Nicomachean Ethics*. According to Aristotle, the raw material for ethical knowledge is the diverse experience of the individual or what he learns from the community or the wise; and we begin from intuitions of good and evil in particular ends and means. Reflective people proceed from there, by induction from masses of experience, to more general value statements about ends and means. At the highest level the philosopher seeks to organize the entire range of such conclusions in a unified system, involving a supreme end, 'happiness' (*eudaimonia*), and a hierarchy of subordinate ends and means. Now the man of practical wisdom in his most enlightened form can deliberate on action by working downwards from the most general ends, deducing what practical rules and acts will best satisfy these ends in a given society or a particular situation. This is a brief account which leaves out the abundant details and illustrations provided by Aristotle, as well as any discussion of ambiguities in his theory. The only point to be made here is that Aristotle is confident that man has the capacity to arrive at true conclusions at every step by his natural understanding – not every man, but the wiser, and not with scientific certainty but sufficiently for practical purposes.

Ghazālī, on the other hand, does not think that natural understanding is useful for most of the steps required; on the contrary, it is more likely to lead

106 *Ibid.*, I, 140–4. See R. Paret, 'Istiḥsān and istiṣlāh', *EI*², especially 257, and Laoust, *Politique de Ġazali*, pp. 166–71.

us astray because it is itself liable to be led astray by desires. At the initial stage it can only inform us of short-term good and evil, whatever is fitting or repugnant to our personal ends as we see them. To know our ultimate ends and the effective means to them we depend completely on the guidance of God, provided in scripture. The rules for action are given piecemeal, on the whole, and must be followed as they come; and we must be cautious in generalizing them, although we have seen Ghazālī doing so at one point with his five purposes of the Law. Deliberation, whether to arrive at rules of action or individual decisions, then proceeds from quite different premises from Aristotle's: not from constructions of human wisdom or philosophy but from the revealed Law. After this point, however, Ghazālī allows the use of human reasoning to draw further conclusions from the scriptural premises, by the methods of analogy and a narrowly restricted *istiṣlāh*.

13

Ghazālī's thought on the sphere of ethics surveyed here has shown itself internally consistent. The leading themes of his theology are the omnipotence of God and the complete dependence of man; the corresponding themes in *fiqh* are the dominant rôle of revelation and the subordinate rôle of natural reason in giving guidance for external action.

But this part of ethics is only 'the beginning of guidance',[107] which leads on to 'the science of states of the heart', dealing with the cultivation of the virtues and inward purification, the chief means to man's salvation. In this sphere, many questions about the method of knowledge of virtue can be asked. How do we know the necessity of acquiring virtue? How do we know its essence and kinds, its causes, the methods of attaining it? Some of the answers are given or suggested in Sherif's book. He shows the relation of Ghazālī's thought to philosophy, and to the culminating science and practice of Sufism. But we shall not pursue these questions here. They have been mentioned only to give perspective to the part of Ghazālī's ethics that has been described.

His general attitude to the functions of revelation and reason in ethics can best be summarized in his own words in *Munqidh*:

> In sum, prophets are the doctors of heart ailments. The only beneficial function of intellect is to teach us that fact, bearing witness to the veracity of prophecy and its own incompetence to grasp what can be grasped by the eye of prophecy; it takes us by the hand and delivers us to prophecy as the blind are delivered to guides and confused patients to compassionate doctors. Thus far is the progress and advance of

[107] *Bidāyat al-hidāya*, the title of a short book of Ghazālī serving as an introduction to *Iḥyā*ʾ.

intellect; beyond that it is dismissed, except for understanding what the doctor imparts to it.[108]

Thus, independent reason is indispensable for the first steps in apologetics, since revelation cannot authorize its own authority, as the Muᶜtazilites had never tired of pointing out. Revelation then takes over the bulk of the task of ethical guidance, being supplemented by reason only in its dependent functions of interpretation and drawing out implications.

Ghazālī would no doubt have liked us to conclude with another quotation which comes to mind, the last of the beautiful 'light verses' of the twenty-fourth *sūra* of the Qurʾān:

> And to whomsoever God assigns no light, no light has he.[109]

In his view the light of ethics comes only from revelation, except for that mystical light which comes directly to a few by inspiration. But this interpretation begs the question: may not intellect be a part of the divine light, as it has been considered by so many Muslim, Christian and Jewish thinkers in the Neoplatonic tradition? Such a question is too large to enter into here. But I think it permissible to end on this personal note of scepticism about Ghazālī's exclusion of independent human reason from the operations of ethical judgement.

[108] *Munqidh*, 146.

[109] Qurʾān, xxiv, 40: *wa man lam yaf ᶜali llāhu lahu nūran fa mā lahu min nūrin*. Eng. trans. A. J. Arberry, *The Koran interpreted*, 2 vols. (London, 1955).

12

REASON AND REVELATION IN IBN ḤAZM'S ETHICAL THOUGHT

I

Normative ethics (*akhlāq*) in the sense of wise advice for a good and happy life, was written about by Ibn Ḥazm in two well-known books, *Ṭawq al-ḥamāma* ('The dove's neck ring') and *Mudāwāt an-nufūs* ('Cures for souls'). The following article, however, is not concerned with his views on ethics in that sense, but with his answers to fundamental questions of modern philosophical ethics: the meanings of ethical concepts, the sources of our knowledge of them and of values in practice, the theory of moral motivation. In the religious tradition of medieval Islam, to which Ibn Ḥazm for all his individuality belonged, these questions were not marked off as a separate field of knowledge but fell somewhere between theology and law. More precisely, theology provided the framework of doctrines from which the principles of ethics could be derived, and these principles were applied by jurists in working out Islamic law.

Accordingly, we find Ibn Ḥazm's treatment of philosophical ethics mainly in his major work on theology, the *Fiṣal*, and his major work on jurisprudence, the *Iḥkām*. Both these works were written in the later years of his life, when his theological and legal position as a Zahirite was settled, and together with other works of the same period they supply a unified theory of ethics. His last work, *Mudāwāt an-nufūs*, although of a different literary genre, also throws light on this theory and is consistent with it. All these writings, then, will be used to reconstruct his ethics. But *Ṭawq al-ḥamāma* will not generally be used, because it is a work of Ibn Ḥazm's youth, completed no doubt after he had taken up religious studies in earnest but before he had adopted Zahirism.[1] The dividing line has to be put around A.D. 1027–9, when Ibn Ḥazm was studying in the Great Mosque of Córdoba under the Zahirite Abu l-Khiyār of Santarén. By that time he had already quit politics as his main activity and gone through a few years of religious studies, first as a Shafiʿite, then as a Zahirite. From

[1] On the earlier life of Ibn Ḥazm see especially the introduction of E. García Gómez to *El Collar de la paloma* (Madrid, 1952): also the introductions of Asín and Tomiche to their works cited in notes 2 and 3.

then on he devoted his intellectual and literary life to working out the theory of Islam in its Zahirite form and combating its enemies, and it is with this phase of his thought that we shall be concerned.

In the following systematic account I shall rely on the eminent studies of Goldziher, Asín Palácios, Cruz Hernández, and Arnaldez[2] for the general lines of Ibn Ḥazm's thought, and use the texts of his own works as evidence on his ethical philosophy.[3]

2

In showing the respective rôles of reason and revelation in ethical knowledge according to Ibn Ḥazm we have to start with reason, because in certain directions he regards it as prior to revelation. ('Reason' or 'intellect', *ʿaql*, is used here in a broad sense to include all natural channels of knowledge.) He is neither a fideist nor a mystic, and firmly upholds reason as the starting point of knowledge in three directions relevant to our subject: (i) in justifying revelation itself, and (ii)–(iii) in supplying us with two kinds of primary knowledge related to value – lexical and psychological – though not supplying directly any knowledge of particular ethical values, as will be shown.

(i) The first sources of all human knowledge are the soundly used senses and the intuitions of reason, combined with a correct understanding of a language. From these sources we can gain extensive further knowledge by the use of reasoning in its proper place. The most important knowledge attained by these rational methods is the preambles of revelation. These include certain provable truths about God, such as His existence, unity and eternity, His creation of the world, and the authenticity of the Qurʾān as the Word of God or (what amounts to the same thing) the genuineness of Muḥammad's prophethood (*Iḥkām*, 1:28). In spite of his emphasis on

[2] Ignaz Goldziher, *Die Ẓâhiriten, ihr Lehrsystem und ihre Geschichte* (Leipzig, 1884), pp. 116–69. Miguel Asín Palacios, *Abenházam de Cordoba y su historia critica de las ideas religiosas*, 5 vols. (Madrid: Revista de Archivos, 1927–32), vol. 1. Miguel Cruz Hernández, *Historia de la filosofia espanola: Filosofia hispano-musulmana*, 2 vols. (Madrid, 1957), vol. 1, chs. 5–6. R. Arnaldez, *Grammaire et théologie chez Ibn Ḥazm* (Paris, 1956); idem, s.v. 'Ibn Ḥazm', in *The Encyclopaedia of Islam*, new ed. (Leiden and London, 1960–).

[3] Works of Ibn Ḥazm referred to, in approximate chronological order, and editions used: *Ṭawq al-ḥamāma*, ed. and French trans. Léon Bercher as *Le Collier du pigeon: ou de l'amour et des amants* (Algiers, 1949). *Kitāb al Fiṣal fi l-milal wa l-ahwāʾ wa n-niḥal*, with Shahrastānī, *Kitāb al-Milal wa n-niḥal* in margin, 5 vols. (Cairo, 1308–21 h./1899–1903); re-edition, 5 vols. in 2 (Baghdad, 1960?); the Spanish translation of Asín in *Abenházam*, vols. 2–5, is almost complete and gives page references to the Cairo edition. *Kitāb al-ihkām fi usūl al-aḥkām*, ed. A. M. Shakir, 8 parts in 2 vols. (Cairo, 1346–7 h./1927–8). *Mulakhkhaṣ Ibṭal al-qiyās wa l-istiḥsān wa t-taqlīd wa t-taʿlīl*, ed. S. al-Afghani (Damascus, 1960); used in preference to the extracts from the complete *Ibṭāl* in Goldziher, *Ẓâhiriten*, pp. 207–22, because the *Mulakhkhaṣ* covers the main ideas more widely than the extracts, and omits little of importance. *Kitab al-Maḥaliā*, 11 vols. (Cairo, 1929–34). *Mudāwāt an-nufūs*, ed. and French trans. N. Tomiche as *Épître morale* (*Kitāb al-Aḥlāq wa s-siyar*) (Beirut, 1961); the Arabic title is a matter of opinion.

revelation as the sole source of normative ethical knowledge, Ibn Ḥazm, like Aquinas and many other theologians, is well aware that to make revelation the first source of all religious knowledge is self-defeating, because it leaves nothing but a circular argument on which to base the authenticity of revelation itself. He says this very clearly in a context where he is stating that we must, of course, pay attention to whatever the Qurʾān says confirming the conclusions of the natural sources.

> We are obliged to understand the Qurʾān and accept its contents. Among these, we find it drawing attention to the soundness of the means by which we arrive at knowledge of things as they are: the faculties of intellect and the senses. But I do not mean by this that we can verify by the Qurʾān anything whose truth we had doubted by the comprehension of our intellect and senses. If we did that we should be refuting realities and proceeding on a circular demonstration, by which nothing at all can be confirmed. For suppose we are challenged and asked, 'How do you know that the Qurʾān is genuine?', we can answer only on the basis of true premises attested by intellect and the senses. Then if we are asked, 'How do you know the soundness of intellect and the senses, which affirm those premises?' and we reply 'By the Qurʾān', this is a fallacious proof that refutes realities. Rather we say: 'The Qurʾān draws the attention of ignorant and heedless people and puts an end to the contentions of the stubborn' (*Iḥkām*, 1:66).

(ii) The primary terms of value, such as 'good', 'evil' and 'obligatory' are understood in the same way as we understand the rest of our vocabulary, in any language. A language was given to men by God at the time of their creation, together with the natural endowments of intelligence enabling them to speak, understand and expand language. The Qurʾān and preceding scriptures do not provide us with definitions of the primary terms of value; they simply use them, on the assumption that they have definite 'correct' meanings which are already understood.[4]

Thus, there is a concept of the personal good, in the sense of what is advantageous (*ṣāliḥ*) or a benefit (*fāʾida*) for the subject, what truly satisfies him. We shall come back to this concept shortly.

Then there is the concept of the obligatory (*wājib*), which is taken to mean whatever is commanded by the supreme Commander, who has the power to impose sanctions for disobedience. Since the concept of *wājib* is central in Ibn Ḥazm's theory, it is important to give evidence for his use of it. He does not give a separate definition of it in his glossary of terms, *Iḥkām*, 1:35–52. The nearest approach is his definition of *farḍ*, 'duty': 'that for which the omitter deserves to be blamed and called disobedient to God, the Exalted, and it is

[4] Arnaldez, *Grammaire et théologie*, and Ibn Ḥazm, *Iḥkām*, 1, 29–35.

[synonymous with] *wājib* ["obligatory"], *lāzim* ["necessary"] and *ḥatm* ["imposition"]' (*Iḥkām*, 1:43). The presence of 'deserves' (*istaḥaqqa*) here creates a problem since it imparts an objective quality to the definition of *farḍ* and its synonyms, which is alien to the rest of Ibn Ḥazm's theory. Indeed, the first phrase of the formula (*mā istaḥaqqa tārikuhu l-lawma*) is taken straight from the Muʿtazilite definition of *wājib*.[5] We can obtain a more accurate understanding of the meaning of *wājib* in Ibn Ḥazm from his many refutations of rationalist objectivism in ethics, which will be discussed later: but here is one example to confirm our understanding of *wājib*. In *Fiṣal* Ibn Ḥazm argues against the theory that we can know by reason our obligations of gratitude to other human beings, and he concludes by saying, 'Gratitude is obligatory only towards those persons to whom God Himself has declared it obligatory for us to show ourselves grateful' (3:109; cf. *Iḥkām*, 1:60). But, apart from any particular quotations, the entire ethical and legal theory of Ibn Ḥazm, like those of all the more or less 'traditionalist' thinkers – Shāfiʿī, Ibn Ḥanbal, Ashʿarī, etc. – is based on the assumption that obligation is intelligible only in terms of the commands of revelation.

Similarly, 'evil' (*qabīḥ*) is used as equivalent to what is forbidden or disapproved by revelation, without any objective essence, and unknowable to unaided human reason (*Fiṣal*, 3:101–15). 'Virtue' (*faḍīla*) means obedience to God, and more particularly to the general injunctions to upright living (*Iḥkām*, 1:5; *Mudāwāt*, §§16, 45, etc.), as contrasted with fulfilment of the specific obligations of the *sharīʿa*.

If we are to avoid hopeless confusion about the functions of reason and revelation in Ibn Ḥazm's ethics, it is essential to understand clearly the sharp contrast implicit in his thought between our knowledge of the *meanings* of value terms, which is given to use by our intellectual understanding of language, prior to revelation (although confirmed by it), and our knowledge of the specific *contents* of ethical value, such as virtues and obligations, which is given to us only through revelation, with the supplementary aid of intellect for interpretation in strictly limited ways. To test and illustrate the function of intellect, we may examine briefly a sentence about obligation, which looks like the concept most dependent on revelation.

> It belongs to the intellect only [1] to understand the commands of God the Exalted and [to understand] the obligation [or necessity] (*wujūb*) of avoiding transgression in cases where eternal punishment is to be feared, [followed by two other kinds of rational knowledge] (*Iḥkām*, 1:29).

Here *wujūb* is ambiguous, but on either alternative it is possible to show how it is understood by the intellect. (*a*) If it means 'obligation', we know the

[5] George F. Hourani, *Islamic rationalism: the ethics of ʿAbd al-Jabbār* (Oxford, 1971), p. 39.

obligation of avoiding transgression, etc., analytically, because the later words 'avoiding transgression...to be feared' are part of the definition of *wujūb* in this sense. (*b*) If *wujūb* means 'necessity', as it sometimes does in Arabic, we may rule out logical necessity or any kind of force, since it is obvious that men do not necessarily avoid transgression in these senses. What is left is 'prudential necessity', i.e. the necessity that follows from an agent's rational estimate of his own good (*ṭāʾila*). Now the 'necessity', in this sense, of avoiding punishable transgression is known partly[6] by intellect, according to Ibn Ḥazm, because men know prior to revelation that avoidable pain, such as hellfire, not leading to any further satisfaction, is disadvantageous (*Iḥkam*, 1:28–9). That will now be shown from the general psychology of desires outlined in *Mudāwāt an-nufūs*.

(iii) We can also know independently of revelation some general facts of human psychology which are relevant to our choices of goals. That the personal good is what satisfies a man over the long term is true by definition, as mentioned; but that everyone strives for such satisfaction (conceived in the vaguest terms) is an empirically known fact. In *Mudāwāt* Ibn Ḥazm induces the negative facet of this truth from his lifelong observation of human efforts: that all men aim at freedom from care, *qillat al-hamm*, the *ataraxia* of ancient Greek philosophers.

> I looked for a goal that all people alike approve of and seek, and I found only one, repulsion of care. And on reflection I realized that all alike not only approve of it and seek it; I saw that, in spite of the variety of their desires and pursuits and the differences in their concerns and objectives, they make not the slightest move except in the hope of repelling care, and they speak not a word except with the intention of removing it from their souls (*Mudāwāt*, § 5).

He describes this discovery as 'exalted knowledge', 'a wonderful secret' and 'a great treasure', with which God has illuminated his mind (§ 6), but with no suggestion that he has acquired it from the study of scripture. This is knowledge gained by experience and reflection, as the whole passage shows (§§ 5–7). Perhaps this viewpoint classes Ibn Ḥazm's formal ethics as egoistic hedonism, but as we shall see that name is inadequate as a description of its inner spirit and contents.

He then goes on to tell how he looked for the best means to freedom from care, and how he found all activities defective for this purpose except one: working for salvation in the next life (§ 8). Here too he uses his experience, but also his religious knowledge derived from scripture, concerning the afterlife; so at this point his thought goes beyond reason.

6 'Partly', because revelation alone gives knowledge of the afterlife and its specific sanctions.

3

After these three starting points in rational knowledge, all further religious knowledge, in theology, ethics and law, is derived mainly or partly from divinely inspired sources. These sources for Ibn Ḥazm are the Qurʾān above all, but also the Traditions of the Prophet and his Companions and the *ijmāʿ* (consensus) of these Companions. His Zahirism consists of two major elements: (1) strict literal interpretation of these sources, (2) refusal to extend the message of the sources by dependent rational procedures such as analogy. Yet both in the theoretical formulation and in the application of his Zahirite principles there are elements of reason at every step, which he does not deny. For instance, the principle of literal interpretation is based partly on explicit statements of the Qurʾān, such as the notable verses iii, 3–5, forbidding allegorical interpretation (*taʾwīl*) as a mischievous activity, partly on the simple and direct attitudes of Muḥammad and his Companions, but partly also on a comprehensive theory of human language and its purposes, which has been expounded by Arnaldez in his massive study[7] and need not be gone over here. So, too, in the detailed understanding of the meaning of the scriptural texts one must apply the rules of ordinary language in the context of the speech of Mecca and Madīna in the early seventh century, with the help of the substantial philological knowledge of scholars of Arabic. Thus in writing above that further religious knowledge is derived 'mainly or partly' from revelation, I meant to state precisely that from this point on revealed texts are always an indispensable element in that knowledge, but also that in spite of Ibn Ḥazm's Zahirism elements of reason are present at all levels, within strict limits.

Before we proceed to the distinctive Zahirite features of his ethical theory, we have first to explain a range of ethical doctrine which he shares, more or less, with traditionalist jurisprudence and theology of the regular Sunnite schools, but not with Muʿtazilite rationalism or with Muslim philosophy.

4

Ibn Ḥazm's ethics, like that of most other medieval theologians, is oriented primarily towards the good of the individual, conceived in terms of his long-range happiness. As was stated above, the good for man is defined in these terms, and its most general content, freedom from care, is known from experience to be in fact the aim of everyone. But these two pieces of general

[7] *Grammaire et théologie.*

knowledge do not take us very far in making practical decisions, in ordering our lives. The more urgent questions are, (i) what kind of life constitutes a state of freedom from care? and (ii) what are the means to attain such a life?

(i) From the Qurʾān, which is known to be the Word of God, we learn that there is an eternal afterlife, in which man may either enjoy the Reward of permanent happiness and complete freedom from care in paradise or suffer permanent torment in hell. This is the first overwhelming fact about his future prospects that man learns from revelation. The afterlife must then be his foremost concern, since in comparison with it the present life is insignificant in length and intensity. Its ends in themselves are the same in their nature but transitory, and must be subordinated to any relation they may have as means to attaining eternal felicity and avoiding eternal misery.

(ii) The second overwhelming fact revealed by the Qurʾān is that every individual's salvation or damnation to the two alternative kinds of afterlife is dependent on his conduct in this present life, as judged by God on the Day of Judgement. Therefore man must learn what are the features of conduct that will be rewarded or punished by that Judgement, and his entire present life must be oriented towards fulfilling the rewardable conduct as a means to salvation as described. It is a sign of stupidity and irrationality to prefer the mixed goods of this short life, just because they are immediate, to the pure goods of eternal life. It is like the behaviour of a man who would prefer a day's walk through a countryside of pleasant meadows, with some hazards, in order to arrive at a squalid cottage and live there a hundred years, to a day's walk with some sorrows, at the end of which he would arrive at a splendid palace with servants and gardens, trees and streams, and live there a hundred years (*Iḥkām*, 1:5–6).

But the Qurʾān does not merely inform man vaguely that there is a causal relation between his conduct and his fate in the next life. It also tells him what kinds of conduct will receive Reward and Punishment. In general, the whole of rewardable conduct comes under the heading of obedience to God's commands and prohibitions. This rule is emphasized as the guiding line for all human virtue and obligation, the means to salvation (*Iḥkām*, 1:7 and 29; *Mudāwāt*, chap. 2). But before we go into the details of obedience, three points deserve to be noticed briefly at this general level.

(*a*) While scripture tells us that in fact God rewards obedience and punishes disobedience, Ibn Ḥazm takes pains to declare in many ways that there are no rational limits to God's judgement in this matter. He judges as He pleases, and whatever He judges is just (*Fiṣal*, 3:98 and 105). Human intellect cannot set rules for God's decisions, as the Muʿtazilites suppose, 'who by their intellects "correct" for their Creator, Mighty and Glorious, judgements which their Lord does not make in the way they assert' (*Iḥkām*, 1:28). Indeed, Abū Hāshim, one of the former heads of the Muʿtazilites (d. 932), was shameless enough to use expressions like 'God ought to do so and so'. Ibn Ḥazm asks: then who obliges Him? – since, on his view (although not on Abū Hāshim's), every obligation implies the existence of an obliger (*mūjib*), otherwise there would be an effect without an agent. Only two answers are possible: that the obliger is human, which is impious, or that God obliges Himself. In the latter case, either He can change any obligation and is completely free, as we claim, or else He has committed an eternal act of obliging, which sets up a coeternal being – impious in the direction of fatalism (*Fiṣal*, 3:102–3).

In accordance with this doctrine of God's unrestricted freedom and unquestionable justice, Ibn Ḥazm draws out some of the alternative moral orders that He might have set up for the world. He could have punished the angels, the prophets and believers everlastingly in the Fire, and rewarded the devil and unbelievers everlastingly in heaven (*Fiṣal*, 3:105). He could have imposed on man obligations impossible to fulfil, then punished him for failing to fulfil them; that this is evil is not known by reason, since many theologians deny that they know it thus; it is evil only because it is denied by God in revelation (*Fiṣal*, 3:107). God could justly punish a man for something that He has helped him to do; the denial of this by the Muʿtazilites is sheer anthropomorphism, judging God's justice by what natural reason judges just for man (*Fiṣal*, 3:97).

> And if God the Exalted had informed us that He would punish us for the acts of others...or for our own obedience, all that would have been right and just, and we should have been obliged to accept it (*Fiṣal*, 3:92).

Finally, it is not unimaginable, and quite possible, that God would have commanded us to be unbelievers, to deny Him, to worship idols and commit wrong; however, He has told us that He does not do so in fact (*Iḥkām*, 1:69–70). But God can do anything He wants!

(*b*) As early as *The dove's neck ring* (*Ṭawq*), Ibn Ḥazm had become convinced that the emotional soul (*nafs*) of man left to itself naturally counsels evil (*Ṭawq* 316), and without the help of revelation and reason he inevitably yields to persistent sensual temptations (*Ṭawq*, 318–20, 328, 376). This conviction he gained not only from the Qurʾān (xii, 53/Cairo, Joseph's famous comment on his temptation by the governor's wife and his resistance only with the aid of God), but also from his own experience as narrated in the *Ring*. There is no reason to believe that he changed his belief on this question in his later life. On the contrary, the more deeply we study the *Ring* the more clearly we find in it the elements of personal struggle and sorrow which led its young author into the refuge of a religion that would give him security and tranquillity; and this impression is confirmed by his other personal book, the *Mudāwāt*, as well as by what we know of the rest of his troubled life and passionate character. Even his choice of the Zahirite form of Islam, which may seem odd in such a brilliant and broadly educated man, may be partly explained by his desire for the security of firm textual commands and prohibitions, free from the variety of interpretations and extensions open to the other traditional schools.

(*c*) Concerning the relation between predestination and responsibility, Ibn Ḥazm holds as against the Muʿtazilites that a man cannot choose to be either obedient or disobedient to the divine commands entirely by his own capacity (*istiṭāʿa*) at the time of action; his choice depends on the favour or disfavour of God, who gives or withholds from him the power to act at the moment of action. Thus at the decisive point Ibn Ḥazm is a predestinarian. Yet he thinks at the same time that man is responsible and justly burdened with obligations to obey commands and prohibitions, so long as he has capacity (*istiṭāʿa*) in another sense, that prior to the action he has 'soundness of his limbs and the removal of obstacles', i.e. if he is free from external impediments (*Fiṣal*, 3:32).

Confirmation of his view is found in several other passages, of which the following is perhaps the clearest. He starts from the Muʿtazilite use of Qurʾān, iv, 81, to support their doctrine of human free will: 'If anything good happens to you, it comes from God, but if anything evil happens to you, it is from yourself.' The first half of this quotation does not serve their purpose, and Ibn Ḥazm accepts it willingly. With regard to evil, he draws attention to the preceding verse, iv, 80, 'Say to them that everything comes from God', and lays it down that the meaning of 81 must be consistent with this general principle. Then he explains the words on evil thus:

> We deserve punishment for the moral evil that appears to proceed from us as its subject, by which we are guilty of rebellion against God, according to the decrees of His providence, which is justice and truth itself
>
> (*Fiṣal*, 3:92–4: quotation from 94; cf. also 3:51, 104).

This explanation brings together the same elements of responsibility and predestination as were asserted in the previous statement of his doctrine. Whether he succeeds in harmonizing these two elements is open to question, but it is not my concern to discuss his position critically. The fact that concerns us in a historical account is that in all ethical contexts he regards man as responsible for his own actions and liable to Reward and Punishment accordingly. In any case, for Ibn Ḥazm God's disposition of the moral order is just, for reasons given under (*a*) above.

5

Since obedience to God's commands leads to salvation, and revelation specifies what obedience consists of, the most important practical tasks for man are to find out what revelation prescribes and then to do it faithfully at all times and in all circumstances. At this point, Ibn Ḥazm is not altogether consistent in his terminology. Sometimes he speaks of 'the virtues' (*faḍāʾil*, sing. *faḍīla*), as synonymous with all acts of obedience (*ṭāʿāt*), and the vices as synonymous with all acts of disobedience (*Mudāwāt*, §§16, 185; *Ṭawq*, 404). In other instances he divides the obligatory (*wājib*, coextensive with acts of obedience) into two classes, *faḍīla* and *sharīʿa* (*Mudāwāt*, §45). This division corresponds with the division of subject matter in his two books, *Mudāwāt* and *Iḥkām*. In *Mudāwāt* he is treating the general virtues – generosity, continence, courage, justice, etc., where no specific act is commanded by scripture, but rather to behave in a certain spirit, and he speaks here about virtue and virtues. *Iḥkām* is a treatise on jurisprudence, in which he concentrates on the justifications for the specific obligations of the *sharīʿa*, such as the rules for prayer and other matters prescribed by religious legislation. So it will be more convenient to take *faḍīla* and 'virtue' in the more restricted sense, in order to distinguish what is said about each of the two types of obligation.

Ibn Ḥazm expresses many value judgements on the virtues and vices in his two books of normative ethics, *Ṭawq* and *Mudāwāt*. A close study of what he has to say would be of interest in other contexts – biographical or social-historical – but would be out of place in the present outline of his ethics as a theoretical construction. Only a few general observations may be offered, for the sake of giving some body to this construction. In *Mudāwāt* (§§89–92) he defines and discusses four virtues, three of which are the same as those chosen by Plato in his *Republic*: courage, continence and justice, although his definitions differ from Plato's. For Plato's 'wisdom' he substitutes 'generosity' (*jūd*), a virtue highly esteemed among the Arabs. But wisdom, intelligence and knowledge receive plenty of commendation throughout the book, in fact it *is* primarily a book of practical wisdom.[8] In another place (§26) he says that all the virtues are summed up in two Traditions of the Prophet, his saying 'Do not be angry' and his command to desire for others what we desire for ourselves. In *Ṭawq* he praises fidelity above all other virtues of love and friendship (2, 198–200, 208–10) and thinks this has been his own particular

[8] Cruz, *Filosofia hispano-musulmana*, I, 282, is mistaken in including wisdom among the four cardinal virtues listed by Ibn Ḥazm, and in saying that the Greek *sōphrosunē* is specified by him as 'generosity'. The two latter are listed separately, as *ʿiffa* and *jūd* respectively, and wisdom is not mentioned in §§89–92.

merit (296). He regards lying as the greatest vice (140–4). In *Mudāwāt* (§§96–114) he discusses his own faults and merits at length and frankly; his faults are grouped around excesive pride, and include his passion for triumphing in argument and proneness to anger (§97), both of which brought him into much trouble in his relations with other scholars.

'The sum of the virtues and avoidance of vices is obedience to God, Mighty and Glorious' (*Iḥkām*, 1:5). Even in *Mudāwāt*, a book of reflective wisdom drawn from Ibn Ḥazm's own experience, he makes it clear that the supreme end is to be attained only by such obedience. In the heading of chapter 2, which he calls 'an important chapter', he asserts that the whole of intelligence and tranquillity consists of 'casting aside attention to the words of men and paying attention [only] to the words of the Creator, Mighty and Glorious', i.e. to revelation (before §13). And although the spirit and style of this book make it inappropriate to quote scriptural texts at every turn, as he does in his Zahirite legal works, there is no inconsistency between the virtues emphasized in it and those emphasized in the Qurʾān, which was after all the piece of literature that had been most deeply formative of his mind during at least thirty years before the *Mudāwāt*, and perhaps also in his early childhood. We should also recall that the supreme goal of man is stated in this book to be freedom from care, and that this is to be attained mainly in the next life and worked for as the principal activity of this life (§4); and it is implicit in these ends and means that the specific means is practice of the religious virtues. Thus, in spite of first impressions, there is no sense in which *Mudāwāt* can be described as a 'secular' book, even to the extent that *Ṭawq* can be. At the same time, Ibn Ḥazm points out in passing that the quest for salvation also brings joy in this life, through 'freedom from care for what other people are concerned about, and respect from friend and enemy' (§4).

While the emphasis in the conception of virtue is on obedience to revelation, Ibn Ḥazm leaves a place for philosophy too in the work of cultivating virtue. In *Fiṣal* he writes that

> in reality the meaning and result of philosophy and the aim intended in studying it are nothing other than the correction of the soul, achieved both by practicing the virtues and good conduct in this life, which leads to salvation in the other life, and by good social organization, domestic and political. Now this and nothing else is also the aim of the religious law (*sharīʿa*).

This is admitted by all parties – philosophers and lawyers (1:94).

Questions arise as to what he means here by philosophy, and how a theologian with such an insistence on scripture as the only authoritative source of values could find any use in philosophy, which was by definition regarded as a secular science. The answer to the question on meaning is, I believe, to be learned from the quotation, where he mentions the three *practical* branches of philosophy according to the Aristotelian tradition: personal ethics, household or family management (the original 'economics'), and politics. We find them distinguished and treated as normative knowledge or wisdom in books of 'ethics' such as *Tahdhīb al-akhlāq* of Miskawayh (*d. c.* 1030), where the original rationalistic theories of Greek ethical philosophy are in the background and the interest is rather in advice for the virtuous life; yet such books were still classed as 'philosophy'. We can now answer the question on the use of such philosophy. Ibn Ḥazm's own final book *Mudāwāt an-nufūs* almost fits into this type, and it is not hard to reconcile this sort of 'philosophy' with his theory of the virtues. For these are viewed, as we have seen, as the more general obligations, not specified precisely by *sharīᶜa* laws; therefore there is legitimate scope for human wisdom to supply guidance on the details, using all the resources of pertinent rational sciences.

> The definition of reason (*ᶜaql*) is practice of obedience and the virtues, and this definition implies avoidance of disobedience and the vices (*Mudāwāt*, §185).

For Ibn Ḥazm, reason when properly used is not opposed to revelation, it is simply put at its service in any useful direction.

It should further be noticed that all his advice on virtue conceives it as a means to the good of the individual. There is no idea of virtuous activity as an end in itself, done for its own sake and constituting its own reward. And, although our fulfilment of virtues and other obligations may contribute in fact to the good of society, that is not their essence: it is simply obedience to the divine will, as expressed in revelation. That is not to say that Ibn Ḥazm is not concerned with the good of the *umma*, the earthly community of Muslims; indeed his own efforts in writing books to guide them show that he is. But his concern is now with the salvation of each individual member of the *umma*. In his youth he had engaged passionately and often dangerously in politics, hoping to help the restoration of a stable Umayyad dynasty such as had created the conditions for a wholesome Muslim community in Spain for so long in the past. But, like Ibn Khaldūn in North Africa three centuries later, he had given up political struggles as useless in the conditions of his environment, and directed most of his later life to intellectual efforts to help individual Muslims find their own way to the true end of life.[9] There is a maxim in *Mudāwāt* (§45) which, although not perfectly apposite, is worth

[9] *Fiṣal*, IV, 87–111 and 163–71, goes over the classical questions on the caliphate (rights of succession, etc.), but with little originality and few remarks about the purpose of the institution in serving the *umma*.

quoting because it illustrates a general trend in his thought: 'Beware of pleasing others by actions which harm your own soul, and which are not made obligatory for you by the *sharīʿa* or virtue.' The imperfection in this quotation is that it probably refers to antisocial actions demanded by others for selfish ends. It therefore does not display a case of 'personal' virtue being preferred before 'social' virtue by Ibn Ḥazm – indeed, such a case may be hard to find in his writings, since he has no tendency to see a conflict between these two kinds of virtue or to make a problem out of it. Still, the quotation shows well enough where he places the priority in true human interests.

While *Mudāwāt* is about the general virtues, the more specific obligations of the *sharīʿa* are dealt with in *Iḥkām* in a theoretical way, in *Kitāb al-Muḥallā* in detail, and in other religious works in various controversial contexts. It should be understood that *Iḥkām* is not confined to the *sharīʿa* obligations but spans 'the sources of [ethical] judgements in religion' (*uṣūl al-aḥkām fi d-diyāna*) (1:8). But here I shall draw upon it only for some remarks on the *sharīʿa*, since the other kind of obligations (virtue) has already been discussed. In the sphere of *sharīʿa* it is even clearer that the obligations are derived from a positive divine Law exclusively. God, addressing man through the Prophet in the Qurʾān and the Traditions, imposed divine Laws (*sharāʾiʿ*) on man for his salvation and obliged us to follow them (*Iḥkām*, 1:9–10).

> Whatever we have said, we have not said at random. We have not uttered a word on all this subject that is not drawn from what God the Exalted has said, as a witness to its truth, and what the intellect has distinguished (*mayyazahu l-ʿaql*), understanding its reality, praise to God, Lord of the worlds (*Iḥkām*, 1:6).[10]

Even while asserting emphatically the revealed source of all ethical judgements, Ibn Ḥazm does not neglect to mention the rôle of reason in 'distinguishing', i.e. understanding accurately the meaning of the sacred text. This is a derivative but important rôle. For Ibn Ḥazm it consists above all of understanding the text in a literal sense wherever possible, and stopping there. This is where as a Zahirite he parts company with the majority of Sunnite traditionalists in medieval Islam. His Zahirite doctrines in law and theology have been sufficiently explained in the books of Goldziher and Arnaldez in particular (see note 2), and it will be unnecessary to elaborate them here. But a little more will be said on them in the next section, in explaining what it is that Ibn Ḥazm wants to deny, and why.

[10] Cf. *Iḥkām*, 1, 10 and *Mulakhkhaṣ*, 5: the whole of religion is drawn from revelation.

6

The last section has expounded Ibn Ḥazm's theory of obligation in positive terms, showing its entire dependence in content on the will of God as revealed in scripture. In the present section we shall turn to his polemics against the false uses of reason in ethics and law. And we shall here divide reason into two kinds, which he attacks in different ways although holding basically the same objection against both. (i) 'Independent reason' is here defined as the attempt to arrive at value judgements without any source in revelation at all. (ii) 'Dependent reason' is defined as the attempt to extend the legal knowledge derived from revelation by illegitimate methods. I am using these two expressions as convenient stipulated names for two kinds of reason which he attacks, not for all possible uses of reason; for, as has been and will again be mentioned, Ibn Ḥazm allows certain uses of reason at vital points in his system.

(i) It has already been shown (in 4) that no limits can be set in terms of supposed 'objective' standards of value to the general moral order that God could have set up for the world. Now the same thing has to be shown with regard to the specific obligations of man (whether virtues or *sharīʿa* laws matters little in this context). But before we come to his refutations concerning particular obligations, some theoretical statements of his position will be useful. The general position is that there are no such characters as good or evil, obligatory, just or unjust 'in essence', but only as descriptions of what is commanded, approved, etc., by a judge; and that the only qualified judge is God, the Creator and Lord of the World (*Fiṣal*, 3:100–2): this is theistic subjectivism. Consequently, the human intellect does not have the power to attribute any such characters to things, people or acts independently of the Word of God. In *Iḥkām* there is a clear statement of the limits of the human mind in this sphere:

> The intellect only distinguishes between the qualities (*ṣifāt*) of existing things, and informs him who seeks its guidance of the facts concerning the properties (*ḥaqāʾiq kayfiyyāt*) of actual objects, and of the distinction from them of what is impossible. But whoever claims that the intellect makes lawful or forbids (*yuḥallilu aw yuḥarrimu*) or that the intellect provides obliging causes (*yūjiba ʿillalan mūjibatan*) for the existence of all acts – laws or others – manifested by God the Exalted Creator in this world, is in the same condition as he who denies the need for the intellect altogether
>
> (1:27; cf. *Fiṣal*, 1:98; 3:98).

Ibn Ḥazm is here drawing a distinction, accepted by many modern ethical philosophers, between 'descriptive facts' and 'values', although his theological explanation of the latter is not one that is acceptable to most of our Western contemporaries.

Such a statement as the one quoted above sounds dogmatic, but Ibn Ḥazm had found his reasons for reaching his conclusion in the failures, as he viewed them, of the Muᶜtazilites to justify the rules of morality and law by any rational arguments. His manner of disputing their claims is best shown by several examples, mostly from a few pages in *Fiṣal* (3:105–30) where he deals directly with this problem in its detailed aspect.

(*a*) Enmity between animals is not condemned as evil and wrong; yet it would be, if enmity as such were evil and wrong – it would be so wherever it existed. Thus enmity has these attributes not in itself but only when declared evil by God (105; cf. 128–30 on the injustices of animal life).

(*b*) The golden rule that it is always evil to do to others what you would not want them to do to you is disproved by many examples, such as the laws of marriage in Islam, by which it is permitted and good for a man to marry up to four women at a time, but not for a woman to marry more than one man at a time, in spite of the feelings of jealousy that arise in women's hearts as much as in men's (106).

(*c*) Likewise the laws of inheritance allot to males twice the shares of females, regardless of the wealth or poverty or earning capacity of individual heirs (107).

(*d*) The Muᶜtazilites claim that it is known by reason that ingratitude to benefactors is always evil and disapproved. 'We reply that God is the only real benefactor, since He has created us and every benefit we enjoy, so there is no rational obligation of gratitude to any human being. And there is no [human] benefactor except him whom God the Exalted has named as such, and gratitude to a benefactor is obligatory only after God the Exalted has made such gratitude obligatory; in that case it is obligatory and not otherwise' (107–8; quotation from 108). Another answer is given elsewhere: suppose a beneficiary faces a former benefactor in war (presumably religious war), is it his duty to try to kill him or not? The 'rule of reason' would have to deny it, but we know by *ijmāᶜ* that it is his duty (*Iḥkām*, 1:60). In another example on gratitude, a Muslim who enslaves non-Muslims and makes them work hard on menial tasks is within his rights so long as he provides for them in the minimum lawful ways; and if he then emancipates them it is for them to be grateful to him! But if another Muslim enslaves some Muslims, treats them well and gives them a good religious education, he does all this without any right, and if he abuses one of their women he is liable to death by stoning, regardless of any former benefits for which he would normally deserve gratitude (*Fiṣal*, 3:108–9).

(*e*) The obligations of obedience to parents are limited and assigned by divine Law, not by any natural reasons (107–9).

(*f*) If it is said 'Lying is always evil', we can point out cases where it is commanded by the Law: to conceal a fugitive and his possessions from an oppressive government, to mislead an enemy in war, to avoid hurting one's wife's feelings and causing her to withdraw her love. It is not that God can make lying good *against* reason; rather it is impossible for God's commands to be irrational, as the Muᶜtazilite 'principles of reason' seem to imply that they might be (109–10).

(*g*) When they claim that wrongdoing (*ẓulm*) is always evil, we ask them to define 'wrongdoing', and all they can do is to produce a list of types of acts such as killing, taking another's property, suicide, allowing one's wife to other men, etc. But in every case we can show them exceptions that are lawful, without any difference in the type of act as a mere physical event (110–11).

Other examples can be found easily, but these will be enough to illustrate Ibn Ḥazm's methods of argument against Muᶜtazilite rationalism in ethics. It will be apparent that the main method is to show that the ethical conclusions of their supposed reason are always overturned by some cases prescribed differently by revelation. Looking at these arguments from a detached position outside the religion and the period, we can readily point out that many of them beg a rather large question: if the laws of a religion conflict with the intuitions of ordinary morality, as they seem to do in some of the examples in (*b*), (*c*) and (d) at least, could that not be taken as evidence that these laws are not from a divine source? In face of this question, several positions can be taken. The dominant attitude of medieval Christendom was to seize upon the weaknesses of Islamic law eagerly as proofs of the falsity of the Muslim claim to a genuine revelation. Fortunately, the ferocious hostility of that era against Islam has almost disappeared, but it remains legitimate to raise the moral and religious questions involved in the international debate on world religions which is and must be increasingly a part of the intellectual life of our times. For convinced Muslims, however, the possible attitudes are more limited. In the classical world of Islam, the revelation given to Muḥammad was beyond question. It was a fixed starting point of argument, and the only flexibility on this side came from the various possibilities of interpreting the revealed obligations. And in disputes on this issue, traditionalists like Ibn Ḥazm and Ghazālī, who had only to follow scripture closely, were in a far stronger position than the Muᶜtazilites, who had to reconcile scripture with a rational system based on other considerations. Modern Muslim liberals, however, have been resuming essentially the same task as the Muᶜtazilites in a more favourable intellectual environment, and it is doubtful that they will meet today any opponent within Islam combining the education and confidence of an Ibn Ḥazm, and willing and able to use the literal interpretation of scripture to put an end to all opposing moral argument.

There is, however, another strand in Ibn Ḥazm's method of argument, more like an undercurrent, which is powerful but not fully brought to the surface. This is illustrated by our example (*f*) on lying. Although he refutes the Muʿtazilite generalization 'Lying is always evil' by flat assertions based on the Law of Islam, which is his 'official' method, the rational ethical reasons for the Law's commands become apparent in this case. For the generalization is too sweeping to be accepted by most ethical theories, and needs refinement. ʿAbd al-Jabbār (d. 1025) in his fully developed Muʿtazilite ethics ran into difficulties with regard to lying, because he was unwilling to make concessions. On other questions he was able to be more flexible by applying the theory of prima facie obligations, which allowed for conflicting ethical considerations and differing final judgements to fit different cases.[11] Yet in the end the ethical intuitionism of the Muʿtazilites did not carry conviction in most of classical Islam, perhaps because its elaborate set of ethical intuitions had no unifying principle, such as modern utilitarianism has, and at the same time appeared dogmatic and arbitrary. To the classical Muslim, the Qurʾān appealed as a surer basis for ethical judgements because of its divine authority; and no further unifying principle seemed necessary in the face of that outstanding source.

7

We can turn next to consider a more technical use of independent judgement which Ibn Ḥazm rejects: the use of legal judgement known as *istiḥsān* or *raʾy*. *Istiḥsān* is literally 'thinking good', and it was used as a judgement of equity where the *sharīʿa* gives no explicit guidance. This term was used more particularly by the Hanafite law school. *Raʾy* is 'opinion'; it had been used in the same sense in earlier times, but had dropped out of currency by Ibn Ḥazm's day. He says that these words, as well as *istinbāṭ*, 'discovery', have the same connotation: 'judgement according to what the judge thinks more advantageous (*aṣlaḥ*) in its consequences and in itself' (*Iḥkām*, 6:16). (This definition reminds us of the Malikite term *istiṣlaḥ*, 'thinking in the public interest', which Ibn Ḥazm does not attack directly – perhaps out of prudence, since the school of Mālik was dominant in Andalusia.)

He raises several objections to this practice in Islamic law, by whatever

[11] Hourani, *Islamic rationalism*, pp. 32–4, 76–81.

name it is called. Probably the most basic objection is that it does not even reach the level of rational judgement, but is nothing more than the result of following desires and fancies, without proofs (*Iḥkām*, 6:17; *Mulakhkhaṣ*, 5, 50–1, 56). And since different judges have different natures and desires, *istiḥsān* leads to disagreements about the law, which is a deficiency in religion (*Iḥkām*, 6:17; *Mulakhkhaṣ*, 5). Worse still, there is no way to resolve this kind of disagreement, for what difference is there in authority between what you approve and what someone else approves, or between what he approves and what you disapprove? What makes one such opinion closer to the truth than another? (*Iḥkām*, 6:21).

The supporters of *istiḥsān* and *raʾy* claim in their support the Tradition: 'Whatever the Muslims think good (*raʾāhu ḥasanan*) is good in the eyes of God.' This Tradition, he retorts, does not have a sound *isnād*. And even if it did, it would only support *ijmāʿ*, for it does not refer to some of the Muslims rather than others. When they disagree, their opinions are on the same level of authority and contradictory, so, according to their view, we should be commanded to do contradictory acts (*Iḥkām*, 1:18–19).

In short, Ibn Ḥazm condemns a view which looks to him like human subjectivism in ethics. 'What is true is true even if people condemn it, and what is false is false even if people approve of it' (*Iḥkām*, 1:17). But this judgement does not lead him back to the human objectivism of the rationalists, which we have seen him attacking just as strongly, but to the theory of revelation as the only valid source of value judgements. 'He who gives a decision by *raʾy* does so without knowledge. There is no knowledge in religion except from the Qurʾān and the Traditions' (*Mulakhkhaṣ*, 56). I have often named this position 'theistic subjectivism', because it makes values ultimately dependent on the will of God rather than on any facts in the natural order of the world. But it should be mentioned that from another point of view the position appears to a believer as objective: in the sense that, given revelation as the source of all ethical truth, he has before him something that he can know by a science (philology), namely the meaning of revelation. In other words, ethics is reduced to positive law, in which the proper object of study is texts. This is why Ibn Ḥazm can assign to reason an essential place in his ethical theory, while being antirationalist as against theories of ethical knowledge by natural reason independent of scripture.

8

A special problem of theodicy arises from Ibn Ḥazm's position that ethical decisions cannot be correctly made either by independent reason or any other form of independent judgement, but only by the guidance of revelation. What about people who have lived, live or will live beyond any knowledge of revelation? How are they able to make moral judgements, and how does God judge them? It will be seen that there are two questions here, but since they are closely interconnected it is possible to give a single account of Ibn Ḥazm's answers. These are somewhat complex, but not obscure.

It is fair to say that Ibn Ḥazm's first thought on any problem of this kind is that God can do what He wishes: thus He can leave men without any sound means of ethical judgement, and then He can punish them, without entitling us to call Him 'unjust' – for who is man, to pass judgements on God? The only questions that arise, then, concern what dispensations He has actually made, and the answers can be known only through scripture (*Iḥkām*, 1:54).

The problem had been posed by the Muʿtazilites with special reference to the state of mankind before the coming of Islam, since the people of antiquity were supposed to have been certainly beyond the reach of the true revelation. Ibn Ḥazm turns aside the force of this objection by asserting that men were never without a Law, on the basis of the Qurʾān's rhetorical question: 'Does man think he would be left to wander at random?' (lxxv, 36). Adam was a prophet and received commands and prohibitions. Therefore the intelligence of mankind as a whole never had an occasion or a need to make judgements on what was disapproved or permitted before the existence of a Law (*Iḥkām*, 1:58–9).

This particular form of the discussion, however, avoids the main issue; for there certainly have been, are and will be some people beyond the range of revelation through no fault of theirs, and Ibn Ḥazm admits this (*Iḥkām*, 1:60). Such people's judgements of value are comparable to those of children: they simply lack the means to know anything as prohibited or even permitted, for their intellects without revelation supply no valid guidance (*Iḥkām*, 1:59). Therefore they will not be held responsible and punished for what is not in their power, as the Qurʾān proclaims (ii, 286; etc.). On the other hand, those who have heard revelation but ignored or forgotten it will certainly be held responsible (*Iḥkām*, 1:60–5).

So far Ibn Ḥazm's answer seems 'reasonable', in the sense of agreeing with common conceptions of justice. But it would not be in character for him to stop here. In at least two places he reminds us that God not only can but sometimes does make inexplicable decrees. He has favoured the nations of Islam by sending them a prophet to summon them to the true religion, whereas Africans, Chinese and Europeans have heard only critics of Islam; thus He has given a better chance of paradise to some people than to others, without any difference in initial deserts. This is one of many examples that show the falsity of the Muᶜtazilite claim that God's actions always accord with our notions of justice (*Fiṣal*, 3:104). In the other passage he poses a borderline case and answers it in a way that seems shocking to a modern mind. He imagines a saintly man who seeks God and does everything good, but who lives in remote islands where he hears only distorted and malicious accounts of Muḥammad; and he dies doubting or denying his prophethood. 'Then is not his course to the Fire, eternal, everlasting, endless? If anyone doubts this he is an unbeliever and a polytheist, by the *ijmāᶜ* of the Community.' Then he imagines a Jew or a Christian who has killed Muslims and committed every sin; after that he becomes a Muslim and dies as such. 'Is he not among the people of paradise?' This too is a decision of *ijmāᶜ*, to doubt which is unbelief. The intellect has no way to work out these incalculable and unexpected value judgements; the only way to know them is from scripture (*Iḥkām*, 1:56). We may wish that Ibn Ḥazm had at least been more charitable to the saintly non-Muslim and counted him among those who had not had a chance to appreciate Islam; but he thought he had the backing of *ijmāᶜ* for his judgement, and it is rather typical of his combativeness to use such an argument. (Besides, the Muᶜtazilites had not survived in Andalusia and made an all too easy target.)

9

(ii) If Ibn Ḥazm fiercely opposes Muᶜtazilite and other uses of independent reason to make value judgements, he is no less strongly opposed to certain uses of reason by most of the law schools to make legal judgements, starting from texts of scripture. These 'dependent' uses which he finds illegitimate are *qiyās*, 'analogy' and *taᶜlīl*, 'giving reasons'; the latter is subordinate, in the sense that it supplies reasons for a *qiyās*. In this opposition he takes his stand with the Zahirites against all the other law schools. Since this is not a technical article on Islamic law, I shall only go over this question in its main lines, drawing upon *Iḥkām* and *Mulakhkhāṣ Ibṭāl al-qiyās*.

Qiyās is defined as 'judgement on matters on which there is no text, on a level with (*bi-mithli*) those on which there is a text or *ijmāᶜ*' (*Mulakhkhaṣ*, 5). Ibn Ḥazm has several objections to this practice, two of which are more fundamental than the rest, according to his way of thinking. The first is that there is no scriptural authority for *qiyās*. The Qurʾān does not prescribe it, and those Traditions which have been claimed to support it are historically unsound – he goes into the details in a few pages (*Mulakhkhaṣ*, 6–9). The second objection is that *qiyās* is not needed, because all of the Law is present in texts of scripture (*Iḥkām*, 1:10; 8:2–3; *Mulakhkhaṣ*, 5). This assertion may seem surprising, in view of the vast range of situations in human life that a Law claiming completeness needs to cover. However, there are several features in Ibn Ḥazm's theory of jurisprudence which make his position more tenable. (*a*) We can recall the distinction made in *Mudāwāt* (see 5 above) between the obligations of virtue and those of the *sharīʿa*, which limits greatly the range of situations that *sharīʿa* law has to cover. (*b*) He argues in detail for the Zahirite position that all expressions in scripture must be interpreted in their most general sense (*ʿumūm*) without further inquiry, unless a proof can be presented requiring us to restrict the meaning (*khuṣūṣ*) in a particular passage (*Iḥkām*, 3:97–160).[12] Obviously, this principle allows the texts to cover the maximum range of cases. (*c*) The Traditions tell us that whatever scripture is silent about is neither a duty nor forbidden, and the Qurʾān says that everything on earth was made for man: so everything is permitted except what is expressly commanded or forbidden. The partisans of *qiyās*, Ibn Ḥazm alleges, maintain that any act that scripture is silent about is not permitted, unless it is analogous to another act that is expressly permitted; but this ruling is at variance with the Traditions (*Mulakhkhaṣ*, 44–5). *We* might also point out that it needlessly restricts human freedom; but it is against Ibn Ḥazm's principles to make this value judgement out of his own head; for him, it must come from the Prophet if it is to carry any weight, and it comes in his saying *Dharūnī mā taraktukum*, 'Let me off [passing judgement] on what I have left for you [to do freely]' (*Mulakhkhaṣ*, 44).

After working out these two fundamental objections to *qiyās*, that it is unauthorized and unnecessary, Ibn Ḥazm might have been satisfied. But he was not one to give up before scoring all possible debating points. So he has to show that, even if *qiyās* were authorized and useful, the kinds of justification that have been given for particular cases are weak. He says they are two.

(*a*) Mere resemblance between a case mentioned in a text and the case under consideration. The trouble with this is that everything resembles everything else in some respect, so there would be no limits to what anyone could claim, and ethical judgements based on religious texts would become worthless (*Mulakhkhaṣ*, 5, 40).

(*b*) *Taʿlīl*, transfer of the divine reason for the decision in the textual case to another case where the application of the same reason seems fitting. (The stock example: wine is prohibited in scripture, because it is intoxicating – the *ʿilla* or 'reason'. Beer is not mentioned in scripture but is also intoxicating so the same *ʿilla* applies to it; therefore beer too must be prohibited, by the argument of *qiyās*.)

[12] See Goldziher, *Ẓâhiriten*, pp. 120–3; Arnaldez, *Grammaire et théologie*, p. 131.

Among the several objections of Ibn Ḥazm to *taʿlīl*, it will be convenient to begin by dismissing one which is based on a quibble about definitions of terms. In *Iḥkām* (8:99–101), he defines a few related terms, and he takes *ʿilla* to mean 'any quality that necessitates a thing by an immediate necessity, where the cause (*ʿilla*) is not separated at all from the effect (*maʿlūl*), as fire is the cause of burning, or snow is the cause of chilling, where one of the two does not occur without the second at all, and one is neither before nor after the other at all' (99). Taking *ʿilla* in this sense of 'efficient cause', Ibn Ḥazm then objects that if God had such causes for His Laws, He would be compelled to make them, which is inadmissible (102). Also, to avoid an infinite chain of such causes, God Himself must initially have taken decisions without any causes (98). Further, intoxication cannot be the *ʿilla* for the prohibition of wine, for in that case it would have caused its prohibition always, as fire causes heat (106). Now, if Ibn Ḥazm chose to restrict *ʿilla* to the meaning 'efficient cause' – which is in fact one common use in *kalām* – he was perfectly able to understand that the Sunnite jurists – Shafiʿites and others, not Muʿtazilites – used it as 'reason' in the purposive sense. Or he could have discussed the question in terms of *gharaḍ*, which he himself defines as that which an agent aims at by his act, and which follows after that act necessarily (100). So, in the case of alcoholic drinks, to say that the *gharaḍ* of the prohibition is avoidance of intoxication amounts to the same as saying that intoxication is the legal *ʿilla* for the prohibition of these drinks.

But in other passages Ibn Ḥazm forgets his special definition of *ʿilla* and criticizes *taʿlīl* in the ordinary legal sense on the grounds that really matter to him. The basic criticism is that there is no textual proof that there is an *ʿilla* for any of God's judgements (*Mulakhkhaṣ*, 5; *Iḥkām*, 8; 102). In other places he softens his stand a little by saying that in particular cases the Qurʾān may specify a *sabab* or 'cause' for a decision, e.g. theft is the *sabab* for cutting off the thief's hand. But such causes apply only to the case mentioned (*Iḥkām*, 8:77; 102). No pattern of *taʿlīl* can be found in the divine commands (*Mulakhkhaṣ*, 47–9). The practice of *taʿlīl* is a human operation which has led to arbitrary judgements, by which lawyers have abandoned the decision of the Qurʾān and turned what was approved into something disapproved (*Mulakhkhaṣ*, 10). He gives examples of inconsistency and arbitrariness in claims of *ʿilla* (*Iḥkām*, 8:114).

Thus all *qiyās* is arbitrary (*Iḥkām*, 8:42ff.). The Laws are either found in texts or they do not exist; there is no place for analogies (*Iḥkām*, 8:2–3). The Qurʾān says: 'today I have perfected for you your religion and completed for you my blessing' (v. 3). If the protagonists of *qiyās* assert that they are drawing out the particular laws (*furūʿ*) from the principles (*uṣūl*) given by scripture, Ibn Ḥazm denies that there is any such distinction; all the Laws are *uṣūl*, such as those prescribing prayer, pilgrimage, etc. (*Iḥkām*, 8:3). Here, presumably, he means by *uṣūl* 'sources' rather than 'principles', for in his theory we cannot group together the Laws of God under 'principles': that would only be another instance of human meddling, whereas each Law is valid in its own separate right because it is prescribed by God and for no other reason. Finally, *qiyās* has proved harmful because by its arbitrary nature it has led to many disagreements among lawyers (*Iḥkām*, 8:48–76).

Now that everything has been said against various uses of dependent reason, we may ask whether any kind is left as legitimate. The answer is: interpretation of scripture, in accordance with the laws of logic and the evidence of philology and the senses. The rules for interpretation are set by the Zahirite method, which is itself based on both scripture and reason.

10

It can never be a simple matter to classify such an individualist as Ibn Ḥazm among the schools of thought in classical Islam. But a few conclusions emerge from the preceding account about his place in the history of Islamic ethics. It will have become clear that the centre of his concern was to uphold the autonomy of God as the sole source of value judgements, against the rationalist objectivism of the Muʿtazilites. Reason cannot independently decide questions of right and wrong: this is his primary message. But reason is competent and necessary wherever description or explanation of facts is called for, and must be used actively in the service of obedience to revelation, the sole path to salvation. All this he holds in common with the main stream of Sunnite law and *kalām* that was opposed to Muʿtazilism. He is the most eminent forerunner of Ghazālī in his discriminating appreciation of human reason as a tool to be used actively within the framework of Islam as conceived in this main Sunnite tradition, although he differs from Ghazālī in many other respects.

In the religious milieu of his time, his Zahirism appeared as a sharp divergence from the methods of the other schools of law and theology. But within the total frame of his ethical system it looks to us more like a minor deviation from the main stream.

13

THE BASIS OF AUTHORITY OF CONSENSUS IN SUNNITE ISLAM

I

The primary doctrine of consensus (*ijmāʿ*) in Sunnite Islam is simply this: that the unanimous opinion of the Sunnite community in any generation on a religious matter constitutes an authority (*ḥujja*), and ought to be accepted by all Muslims in later times. The importance of the doctrine in theory and practice was recognized particularly in classical Islam, and has been much emphasized, and in some respects exaggerated, by modern orientalists since the studies of Snouck Hurgronje (see § 17).

This being so, it was natural that serious thought should be given to the fundamental question: 'What is the basis on which this authority of consensus rests?' Or, what facts about Islam and the world legitimize it? This is the question known in Arabic as *ḥujjīyat al-ijmāʿ*, 'the authoritativeness of consensus'. Much was written about it in classical Islam, as we shall see, and more variety has been added by modern Muslims. We should also expect to find some extensive historical study of the question by modern orientalists. But what has been written has generally been too brief, forming a part of a wider survey of Islamic consensus, or of Islamic law as a whole.[1] The question has usually been thought to have been sufficiently dealt with by quoting the famous Tradition: 'My Community does not agree on an error', which was the major basis accepted for a thousand years. The historical weight of this Tradition, however, should not obscure the existence of a considerable variety of opinion and expression in the past. The question seems to deserve treatment in a monograph which will, it is hoped, illuminate it by concentrating on it as a subject by itself and referring to other aspects of consensus only when they are seen as relevant.[2]

[1] References to standard works by modern Muslims and orientalists are given in §§ 14–15 and 17–18.

[2] The closest to monograph treatment known to me to date is found in an unpublished doctoral dissertation by M. Z. Madina, 'The classical doctrine of consensus in Islam' (Chicago, 1957). The first two chapters deal with the basis of consensus in the Qurʾān and Traditions, as worked

2

The subject will be treated primarily as intellectual history, showing the development of arguments in successive periods by leading thinkers. The social and religious background will be mentioned as helping to explain the tendencies of classical and modern ages. But the main purpose of this article is not to explore the practical and other causes which created a favourable or unfavourable climate for the doctrine of consensus, but to review the justifying *reasons* accepted (or doubted) by Muslim jurists. Obviously to any intellectual class these are of great weight as causes of conviction. They have a logic of their own which makes their relations with each other, sometimes over periods of centuries, often more significant than their relations with contemporary events and conditions. This is particularly true for classical Islamic thought, in an environment which changed comparatively little over a long time, and in which on the other hand there was a continuous intellectual tradition making it normal for later thinkers to be thoroughly familiar with what their predecessors of all periods had written.

Critical comments on the arguments used will also be made. These will be given from the standpoint of a non-Muslim trying to find out what would be logically valid on this subject, given the basic Islamic assumption that the true religion was revealed by God to Muḥammad in the Qurʾān. Thus no assumption is being made at all that consensus is an essential part of Islam, nor even that the Traditions of the Prophet are so, though they will be considered seriously. Still less is it assumed that every opinion of individual Muslim scholars like Shāfiʿī or Ghazālī reflects accurately the original religion of Islam, however widespread their influence may have been. This approach needs no apology. It seems to me the only way to contribute to a further understanding of Islam, by Muslims and non-Muslims alike. A historical account alone will not do this, for however much it may clarify what Muslims in the past have actually thought, and why, it will leave us with no estimate of the Islamic validity of all this thought.

No reference will be made to Shiʿite theories, except incidentally as influencing Sunnite thinking. It is felt that the latter can be studied as a fairly self-sufficient unit. 'Islam' and its adjectives will be used conventionally as referring to the Sunnite tradition.

out by Muslim scholars. I have found these chapters helpful as far as they go. ʿAli ʿAbd ar-Rāziq, *al-Ijmāʿfi sh-sharīʿa al-Islāmiyya* (Cairo, 1948), ch. 3, brings together many quotations, but offers little analysis.

3.1 CLASSICAL ISLAM

The practice of following consensus, as distinct from theories about it, goes back to pre-Islamic Arab society, in which the force of public approval generally backed any man's adherence to the *sunna*, the customary way of the ancestors. *Sunna* in this ancient sense means what Joseph Schacht called 'the living tradition', and as he pointed out it is closely connected with the idea of consensus.[3]

The Prophet imposed a sharp break with tradition, changing the concept of the community as well as many customary practices, and while he lived the practice of following consensus was largely superseded among Muslims by obedience to the judgements of the Qurʾān and Muḥammad. But there can be little doubt that a good deal of consultation went on before he made a decision, far more than is represented in the hero-worshipping biographies of Ibn Isḥāq and others. And in any case, whatever may have been his own practice, there is no reason to think he discouraged his Companions from making agreed decisions during his absence or after his death. Thus it was normal that the first Caliph was elected by some kind of informal consensus, and this long-remembered event set the tone for many later proceedings. Without the Prophet, the early Muslims naturally reverted to a sensible procedure of their ancestors, only changing the source of public authority from the tribe to the religious community or *umma*.

When the Umayyad dynasty came to power, they found support for their own legitimacy in the oath of loyalty, which supposedly bound the whole community to them and sanctioned their régime with unanimous public acclaim. Thus the state in the first century of Islam was not unfavourable to the idea of consensus of the Muslims, backing the ruling family. The early scholars from their side welcomed the idea of consensus in the sphere of law, as they were the mouthpieces and formulators of it, and during the first century they were able to develop it as a 'living tradition', unhampered as yet by the weight of prophetic Traditions or of past consensus. Above all, there was a compelling religious reason, soon felt by all thoughtful Muslims: the need for a continuing human authority that would bind the community together by enlarging the nucleus of practice and belief established by the Prophet, through new interpretations and extensions. This need was felt desperately after the disastrous schisms between Sunnites, Shīʿites and Kharijites over the question of the Caliphate. Since the Sunnites could not find

[3] *Origins of Muhammadan jurisprudence* (Oxford, 1950), p. 58; and in *Law in the Middle East*, ed. M. Khadduri and H. J. Liebesny, I (Washington, 1955), 30. I. Goldziher, *Muhammedanische Studien* (Halle, 1888), reprinted (Hildesheim, 1961), II, 11ff.

such an authority in an official priesthood, lacking in Islam, nor in the leadership principle sponsored by the Shīʿites, they naturally turned to the Community itself as the authority that would unite the faithful, all but the heretics, in a common body of law and doctrine.

These are some of the aspects of early Islam which made consensus apt to be accepted in practice. But there was no conscious formulation of a theory at this time. It is probable that neither the Qurʾān nor any genuine Tradition contains such a formulation.[4] Nor were the lawyers of the first century yet ready to frame theories to justify their evolving practice.

3. 2

Theories arose in the eighth century A.D., as part of the general growth of the science of Islamic jurisprudence (*uṣūl ash-sharīʿa*). Various questions were posed about consensus. What was the constituting group whose unanimous opinion was binding: the entire Community or the learned? On whom was consensus binding: on all future generations of Muslims or something less than that? On what subjects: religious practice or doctrine or both? Was 'independent' consensus authoritative, i.e. consensus which went beyond interpretation of the sacred texts to make new rulings not derived from them? What sanctions should enforce conformity to consensus? All these questions, though prominent in the classical writings, will not be discussed here, except in so far as differences in the answers given to them affect the answers given to our question.

For convenience of reference, a standard definition of consensus is quoted here from a classical source:

> the agreement of independent scholars of Muḥammad's Community in a particular period upon a legal decision.[5]

This gives the constituting group and the range of subjects. But there was by no means an agreement on either of these points. With regard to the constituting group, for instance, Shāfiʿī thought of it as the entire Community,

[4] This is an opinion, which will be supported in the course of the chapter. Meanwhile, since a decision on the order of treatment has to be made, this opinion provides one reason why these two sources are not being examined at the present stage as bases for consensus. Another reason is that their significance for our subject depends largely on the varying interpretations given of them, so it will be more accurate to examine them in the contexts of their interpreters through the centuries. Some judgements can then be made about the soundness of the interpretations in relation to the original sources.

[5] Muḥammad b. Ḥamza al-Ghaffārī (d. A.D. 1430/31), *Fuṣūl al-badāʾiʿ fī uṣūl ash-sharāʾiʿ*, quoted by ʿAbd ar-Rāziq, *Ijmāʿ*, p. 6: *ittifāqu l-mujtahidīna min ummati Muḥammadin (ʿalayhi s-salāmu) fī ʿaṣrin ʿalā ḥukmin sharʿī*.

except on technical matters, while the Hanbalites confined it to the Companions of the Prophet. In most of the discussions about the basis of consensus, however, the group is not specified, and the proofs relied on might apply to any group. Therefore I shall not specify unless required by the argument to do so. With regard to subjects, the definition given is narrower than what was in fact the full range, since consensus determined not only questions of law but also a few essential elements of doctrine, such as a Muslim could not deny without going against the minimum creed of the religion. Nevertheless it is true that consensus was used more widely to determine matters of *sharīʿa* law, i.e. matters of religious-legal practice.

The question with which we are concerned, about the basis on which the authority of consensus rests, is quite a sophisticated one, and for that reason was probably not the first in time of the questions raised by the legal theorists. We do not know what occasioned its first being asked. One obvious possibility is that it was stimulated by the challenge of Shiʿism. The Shīʿites claimed authority for their *imāms*, on the basis of the divine grace bestowed on the house of ʿAlī to make infallible religious judgements. Over against this formidable claim, the Sunnites had to defend the rightness of their community as a whole. And since they could not do this on issues where there was dissension among themselves, their unanimous judgements were evidently the thing for which they might most easily claim divine guidance and religious authority. But we must hesitate to explain the origin of Sunnite statements on this question as a response to a Shīʿite challenge, because the first statements arose in the early ʿAbbasid period, when Shiʿism was in a dormant phase, and had not yet organized a militant intellectual propaganda.

Before proceeding to a survey of the bases of support mentioned in history in favour of consensus, it will be useful at this point to set forth a table of the main logical types into which they fall.

(a) *A text without a reason:* i.e. a statement of Qurʾān or Tradition urging Muslims to follow consensus, but giving no argument for doing so.

(b) *A reason without a text:* i.e. an argument for following consensus which does not explicitly quote scripture. This heading, however, includes two sub-types with a significant theological difference between them. (i) A reason independent of anything in scripture. Some suggestions of this sort have been made in the modern age, but without validity as I hope to show. (ii) A reason which is an implication of scripture in its broad meaning, without being relatable to a particular text.

(c) *A text giving a reason.* This type also may be subdivided. (i) A text giving an explicit reason, not requiring interpretation or deduction, such as the

Tradition that asserts the infallibility of the Community. (ii) A text which implies a reason, to be drawn out by scholarly interpretation or deduction.

Obviously the type which best satisfies the requirements of Islamic jurisprudence is (c, i), a text of Qurʾān or Tradition giving a reason in plain language. And this is in fact the type that became historically predominant.

4

The first known attempt to find an intellectual basis for consensus was made by Muḥammad b. al-Ḥasan ash-Shaybānī (A.D. 749–805), a disciple of Abū Ḥanīfa who was one of the earliest Muslim writers of books on jurisprudence.[6] Shaybānī was a cautious advocate of the use of personal judgement (*raʾy*) in law, who nevertheless based his teaching on Traditions wherever possible.[7] In his edition of Mālik's *Muwaṭṭāʾ*, commenting on a particular decision he wrote:

> The Muslims are agreed on this and approve of it, and it is related on the authority of the Prophet that everything of which the Muslims approve or disapprove is good or bad in the sight of Allah.[8]

Thus Shaybānī in generalizing the principle of consensus was careful to base it on a Tradition.

The same Tradition was repeated in later works as supporting consensus, but was not much emphasized on account of certain weaknesses. For one thing, its *isnād* was incomplete, even though it contained the venerable name of ʿAbdallāh b. Masʿūd.[9] Some reserve may also have been felt about the content of the Tradition. For although no doubt its proper interpretation is that the Muslims always *see* correctly what God has laid down as good, it could too easily be misunderstood as meaning that human opinion (*raʾy*), not God's decree, *determines* what is good and bad, and God merely follows with His

[6] See (Ibn) an-Nadīm, *al-Fihrist*, ed. G. Flügel (Leipzig, 1872), 204 (Cairo, 1348 h./1929–30), 287–8. Equally early is an argument of Mālik b. Anas (d. 795) supporting the 'living tradition' of the Madinese with two Qurʾanic passages, but without referring to consensus. See R. Brunschvig, 'Polémiques médiévales autour du rite de Mālik', *al-Andalus*, 15 (1950), 377–435, especially 381–2, 416–17.

[7] 'Shaibānī', *Shorter Encyclopaedia of Islam* (Leiden, 1953).

[8] As translated by Schacht, *Origins*, p. 86. Literally, 'Whatever believers see as good is good with God, and whatever Muslims see as bad is bad with God': *Mā raʾāhu l-muʾminūna ḥasanan fahuwa ʿinda llāhi ḥasanum, wa mā raʾāhu l-Muslimūna qabīḥan fahuwa ʿinda llāhi qabīhun.* Mālik-Shaybani, *al-Muwaṭṭaʾ* (Lucknow, 1297 and 1306 g./1880 and 1888–9), p. 140.

[9] S. Mahmasani, *Falsafat at-tashrīʿ fi l-Islām*, 2nd ed. (Beirut, 1952), p. 118; Eng. trans. F. Ziadeh, with same title (Leiden, 1961), p. 77: with incomplete reference to Sakhāwi, *al-Maqāṣid al-ḥasana*, and Aḥmad b. Ḥanbal, *Kitāb as-sunna*. See also ʿAbdalhai Lakhnawi's commentary on Mālik-Shaybanī, *Muwaṭṭāʾ*, *ad loc.*

approval. And anything approaching this social subjectivism in ethics, or *vox populi vox Dei* in theology, was sure to be rejected by all Muslim scholars as directly contrary to the religion of the Book (see § 16).[10] For if God gives His believers a *furqān*, a means of discriminating between true and false, good and evil,[11] this means is evidently provided in the first place through the *sharīʿa*, not through man's thinking. This was the predominant opinion, at any rate after the work of Shāfiʿī in jurisprudence. Shaybānī's Tradition had a further weakness: it does not refer specifically to the *unanimous* approval or disapproval of the Muslims, thus it is too vague to be a decisive text favouring the doctrine of consensus. But with all these faults it did not fall entirely out of sight, for it did support, however vaguely, the major idea in classical thought about consensus, the idea of its infallibility.

Another argument from the early ʿAbbasid period, which foreshadows the classical argument, is recorded by Shāfiʿī, where he says that those scholars who reject Tradition altogether as a source of law

> acknowledge the consensus on the ground that the Muslims, Allah willing, would not agree on any given doctrine unless they were right, and so their generality (*ʿammatuhum*) could not be mistaken as to the meaning of the Koran, even if individuals might be.[12]

Schacht identifies these 'anti-Traditionists' with the *ahl al-kalām*, by which Shāfiʿī meant the Muʿtazilites. Their argument naturally does not quote a Tradition. Instead, it relies on an implication of the general spirit of Islam and the Qurʾān, quite in the Muʿtazilite manner of rational theology. It starts from the Islamic premises of a benevolent God and an *umma* specially favoured with divine grace.[13] Hence it is inferred that for all of the Muslims to be mistaken would be a contradiction of this divine favour. The inference is not strictly

[10] See ch. 3. A classification of Islamic theories of ethics is given in ch. 2.

[11] *Qurʾān*, viii, 29; xxv, 1. *Furqān* was generally understood in this sense by the commentators. Whether it really bears another sense in the *Qurʾān* is not pertinent to our statement of medieval scholars' reactions. See 'Furḳān', *Shorter Encyclopaedia of Islam*.

[12] Schacht, *Origins*, p. 41, summarizing Shāfiʿī, *Kitāb al-umm* (Bulaq, 1321–5 h./1903–7). VII, 252–3. But I have translated *ʿāmmatuhum* as 'their generality', not 'their majority'. The primary meaning of the verb *ʿāmma* is 'to be general, universal, common, comprehensive', etc., and it could not normally refer so specifically to a majority. 'Their majority' would produce a rather extreme view of consensus: that even a majority of Muslims must be infallible.

The reason for Schacht's understanding 'majority' may have been the apparent difficulty of reconciling the totality not being mistaken with some individuals being mistaken. This would certainly be a contradiction if understood *simultaneously*. But I think the meaning is: 'It is impossible that the Muslims could all be mistaken at once, though it is possible that some individual Muslims may be mistaken *on other occasions*, when there is no unanimity.' This is the classical view of consensus. It is expressed more clearly in Shāfiʿī's statement of his own view, see below, § 5.

[13] See below, § 7, for Qurʾanic support, quoted in later times.

justified, for God may favour a people with blessing but stop short of making them infallible.

This argument is interesting as coming from the Muʿtazilites, for the idea of a divine guarantee of the rightness of the *umma* comes close to assuming predestination of the *umma*'s decisions, which we should expect to be contrary to the Muʿtazilite principle of man's power to choose, including the power to choose error. It would not, however, be fair to refer to this as a definite doctrine, since all we have as evidence is brief statements of Shāfiʿī about some barely identified early thinkers, to whose general position he was himself opposed.[14]

5

When we come to Shāfiʿī (767–820), we are dealing for the first time in Islamic history with a thoroughly systematic jurist whose views are well known from substantial writings of his own. The root idea of his jurisprudence may be described as theological positivism, the theory that the entire law of Islam is to be derived ultimately from sacred or sanctified sources, the Qurʾān and Traditions respectively. Analogical reasoning (*qiyās*) was not hard to fit into this theory, since it was no more than deduction, drawing out the implications of scripture, and thus akin to interpretation of scripture. But to follow human consensus as a legal source seemed somewhat remote from scripture, hence it is not surprising that Shāfiʿī was lukewarm about it. Since it was too well entrenched in his time to be rejected (and he may never have thought of that), he accepted it with qualifications[15] and sought to justify it by proofs within the framework of his system.

As might be expected, Shāfiʿī looked for a proof in the Qurʾān. It is related that he searched the Book for three days, before he settled upon iv, 115:

> But whoso makes a breach with the Messenger after the guidance has become clear to him, and follows a way other than the believers', him We shall turn over to what he has turned to and We shall roast him in Gehenna – an evil homecoming![16]

[14] Cf. a parallel early Christian argument for the infallibility of the Church, by Tertullian: 'Suppose now that all the Churches have erred... This would mean that the Holy Spirit has not watched over any of them so as to guide it into the truth, although He was sent by Christ, and asked from the Father for this very purpose – that He might be the teacher of truth.' J.-P. Migne, *Patrologiae cursus completus, Series Latina*, II (Paris, 1878), 40: in 'De praescriptis', ch. xxviii, as translated by P. J. Toner, 'Infallibility', *Catholic Encyclopaedia*, VII (New York, 1910), 793, with mistaken reference (here corrected).

[15] See Schact, *Origins*, pp. 88–94, for Shāfiʿī's attitude to consensus.

[16] Trans. A. J. Arberry, *The Koran interpreted*, 2 vols. (London, 1955), as for all *Qurʾān* quotations. Verse references to Flügel and Cairo editions, e.g. iii, 98/103. Third line: *wa yattabiʿu ghayra sabīli l-muʾminīn*. See I. Goldziher, *Vorlesungen über den Islam* (Heidelberg, 1910), pp. 53–6, on Shāfiʿī's search.

The verse is understood as a direct injunction to follow consensus, without the mediation of any reason such as its infallibility. The proof depends on an identification of the 'way of the believers', referred to obliquely in the verse, with the unanimous consensus of the continuing Muslim community. This is where its weakness lies, for the phrase is capable of other interpretations: e.g. 'the way of the believers' may mean 'the way laid down *for* them in scripture'. The story of Shāfiʿī's lengthy search, if true, must be understood to mean, not so much that he needed three days to light upon the relevant verses in the Book, with which he was perfectly familiar, but rather that he hesitated that long before accepting any verse as a proof.

Shāfiʿī also quotes two Traditions ordering Muslims 'to hold fast to the Community'.[17] The interpretation he gives of these Traditions shows how he makes them a basis for the authority of consensus:

Q.: What is the proof for the authority of that on which men are agreed? A.: When the Prophet ordered men to hold fast to the community of Muslims, this could only mean that they were to accept the doctrine of the community; it is reasonable, too, to assume that the community cannot as a whole be ignorant of a ruling given by Allah and the Prophet. Such ignorance is possible only in individuals, whereas something on which all [Muslims] are agreed cannot be wrong and whosoever accepts such a doctrine does so in conformity with the *sunna* of the Prophet.[18]

This answer of Shāfiʿī is important and deserves careful scrutiny. The 'question' interprets the Tradition in a more specific sense than is apparent, understanding it as authorizing a cumulative, irrevocable obligation on all Muslims to accept every consensus. In his answer Shāfiʿī gives a reason, amounting to the same argument which he had found in the opponents of Tradition. It is, in fact, the later proof by infallibility, but stated as an argument, not as the Tradition 'My Community does not agree on an error'. Now this Tradition would certainly have been quoted by Shāfiʿī if it had been available to him, for it would have provided the ideal proof from his positivist viewpoint. Hence Schacht concludes that he did not know it – an inference which is unavoidable, except for the possible alternative that he had heard it but did not accept it as genuine.[19] In either case it is significant for Shāfiʿī's thought that he accepted the doctrine of infallibility even without a Tradition. The significance of this fact for the history of the Tradition itself is even greater, as will be pointed out (§ 19).

[17] *Risāla*, ed. M. Shakir (Cairo, 1358 h./1940), 402, 473–4; trans. M. Khadduri, *Islamic jurisprudence: Shāfiʿī's Risāla* (Baltimore, Md., 1961), pp. 253, 286.
[18] *Umm*, VII, 271–2, as translated by Schacht, *Origins*, p. 90. Cf. *Risāla*, 472–3.
[19] *Origins*, p. 91.

6

After Shāfiʿī, and to some extent due to the force of his thought, there arose the great collections of Traditions, the standard commentaries on the Qurʾān, and the classical formulations of Sunnite jurisprudence in the compendia of the four schools. Consensus came to be accepted by all jurists as one of the four sources of law. Among the major practices imposed by consensus on lawyers was that of *taqlīd*, consultation of the standard law books of one's own school, with a corresponding abstinence from *ijtihād*, the use of one's own judgement in discovering the law. The underlying assumption was that the standard decisions of the schools in detail were themselves now authorized by consensus and could not be overriden. While the growth of a body of law by precedent is familiar in other systems, in Sunnite Islam the doctrine of consensus and the almost complete closing of the gate of *ijtihād* produced an unusually static law, within the spheres where it operated, such as family law, obligations and contracts, religious trusts (*awqāf*). But the situation was generally accepted and even welcomed by the legal profession from the ninth to the nineteenth centuries, except for a few original thinkers like the Zahirite Ibn Ḥazm and the Hanbalites Ibn Taymiyya and Ṭawfī. This general compliance is reflected in the attitude of the majority of jurists towards the basis of consensus, which was thought of as something to be established, not rejected. Even Zahirites and Hanbalites only thought of limiting it.

In the sphere of dogma the weight of consensus was less heavy, because there was less agreement in fact, and because many leading theologians, philosophers and mystics were disinclined to claim the existence of a consensus on points of belief beyond the minimum necessary for unity. After the schismatic conflicts of early Islam it was commonly felt as desirable to allow latitude in interpreting scripture, on matters which did not affect practice. For after all it was the way of life, the *sharīʿa*, which for Muslims constituted the core of Islam.

It would be an arduous task to make a complete survey of all that was written about the basis of consensus in the voluminous literature of Islamic law. It will be sufficient here to discuss some of the main texts and arguments that were relied upon, and the opinions of a few leading thinkers, and especially of the Shāfiʿīte Ghazālī (1058–1111), whose treatment of the subject is the most thoroughgoing in classical Islam. We may take our starting-point from a concise statement by him. After defining consensus as 'agreement of the Community of Muḥammad, especially on a religious question', he writes:

Its authority is based on the impossibility of error by the Community; this is the whole matter. That it is an authority may be known by the Book, or by universally accepted Tradition (*sunna mutawātira*), or by intellect (*ʿaql*). As for consensus, it is not possible to establish consensus by it.[20]

The four methods of proof mentioned here are parallel to the four standard sources of Islamic law; Qurʾān, Tradition, analogical deduction from scripture (*qiyās*), and consensus. The general correspondence of *ʿaql* with *qiyās* will appear when we come to the intellectual argument (§9).

7

Several verses of the Qurʾān are cited by medieval scholars in support of consensus. iv, 115, the one blessed by Shāfiʿī, is felt by Ghazālī[21] to be the strongest, but he does not consider it to be a *naṣṣ*, a decisive textual proof. Of the commentators, Ṭabarī (839–923) does not apply the verse to consensus; Bayḍāwī (d. 1286?) does so, but with little discussion; while Zamakhsharī (1075–1144) does so with a reason, that the verse links disobedience to the Prophet with divergence from 'the way of the believers'.[22] The last point is also made by both Ibn Ḥazm (994–1064) and Ibn Taymiyya (1263–1328),[23] but with a different emphasis, corresponding to their positivist purposes: to show that 'the way of the believers' (understood as their consensus) is never independent but is always based on the Prophet's revelation or *sunna*, and 'there is no decision of consensus which has not been previously expounded clearly by the Prophet'.[24] Ibn Taymiyya sees well that 'the way of the believers' may refer to the way laid down *for them* by the Prophet. But he does not see that it may mean *only* this, with no reference to the beliefs actually held *by them* at any time – and still less to their unanimous beliefs.

[20] *al-Mustaṣfā min ʿilm al-uṣūl* (Cairo, 1356 h./1937), I, 110, 111. For Ghazālī's views on other aspects of consensus, see I. Goldziher, 'Über iǵmā', *Nachrichten von der Königl. Gesellschaft der Wissenschaften zu Göttingen*, Phil.-hist. Kl. 1916, pp. 81–5.

[21] *Mustaṣfā*, I, 112.

[22] Ṭabarī, *Tafsīr*, ed. M. Shakir (Cairo: Maʿarif Press, n.d.), VII, 204–5. Bayḍāwī, *Anwār at-tanzīl wa asrār at-taʾwīl*, various editions, *ad loc*. Zamakhsharī, *al-Kashshāf ʿan ḥaqāʾiq at-tanzīl* (Calcutta, 1856), I, 321.

[23] Ibn Ḥazm, *al-Iḥkām fī uṣūl al-aḥkām* (Cairo, 1925), IV, 131–2. Ibn Taymiyya, *Maʿārij al-wuṣūl ilā maʿrifat anna uṣūl ad-dīn wa furūʿahu qad bayyanahā r-rasūl* (Cairo, 1318 h./1900), 19, 30–2; French trans. H. Laoust, *Contribution à une étude de la méthodologie canonique de Taḳī-d-dīn Aḥmad b. Taimīya* (Cairo, 1939), pp. 84, 99–101.

[24] *Maʿārij*, 31: Laoust, p. 102. Another Hanbalite, Najm ad-dīn aṭ-Ṭawfī in an extensive but erratic criticism of this verse as a proof of consensus, makes at least one good point: that 'the way of the believers' may be best understood in terms of the preceding verse, which has referred to 'him who bids to freewill offering, or honour, or setting things right between the people'. *Risāla fī riʿāyat al-maṣlaḥa*, ed. A. Khallāf in *Maṣādir at-tashrīʿ al-Islāmī fī mā lā naṣṣa fīhi* (Cairo, 1954), p. 102.

But this is the crucial question, which is not settled by any argument of the commentators or theologians, as far as is known to me. Perhaps this is why Ghazālī thought the verse less than a *naṣṣ*.

Of similar intent is iii, 98/103:

And hold you fast to God's bond, together, and do not scatter; remember God's blessing upon you when you were enemies, and He brought your hearts together, so that by His blessing you became brothers.

The application is stated concisely by Sayf ad-dīn al-Āmidī (1156–1233): 'God has forbidden separation, and disagreement with consensus is separation'.[25] This verse has considerable merits in its directness: it does enjoin the Muslims to keep together, and calls this brotherly unity of hearts a blessing of God. Certain words used would have effective associations for later Muslims: *tafarraqū*, 'scatter', suggests the sects (*firaq*) into which the Community became divided when they failed to attain or follow consensus; *jamīʿan*, 'together', suggests *ijtimāʿ* and *ijmāʿ*. The verse does not mention the Prophet, and so it is without the distracting element which complicated the discussions of iv, 115. But in spite of these advantages it was not much relied upon by medieval authors. This may have been because it was felt that 'God's bond' is rather a reference to the Qurʾān than to consensus. It must also be said that the precise doctrine of consensus can hardly be found in the verse; but this was not the kind of consideration to deter a medieval commentator.

Two other verses were often cited, both demonstrating the divine favour bestowed on the Community.

(a) You are the best nation ever brought forth to men, bidding to honour (*al-maʿrūf*). and forbidding dishonour (*al-munkar*), and believing in God... (iii, 106/110).

Pazdawī (*c*. 1009–1089) says: 'Their excellence (*al-khayriyya*) implies the rightness of their consensus'.[26] Bayḍāwī says:

The verse has been used to prove that the Agreement of the Believers is a source of Law; for the verse makes it certain that they enjoined everything right and forbad everything wrong, the article here [with *maʿrūf* and *munkar*] being universalizing. Now were they to agree to what is false, their conduct would be the reverse.[27]

It is a fair criticism of these learned doctors to say that they have turned a general statement into a universal one. They have made a leap which is

25 *al-Iḥkām fī uṣūl al-aḥkām* (Cairo, 1914), 295.

26 *Kanz al-wuṣūl ilā maʿrifat al-uṣūl*, with commentary of ʿAbd al-ʿAzīz al-Bukhārī, in *Kashf al-asrār* (Constantinople, 1307–8 h./1889–90), III, 975. Cf. also Ghazālī, *Mustaṣfā*, I, 111; Āmidī, *Iḥkām*, I, 311; Ibn Taymiyya, *Maʿārij*, p. 17.

27 *Anwār at-tanzīl*, *ad loc*., as trans. by D. S. Margoliouth in *Chrestomathia Baidawiana* (London, 1894). Margoliouth calls it 'very feeble evidence'.

not justified by the text, and which they would never have thought of unless the doctrine of consensus had already been present to their minds.

(b) Thus We appointed you a midmost nation (*ummatan wasaṭan*) that you might be witnesses to the people, and that the Messenger might be a witness to you;...

(ii, 137/143).

Taken in its context, *wasaṭan* appears to mean 'in the middle', between other people whom the Muslims will witness against and Muḥammad who will certify the Muslims as reliable witnesses. This is well explained by Zamakhsharī:

Some nations have chosen to reject the Prophet's mission. On the Day of Judgement God will ask the prophets [sent to other nations] if they have delivered their messages, and the Muhammadan Community will then be summoned as witnesses...Then Muḥammad will be summoned and questioned about the condition of his Community, and he will certify it (*yuzakkīhā*) and testify to its justice (*ʿadālatihā*) [i.e. its qualification to be a witness, *ʿadl*].[28]

If this is correct, then the Community is at least proclaimed superior to other nations and possessing the sense of justice and the good character required in witnesses. Bayḍāwī and Ibn Taymiyya both reason that the Community's being appointed as certified witnesses implies that they cannot as a Community give false testimony, hence their unanimous opinion is always free from error.[29] This is stretching the meaning of the verse rather too far, because the qualification of a witness is something less than to be infallible.

Wasaṭan is also often interpreted, by Ṭabarī and Bayḍāwī for example,[30] as 'holding to the mean', in the Aristotelian sense of moderation between vicious extremes. This interpretation would strengthen the argument for the perfection of the Community; but it probably reads too much into the word in its Qurʾanic context.

A few more verses were sometimes listed in support of consensus, but add no strength to those already mentioned.[31]

Reviewing the arguments from the Qurʾān as a whole, we can conclude that none of them is quite decisive. Some verses undoubtedly recommend

[28] *Kashshāf*, I, 110; followed by Bayḍāwī, with less clear expression. The attribution to the *Qurʾān* of the technicalities of later Islamic law is anachronistic, but the general argument may stand.

[29] Bayḍawī, *Anwār*, *ad loc.*; Ibn Taymiyya, *Maʿārij*, 81–4: Laoust, p. 19. Ṭawfī, *Risāla*, 103 objects that infallibility in giving true witness does not imply infallibility in judging right and wrong.

[30] Ṭabarī, *Tafsīr*, III, 141–5; Bayḍāwī, *Anwār*, *ad loc.*

[31] E.g. iv, 59/62, enjoining obedience to God, the Messenger 'and those in authority (*ulī l-amr*) among you'. It was disputed whether the last phrase refers to rulers or religious authorities or both. If the second, the text might be a support for obeying consensus. See below, § 13 on Muḥammad ʿAbduh's interpretation.

unity to the Community, while others commend the Community as a superior people. But to conclude from either kind that the Qurʾān makes it a duty for Muslims to follow the accumulated consensus of all past generations is a step beyond anything that the scripture of Islam would seem to warrant, taken by itself without preconceptions derived from later writings or felt needs.

8

Ghazālī's opinion was that the *sunna* of the Prophet, as known by Traditions, provides the strongest proof of the authority of consensus.[32] Of the several Traditions used, two have been mentioned before. 'Hold fast to the Community' had the prestige of Shāfiʿī's backing. It has a similar force to Qurʾān iii, 98/103, as a clear general recommendation of Islamic solidarity. 'Whatever believers see as good is good with God', etc., has the defects previously pointed out. It is cited by Āmidī[33] but not by Ghazālī.

The group of Traditions on which most reliance was placed were those which make a plain assertion of the infallibility of the Community. The wording varies slightly in two different versions: (a) 'My Community does not agree on a mistake (*khaṭa'*)' or (b) 'on an error (*ḍalāla*)'. The first version was regarded as weak in its *isnād*, and is not listed by Wensinck from any of the standard collections. The second was accepted as sound, and is listed by Wensinck.[34] But there is no significant difference between *khaṭa'* and *ḍalāla*.[35] Another Tradition which was thought to yield the same conclusion is:

There will always be a group in my Community maintaining the truth, unharmed by deserters and dissenters, until the Judgement of God arrives.[36]

This was understood to imply that whenever the Community is unanimous it cannot be on an error. Ibn Ḥazm objects that the Tradition only asserts that a wrong view will always have opponents disagreeing with it, and says nothing about the state of agreement.[37]

Of the various Traditions giving the same meaning, Ghazālī concludes that the common meaning is certainly authentic (*mutawātir bil-maʿnā*), even if each

[32] *Mustaṣfāʾ*, I, 111. [33] *Iḥkām*, I, 313.

[34] A. J. Wensinck, *Concordance et indices de la tradition musulmane* (Leiden, 1933–), I, 93–6, and *A Handbook of early Muhammadan tradition* (Leiden, 1927), pp. 47–8, s.v. 'Community'. See Madina, 'Classical doctrine', pp. 36ff.

[35] This is Ghazālī's position, *Mustaṣfā*, I, 113, as against a rather arbitrary distinction made by Ibn Ḥazm, *Iḥkām*, iv, 131.

[36] Wensinck, *Concordance* and *Handbook*, I, 93–6. Various versions are given by Ibn Ḥazm, *Iḥkām*, iv, 130–1.

[37] *Iḥkām*, iv, 131. The same argument has been used recently by M. Asad, *The principles of state and government in Islam* (Los Angeles, 1961), p. 38; answered by K. A. Faruki, *Islamic jurisprudence* (Karachi, 1962), p. 154.

one by itself is not.[38] And this was the general opinion of Sunnī jurists. When once their authenticity was thus accepted, by the traditional tests of *isnād*-criticism, the doctrine of infallibility seemed to be on an unshakable basis, since the assertion of the Traditions was plain and not open to doubts of interpretation. And so things remained, putting at rest all questions about the authority of consensus, until modern times when the question of authenticity has been raised again. Criticisms on this score will be reserved for a later section (§ 19).

9

The 'intellectual proof' mentioned by Ghazālī[39] amounts to an argument by analogy with something universally admitted by Muslims. In the sphere of *ḥadīth* criticism it was admitted by all that some Traditions (those known as *mutawātir*) could be accepted as certainly reliable on the ground that they were accepted by all the Companions, and these were sufficiently numerous so that they could not all have been deliberate liars or all mistaken. For the same reason, it was argued, when the Companions agreed unanimously that a judgement in law or theology was certainly correct (*maqṭūᶜan bihi*), they could not all have been liars or mistaken.

Ghazālī thinks the argument is weak, because a number of people sufficient to constitute *tawātur* evidence for historical reports, such as the Traditions of Islam, may yet be mistaken in the different sphere of legal and theological judgements. For example, the Jews or Christians are numerous enough as historical witnesses of events in the past, but their unanimous agreement in their respective communities that Muḥammad is not a prophet is not above error; in fact it is erroneous. There is a difference in the two spheres. The condition for a *mutawātir* Tradition is that it must be based on sensation or some other kind of immediate perception of the witnesses, where there is no possibility of divergence between the perceptions of different persons. In the case of consensus, on the other hand, the object of agreement is a matter of theory (*naẓarī*), e.g. whether a legal judgement is correct, on which competent people may hold divergent opinions; 'and it is not impossible in the usual course of events (*fi lᶜāda*) that a group constituting *tawātur* [on Traditions] should be unanimously mistaken about this'.

Here Ghazālī uses the terminology of the Ashᶜarite theologians, in which any regularity in the world is attributed to God's 'habit' (*ᶜādat Allāh*), not to 'nature' (*aṭ-ṭabīᶜa*).[40] He means to say that, according to the laws of valid

[38] *Mustaṣfā*, I, 111–12. See Madina, 'Classical doctrine', pp. 48–50. [39] *Mustaṣfā*, I, 114.
[40] See Ibn Rushd, *Tahāfut at-tahāfut*, ed. M. Bouyges (Beirut, 1930), 531–2; L. Gardet and M. Anawati, *Introduction à la théologie musulmane* (Paris, 1948), p. 353.

evidence in the world as it is ordinarily, a *tawātur* group would not guarantee the correctness of a community's theoretical judgement. The infallibility of the consensus of the Muslim Community is, therefore, only guaranteed by a divine favour (*karāmat Allāh*), a 'breaking of habit' (*kharq al-ᶜāda*) by God which amounts to a miracle. Such a miracle was not granted to any other community. Its existence in the case of Islam cannot be inferred from any fact of ordinary experience or any principle of pure reason;[41] it is known only through the positive divine sources (*samᶜīyāt*) – in this case through Traditions.

Ghazālī's criticism of the 'intellectual proof' can be accepted. Indeed we may go further, by realizing that even the first leg of the analogy, the *mutawātir* Tradition, can no longer be regarded as stable. Historians today take a rather more sceptical view of 'unanimous' reports handed down orally from a distant past, whether in Islamic or other civilizations.

The early argument of rational theology, attributed by Shāfiᶜī to the Muᶜtazilites (above, §4), was apparently not revived in later Islam. That argument started from the premise of the divine favour of God to Muslims, known generally from the Qurᵓān. Later theology, more systematic and positive, was not content with such a vague premise but sought for specific passages in the revealed sources to substantiate the divine favour. In any case, any tendency to develop this type of argument was half-hearted, after the acceptance of the Traditions which stated unambiguously that the Community was not liable to error.

10

It was evident to the jurists that the authority of consensus could not be based on a consensus of the same kind, as this procedure would set up a vicious circle, or (in another metaphor) an infinite chain.[42] But evidently the classical theory which relies on Traditions was attacked on the ground that it involuntarily commits this fallacy. Ghazālī states and answers the attack as follows:

Objection: 'You have proved consensus by the Tradition, then proved the soundness of the Tradition by consensus. Granting that there was a consensus on its soundness,

[41] Cf. Ṭawfī, *Risāla*, 107: 'If consensus were an authority, this would be either by the essence of the consenters or by the witness of scripture to their infallibility. The first is invalid: the consenters are not infallible by their essence, because no impossibility follows for their essence from the supposition of their lack of infallibility.'

[42] See Ghazālī, *Mustaṣfā*, I, 111, quoted above, §6; Ṭawfī, *Risāla*, 103; Shawkānī, quoted without reference in A. ᶜAbd ar-Rāziq, *Ijmāᶜ*, p. 39; M. al-Khudari, *Uṣūl al-fiqh*, 3rd ed. (Cairo, 1937), p. 279.

what is the proof that what they have agreed to be sound is sound in fact? And what is the dispute about but this?'

Answer: This is not so. We have proved consensus by the Tradition, but the soundness of the Tradition by the absence through the centuries of objections to it and disagreement with it, whereas the usual course of events (*al-ʿāda*) requires a denial that a decisive principle by which sure decisions are made could be established by a Tradition of unknown soundness. So we know by the usual course of events, not by consensus, that a Tradition is decisive (*maqṭūʿan bihi*).[43]

The objection is clear enough. It proceeds on the assumption that the Tradition, supporting the authority of consensus, is to be accepted on the strength of a second consensus, that of all the witnesses unanimously attesting the veracity of the Tradition. But this second consensus has no weight unless some reason has already been given to believe that consensus hits the truth. As this is the very point at issue, the second consensus takes us no further forward than the first.

Ghazālī's answer can best be understood in the light of the concepts of *tawātur* and *ʿāda* explained in the last section. Where he writes 'This is not so' he is denying that the Tradition is proved authentic by a consensus in its favour. It is authenticated, he says, by *mutawātir* evidence, which is considered sound not through mere unanimity of opinion but because it is a result of very many witnesses' hearing and seeing the Prophet speaking, or hearing the first-hand witnesses reporting it to them, and the absence of any contrary witness. Thus the Tradition is known to be sound by the rules of historical evidence in the ordinary state of the world (*ʿāda*). An important principle of law, such as consensus, he concludes, could not be based on anything less solid than this.

Perhaps Ghazālī's argument can be made clearer by a reference to a Roman Catholic argument in a closely analogous situation. The doctrine of the infallibility of the Church (not the Pope) has been attacked on the ground that it rests on statements of a scripture, and that the authenticity of that scripture is guaranteed, in turn, by a Church regarded already as infallible. A writer in the *Catholic Encyclopaedia*[44] has refuted the charge of a logical vicious circle by delineating the correct argument carefully in three steps.

(a) It starts from the scriptures 'merely as reliable historical sources', which give us a trustworthy report of Christ's sayings and promises.

(b) 'Christ's promises to the Apostles and their successors in the teaching office include the promise of such guidance and assistance as clearly implies infallibility.'

[43] *Mustaṣfā*, I, 112.

[44] P. J. Toner, 'Infallibility', *Catholic Encyclopaedia*, VII (New York, 1910), 701.

(c) Proceeding from here, it is possible 'to rely on the Church's authority for proof of what writings are inspired'.

The decisive feature of this argument is that no assumptions of an infallible community or an inspired scripture are made at the first step. It is based on ordinary historical evidence, such as (it is claimed) would convince any intelligent person.

The argument is unassailable on logical grounds. Any criticism has to be directed at the truth of the premises or of the assumptions behind them.

The fallacy suggested in the preceding objections is that of infinite regress. It is quite possible, however, to have a single regress without leading to infinity. An instance is to be found in Ibn Khaldūn's justification of consensus as a source of obligations.

> Then consensus takes its place next to those two [Qurʾān and *sunna*], because of the consensus of the Companions to disapprove of those who disagreed with them; and they would not have done so without a positive basis (*mustanad*), because such men do not agree [upon anything] without a firm proof.[45]

The argument can be analysed as follows:

(a) The consensus of the Community is authoritative because it has been validated by the precedent established by the Companions in consensus.

(b) The Companions' consensus is based, not on another consensus, but on their correct understanding of the positive sources amply available to them, i.e. the Qurʾān and the *sunna* of the *Prophet*.

There is nothing logically vicious here. But Ibn Khaldūn may have felt it to be too complicated, for he immediately adds: 'There is also the evidence of textual proofs that the Community is infallible.' Here he refers to the standard Traditions.

Ibn Khaldūn, however, rather spoils his record in another passage, where he is dealing with the authority of the *sunna*, and justifies it by consensus: 'The *sunna*, as it has been transmitted to us, is justified by the [Companions'] consensus on the obligation to act in accordance with its sound parts, as we have mentioned.'[46] This is circular, for he has just said that the authority of the Companions' consensus rests on the positive basis of the Qurʾān and *sunna*.

45 *al-Muqaddima*, ed. E. Quatremère, *Prolégomènes d'Ebn Khaldoun* (Paris, 1858), III, 17. Cf. 18–19 for a shorter repetition. My translation owes something to that of F. Rosenthal, *The Muqaddimah* (London, 1958), III, 23–4.

46 Quatremère, III, 18, with a reference to 17. Rosenthal, III, 25 and 23. The passage referred to, 17, shows that the consensus mentioned is that of the Companions. This does not avoid the circularity.

II

Before we pass from classical Sunnite Islam we should take note of the special viewpoint of the Hanbalites on the sources of law, which led them to a different emphasis in the proofs of the authority of consensus.[47]

The Hanbalite movement may be described as a protestant reformation, in another sense than the Shafiʿite and Zahirite movements. In Hanbalism the stress is less on the texts of revelation as understood by contemporary scholarship, and more on the texts as understood by the earliest Muslims (*salaf*), the Companions of the Prophet, and on his life as imitated in their practice. It was felt that the primitive Community knew far more about the Prophet's ways of living and judgement than anything that has been preserved in surviving oral tradition or written records, and that later generations in turn know far more about that primitive Community than they know directly about the Prophet. The primitive Community is thus an indispensable link of knowledge between the Founder of Islam and Muslims of later times.

We may consider the implications of this doctrine for the theory of consensus as worked out in the thought of the most systematic Hanbalite jurist, Ibn Taymiyya. The first point to notice is the de-emphasis on the consensus of the later Community as a source of law, for it was precisely the overworking of this source by the other schools that was believed to have led to wandering from original Islam and unlicensed developments of the teachings of God and the Messenger. In spite of the Tradition 'My Community does not agree on an error', which he does not reject, Ibn Taymiyya feels that infallibility is an unconvincing doctrine when applied to the entire continuing Community of Muslims, liable as it is to the weaknesses of humanity. Why should they not be in error, unless they are close to a Prophet? Here Ibn Taymiyya was influenced by the Shiʿite theorist Ḥillī, who defined consensus in terms of agreement with the thoughts of a living *imām*. For the Sunnites, correspondingly, the only consensus that could be convincingly held infallible according to Ibn Taymiyya, was that of the Companions of Muḥammad.

In this view, the Tradition was thought to be backed by precise reasons showing why the Companions in particular were so authoritative. Two qualities commended them. One was their unequalled moral probity. It was a characteristic thought of Sunnite Islam that grace has diminished with distance from the Prophet. This was expressed in the Tradition, 'The best men are those of my generation, then those who follow them. Then falsehood wil

[47] This section owes much to the classic study of H. Laoust, *Essai sur les doctrines sociales et politiques de Taḳī-d-dīn Aḥmad b. Taimiya* (Cairo, 1939), pp. 239–42.

spread.'[48] The other quality, closely linked with the first, was their nearness to the Prophet, which enabled them to have a unique personal knowledge of his teaching, his manner of life and thinking, and the circumstances in which he received revelations and gave injunctions.[49] The conclusion to be drawn, then, was that those men would be extremely unlikely to be unanimously in error regarding the original teachings of Islam.

This argument follows a line of historical source criticism, not needing the intervention of any special providence to establish freedom from error, except in so far as the goodness of the Companions might be thought providential. The conclusion, infallibility of the Companions, is more limited than the standard doctrine, and takes a more cautious attitude to evidence; and it is surely stronger for that reason.

12 MODERN ISLAM AND WESTERN SCHOLARSHIP

So there remained in the later classical period two traditions, side by side in permitted disagreement (*ikhtilāf*): the 'catholic' majority supporting the continuous authority of the Community by scriptural proofs, and the Hanbalite 'protestants' not denying the proofs but restricting their application to the authority of the Companions, by reason of their blessed closeness to the Prophet.

In modern Islam, beginning in the nineteenth century, the whole situation has changed: not as yet through new proofs of any value, as will be shown, but by virtue of a changed attitude to consensus itself as a source. For, whereas classical intellectuals had been mainly concerned to *preserve* their Islamic world as they knew and loved it, and had found in consensus an effective means thereto, the distinctively modern trend has been to *adapt* the contemporary Islamic world to new conditions of life, without departing from the basic ideas of original Islam. Seeing, therefore, a barrier to adaptation in the classical doctrine of the authority of all past consensus, modernists have often striven to find it no part of original Islam. This effort has had a note of urgency, lacking in the corresponding discussions of infallibility in Catholic circles, on account of the different subject-matter of consensus in Islam. The pronouncements of the Catholic church that have been claimed as infallible

48 As quoted by Ibn Khaldūn, *Muqaddima*, I, 393, as trans. F. Rosenthal, I, 447. Many references in Wensinck, *Handbook*, p. 48. In the ordinary Sunnite view the spread of falsehood would not be universal, so that this Tradition does not contradict 'My Community does not agree on an error.'

49 Ibn Taymiyya, *Maʿārij*, 35–6: Laoust, *Contribution*, p. 110. Cf. the saying of Abū Ḥanīfa, 'An hour's session of one of them the Companions with the Prophet, blessing and peace on him, is better than the learning of years.' Quoted by M. Abu Zahra, *Abū Ḥanīfa*, 2nd ed. (Cairo, 1955), p. 315, without reference to source.

have been mostly on matters of theology, supposedly eternal verities which could, at any rate, be allowed to stand unchanged for a very long time. By contrast, the subjects dealt with by Islamic consensus have been mainly practical ones, as has been seen, calling for repeated decisions in action which would affect individuals and the community from day to day, or from year to year. Thus the doctrine of consensus has been under continual review by modern Muslim lawyers and social thinkers, rather than theologians. For illustration of modernist thought concerning the basis of consensus I shall consider the theories of two reformers, Muḥammad ʿAbduh and Kemal Faruki.

13

The Egyptian ʿAbduh (1849–1905) understood Islam as a revealed religion, which at the same time encouraged full use of reason within the natural order and pursuit of the public interest (*maṣlaḥa*) as the primary end of action.[50] In other words, he proclaimed independent thinking (*ijtihād*) as the right and duty of those competent to perform it in every age, and denied that priority in time necessarily meant superior wisdom, except in the case of the Companions and Successors. Indeed, later ages have had two persistent reasons to modify decisions by their predecessors: one is the growth of understanding through experience, and learning from their mistakes,[51] the other is the constant change of historical circumstances, which makes obsolete and harmful many rules of life which were suitable to former conditions. Hence ʿAbduh considered it one of his chief aims 'to liberate thought from the shackles of traditionalism (*taqlīd*)',[52] the following of past authorities without reflection, out of reverence for the past.

ʿAbduh made it quite clear that he included in this liberation the freedom of Muslims from the obligation to follow past consensus merely as such, and so went on record as opposing the classical doctrine of consensus. His view is stated in the *Manār commentary* on Qurʾān iv, 59/63:

> O believers, obey God and obey the Messenger and those in authority among you..

This sentence had sometimes been taken as supporting obedience to consensus but more often not used for this purpose because of the difficulty of equating 'those in authority' (*ūlī l-amri*) with the Community as a whole or its learned representatives. ʿAbduh, however, takes the phrase as meaning all the Muslims

[50] See A. Hourani, *Arabic thought in the liberal age* (Oxford, 1962), pp. 139ff.; C. C. Adams, *Islam and modernism in Egypt* (Oxford, 1933).

[51] *Risālat at-tawḥīd*, ed. M. Rashid Rida, 4th ed. (Cairo, 1371 h./1951–2), pp. 158–9; Fr. trans. B. Michel and M. ʿAbd ar-Rāziq, *Rissalat al-tawhid* (Paris, 1925), p. 108.

[52] M. Rashid Rida, *Taʾrīkh al-ustādh al-imām ash-shaykh Muḥammad ʿAbduh* (Cairo, 1931), I, 11

leaders of the Community – rulers, generals, scholars, etc. – and thinks the verse enjoins obedience to them when they are in agreement on a real interest which is not contrary to scripture.[53] But this obedience is not unlimited in time. Inevitably the consensus of one age conflicts with that of another, and even a single age may revise its consensus if it finds that in the public interest.

For their obligation to obey consensus is due to the public interest, not to infallibility as asserted in the [books on] principles of law; and interest appears and disappears, and varies with different times and conditions, such as strength and weakness [of the Community], etc. This is different from the disobedience to consensus which the early Muslims forbade, by which [consensus] they meant the true views of religion attained by the Companions and Successors, without any disagreement being reliably reported of any of their learned men. And the apparent meaning of Shāfiʿī in his *Risāla* is that this is the consensus which is reckoned as valid, and I think Aḥmad [b. Ḥanbal] held the same view. Clearly it is unreasonable to hold that the men of the first age agreed on a religious matter without its becoming a principle of religion. But what has this to do with the sayings or silence imputed to independent scholars after them, on matters which were unheard of in the best centuries – especially when the rest of the Muslims did not agree with these scholars?[54]

ʿAbduh's view as stated here shows several affinities. Its theological method is Muʿtazilite, since the conclusions are deduced from a view of what Islam is as a whole, a religion of reason, rather than worked out by close philological interpretation of revealed texts. In its ethical theory it is utilitarian, holding the public interest as the supreme standard of value (and thus also the goal of the religion of reason). And in its conclusion it is Hanbalite, accepting as permanently valid only the consensus of the earliest Muslims, without denying a limited weight to later consensus. This Hanbalite aspect was developed by ʿAbduh's disciple Rashīd Riḍā, as is well known.

But the shaykh had to face the classical textual 'proofs', and it is of interest to inspect how he dealt with them. His comments on Qurʾān ii, 137/143 and iii, 106/110 make no reference to consensus. In iii, 98/103 he takes 'God's bond' to be the Qurʾān itself, and 'holding fast...together' to it to be the desirable unity or consensus in following it.[55] 'The agreement is just the holding fast' (*wa innamā l-ijtimāʿu huwa nafsu l-iʿtiṣām*). Thus consensus has no separate authority. He understands iv, 115 as referring to 'the way of the believers' in the Prophet's time, not later. He is conscious that this verse has been used as a basis for the authority of consensus in the classical tradition but does not accept that it is so; adding that the only verse which proves 'the

[53] Ed. M. Rashid Rida, *Tafsīr al-Qurʾān al-ḥakīm* (Cairo, 1927–36), v, 180–1.
[54] *Tafsīr*, v, 208–9.
[55] *Tafsīr*, IV, 19–20.

real consensus' is iv, 59/62, enjoining obedience to those in authority.[56] His interpretation of the latter verse has been explained above.

In the course of his lengthy comment on Qurʾān iv, 59/62 ʿAbduh brings up the Tradition 'My Community does not agree on an error' and its variants, and discusses the classical use of it to support the claim that a consensus must never oppose an earlier consensus.[57] He gives two reasons why the Tradition does not prove the claim. (a) The consensus of the classical jurists, which has traditionally been held authoritative, cannot be considered to be the same as the consensus of the Community. So if the latter is pronounced infallible by the Tradition, the former is not necessarily so, and the traditional practice of *taqlīd*, relying on the opinions of the founders of the four law schools, breaks down.

(b) The consensus of any group is a result of a process of independent judgement (*ijtihād*) by each individual. But an intellectual mistake (*khaṭaʾ*) in *ijtihād* is not reckoned as a moral error (*ḍalāla*); if the *mujtahid* is qualified and tries hard to arrive at the truth, he is doing his duty.[58] Thus there could be a unanimous 'mistake' (*khaṭaʿ*) by the qualified scholars which would not be a unanimous 'error' (*ḍalāla*); so that the Tradition does not rule out the possibility of mistakes and permissibility of revising consensus.

Of these two reasons, (a) makes a fair point, though it does not seem decisive. The working definition of 'the Community' in this context has given rise to a vast amount of discussion in classical and modern times. It would be idle to attempt to go into this question here, and it is preferable not to offer a firm opinion. All I shall say is that, even if ʿAbduh's argument is accepted it does not deny the infallibility of *someone or other*, whether the whole Community or representatives of it, so that the doctrine of cumulative consensus, in some form or other, is untouched. Perhaps this is why ʿAbduh thought a second argument necessary. (b) seems plainly weak, since it depends on an untenable distinction between the words *khaṭa'* and *ḍalāla*, and in any case the Tradition exists in the form *khaṭa'* – though less well attested by its *isnād*, as mentioned above (§8).

In sum, ʿAbduh dealt prudently with the Qurʾanic proofs, but appears to have been floundering in face of the standard Tradition. As an honest scholar equipped only with the classical apparatus of historical criticism, he did not have the means to challenge its authenticity. All he could do was to reinterpret it in a sense that would render it harmless to his modernist understanding of Islam, but in doing so he could not stand up to the objections of even th

[56] *Tafsīr*, v, 417. [57] *Tafsīr*, v, 209.

[58] An allusion to the well-known Tradition: 'If the judge after exerting his mind makes a right decision, he will have a double reward; and if he makes a wrong decision he will still have a single reward.' Bukhari, *Saḥīḥ*, 96: 21. Wensinck, *Concordance*, s.v. '*ijtahada*'.

old-fashioned philology. This is typical of the difficulties of early Islamic modernism, as shown by Sir Hamilton Gibb in his masterly critique, *Modern Trends in Islam.*[59] As for ʿAbduh's own limited doctrine of consensus, it is very sensible like all his practical teaching, but can hardly be drawn precisely from the Qurʾanic injunction 'Obey...those in authority among you' (iv, 59/63) as he claims. Here, as in other interpretations, the shaykh's idealism outran his scholarship. A just assessment of the *Manār Commentary* has been given by Aḥmad Amīn (1886–1954):

It is a practical commentary, expounding the present and explaining its causes; a moral one, summoning men to action according to the principles of Islam and showing it as the source of happiness in all ages; and a spiritual one, summoning to elevation of the soul to the higher world.[60]

14

A contemporary Pakistani thinker, Kemal A. Faruki, takes a somewhat similar position to ʿAbduh's, and with the same end in view, to allow for the operation of a consensus that would be a vehicle for change in Islamic society, not a petrifying force.

Thus, like ʿAbduh, he thinks that scripture upholds the authority of consensus, but in a limited sense.[61]

Faruki accepts the usual texts of Qurʾān and Traditions as proofs that the Islamic Community is infallible in some sense, but seeks to determine the limits of this infallibility as intended by scripture. He argues from general considerations of theology and ethics, in the manner of the Muʿtazilites. First of all he points to the contrast between God and man, indicated by many verses of the Qurʾān. God alone has unlimited infallibility. The limits of man's infallibility in matters of ethical and legal judgement are set by the variation of circumstances in different times and places, and the judgement that is right for one age or country is necessarily not so for other ones that differ in ethically relevant respects. Thus the infallibility of consensus can mean at most that its collective judgement is always sound for the local and temporal conditions for which it is intended.

Consequently, we must acknowledge, without hesitation, the correctness of a past *ijmāʿ* of the community within its given time-space context, i.e. presence, and yet, at the same time, we are fully entitled, indeed obliged, to exert fresh *ijtihād* and come to fresh *ijmāʿ* rulings on the same problems, when necessary, within the changed presence, or time-space context, of the living community.[62]

59 (Chicago, 1947), pp. 68–84. 60 *Zuʿamā al-iṣlāḥ fi l-ʿasr al-ḥadīth* (Cairo, 1949), p. 329.
61 *Ijmāʿ and the gate of ijtihād* (Karachi, 1954), and *Islamic jurisprudence* (Karachi, 1962).
62 *Islamic jurisprudence*, pp. 156–7.

Thus Faruki neatly avoids the dubious exegeses of Muḥammad ʿAbduh, by basing his argument on legitimate general considerations. Applying such considerations to the standard Tradition, he is saying that 'error' – and its opposite 'rightness' – must be understood as relative to time and place. Now ethical relativism in this sense (not to be confused with subjectivism) is indeed obvious to anyone who thinks about morality, and has been accepted by most ethical philosophers, from Aristotle onwards. So it is reasonable to believe that Muḥammad allowed for it in the saying 'My Community does not agree on an error'.

Faruki is not troubled by any doubts about the authenticity of the Traditions. Yet it is just here that the Achilles' heel of any Islamic argument for infallible consensus lies, as will be shown toward the end of this article (§19).

15

These are two examples out of many modernists, with various shades of opinion on consensus. On the other side are those Muslim scholars who have accepted the traditional view of it on the traditional grounds. A well-expressed statement of their view is that of Muḥammad al-Khuḍarī (d. 1917).[63] In between the extremes there are scholars who are content to report the traditional view, without any apparent conviction of their own.[64] This happens, presumably, because on one hand they feel it impossible to deny or ignore the classical doctrine, while on the other hand they do not see consensus as an active procedure of modern Islam and have no wish to revive the binding force of the consensus of the past.

16

It is time now to look in another direction, and ask whether western scholarship has anything to contribute to the question. I shall begin with a plausible argument for infallibility which might be derived from a certain western theory of ethics. This is the theory known as conventionalism or social subjectivism, which was held by some Greek sophists and attacked by Plato, was restated by Hume, and is quite popular in our time. The basic assertion is that in any community the standards of right and wrong are set by the general opinion, sentiment and traditions of the community, i.e. that communal attitudes define value. In our context we cannot do better than quote the statement of this view by the Turkish sociologist Ziya Gökalp (1876–1924), whose outlook owed much to the writings of Émile Durkheim

[63] *Uṣūl al-fiqh*, pp. 279–80.

[64] E.g. Mahmasani, *Falsafat at-tashrīʿ fī l-Islām*, pp. 117–18, Eng. trans., pp. 76–7.

Value...reflects the emphasis society places on certain things which do not intrinsically have the properties implied in the value judgements. The family believes in the respectability of the father, the nation in the sacredness of the soil or of the flag. Therefore, the validity of a value judgement is not determined by its correspondence to a physical object in the external world, but by its correspondence to a social reality which exists in the minds of people. In other words, what the value judgement refers to is found, not in the nature of things but in the beliefs of society.[65]

From this theory the infallibility of the community follows as a logical consequence. For, since the approval of a whole community is by definition what *makes* a practice right for its members, any unanimous consensus of that community necessarily prescribes the right; hence the community is infallible in its moral judgements.

Such an argument could be applied to the Community of Islam as the standard-setting group for Muslims. Islamic textual support for it might then be found in the Tradition quoted by Shaybānī, 'Whatever believers see as good is good with God', etc. (above, §4), understanding 'good with God' as 'really, necessarily good', so that the whole sentence would be merely a religious way of expressing the social subjectivist definition of value. To my knowledge no Muslim has in fact applied the argument to Islam, including Gökalp for whom the primary value-creating community was the nation (*millet*), not the international Muslim *ümmet*.[66] But I have made the application here, to show the complete range of possible theories.

It should be noted that the argument, if correct, would prove not merely the limited infallibility upheld by the Muslim reformers but the cumulative infallibility of classical Islam. For, since the existing social consensus would always set the standard of right, no criticism of it could be right and no departure from it could ever be justified, except where the consensus has set limits to its own validity.

There are, however, two absolutely fatal objections to the whole theory, from the directions of modern ethical philosophy and Islamic theology. From

[65] *Turkish nationalism and western civilization: selected essays of Ziya Gökalp*, Eng. trans. and ed. N. Berkes (London and New York, 1959), p. 148.

[66] Cf. *Turkish nationalism*, p. 185, foot, with p. 224, top. See also p. 171, foot. But Gökalp seems to have been aware of the corresponding implication within the national community, for he developed a doctrine of *örf* (Arabic *ʿurf*) in the nation which parallels the doctrine of infallible *ijmāʿ* in Islam. *Örf* is the collective social consciousness, 'both social rules of conduct and the social conscience (*vicdan*)' (p. 153). The translator renders *örf* as *mores*. So 'there can never be rejected *mores*. *Mores* are those rules which are accepted by the whole community'. (*Ibid.*). Gökalp even quotes the Tradition: 'Whatever the believers (*sic*, *al-muʾminūna*) see as good is good with God', in support not of Islamic *ijmāʿ* but of national *örf* (p. 194). This is rightly called 'a highly arbitrary interpretation' by U. Heyd, *Foundations of Turkish nationalism* (London, 1950), p. 87, n. 2. In general see Heyd, *Foundations*, pp. 50ff., 85–8, and Gibb, *Modern trends in Islam*, p. 92.

the side of ethics, the objection is that the definition of value from which the reasoning proceeds is untrue; for we speak about values in many ways which this definition is unable to account for. In Gökalp's first example quoted above, 'respectability' implies a characteristic of the father as deserving respect; and it is *what* the family believes, so that this value which they attribute to the father cannot be their own state of mind in believing. Similarly, the sacredness of the soil, whatever it may be, is evidently not the same thing as the nation's belief in the sacredness of the soil. Again, if a particular community's beliefs were the final criterion of real values, it would be impossible to criticize the 'accepted' values or value beliefs of that community; all ethical dialogue between communities, and all ethical progress, would then be impossible. (This is not merely a practical objection; it states a discrepancy between the theory and the facts of usage.) It is possible to escape from these objections by defining value in terms of a moral *emotion* of approval rather than an intellectual *belief*. This meets with its own difficulties, but it is not necessary to go into them here; for this variant of the theory can lead to no conclusion about infallibility, since it is meaningless to speak of emotional attitudes as fallible or infallible.[67]

The valid theological objection (stated briefly above, §4 in connection with Shaybānī) is that the definition of value, from which the theory begins, conflicts with that which is implicit in the scriptures of Islam.

Two views are possible of the ethical theory implicit in the Qurān. (a) There is an objective good, a 'natural right', which the Qurʾān and the Prophet enjoin man to follow, and to some extent reveal to him. This is the Muʿtazilite view. (b) The good is simply equivalent to the law of God as stated in scripture; God determines it by His will. This is theistic subjectivism, the prevailing view of classical Islamic jurisprudence and theology. Now neither view is reconcilable with the theory of social subjectivism, that man by his judgement makes right and wrong. It is not hard to find in the Qurʾān itself opposition to this idea. For example,

> Prescribed for you is fighting, though it be hateful to you. Yet it may happen that you will hate a thing which is better for you; and it may happen that you will love a thing which is worse for you; God knows, and you know not (ii, 212/216).

[67] This is as far as we can go here in criticism of social subjectivism. Any reader who sees the difficulties raised will not need further convincing; while one who does not would need a more elaborate treatment. See the brief discussion in my *Ethical value* (Ann Arbor, Mich., and London, 1956), pp. 29–31, and the works of W. D. Ross and others referred to in the notes there. To discuss what the truth about value is would also take us far beyond our present concern.

I think the major point was seen by Ṭawfī in the thirteenth century: see the quotation from him above, note 41.

('You' here is plural, and refers to the whole community.) All the verses that mention God's guidance to man surely include moral guidance, divine not human; e.g.

and God guides whomsoever He will
  to a straight path (ii, 209/13),

and whomsoever God guides,
  he is rightly guided (xvii, 98/97).[68]

Those verses which call the Muslims 'the best nation' and 'a midmost nation' imply the existence of a standard of merit – independent of the 'accepted values' of any nation – by which it is possible to make comparisons of value *between* nations.

The Tradition 'My Community never agrees on *an error*', implies by its very wording that error and truth in ethics and law, whether (a) objective or (b) God-created, correspond to something independent of the Community's opinion. If the saying is genuine, it is further evidence that Muḥammad did not think in terms of values created by the Community itself. The Tradition 'Whatever believers see as good is good with God' etc., should probably be interpreted thus: the Muslims as a whole always see correctly what God has revealed or laid down as good. But since the Tradition might be understood in the other way, mentioned above, it would beg the question to take it as an additional piece of evidence for our view.

17

The next contribution of western thought to settling the problem of the authority of consensus consists in a new statement of the basis on which it rests by the Dutch orientalist C. Snouck Hurgronje (1857–1936), and a criticism by him of that supposed basis. He thought that the real basis of the doctrine was the consensus of the Muslim community; then he pointed out that this construction falls into a vicious circle, because the basis itself has not yet been proven a valid authority.

Since Snouck also laid great emphasis on the importance of consensus as 'the foundation of foundations'[69] of the whole system of Islamic law, his

[68] The question of the general ethical assumptions of the Qurʾān is not dealt with, in the way required here, by T. Izutsu, *The Structure of ethical terms in the Koran* (Tokyo, 1959), or by Salih Shammaʿ, *The Ethical system underlying the Qurʾān* (Tübingen, 1959). For detailed evidence from the Qurʾān, see ch. 3, 'Ethical presuppositions of the Qurʾān'.

[69] 'Le droit musulman', *Revue de l'Histoire des Religions*, 37 (Paris, 1898), reprinted in *Œuvres choisies – Selected works*, ed. G.-H. Bousquet and J. Schacht (Leiden, 1957), p. 289. Similar statements on pp. 56, 225–7, etc. See below in this section for quotation of his reasons and discussion.

criticism of the basis of consensus would, if correct, completely undermine the system as he understood it. Whether he realized this momentous effect or not, his argument deserves examination both for its own interest and because of the continuing influence of his writings, especially in the West.

Snouck's criticism of the basis of consensus is contained in two statements in an essay on Islamic law, published towards the end of the nineteenth century.

(a) The first statement is brief and must be understood as only preliminary. It is prefaced by a mention of the need that had been felt by Muslims after the time of the Prophet for a continuing source of answers to questions about their religion, that would be as indubitable as the words of the Prophet had been to his Companions. As a result,

> Just as the Catholic church, seeking a source of truth [that would be] always available, came to declare itself infallible, in the same way the Muslim community was led to declare itself raised above all error. Such a doctrine evidently rests on a petitio principii.[70]

Taken at its face value, the statement treats the Muslim (or Catholic) community's declaring itself infallible as part of its own 'doctrine' about the basis of infallibility. This is where the doctrine is said to fall into the fallacy of petitio principii (or vicious circle), in resting consensus on the consensus of the very people concerned.

Now it is certainly a fact that the Muslims have been the people to declare their own infallibility; this is natural, since they are the ones most concerned and most disposed to do so. But the doctrine does not 'rest on' the fact of their declaring it. As a doctrine it can only be said to 'rest on' the *reasons* given for it by its own adherents. Thus there is no evident vicious circle, and Snouck's criticism up to this point cannot be regarded as adequate. He probably intended it as nothing but a compressed assertion of his position, since he goes on to a more elaborate statement which does take account of the Muslim reasons.

(b) Snouck knew well that many Muslim scholars had been very conscious of the necessity of avoiding a vicious circle, and in their theories had based consensus on scripture. What he tries to show next, therefore, is that according to their own teaching the proper understanding of scripture itself was based on consensus, so that, in spite of their intention to avoid a vicious circle, they involuntarily fell into one in a more complex manner than they could see.

But before we come to his second statement which explains the vicious circle

[70] *Œuvres choisies*, p. 226.

precisely, it will be useful to interpose another quotation which shows more broadly in what ways he thought consensus was the foundation of the whole system of Islamic law. Writing of the need for consensus in early Islam, Snouck poses a list of questions which urgently called for answers in a community that recognized a divine revelation.

What guarantee was there for later generations that there was in Arabia someone called Mohammed who for twenty-three lunar years preached in God's name? Or: Is the book at present known as the Coran really the collection of Mohammed's sayings? Have the often obscure contents of this Coran been well understood? Are the explanations of the *sunna* correct? Are the Traditions which acquaint us with the *sunna* authentic? Are those which are considered canonical really superior to those which have been rejected? Is the manner in which they are applied in the community sound, or must they be interpreted in quite a different way?[71]

He then mentions consensus as the authority which answers these questions.

It can be admitted that *in general* consensus has in the past performed these important functions with regard to the textual sources. It has been the human agency which has certified the authenticity and meaning of scripture for Muslims, and thus made laws and doctrines finally official, i.e. part of the enforceable public practice or belief of the Muslim community. In this way it has played a large rôle in preserving such unity as Islam has enjoyed in the world; it has been the cement (not the foundation) of the Islamic structure. It can also be admitted that its right to exercise these functions has usually been accepted by Islamic jurisprudence in the past. But the claim that consensus rightfully authenticates and interprets *all texts*, including those which are supposed to authorize consensus itself, leads at once to a vicious circle and requires to be challenged.

All the questions posed by Snouck in the last quotation concern two matters: the *authentication* and the *interpretation* of scripture (Qurʾān and Traditions). We have previously seen (§ 10) how in the Middle Ages someone found a vicious circle in connection with authentication, of the form: consensus, based on Tradition, authenticated by consensus, and how Ghazālī answered him by denying the last step. We have now to see how Snouck found a similar circle in connection with interpretation, and to supply an answer. The quotation which follows is what was referred to near the beginning of this section as his second, deeper statement.

It [consensus] is the fundamental axiom of dogma and law in Islam. Attempts have been made to demonstrate it by the Qurʾān and the *sunna*, but it is impossible to hide the fact that this is to go round in a vicious circle. Only the infallible community can

[71] *Ibid.*

explain the *sunna* and Qurʾān accurately; it is then completely idle to claim to establish the infallibility of the community by the authority of the Qurʾān and the *sunna*. Nevertheless *ijmāʿ* has its *loci probantes*.[72]

Is it true *for all cases, including the texts supporting consensus*, that 'only the infallible community can explain the *sunna* and Qurʾān accurately?' i.e. is it true according to Islamic belief? That is the crucial question that has to be settled. As a basis for an answer, let us recall that for all Muslims the Qurʾān has a definite meaning, or more than one level of meaning, which was determined by God who revealed it. There are parts whose meaning at the highest level (*taʾwīlahu*) is understood by God alone, and which men are discouraged from trying to penetrate (iii, 5); but even in these parts the meaning is there, once for all. In the rest, it is for men to *discover* the meanings, insofar as their knowledge and intelligence permit, but in no sense to create them, either individually or as a community.

In the Traditions, the meaning is that intended by Muḥammad, and the situation is the same except that there is little symbolism and no discouragement to full understanding.

Now, many parts of these texts are addressed to individuals, and most of them are evidently meant to be understood by individuals and capable of being understood by them, sometimes with complete accuracy. These are natural assumptions which we make when we read them. So far as I know, there is no authority for the blanket statement that 'only the infallible community can explain the *sunna* and Qurʾān accurately'. Indeed, it is logically impossible, if taken in a strict sense, for a consensus is made up of the individual interpretations of *mujtahids* prior to it, and unless all these were accurate the consensus would not be so.

But even if Snouck's statement is taken as applying only to the situation *after* consensus, it is still not true of all texts. For three classes of texts may be distinguished. (a) Those whose meaning is clear to all individuals, so that even if there *is* consensus on them an individual can still penetrate them directly for himself. (b) Those on whose interpretation individuals might hesitate, but which have been settled by the consensus of former *mujtahids*. Such, for example, are the texts attributing to God anthropomorphic qualities, which it is agreed He cannot have in a physical sense. This middle class is the active zone of consensus (*ijmāʿ* in the technical sense), though even here competent individuals like the classical commentators may quite well interpret the meaning for themselves, in accordance with consensus but penetrating behind it to the reasons for it. (c) There are texts on which no consensus has

[72] *Ibid.*, p. 227.

been reached, and it is for qualified individuals to judge the meanings as best as they can.

To which class do the texts supporting consensus belong? Some belong to (a), for instance the Tradition 'Hold fast to the Community', whose meaning is probably plain to every Muslim, as well as approved by past consensus. Some belong to (c), such as the Tradition 'My Community does not agree on an error', where there are different interpretations of the extension of the Community and the range of subjects judged by it without error (see § 3.2). Therefore consensus does not guarantee the interpretation of this most important text; and there are others in the same case, as has been seen. But *no* relevant text belongs to (b). Indeed no valid support for consensus could possibly be found in this class, because that would be 'to base a thing on itself', as Arabic writers on the subject say.

Since Muslim scholars have seen the fallacy so regularly, it seems strange that Snouck attributed it to them, by assuming that *all* the *loci probantes* fall in class (b). Apparently he thought the entire interpretation of Islamic scripture had been fixed by consensus, so that a Muslim of later ages was bound hand and foot to it and could not move a step without it. This has never been wholly true even in the most conservative periods. Possibly his emphatic declarations that consensus is 'the foundation of foundations' of Islamic law inhibited him from admitting that the doctrine of consensus itself had a solid foundation in scripture. That for him would have been circular, because he could not see that a scripture could have any meaning but that put into it by an interpretation governed by consensus. The difficulty vanishes when we see scripture as the believer does, as a good with God-given meanings, allowing for more or less 'objective' or 'correct' interpretations. The texts on which the authority of consensus rests are thus regarded as having a true interpretation which supports it in fact, and it is held that this interpretation can be seen – or rather cannot avoid being seen – by any fair-minded, normally intelligent and sufficiently educated individual. Consensus is therefore like a medieval sultan, wielding great executive power in fact, but one which is theoretically delegated by a caliph as the primary source of authority.

Whatever the importance of consensus in the classical system, Snouck's conception of it as the theoretical foundation of the system pays a high price in philosophical and theological difficulties. For this conception allows only two alternatives, both of which have now been seen as untenable. Either consensus rests on another consensus of the same kind, leading to the petitio principii which he has pointed out. Or consensus is itself an ultimate foundation carrying its own authority. This makes it like the tortoise on which stands the elephant, on which the world rests: the pile falls into space, because consensus by itself has no authority to support anything else.

Why this is so has been explained in the preceding section (§ 16) where it was maintained that the consensus of the community does not by definition create values, either in fact or according to the Qurʾān.

18

Other orientalists have not followed Snouck in his provocative argument concerning the basis of consensus. Their own statements on this point have sometimes been lacking in clarity or decisiveness. Ignaz Goldziher (1850–1921), after quoting the main Tradition and Qurʾān iv. 115, adds: 'Other theologians regarded the validity of *ijmāʿ* as a postulate [Postulat] of sound human understanding, and made no effort to search for written proofs of it'.[73] The meaning of this 'postulate' is not further explained, and no references are given. David Santillana (1855–1921) says of consensus that 'it is founded on a kind of diffused inspiration, by which the community of believers never loses contact with the Truth, i.e. God'.[74] This is more like a formulation of what consensus *is* than of what it is founded on. He also refers to the textual bases in Qurʾān and Traditions. The truest statement is a simple one by Louis Gardet. After mentioning the historical origin of the doctrine in the practical needs of the community, he writes: 'From the point of view of Islam, however, a politico-religious conception could not be fully legitimate without a scriptural basis.'[75]

Where Snouck has been very influential on later scholars is in bringing them to full awareness of the important functions of authentication and interpretation performed by consensus and, less fortunately, in leading them into ambiguous claims of fundamentality. Two quotations will illustrate the trend.[76]

(a) Gotthelf Bergsträsser (1886–1933):

These four roots (*uṣūl*) are disparate: two sources, one method and one court of appeal (Instanz). Herewith it is admitted that the last [consensus] is the really decisive one, guaranteeing the authenticity of the other two and determining their interpretation (just as in the Catholic church the authority of the church comes historically *after* the Bible, but systematically *before* it, since it guarantees its divinity and establishes its interpretation in a binding way).[77]

[73] *Die Ẓâhiriten* (Leipzig, 1884), p. 33, n. 1.
[74] *Istituzioni di diritto musulmano Malichita* (Rome, 1925), I, 41.
[75] *La cité musulmane* (Paris, 1954), p. 121.
[76] Cf. also Santillana, *Istituzioni*, I, 41; Schacht, *Origins*, p. 2.
[77] *Grundzüge des islamischen Rechts*, ed. J. Schacht (Berlin and Leipzig, 1935), p. 14.

(b) Sir Hamilton Gibb:

Indeed, on a strict logical analysis it is obvious that *ijmāʿ* underlies the whole imposing structure and alone gives it final validity. For it is *ijmāʿ* in the first place which guarantees the authenticity of the text of the Koran and of the Traditions. It is *ijmāʿ* which determines how the words of their texts are to be pronounced and what they mean, etc.[78]

Both statements are illuminating and valid if understood aright. But after the analysis of Snouck presented above it will not be necessary to explain how such words as 'decisive', 'guarantees', 'determines', 'underlies' and 'gives validity' must be qualified if they are not to give wrong ideas of the basic relations of consensus and scripture.

The over-emphasis by orientalists on consensus in general has not gone without protest from Muslim scholars. Muḥammad Abu Zahra in particular has criticized six points, including the claim that consensus has priority over scripture.[79] His remarks have provided a lively stimulus to the writing of this article, for they have made apparent the wide divergence between what orientalists and Muslims have been thinking on the theory of classical consensus.

19

We have explored some blind alleys, not (it is hoped) without profit to the general understanding of the subject. Next we shall follow the path of the orientalists in a more valid direction: their criticism of the authenticity of Traditions attributed to the Prophet. Since the main weight of proof for consensus has always been placed by Muslim scholars on the Prophetic Traditions which assert plainly the infallibility of the Community, well-founded criticism of the claim that these Traditions spring from the Prophet is a serious matter.

In his classic *Muhammedanische Studien*,[80] Goldziher raised doubts about the whole corpus of Traditions, applying modern methods of historical source analysis to show how most of them must have arisen in late Umayyad and early ʿAbassid times. His conclusions have been accepted by western scholars, and, as Schacht has written, 'This brilliant discovery became the cornerstone of all serious investigation of early Muhammadan law and jurisprudence...'[81] Schacht has followed with a more intensive investigation of legal Traditions, in *Origins of Muhammadan Jurisprudence*, and has confirmed Goldziher's conclusions for that particular class.

[78] *Mohammedanism* (Oxford, 1949), p. 96.
[79] *Abū Ḥanīfa*, pp. 321–3.
[80] II, 1–274, 'Ueber die Entwicklung des Ḥadîth'.
[81] *Origins*, p. 4.

The Traditions on the freedom of the whole Community from error have not escaped criticism, and we have seen above the unavoidable inference from the silence of Shāfiʿī with regard to them: that he either did not know them or did not accept them, since if he had he would certainly have quoted them as the best possible support for consensus. This argument applies to all forms of the Tradition having the same meaning; and it throws grave doubt on the authenticity of the Traditions, since a Tradition on such a vital subject not known to Shāfiʿī is under suspicion of having been created later.

But further, since both the Muʿtazilites and Shāfiʿī give the idea of the main Tradition in almost the very words used in it (see §4) we are led to see the genesis of the Tradition out of the previously circulating idea. In other words, if the record of the idea precedes the record of the Tradition, there is a suspicion that the Tradition arose after the idea and in order to substantiate it. This argument by itself is not conclusive, for we can never be sure of a *post hoc, ergo propter hoc* argument, and it is always possible that a genuine Tradition existed unknown to Shāfiʿī. But the argument is circumstantially strong, in combination with other facts.

One such fact is that the Tradition was disputed in the time of Naẓẓām (d. 835–45), just the time when a new Tradition might have arisen as a result of the impetus given by Shāfiʿī and his school.[82]

Another ground for suspicion lies in the use of the phrase 'my Community' (*ummatī*) in all these Traditions. Did the historical Muḥammad ever refer to the Muslims in these terms? The phrase seems altogether more possessive and Messianic than anything to be found in the Qurʾān, which never describes the Muslims to Muḥammad as 'your Community', or in the Covenant of Madīna.[83]

Again, the assertion that the Muslim Community of all future times would never commit a unanimous error seems far to exceed anything that a man could normally know, and such a claim does not accord with the real Muḥammad's humility and his awareness of his human limits, as they appear to us from the Qurʾān. From the very fact that this claim is made in a Tradition, we know that it is not attributed to Muḥammad's revealed knowledge, but is supposed to be a part of his merely human knowledge. With all his wisdom, how on earth could he know such a thing? It is true that the

[82] Ghazālī, *Mustaṣfā*, I, 112. It is true that Ghazālī says the Traditions were *never* denied *before* the time of Naẓẓam. But as he is relying on the traditional *isnād* evidence, which modern scholarship has found good reason to question, we are justified in disregarding his statement about early Islam, and attaching greater weight to his testimony that the Traditions *were* denied in the time of Naẓẓam – a period which he knew better through its literary remains.

[83] Ibn Isḥāq, *Sīra*, ed. F. Wüstenfeld, *Das Leben Muhammed's nach Muhammed b. Isḥāķ* (Gottingen, 1858–60), 341–4; tr. A. Guillaume, *The life of Muhammad* (Oxford, 1955), pp. 231–3.

Tradition appears in a more elaborate variant, 'I begged God the Exalted that my Community might never be united on an error, and He granted it to me,'[84] and this version seems made to order to answer the objection, by bringing in an element of revelation. But, once our critical judgement of Traditions is aroused, it is precisely such a feature which leads us to think it *was* made to order, literally, for exactly this purpose. Thus it appears merely as a later stage in the life-cycle of this cluster of Traditions.

Finally, we have seen that the Qurʾān contains no clear text on the infallibility of the Muslim Community, as Muslim scholars have often admitted. But if this doctrine had been intended originally as a part of Islam, and one which would inevitably have the most far-reaching effects on its religious law, is it likely that it would have been left to the Prophet to state in Tradition, and never once proclaimed in the Qurʾān as a part of the revealed religion? If the answer is No, as is reasonable, it must be concluded that it is unlikely that the doctrine is part of original Islam, and that the Tradition is not genuine.

Now, since every form of the Tradition is subject to one or more of these objections, it is no use saying that the sum total of them guarantees that the Prophet really spoke of infallibility, though the words are uncertain. For a sum of weaknesses is weak, not strong.

Up to the present, the fundamental researches of Goldziher and Schacht on the Traditions of Islam have had little impact on the thinking and writing of Muslim scholars. There is thus once more a great gap between the attitudes of western and Muslim scholars, the one party not counting the Traditions 'Muhammadan', the other still quoting them as authorities for *sharīʿa* law, without considering the grave doubts that have been cast upon them.

20

This article has led to two major conclusions.

(a) Any sound basis for the authority of an infallible, cumulative consensus, as a definite institution of Islam, must be found in a text of Islamic scripture. On this principle the classical Muslim scholars were right.

(b) No such basis can be found in the Qurʾān, or in any Tradition that can be regarded with confidence as authentic. This is what modern scholarship leads us to think.

Using these two conclusions as premises, we arrive at a third: that there is no sound basis for the traditional doctrine of consensus in Islam.

[84] Quoted by Ghazālī, *Mustaṣfā*, I, 111.

This last conclusion is not at all disastrous for the religion of Islam, either as a system of belief – so long as it continues to be solidly based on the Qurʾān, at least – or as a system of practice, where traditional consensus was only a barrier to modern change. Indeed, it is now nearly a century since Muḥammad ʿAbduh started to break away from *taqlīd*, and in the meanwhile the Muslim peoples have done very well without such a restraint. But they have not until now found a sufficient theoretical justification for ignoring past consensus. Perhaps the present study will be helpful in that direction, the more so as it has not been written with any practical purpose in mind or any foreknowledge of what conclusions would be reached.

It has occurred to some Muslim thinkers, such as Kemal Faruki, to consider a revocable consensus one of the principles of Islamic law. This sounds more reasonable, and we have looked with respect at Faruki's argument for it. Still, this consensus remains infallible within its limits of time and space, for Faruki accepts the Tradition as authentic. Now even this must be abandoned if the Tradition is not authentic.

All that remains possible, then, is a consensus that is revocable and fallible. But this should provide quite enough authority for the needs of the religious community. The Qurʾān, as has been seen, does contain positive injunctions to Muslims to maintain solidarity, to stick together in following the path of Islam. The fulfilment of these injunctions can be carried out by the worldwide Muslim community in any way it sees fit, in accordance with its vision of its religious interests and obligations. In pursuing these ends, Muslims can accept what they find beneficial from the institutions of the past, or create new institutions, such as ecumenial councils of religious leaders. Whatever is generally agreed upon will surely constitute an effective unifying consensus until it is revised, but there will be no need to think that Muḥammad made it irrevocable or infallible.

14

IBN SĪNĀ'S 'ESSAY ON THE SECRET OF DESTINY'

On several occasions in his writings Ibn Sīnā discusses the problem of destiny (*al-qadar*), by which he means primarily the problem of reconciling the divine determination of human acts and characters with the rewards and punishments of the after-life, in such a way as to safeguard God's justice to man. This aspect of the problem of theodicy had arisen long before his time out of statements of the Qur'ān and Traditions, and had been settled in their own fashions by Mu'tazilite and predestinarian theologians. Ibn Sīnā as a philosopher could hardly avoid offering a solution, if only to satisfy the doubts of his Muslim public; but he goes beyond a perfunctory answer, and seems to show a genuine interest in finding an intellectually convincing solution consistent with his own philosophy. As would be expected, he interprets the data of the problem in his own terms and comes up with a distinctly Neoplatonic answer, while taking care to express this in a way that might have a chance of acceptance in his religious milieu, Muslim Iran of the early eleventh century A.D.

The word 'destiny' in the title and text of this article is used as a deliberately ambiguous translation of Arabic *al-qadar*. Omitting complexities, we may for our purpose distinguish two main significations of the word in the religious context of earlier Islam. The older usage is 'predestination' of human acts and characters by a freely willed decision of God for each person. This is the apparent meaning of the word in the Qur'ān and Traditions, and it was understood thus by Muslim theologians. But *al-qadar* also came to be used by Muslim philosophers in their own sense: 'determination' of man's life as a part of a cosmic system in which God causes His effects by the necessity of His nature and their natures. As in other cases, the philosophers found it convenient to employ an accepted Islamic term in a new way rather than draw attention to their own innovation of thought by inventing a new term. I shall therefore distinguish 'predestination' and 'determination' where it is required for analysis, but in many places it will be more suitable to use 'destiny', to reproduce as nearly as possible the full associations of Ibn Sīnā's language.

Apart from the passages occurring in longer works on other subjects, which will be referred to below, Ibn Sīnā wrote two monographs on destiny which have survived. One is *Risālat al-qadar* 'Essay on destiny'.[1] This is written in a florid, rhetorical Arabic, with a vocabulary which would place it beyond the reach of readers unlearned in Arabic literature. It is one of a group of mystical works which Ibn Sīnā presented as the wisdom of the mythical Ḥayy b. Yaqẓān. I shall refer to it, but it is not the subject of this article. The other monograph, of unknown date, is *Risāla fī sirr al-qadar*, 'Essay on the secret of destiny'.[2] This opusculum too is difficult, but for different reasons. One is extrinsic: the faulty state of the Hyderabad edition, which has been the most accessible version so far. Two further reasons are intrinsic to the essay as its author wrote it: the order of the argument is not altogether logical, and the exposition is very concise. The work therefore stands in need of elucidation, and I shall try to provide this in the present article. Ibn Sīnā's general thought on the problem of destiny will be described to the extent that is needed for this purpose. Finally I shall discuss the problem of Ibn Sīnā's style of philosophical writing in the essay.

EDITIONS AND MANUSCRIPTS

Of the two printed editions referred to above in note 2, that of Cairo (1910) was unavailable to me, while that of Hyderabad (1934) is not very satisfactory. I therefore made a new provisional text, based on four good manuscripts out of fourteen listed in bibliographies.[3] This edition was published as part of my original article, and I must refer readers of Arabic to those pages.[4] It has proved impracticable in contemporary economic conditions to incorporate Arabic script and notes in the present book. But the analysis of the Essay which follows the translation refers exclusively to this translation and is fully intelligible, I believe, in terms of it.

[1] Ed. and paraphrased by A. F. Mehren, *Traités mystiques...d'Avicenne*, IV (Leiden, 1899).

[2] In *Majmūʿat rasāʾil ash-shaykh ar-raʾīs*, ed. A. A. al-ʿAlawi (Hyderabad, 1353 h./1934), fourth treatise. Also in *Majmūʿat ar-rasāʾil* (Cairo, 1328 h./1910), 243–9. Translated from the Hyderabad edition by A. J. Arberry in his *Avicenna on theology* (London, 1951), pp. 38–41 'Predestination'.

[3] See C. Brockelmann, *Geschichte der arabischen Litteratur*, I[2] (Leiden, 1943), p. 456; *Supplementband*, I (Leiden, 1943), no. 49; G. Anawati, *Muʾallafāt Ibn Sīnā* (Cairo, 1950), no. 181, pp 240–1; Y. Mahdavi, *Fihrist nuskhahā-ye muṣannafāt Ibn-i Sīnā* (Tehran, 1954), pp. 9–10 Hyderabad, editor's note after the text.

[4] Ibn Sīnā's "Essay on the secret of destiny", *Bulletin of the School of Oriental and African Studies*, 29 (1966), pp. 25–48.

TRANSLATION[5]

Ibn Sīnā, 'Essay on the secret of destiny'

In the name of God, the Merciful, the Compassionate.

Someone asked the eminent *shaykh* Abū ʿAlī b. Sīnā (may God the Exalted have mercy on him) the meaning of the Ṣūfī saying, 'He who knows the secret of destiny is an atheist'. In reply he stated that this matter contains the utmost obscurity, and is one of those matters which may be set down only in enigmatic form and taught only in a hidden manner, on account of the corrupting effects its open declaration would have on the general public. The basic principle concerning it is found in a Tradition of the Prophet (God bless and safeguard him): 'Destiny is the secret of God; do not declare the secret of God'. In another Tradition, when a man questioned the Prince of the Believers, ʿAlī (may God be pleased with him), he replied, 'Destiny is a deep sea; do not sail out on it'. Being asked again he replied, 'It is a stony path; do not walk on it'. Being asked once more he said, 'It is a hard ascent; do not undertake it'.[6]

The *shaykh* said: Know that the secret of destiny is based upon certain premises, such as [1] the world order, [2] the report[7] that there is Reward and Punishment, and [3] the affirmation of the resurrection of souls.

[1] The first premise is that you should know that in the world as a whole and in its parts, both upper and earthly, there is nothing which forms an exception to the facts that God is the cause of its being and origination and that God has knowledge of it, controls it, and wills its existence; it is all subject to His control, determination, knowledge, and will. This is a general and superficial account, although in these assertions we intend to describe it truly, not as the theologians understand it;[8] and it is possible to produce proofs and demonstrations of that. Thus, if it were not that this world is composed of elements which give rise to good and evil things in it and produce both righteousness and wickedness in its inhabitants, there would have been no completion of an order for the world. For if the world had contained nothing but pure righteousness, it would not have been this world but another one,

[5] I have inserted numbers and letters in square brackets, to show what seem to be the divisions of the argument and to facilitate the analysis.

[6] These Traditions do not explain the meaning of the original saying, they merely reaffirm the prohibition.

[7] 'Report' (*ḥadīth*) seems to hint that afterlife Reward and Punishment in the usual sense are only traditional doctrines, not known by science. This view is confirmed below, and elsewhere, e.g. *Shifāʾ: Ilāhiyyāt*, IX, ed. I. Madkour, M. Y. Musa, S. Dunya and S. Zayed (Cairo, 1960), ix, ch. 6, 414ff.

[8] 'Truly', i.e. according to the Neoplatonic system of causal determination, not the voluntaristic conceptions of *kalām* – Muʿtazilite and other. Thus Ibn Sīnā's 'destiny' should not be called 'predestination'.

and it would necessarily have had a composition different from the present composition; and likewise if it had contained nothing but sheer wickedness, it would not have been this world but another one. But whatever is composed in the present fashion and order contains both righteousness and wickedness.

[2] The second premise is that according to the ancients Reward is the occurrence of pleasure in the soul corresponding to the extent of its perfection, while Punishment is the occurrence of pain in the soul corresponding to the extent of its deficiency. So the soul's abiding in deficiency is its 'alienation from God the Exalted',[9] and this is 'the curse', 'the Penalty', [God's] 'wrath' and 'anger', and pain comes to it from that deficiency; while its perfection is what is meant by [God's] 'satisfaction' with it, its 'closeness' and 'nearness' and 'attachment'. This, then, and nothing else is the meaning of 'Reward' and 'Punishment' according to them.

[3] The third premise is that the resurrection is just the return of human souls to their own world: this is why God the Exalted has said, 'O tranquil soul, return to your Lord satisfied and satisfactory'.

These are summary statements, which need to be supported by their proper demonstrations.

Now, if these premises are established, we say [*a*] that the apparent evils which befall this world are, on the principles of the Sage,[10] not purposed for the world – the good things alone are what is purposed, the evil ones are a privation, while according to Plato both are purposed as well as willed; [*b*] and that the commanding and forbidding of acts to responsible beings, by revelation in the world, are just a stimulant to him of whom it was foreknown [by God] that there would occur in him [performance of] the commandments, or (in the case of a prohibition) a deterrent to him of whom it was foreknown that he would refrain from what is forbidden. Thus the commandment is a cause of the act's proceeding from him of whom it is foreknown that it will proceed, and the prohibition is a cause of intimidation to him who refrains from something bad because of it. Without the commandment the former would not have come to desire the act; without the prohibition the latter would not have been scared. It is as if one were to imagine that it would have been possible for 100 per cent of wickedness to befall in the absence of any prohibition, and that with the presence of the prohibitions 50 per cent of wickedness has befallen, whereas without prohibitions 100 per cent would have befallen. Commandments must be judged in the same way: had there been no commandments nothing of righteousness would have befallen, but

[9] All the words put here within quotation marks are Islamic religious expressions which Ibn Sīnā is interpreting in his own way.
[10] *al-ḥakīm*, the epithet of Aristotle.

with the advent of the commandments 50 per cent of righteousness has occurred.

[*c*] As for praise and blame, these have just two objects. One is to incite a doer of good to repeat the like act which is willed to proceed from him; the second is to scare the one from whom the act has occurred from repeating the like of it, and [ensure] that the one from whom that act has [not] occurred will abstain from doing what is not willed to proceed from him, though it is in his capacity to do it.

[*d*] It is not admissible that Reward and Punishment should be such as the theologians suppose: chastisement of the fornicator, for example, by putting him in chains and shackles, burning him in the fire over and over again, and setting snakes and scorpions upon him. For this is the behaviour of one who wills to slake his wrath against his enemy, through injury or pain which he inflicts on him out of hostility against him; and that is impossible in the character of God the Exalted, for it is the act of one who wills that the very being who models himself on him should refrain from acts like his or be restrained from repeating such acts. And it is not to be imagined that after the resurrection there are obligations, commandments, and prohibitions for anyone, so that by witnessing Reward and Punishment they should be scared or refrain from what is proscribed to them and desire what is commanded to them. So it is false that Reward and Punishment are as they have imagined them.

[*e*] As for the [system of] penalties ordained by the divine Law for those who commit transgressions, it has the same effect as the prohibitions in serving as a restraint upon him who abstains from transgression, whereas without it it is imaginable that the act might proceed from him. There may also be a gain to the one who is subject to penalty, in preventing him from further wickedness, because men must be bound by one of two bonds, either the bond of the divine Law or the bond of reason, that the order of the world may be completed. Do you not see that if anyone were let loose from both bonds the load of wickedness he would commit would be unbearable, and the order of the world's affairs would be upset by the dominance of him who is released from both bonds? But God is more knowing and wiser.

PROBLEMS OF INTERPRETATION

The text and translation presented above are, I believe, clear enough in the meaning of the individual sentences. But the meaning in general is still not clear. What is the problem of the essay? What are the steps in the argument, and the conclusion? To answer these questions, we have to deal with the two intrinsic kinds of obscurity mentioned at the beginning of this article, the illogicality and excessive brevity of the essay; and we may begin by specifying these apparent defects.

[1]–[3] are the three 'premises' (*muqaddamāt*), which are initially stated together and then explained briefly in the same order. Now the peculiarity of this order is that it is logically inappropriate, because [2] entails [3] as its condition; [3] should therefore have been stated before [2]. The 'Reward' and 'Punishment' spoken of in [2] are certainly states of the soul after death; this is proved both by the terms used, *thawāb* and *ʿiqāb*, which are not applied to ordinary rewards and punishments, and by what is said about them in [*d*] and in other works of Ibn Sīnā. Thus [3], the existence of an after-life, is basic to [2]. Further, what is said in [2] about this Reward and Punishment is determined by the character of the after-life described in [3]: it is 'a return of human souls to their own world' (without bodies), therefore Reward and Punishment can only be of souls alone. Thus the natural order of premises in this context would be: [3] there is an after-life of the soul; [2] in that life souls receive a certain kind of reward and punishment.[11]

When we turn to the sections listed [*a*]–[*e*], further problems of order emerge. What is the relation of these sections to [1]–[3]? The only clue given is at the beginning of [*a*], 'Now if these premises are established, we say...' This is insufficient. We are not shown which of the lettered sections follow from which of the three premises, or whether there is some other relation between them. Actually the lettered sections make the best sense when taken as further explanations of the premises, or answers to objections against them, and this is how I shall take them in reconstructing the argument. But even if this is granted, the order of the five lettered sections does not correspond in a simple way to the order of the premises. Four of them, [*a*], [*b*], [*c*], and [*e*], are connected in their subjects with [1], in a way which will be shown, but their series is interrupted by [*d*], which is connected with [2]. The order of my exposition will therefore be as follows:

[1], [*a*], [*b*], [*c*], [*e*]
[3]
[2], [*d*]

[11] This correction would not be justified if the author were here concerned with *proving* an afterlife *from* Reward and Punishment as previously known facts, used as evidence. He might then conceivably have reasoned in the order of entailment: '[2] we know that there are Reward and Punishment of the soul after death; [3] such Reward and Punishment entail a life of the soul after death'. But in this essay Ibn Sīnā is taking the existence of an afterlife of the soul as an accepted premise. The appropriate order of exposition is therefore from the general assertion of a state [3], the afterlife, to a specification of that state [2], certain experiences in that life. I have called Ibn Sīnā's order 'logically inappropriate' rather than simply 'illogical', just for this reason, that in another context [2] entails [3] would have been logical.

The brevity of the essay as a quantity is self-evident. But it is necessary to point out some features of this brevity which add to the work's obscurity. 'The secret of destiny', if known, would certainly solve some problem, by bringing to light an understanding of destiny which is now hidden from most human minds. This much can be gathered from the introductory paragraph. But we are not told what the problem is. We are taken straight into three 'premises', on which the secret is said to be 'based'. Then perhaps we may find out what the problem is when we come to the conclusion, to which the premises will lead. But there is no conclusion either! So both the problem and its solution have to be inferred from the premises and from what we know of Ibn Sīnā's concerns and ways of thinking in other writings. Besides, the whole argument is very concise at every stage, and also needs to be filled out from the thought-world of the philosopher. He himself is conscious of this, as can be seen in two places where he says he is only giving a general summary of the premises without their proofs.

By now it will be natural to wonder why the essay has these peculiarities, and Ibn Sīnā's introduction may have suggested a reason. But it will be less prejudicial to the understanding of the essay's main content if we leave that question in suspense, and first examine the content in itself, seeking out what is intelligible in it without having come to any conclusions about the cause or causes of its recondite presentation. The main argument will therefore be set out next in the reconstructed order mentioned above, and the missing elements will be supplied, by inference from what is stated here and in other works. The reconstruction is, of course, a hypothesis, but it will be presented categorically; its probability can then be judged from its internal coherence and its consistency with Ibn Sīnā's thought as a whole. After that we can consider his introduction and the question mentioned above.

ELUCIDATION

The first task must be to find out what the problem is which the essay is trying to solve. This can best be done by considering the premises on which the secret is said to be based. What is meant by 'basing a secret on premises'? I think the three premises are three propositions which, if they are all accepted as true, lead to a serious question. If we set the propositions in their classical Islamic context, the question to which they lead comes easily to mind:

If [1] all events in the world are caused by the power (*qadar*) of God,
and [3] there is an afterlife,
and [2] in the afterlife men are rewarded and punished,
Then how can God be good? And in particular how can He be just to man?

This is the classical problem of evil, with its special form the problem of divine justice. The latter had been brought to the fore by Muᶜtazilite theologians as early as the end of the eighth century, as a result of studying the difficulties raised by the Qurʾān; and it was still being discussed in Ibn Sīnā's time by the Persian Muᶜtazilite ᶜAbd al-Jabbār (*c.* 937–1025), chief justice of Rayy, whose great work *al-Mughnī* was very probably known to him.[12] The problem is stated concisely by Ibn Sīnā in his *Ishārāt*: 'If there is destiny why is there Punishment?'[13] It is also the primary topic of *Risālat al-qadar*, in which Ibn Sīnā's travelling companion was unable to reconcile destiny with Reward and Punishment, and so came to doubt destiny.[14] Ibn Sīnā's solution is not that of a Muᶜtazilite theologian but of a Muslim Neoplatonic philosopher. It is reached by interpreting the premises in his own terms and answering objections that might be raised.

[1] Ibn Sīnā asserts emphatically the complete determination of the world by God. We must understand this *qadar* in the Neoplatonic sense of the necessary emanation of everything else from the Supreme Being. Thus it is clear that in seeking a solution to the problem of divine justice he is not going to abandon or weaken this doctrine of destiny, even though he understands it very differently from theological 'predestination'. Then he mentions that this world which proceeds from God necessarily contains evil as well as good. The reason for this is indicated only briefly here: that without evil 'there would have been no completion of an order for the world', and 'it would not have been this world but another one'. This explanation is inadequate, because it prompts the question, Why did it have to be this world just as it is, and not another one? Ibn Sīnā appears here to beg the whole question of the existence of evil in a world made by an omnipotent God.

But we find his answer expounded more fully in the 'Metaphysics' of *ash-Shifāʾ*, along the following lines: A perfect, all-powerful Creator necessarily fulfils the maximum good in every possible variety of ways.

So if someone objects, 'It was possible for the First Governor to have brought into being pure good, free from evil', we answer: That was not possible in this sort of existence. If it was a possibility of absolute existence, on the ground that there is a kind of absolute existence free [from evil], it was not this present kind; it was something which had already emanated from the First Governor and existed in the intellectual, psychic, and

[12] See *Mughnī*, VI.i, 'On justice and injustice'.

[13] *faʾin kāna l-qadar falimā l-ᶜiqāb?*, *Kitāb al-Ishārāt*, ed. S. Dunyā, with Ṭūsī's Commentary (Cairo, 1379 h./1960), 742. French trans. A.-M. Goichon, *Livre des directives et remarques* (Paris, 1951), p. 463. Eng. trans. S. Inati, Ibn Sīnā, *Directives and remarks* (Toronto, 1984).

[14] Ed. Mehren, Arabic, pp. 1–2. For another form of the problem of divine justice, the uneven distribution of worldly fortunes, see *Risālat al-arzāq*, ed. H. Ritter, *Majallat al-Majmāᶜ al-ᶜIlmī al-ᶜArabī* (Damascus), 25 (1950), 203–9.

celestial spheres, and there remained as a possibility the present sort – i.e. our world, compounded of form and matter.[15]

The causes of evil are found only in the sublunary sphere, a minute part of the total universe, which contains matter. And even here there is far more good than evil, which strikes only a minority of individuals, leaving the majority untouched by real evil and allowing the preservation of the species.[16] Consequently God is producing more good and less evil by creating this sphere than by refraining from its creation.[17]

The outpouring of good does not require that a predominant good be abandoned because of a rare evil; for its abandonment would be worse than that evil, because the privation of that [good] which is capable of existing in the character of matter is a double privation and thus worse than a single one.[18]

So this is how the creation of our mixed sphere 'completes the order' of the world as a whole.[19] To have refrained from producing it would have been 'a greater fault in the total order of good'.[20] Why evil is unavoidable in a sphere which has matter will be explained shortly in connection with [*a*].

[*a*] is a very brief discussion of a further point about the relation of a perfectly good God to evil, so the passage goes naturally with [1]. It has been stated as true in [1] that everything in the world is willed (*murād bihi*) by God; and it has been suggested, though much too briefly, how this fact can be reconciled with the existence of a certain amount of evil which God cannot avoid. But this position suggests a further problem. Does God really purpose (*qaṣada*) these things which He cannot help creating? To will something is to perform the mental act which carries over into an external change in the world; it is to create or to do. To purpose is at least to intend a certain result, consciously aware of what will be effected by the act of will, and possibly also to desire it. Now God as conceived by a Hellenistic philosopher necessarily wills everything that exists, good and evil. But it is an open question whether He purposes everything. Does He in any sense purpose the evil which he creates?

Ibn Sīnā contents himself with stating the different answers which he attributes to Aristotle and Plato: of the former, that the evil is not purposed,

[15] *Ilāhiyyāt*, IX, ch. 6, 421.

[16] *Ilāhiyyāt*, IX, ch. 6, 417.

[17] *Ibid.*, 418, 421.

[18] *Ibid.*, 418. The double privation is of the good that is normally found in material things and the good that might conceivably have existed in place of the evil. The single privation is of the latter only.

[19] *Sirr al-qadar*, [1]; *Ilāhiyyāt*, II, ix, ch. 6, 421.

[20] *Ilāhiyyāt*, IX, pt. 6, 418. Cf. *Dānesh-nāme-ye Alāʾī*, French trans. M. Achena and H. Massé, *Le Livre de science*, I (Paris, 1955), 215. Cf. St John of Damascus, *De Fide Orthodoxa*, IV, 21: God created people who He knows will sin; but if He had refused to create them, evil would have won a victory in preventing the creation of some people with potentialities for good.

of the latter, that it is. He does not give his own preference. This reticence seems strange, since the question raised here poses a more acute dilemma than what has gone before. For, if Aristotle is understood as saying that God in no sense purposes evil, God seems unable to control fully what He wills by His conscious mind; while according to the view ascribed to Plato His will is controlled by His purpose, but this purpose now appears as partly sinister, with evil entering the very heart of God. But before we try to decide why Ibn Sīnā gives no opinion of his own here, it will be useful to turn again to what he teaches about evil in other works.

In his discussions on providence (*al-ʿināya*) in the 'Metaphysics' and elsewhere Ibn Sīnā explains that in the material conditions of this world many things can only give their advantages at the risk of evil incidentally arising from them. The stock example is fire. Its burning power is precisely 'the aim that is purposed from fire', but the movements of things in the world inevitably bring it occasionally into conflict with other things like flesh which are damaged by it.[21] Another example is taken from human society: a certain amount of inequality in skills among men is necessary so that they will have mutual needs, which are the basis of the social order.[22] Thus in each case the good effects are of the essence of the thing, while the evil is incidental.

> And because this is known in the First Providence, it is as if 'purposed incidentally' (*ka ʾl-maqṣūdi bi ʾl-ʿaraḍi*), so that evil enters into destiny incidentally, as if it were so to speak 'pleasing to it incidentally'.[23]

Thus evil may be said to be 'intended' by God, in the sense of intention defined by Henry Sidgwick as 'including not only such results of volition as the agent *desired* to realize, but also any that, without desiring, he foresaw as certain or probable'.[24] But it is not desired by Him, i.e. 'purposed essentially'. Presumably Ibn Sīnā wanted to make out that God is conscious of the evil He produces without being blameworthy for it.

We can now see how the statements attributed to both Aristotle and Plato could be harmonized with Ibn Sīnā's position, by defining 'purpose' in narrower and wider senses respectively. Aristotle's statement is right in the sense that evil is not desired by God, 'purposed essentially' or for its own sake, while Plato's statement is right in the sense that evil is intended by God, 'purposed incidentally' to what He desires – and unavoidably if the greater good is to be fulfilled. Ibn Sīnā might have shown in the present text how

[21] *Ilāhiyyāt*, IX, ch. 6, 420–1. Cf. Plato, *Timaeus*, 73ff., for the original example: bone in the body is useful by its hardness, but this involves inflexibility which makes it liable to be broken. For a short critical comment on this type of argument, see chapter 15, 'Averroes on good and evil'. [22] *Arzāq*, 206. [23] *Ishārāt*, II, 736; trans. Goichon, p. 460.

[24] *Methods of ethics*, seventh edition (London, 1907), p. 60, note 1; cf. p. 202.

both the ancient philosophers were right in different senses, but perhaps he thought the matter too complex to explain satisfactorily in a short essay. Whatever his reasons for silence, a contemporary reader already familiar with his ideas would probably have been able to recall the distinction between the two senses of *qaṣada*, and consequently to work out quite easily Ibn Sīnā's relation to Aristotle and Plato on this question.

[*b*] is continuous with [*a*] in syntax, since both are coordinate object-sentences following the main verb 'we say'. Both sections deal with problems arising from the divine omnipotence asserted in premise [1], but they are two distinct problems. [*a*] has discussed briefly a moral objection to divine omnipotence, that it seems to make evil purposed by God. [*b*] discusses a more 'scientific' objection, that if God is omnipotent His commands and prohibitions to men cannot be explained by any purpose. It is hard to see why Ibn Sīnā has run these two sections together in this manner without a break. Perhaps one objection to divine omnipotence suggested another one by a rather free association of ideas, and the distinction between God's purpose and His will recalled another well-known distinction, between His will and His command.[25]

[*b*] is concerned with the objection that if human acts were determined (or predestined) the commands and prohibitions issued to men in revelation would be useless, for God would not exhort and try to persuade people whose acts were already fixed in advance. This was a Muᶜtazilite objection[26] – indicating once more that the theologians whom Ibn Sīnā was confronting in Iran of the early eleventh century were of Muᶜtazilite and associated Shīᶜite tendencies, not predestinarian Ashᶜarites who had scarcely been heard of in

[25] The distinctions that have been made can be clarified by a diagram:

Willed by God (everything)

Purposed, i.e. intended by God (everything)	[Not purposed, i.e. not intended by God (no members of class)]
Purposed, i.e. intended by i.e. intended and desired by God (includes commanded acts done by man). Aristotle denies evil is purposed in this sense.	Purposed incidentally, i.e. intended but not desired by God (includes forbidden acts done by man). Plato affirms evil is purposed in this sense.

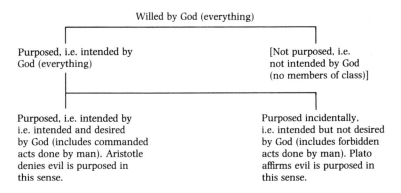

[26] See A. N. Nader, *Le système philosophique des Muᶜtazila* (Beirut, 1956), pp. 263–4 and references in note 1, p. 264.

that country and time.[27] Ibn Sīnā's answer is that the commands and prohibitions of God are themselves parts of the grand causal system which governs the universe, for they act as stimulants and deterrents to men's minds. The effect of the commands accompanied by promises of rewards, and of the prohibitions accompanied by threats of sanctions, is that human wills perform the commands and respect the prohibitions in far more instances than they would have done without these stimuli. In a modern-sounding example Ibn Sīnā illustrates his doctrine by imagined percentages of increased efficacy. He supposes that without the help of revelation men would be completely wicked, but with its help half of them can be rescued.

[*c*] makes the same point about praise and blame as [*b*] has about commands and prohibitions. They are stimuli to future action, and so have a place in a determined world. We must understand the praise and blame referred to as those of scripture for certain acts, if we are to see this section as relevant to the main question. The point is once more to find a purpose in an aspect of God's revelation which might appear useless in view of His determination of human lives.

[*e*] makes the same point with regard to the earthly punishments ordained by scripture (*al-ḥudūd*). They are indispensable as sanctions, to restrain those people who would not be restrained by their own rational appreciation of the social order. Ibn Sīnā's attitude to the sanctions of the next life is quite different, as will be seen.

[3] There is a resurrection, though it applies only to human souls. Ibn Sīnā makes it evident in the 'Metaphysics'[28] that he does not believe in the resurrection of bodies. It is something reported in revelation, but not known by reason or cared for by the wise.

[2] The second premise was originally stated as 'the report that there is Reward and Punishment'. This doctrine creates the most acute difficulty about the justice of God, when it is combined with either predestination or determinism, for it means that God punishes men for acts which He has willed them to do. The Muᶜtazilites had solved the problem in the terms in which they had faced it, by denying predestination, and would no doubt have denied determinism as well. Ibn Sīnā, while not accepting traditional predestination, insists on determinism which is central to his philosophy. His solution is different: to deny Reward and Punishment, in the usual sense of requital for deserts imposed by another person. His initial description of this dogma of Islam as a 'report' (*ḥadīth*) now appears significant. Here he reinterprets that

[27] A critical account of later Ashᶜarite claims is made by G. Makdisi, 'Ashᶜarī and the Ashᶜarites in Islamic religious history', *Studia Islamica*, 17 (1962), 37–80, and 18 (1963), 19–40.

[28] *Ilāhiyyāt*, IX, ch. 7, 423.

dogma figuratively, claiming that what are described as the 'Rewards' and 'Punishments' of the other life are in fact the inevitable effects of the soul's own behaviour in the present life. Its pleasures there are like the results of healthy living, its sufferings like the pains of a diseased body.

It should be noticed that Ibn Sīnā attributes this doctrine to the ancient philosophers, and it is at any rate of Platonic inspiration.[29] Yet we know that it is his view, for in the 'Metaphysics' he states it with some elaboration as his own.[30] Why he does not endorse it here will become clear later when the method of the essay has been examined.

Whereas [2] shows briefly the reality of the soul's fate in the next life, [*d*] completes the argument by giving the negative side of this, denying that there is any reward or punishment in the proper sense after death. It is pointed out that there is no place at that stage for stimulation and deterrence, since man is no longer under obligations or on probation. The only conceivable motives for chastising him would be anger and revenge, and these are impossible in God and contradict the ideals of mercy which He himself prescribes to man.[31]

The whole argument may now be resumed.

[Main problem: If God wills man's evil acts, yet punishes him for them, is He not unjust?]

[1] Good and evil are willed by God, as part of the causal order.

[*a*] Aristotle says evil is not purposed by Him, Plato says it is.

[*b*, *c*, *e*] The commands, blame, etc., in revelation, and the prescribed earthly punishments all have causal functions.

[3] There is an after-life of the soul.

[2] Its 'Rewards' and 'Punishments' are effects of the soul's conduct and habits on earth,

[*d*] not rewards and punishments handed out by God.

[Solution: God is not unjust, for He does not punish man after death. In the present life He helps man to improve his soul and so increase its happiness in the after-life.]

Thus Ibn Sīnā has worked out 'the secret of destiny' by upholding the divine determination very firmly and reinterpreting Rewards and Punishments. The solution as presented above follows a logical order and arrives at conclusions which accord with his philosophy. It is beyond the scope of this article to discuss whether it is a convincing solution.

[29] See *Phaedo*, 80–2; *Phaedrus*, 246–56; *Republic*, x, 613–20. But Plato puts his accounts of the afterlife in the form of myths, and includes in them a Judgement and a choice as well as an element of necessity.

[30] *Ilāhiyyāt*, IX, ch. 7, 423ff.

[31] Cf. *Risālat al-qadar*, Arabic, pp. 17–20: God does not need to stick to His word in executing uselessly the exaggerated Promises and Rewards announced in revelation. To imagine Him as a vain despot is the result of weak anthropomorphic analogies.

THE STYLE OF THE ESSAY

After this reconstruction and interpretation of the essay, it is time to inquire why Ibn Sīnā expressed himself in a way which needs so much unravelling. Two lines of explanation suggest themselves: that he wrote carelessly, or that the obscurity was deliberate. These explanations are mutually exclusive for any one utterance (word, phrase, or sentence), because carelessness and deliberation are indirectly contradictory of each other: carelessness implies lack of thought, deliberation implies thought. But there is nothing to prevent careless obscurity and deliberate obscurity from being present in different parts of the whole essay. Let us see, then, what are the arguments favouring each alternative in general, and whether any points of detail can be found as evidence for either of them in particular parts.

In favour of the hypothesis of carelessness, it can be pointed out that Ibn Sīnā claimed to be capable of writing very rapidly,[32] and sometimes wrote much in unpropitious conditions – while accompanying his sovereign on army campaigns, or sitting through a night and drinking wine.[33] The brevity of expression might be largely spontaneous, if Ibn Sīnā was writing for a circle of disciples and friends familiar with his ideas and able to supply for themselves what was implicit. Against these considerations it must be said that Ibn Sīnā is not usually a careless writer, and the present essay is quite precise in its detailed language, except for three insignificant examples of loose grammar (recorded in the notes to the Arabic text). And what are we to think of the illogical order of the argument, and the omission to state the problem and the conclusion? It is hard to believe these are uncontrolled oversights in the work of so great a logician, and we should certainly heed the principle put forward by Leo Strauss for such cases:

> If a master of the art of writing commits such blunders as would shame an intelligent high school boy, it is reasonable to assume that they are intentional, especially if the author discusses, however incidentally, the possibility of intentional blunders in writing.[34]

Ibn Sīnā does not, so far as I know, discuss just this possibility, but there are other indications that point no less surely to a definite method. So let us consider the other explanation, deliberate secrecy.

[32] At the end of the *Risāla fī māhiyyat aṣ-ṣalāt*, 'Treatise on the essence of prayer', two of the manuscripts have a final paragraph in which it is claimed that the work was written 'in less than half an hour, amid many distractions': Mehren, *Traités mystiques*, III, ii, 42. As the treatise covers 15 pages in the edition, this is impossible, in the absence of shorthand dictation. The paragraph is bracketed by Mehren.

[33] Abū ʿUbayd al-Jūzjānī's biography of Ibn Sīnā, in *The Life of Ibn Sīnā*, ed. and Eng. trans. W. E. Gohlman (Albany, 1974), pp. 66–7, 78–9.

[34] *Persecution and the art of writing* (Glencoe, Ill., 1952), p. 30.

Ibn Sīnā's place in the medieval esoteric tradition is well established and can easily be documented. His introduction to *Manṭiq al-mashriqiyyīn* makes an explicit distinction between the author's earlier, Aristotelian books, which were intended for ordinary students of philosophy, and the present 'oriental' work which contains 'the principles of true science'.

We did not compose this book to reveal it to anyone but ourselves, i.e. those who are in our situation. As for the generality of those who pursue this interest, we have already given them plenty, more than they need, in the *Shifāʾ*.[35]

Among the esoteric works is the last part of the *Ishārāt*, which he calls the cream of wisdom, to be withheld from those who would waste it, those not gifted with inspired intelligence, etc.[36] At the end of his study 'On the nature of prayer' he writes, 'I forbid this treatise to be shown to anyone whom passion has led astray and branded his heart'.[37]

But, beside the more 'exoteric' works of philosophy and the more 'esoteric' mystical ones, there is a third group which appear at first sight more popular, presenting subjects in a short and simple manner, but which in fact contain deeper meanings only perceptible to thoughtful readers. This type of work would be useful when it was required or desirable for any reason to write something, on serious subjects like religion and philosophy, that would circulate among a wider public than students of those subjects. The model was the Qurʾān. In the chapter on prophecy of the 'Metaphysics', Ibn Sīnā mentions the mental confusion created in ordinary people by attempts to teach them advanced theology, and says it is the duty of a prophet 'to acquaint them with the Majesty and Might of God the Exalted by means of symbols (*rumūz*) and images (*amthila*)' of familiar things; and 'it is not good for a man to appear openly to possess knowledge of a truth which he is concealing from the public'. 'But there is no harm if his speech contains symbols and allusions (*ishārāt*), to draw persons naturally qualified for theoretical studies to undertake philosophical inquiry.'[38] In 'On the nature of prayer' he says near the end that he would have gone into more detail,

but it was difficult for us to enter upon matters in which it is not good for everyone to receive instruction. For such people we have therefore laid down a clear and straightforward plan, while the emancipated man (*al-ḥurr*) will be satisfied with allusions.[39]

[35] Ibn Sīnāʾs *Introduction to Manṭiq al-mashriqiyyīn*, 4. Cf. Ibn Ṭufayl, *Ḥayy b. Yaqẓān*, ed. L. Gauthier (Beirut, 1936), Arabic, p. 4: 'the secrets of the oriental philosophy mentioned by the eminent *shaykh* Abū ʿAlī b. Sīnā'.

[36] *Ishārāt*, ed. Dunyā, 903–4; trans. Goichon, p. 525.

[37] *Māhiyyāt aṣ-ṣalāt*, ed. Mehren, III, ii, 42.

[38] *Ilāhiyyāt*, II, ch. 2, 443.

[39] *Māhiyyāt aṣ-ṣalāt*, ed. Mehren, III, ii, 42. Immediately after this he forbids the essay to be circulated, as noted above: which seems in conflict with the method just stated, or at least

In the *Ishārāt* he refers to the myth of Salāmān and Absāl, and says that each one of them is an image (*mathal*) of the reader, or of his degree of knowledge if he is one of the initiated. Then he adds, 'Solve the enigma (*ḥilli ʾr-ramza*) if you are able'.[40] This is significant for our problem because it shows *ramz* clearly in the meaning of an 'enigma' or 'puzzle' to be solved, and not merely a 'sign' or 'symbol'.

With this background we can consider the introduction to the essay. Ibn Sīnā is asked to explain, not the secret of destiny but only the meaning of the Ṣūfī saying condemning knowledge of the secret. It is indeed difficult for us to see how the possession of knowledge could make a man an atheist (*mulḥid*), unless we suppose that the truth about destiny implies that there is no god – which is certainly not Ibn Sīnā's view in any of his writings. It is tempting to read *ʿarrafa 'makes known' for ʿarafa* 'knows', to give an easier meaning, that *teaching* the secret is condemned. This is textually possible, but there are factors weighing against it (see line 3, n. 9). In any case the problem comes up again in the three sayings of ʿAlī, which unmistakably discourage *seeking* knowledge. So we must do the best we can with the reading 'knows', and try to understand the saying in the light of Ibn Sīnā's reply.

He says that 'this matter', i.e. the secret of destiny, is an obscure question, knowledge of which would corrupt the general public – by confusing their minds, as we can safely understand from elsewhere.[41] Thus the reason for not teaching them is a fault in their knowing if taught, a confusion in their thinking about religion which could be described as 'atheism'. It is implied in the reply of Ibn Sīnā and the Tradition of Muḥammad quoted that the secret is known to someone, of the rank of a prophet or philosopher. The three sayings of ʿAlī suggest that he too knows it, which would readily be understood since ʿAlī in classical Islam was thought of as a master of esoteric wisdom. We can conclude, then, that the Ṣūfī saying is not meant to discourage everyone from knowing the secret of destiny, but only the vast majority. This interpretation is in line with Ibn Sīnā's general position, illustrated above with quotations from other works.

The opening paragraph thus gives an answer to the question asked at the

unnecessary. It is hardly possible to make a clear-cut division of all of Ibn Sīnā's works into the three types mentioned and to find a consistent policy throughout his writings. The question of his esoteric method is complex and requires further study. On the symbolic method of the 'Ḥayy' cycle of mystical fables see H. Corbin, *Avicenne et le récit visionnaire*, 2 vols. (Tehran and Paris, 1954). For a comprehensive introduction to esoteric writing in Islam see N. R. Keddie, 'Symbol and sincerity in Islam', *Studia Islamica*, 19 (1963), 27–63.

[40] *Ishārāt*, ed. Dunya, 790–3. Goichon, p. 485, translates, 'Ensuite, découvre le sens de l'allégorie, si tu es en capable.' Ṭūsī, commentary *ad loc.* (in Dunya), understands *ar-ramza* as *siyāqat al-qissa*, 'the thread of the story'.

[41] *Ilāhiyyāt*, II, x, ch. 2, 443, referred to above, at note 86.

beginning of the essay, and with that the essay might have ended since its formal subject has been dealt with. But it then takes a surprising turn: Ibn Sīnā goes on to discuss the secret of destiny itself, which he was not asked about and which he has just said would be harmful if declared openly (*iẓhārihā*). The apparent strangeness of his procedure is brought out in the title of the work, whether it is original or not: *Risāla fī sirr al-qadar*. Does one publish an essay on a secret? The conclusion to which we are led almost inevitably is that Ibn Sīnā wants to write about destiny in the only way he thinks permissible: 'in enigmatic form (*marmūza*)' and 'in a hidden manner (*maknūna*)'. This puts the essay in the third group, mentioned above, of 'popular' works which also contain a deeper meaning, not apparent to every reader. Several questions may be raised about this conclusion, which will now be answered briefly in order.

What were Ibn Sīnā's specific reasons for secrecy on the subject of destiny, beyond the vague assertion that plain teaching on it would harm the public? We can find in his own doctrine elements that would be unsettling to less sophisticated Muslims of his time. The whole problem of evil which is raised might not occur to many of them if left to themselves. And those to whom it did occur might be more easily satisfied with a simple answer, in terms of the will of a personal God, than with an answer depending on Neoplatonic premises about a necessary world order and the metaphysical relation of evil to matter. More especially, the denial of afterlife Reward and Punishment in the proper sense might be seriously disturbing to morality and to belief in scripture. Ibn Sīnā's sensitivity on this matter appears from his precautions in discussing it: in [2] he puts his own view in the mouth of the ancient Greek philosophers, while in [*d*] he attributes the conventional view to 'the theologians (*al-mutakallimūn*)', not to the Qurʾān. By contrast, in a work like the 'Metaphysics', which would be read by philosophy students only, he did not need to take such precautions but could state his theory more plainly.

But in view of these dangers, what reasons did Ibn Sīnā have to publish anything at all on the subject in a short, popular form, at the risk of injuring public religion? It is not an adequate answer to say that the purpose lay in the expounding of a hidden meaning to the élite; for they had access to the author's views formulated as clearly as the subject would allow in various places in his straight 'exoteric' and 'esoteric' books. The question is not easy, and any answer must be tentative, in the absence of knowledge about the occasion of the essay; but two lines of approach can be suggested.

First we must notice a circumstantial reason: that 'someone asked' Ibn Sīnā about destiny. If this questioner was a prince or a minister, it may have been difficult for him to avoid a reply altogether. Still, he could have said less, and we have to look for a more interior and positive reason. From what we know of Ibn Sīnā as a sincere scholar it is fair to believe that he wished to make use of every opportunity to hand on a portion of truth to someone; the question is, to whom, in a work such as the essay? I think the key to an answer is given in a passage already quoted about the method of a prophet:

But there is no harm if his speech contains symbols and allusions, to draw persons naturally qualified for theoretical studies to undertake philosophical inquiry.[42]

What this points to is that enigmatic writing is not meant for the accomplished adept but for the novice, to arouse his curiosity and stimulate his intellect to work on the problems involved. The point has been so well put by Leo Strauss, with reference to all this class of writing, that I take leave to quote from him again:

Those to whom such books are truly addressed are, however, neither the unphilosophic majority nor the perfect philosopher as such, but the young men who might become philosophers: the potential philosophers are to be led step by step from the popular views which are indispensable for all practical and political purposes to the truth which is merely and purely theoretical, guided by certain obtrusively enigmatic features in the presentation of the popular teaching – obscurity of the plan, contradictions, pseudonyms, inexact repetitions of earlier statements, strange expressions, etc. Such features do not disturb the slumber of those who cannot see the wood for the trees, but act as awakening stumbling blocks for those who can.[43]

The reverse side of this reason is that Ibn Sīnā must have felt confident enough that what he was writing down here was so garbled that it would not 'disturb the slumber' of those ungifted for such studies. All they would get would be impressions of a profound philosopher discoursing on a God who governs the whole order of the universe and is not vengeful, on the divine purposes in the commands and prohibitions of revelation, on pleasures and pains in a life of the soul beyond the grave. The more questionable opinions that they read were those of pagan philosophers of long before Islam, whose theories could be reported as matters of historical interest, unlikely to undermine the faith of any genuine Muslim.

We may find Ibn Sīnā naïve in his confidence that such writings would not be understood by ordinary Muslims sufficiently to unsettle their faith or provoke a public reaction against philosophy. But it is well to remember that in fact no great reaction came until half a century after his death, and that when it came it was directed not against such essays but against the more professional works, which Ghazālī took pains to understand before criticizing

[42] *Ilāhiyyāt*, II, X, ch. 2, 443.

[43] *Persecution and the art of writing*, p. 36.

them from the standpoint of a Sunnite *ʿālim*. And in general the Greek philosophical tradition was continued in the Islamic world for hundreds of years, without attracting too much adverse attention; the trial and temporary disgrace of Ibn Rushd in twelfth-century Muslim Andalusia was an exception. The discrete caution of the philosophers in publicizing their theories was no doubt one reason for their long survival.

Next we should ask about the methods of concealment used by Ibn Sīnā. We seem to have found three: changing the order, silence and brevity, ascribing views to others. Are there any precedents or parallels in other writers of the classical Islamic and Arabic world, to help to convince us that Ibn Sīnā might have used these devices intentionally, and that readers educated in the same learned tradition would have been on the look-out for them?

With regard to jumbling the order of the argument, several clues, more or less indirect, can be mentioned.

(*a*) Fārābi, Ibn Sīnā's predecessor whose thought had the greatest influence on him, had spoken with approval of Plato's method of teaching philosophy to an inner circle:

> So he chose symbols (*rumūz*) and enigmas (*alghāz*), aiming thereby to compose his sciences and wisdom in a manner that could only be fathomed by those who are meritorious, etc.[44]

Ramz has the initial meaning of 'sign, hint, allusion', and is probably so used here, but *laghz* is more exclusively 'enigma, riddle, puzzle'. The approved Platonic method therefore definitely includes this type of concealment.

(*b*) Speaking of Aristotle's method, Fārābi quotes a supposed letter from Aristotle to Plato in which he gives a defence of his practice of committing his learning to writing, in the following terms:

> If I have written down these sciences and the wisdom contained in them, I have arranged them (*rattabtuhā*) in such an order that only those qualified for them can attain them.[45]

(*c*) We have seen previously a sentence of Ibn Sīnā in another treatise where he speaks of 'solving a *ramz*', i.e. clearly 'an enigma'; so *marmūza* in the present essay can mean 'enigmatic', not just 'in signs' or 'symbols'.

(*d*) In the large Arabic literature on the occult sciences known as *jafr*, one of the methods was the transposition of letters in a word to form another word.[46]

[44] *al-Jamʿ bayna raʾyay al-ḥakīmayn Aflaṭūn al-ilāhī wa Arisṭūṭālīs*, ed. A. N. Nader (Beirut, 1960), 84.

[45] *Jamʿ*, 85.

[46] T. Fahd, 'Djafr', *EI*².

(*e*) Ibn Sīnā himself was partial to acrostics, for he played with another common method of *jafr*, the use of a well-known magic square of nine Arabic letters with numerical values, corresponding to the hierarchy of beings in the universe.[47]

(*f*) In his summary of the Arabic astrological compendium *Ghāyat al-ḥakīm*, Martin Plessner calls attention to the interrupted order of treatment, in which 'subjects which belong together are separated'; and he suggests that this method may be intentional, to make the magical sections less prominent or for other reasons. He also points out that a similar presentation is found in the 'Encyclopedia' of the Ikhwān al-Ṣafāʾ, which is a principal source of *Ghāyat al-ḥakīm*.[48]

(*g*) Maimonides in frankly explaining the methods used in his esoteric[49] work 'The guide of the perplexed' includes the following statement:

> Hence you should not ask of me here anything beyond *the chapter headings*. And even those are not set down in order or arranged in coherent fashion in this Treatise, but rather are scattered and entangled with other subjects that are to be clarified.[50]

(*h*) The sūras of the Qurʾān are notable for the discontinuity of their thought-sequences. However a modern orientalist such as Richard Bell may explain this in terms of early editing,[51] in classical Islam it was taken as certain that the order within each sūra of the Qurʾān was intended in every detail for some divine purpose. Such a model might well encourage a similar feature in a human book of wisdom that was meant to be enigmatic.

These diverse examples should be enough to convince us that a jumbling of order was entirely within the range of devices for concealment which would occur to the minds of Ibn Sīnā and his learned readers. It would, of course, occur to some who were unsympathetic, but it could be hoped that they would not take the trouble to re-arrange, or would be unable to do so for lack of familiarity with the underlying system of thought. Disciples, on the other hand, would have little difficulty in making the re-arrangement, especially since the disorder is not very extensive.

A difficulty might be raised here about the lack of paragraphs in Arabic

[47] See S. H. Nasr, *An introduction to Islamic cosmological doctrines* (Cambridge, Mass., 1964), pp. 209–12, referring to Ibn Sīnāʾs *ar-Risāla an-Nayrūziyya fī maʿānī al-ḥurūf al-hijāʾiyya*, in *Tisʿ rasāʾil* (Cairo, 1908), 134–41.

[48] *'Picatrix', das Ziel des Weisen von Pseudo-Magrītī*, German trans. H. Ritter and M. Plessner (London, 1962), p. lix. The 'Encyclopedia' was earlier than Ibn Sīnā and known to him.

[49] The self-contradiction is in Maimonides. But his explanation will not take the outsider very far. See L. Strauss, *Persecution and the art of writing*, ch. 3.

[50] *Dalālat al-ḥāʾirīn*, ed. S. Munk (Jerusalem, 1929), 3; as trans. S. Pines, *The Guide of the perplexed* (Chicago, 1963), p. 6.

[51] *Introduction to the Qurʾān* (Edinburgh, 1953), ch. 5, and his translation, 2 vols. (Edinburgh, 1937–9), *passim*.

texts. I have inserted paragraphs with numbers and letters, but what indication would readers of Ibn Sīnā's original manuscript have of where the sections of the argument began and ended? This is easily answered: Arabic writers commonly indicated paragraphs by overlines above the opening words, and Ibn Sīnā may have done so. It is not surprising that these have not survived in the copies that have reached our century.[52]

In support of brevity and silence (which we can take together as one method) there is a good precedent in Fārābi's approving statement about the method of Aristotle: that though in general he writes in a plain and straightforward manner, there is much that is recondite, obscure, and complicated – e.g. omission of essential premises of a philosophical argument, omission of one member of a pair, to be understood from the other, etc.[53] With reference to Maimonides, Strauss says:

> Another device consists in silence, i.e. the omission of something which only the learned, or the learned who are able to understand of themselves, would miss.[54]

It seems unnecessary to substantiate this method any further, since it is central to any enigmatic writing.

Lastly, the method of attributing one's beliefs to ancient writers of prestige is a common feature of medieval literature, which appears in many forms. The most pertinent precedent for Ibn Sīnā is again Fārābi, who composed entire books on the philosophies of Plato and Aristotle, whose positions he evidently endorsed.

Any conclusions about the secret meaning of a piece of writing and any reconstruction of its composition must from the nature of the case be accepted with caution, more especially since the challenge of discovering and deciphering a secret is attractive to scholars. But in the light of all that has been shown, I believe we can confidently state at least this much about the 'Essay on the secret of destiny': that the probability of some conscious reserve in the manner of writing it on the part of Ibn Sīnā is very much greater than the probability that the difficulties of the essay are entirely due to his negligence. We have to be less confident in claiming to have discovered correctly the precise nature of his reserve and the inner meaning which he

[52] One manuscript, B(1), in my edition has overlines above certain quotations and the opening words of [c] and [e] – obvious divisions since they start with *ammā*, 'as for...' Another manuscript, B(2), has them for '*The shaykh said*...' and the second and third premises – three major divisions. In neither case can we attach any relevant significance to these crude and incomplete attempts at paragraphing. There is always a hope that one or more of the unexamined manuscripts will have preserved something more original.

[53] *Jamʿ*, 84–5.

[54] *Persecution and the art of writing*, p. 75.

intended his more perceptive readers to see; for we are, after all, not among that group, nor have we had the benefit of oral instruction or of living as contemporaries in his intellectual milieu. What can fairly be claimed, however, is that the interpretation of his meaning given above makes sense and is consistent with the rest of his thought. If this is so, it can stand until a better hypothesis is worked out.

15

AVERROES ON GOOD AND EVIL

Ibn Rushd (Averroes) devoted most of his efforts as a philosopher to expounding and defending the natural philosophy, psychology and metaphysics of Aristotle, and reconciling with them the doctrines of Islam as he understood them. Reflecting these prominent interests, modern Rushdian scholars have exerted themselves primarily in interpreting his thought in these spheres. Little attention has been given to what he had to say on philosophical questions of value and ethics. Yet it would be surprising if he did not have some well-considered ideas on these questions, in view of his background, education and career on both their Islamic and philosophical sides.

Born into a distinguished family of Malikite lawyers, he must from his earliest years have heard problems of Islamic ethics and law discussed around him in his home. He received a thorough education in Malikite *fiqh*, and a large part of his paid career in the public service of the Almohad government was spent in appointments to various posts as a *qāḍī*, including the office of Chief Justice (*qāḍi al-jamāʿa*) of Córdoba. He also wrote a substantial handbook of Sunnite law, *Bidāyat al-mujtahid wa nihāyat al-muqtaṣid*. His philosophical education was equally thorough and must have included a study of Plato's *Republic* and Aristotle's *Nicomachean Ethics*; and he later wrote commentaries on both these works. Further, the importance of the cultivation of the soul must have been impressed on him both by his general education as a Muslim and by his medical education in the Greek tradition with its characteristic analogy of the health of the body and the soul. Finally, in his lifelong struggle against the spreading influence of Ashʿarite theology and of Ghazālī, he had to deal with an important issue on the nature of value which divided him from them. In fact the longest single passage written by him on value and ethics occurs in *Kitāb al-Kashf ʿan manāhij al-adilla*, a semi-popular compendium of theology intended to criticize and replace the Ashʿarite system.

This article reconstructs from Ibn Rushd's writings his views on the main questions related to good and evil which he discussed. From this reconstruction it should become apparent that, although he never wrote out a philosophical system of value and ethics in a substantial and unified form, there is systematic thinking behind his scattered remarks, having consistency and considerable interest. The subject will be treated in two parts.

A. His theory of value in the broad sense, and his treatment of the theological problem of evil as it arose out of his theory of value.

B. His theory of ethics, applying the theory of value to the nature of right action and character and the way or ways of knowing them.[1]

A.

The theory of value is concerned with the nature of good and evil in general, as applied to objects of aesthetic judgement, to human conduct or anything else. The primary philosophical question is: what is the common character found in everything we call 'good'? Or we may ask: what is the opposite character common to all evil things? Ibn Rushd often discussed this problem in relation to a particular kind of value, justice; but it is usually quite easy to transfer his arguments on justice to value in general.

The fundamental question about value to which he addressed himself was whether it is objective or subjective; and he asserted emphatically the objectivist position, that value is something real in the nature of the things valued, a character in them that is independent of the opinion or attitude of whoever is judging them. This view was in line with the major tradition of Greek philosophy. Both Plato and Aristotle had insisted on the difference between appearance and reality; thus, for instance, the fact that someone, or even a majority, thinks a law is just or beneficial does not in itself make it so. Subjectivism as a theory of value did not receive very strong backing

[1] Sources. References are to pages and lines of the editions listed unless otherwise specified. Quotations are from the translations listed; in other cases as translated by myself.

Averroes' commentary on Plato's 'Republic', Hebrew trans., ed. and Eng. trans., E. I. J. Rosenthal (Cambridge, 1956). References to books, chapters and sections.

Commentary on Aristotle's Nicomachean Ethics, Latin trans. in *Opera omnia Aristotelis Stagiritae…Averrois Cordubensis in ea opera omnes, qui ad nos pervenere, commentarii* (Venice, 1560), III.

Summary (Jāmiᶜ) of Aristotle's Metaphysics, in *Rasāʾil Ibn Rushd* (Hyderabad, 1947).

Great commentary (Tafsīr) on Aristotle's Metaphysics, ed. M. Bouyges, *Tafsīr mā baᶜd aṭ-ṭabīᶜa* (Beirut, 1938–51), 4 vols.

Faṣl al-maqal, ed. G. F. Hourani (Leiden, 1959). References to margin numbers (pages and lines of M. J. Müller's edition). Eng. trans. G. F. Hourani, *Averroes on the harmony of religion and philosophy* (London, 1961).

Kitāb al-kashf ᶜan manāhij al-adilla, ed. M. J. Müller, in *Philosophie und Theologie von Averroes* (Munich, 1859).

Tahāfut at-tahāfut, ed. M. Bouyges (Beirut, 1930). Eng. trans. S. Van den Bergh, Averroes' *Tahāfut at-tahāfut* (London, 1954), 2 vols.

Bidāyat al-mujtahid wa nihāyat al-muqtaṣid (Cairo, 1952).

It is no longer necessary to insist on the dangers and difficulties of interpreting a Muslim philosopher arising from esoteric and exoteric writing, expression of opinion in the form of commentary on the ancients, survival of some works only in Hebrew and Latin translations.

in the Graeco-Roman world, and there is no need to describe here the forms which it took.[2]

In the Islamic world, however, subjectivism took a powerful new form, as a result of tendencies arising out of the religion of Islam itself, or at least out of the assumptions of early Muslim thinkers about it. This form was 'theistic subjectivism' or 'ethical voluntarism', the theory that good and evil, justice and injustice, are defined entirely by reference to the commands of God, as revealed to man in the *sharīʿa*. Human acts, for example, are right only when God commands man or recommends to him to do them, without having any intrinsic character which would make them good in themselves. This theory was the implied basis of the whole system of classical Islamic jurisprudence as it was worked out chiefly by Shāfiʿī. It was made explicit in the works of the theologian Ashʿarī, and strongly stated by Ghazālī not long before Ibn Rushd's time. The main argument used to back it was simply the authority of scripture which was supposed to favour it; and though this may not seem to us very convincing philosophically, it was hard to stand up in classical Islam and declare that 'good' had a meaning independent of scripture, and would apply to certain acts or objects even on the supposition that scripture commanded the opposite. With the establishment of the four schools of Sunnite law and the spread of Ashʿarite theology, subjectivism in this form became the dominant theory of value in classical Islam.

In spite of the prevailing climate of opinion, the Muʿtazilites had for long upheld the objectivity of values, in order to maintain the real justice of God in a sense that would have meaning for Muslims. They had, however, been defeated for various reasons.[3] By the twelfth century, though their bare position was remembered, their arguments for it were known to hardly anyone, especially in western Islam where it seems that their books were no longer available (*Manāhij*, 42.16–17). A slender group of Arabic philosophers maintained the Greek theory of objectivism, but they had written little about it. Therefore Ibn Rushd was a very solitary thinker when he upheld this theory with arguments and in open opposition to the Ashʿarite doctrine.

It was just possible for him to do so, because of the intellectual conditions in Andalus in his time. Ashʿarism had not yet become a universally accepted creed among the scholars of western Islam, and Ibn Rushd was fighting to prevent such a result. He enjoyed the favour of the Almohad *amīrs*, who were interested in philosophy. Moreover the philosophical question of value was too abstract to arouse excitement among the public and, though important in itself, it was not one of the most prominent issues between the traditional

[2] See below, p. 253, on a limited form held by some Greek sophists and referred to by Ibn Rushd.
[3] See Ch. 5 above.

ʿulamāʾ and the philosophers. Nor did Ibn Rushd bring it into prominence in his work, being content for the most part with short comments on it in different books. In openly saying what he thought on value, he probably reasoned that if he were going to meet trouble he would do so anyhow over more hotly disputed opinions such as the eternity of the world. The theory of value was not one of those questions on which the Qurʾān yielded conclusive evidence for either objectivism or subjectivism, and no one had been condemned for *kufr* for supporting objectivism. Still, in spite of all explanations Ibn Rushd showed undeniable courage in stating unpopular views on this as on other subjects, nor should it be forgotten that he suffered a brief but sharp persecution on account of his philosophy as a whole.

Ibn Rushd's arguments for his position can be found in places where he takes exception to Ashʿarite subjectivism. The most important passage is *Manāhij*, 113–18, a discussion of divine and human justice. He states the Ashʿarite theory of God's justice as follows:

Concerning justice (*al-ʿadl*) and injustice (*al-jawr*) as applied to God the Glorious, the Ashʿarites have maintained an opinion that is very foreign to reason and scripture... For they have said that the unseen world is different in this respect from the visible world, because, they assert, the visible world is characterized by justice and injustice only by reason of a prohibition of religion against certain acts. Thus a man is just when he does something which is just according to the Law, while he is unjust if he does what the Law has laid down as unjust. But they say: 'As for Him [God] who is not under obligation and does not come under the prohibition of the Law, in His case there does not exist any act which is just or unjust, or rather all His acts are just'. And they are forced to say that there is nothing just in itself and nothing unjust in itself (113.7–15).

To oppose this view, Ibn Rushd brings arguments from both reason and scripture. The best statement of his rational arguments occurs in the sentences which follow what has just been quoted.

This is extremely disgraceful, because in that case there would be nothing which is good (*khayr*) in itself and nothing which is evil (*sharr*) in itself; but it is self-evident that justice is good and that injustice is evil. And associating [other gods] with God would not be unjust or wrong (*ẓulm*) in itself, but only from the standpoint of the Law, and if the Law had prescribed an obligation to believe in an associate of God, then that would have been just... (113.15–19).

In his *Commentary on Plato's Republic* he puts the same objection thus:

For according to this opinion Good and Evil have no definite nature in themselves, but they are good or evil by supposition (I, xi, 3).[4]

[4] Cf. II, vii, 1; *Jāmiʿ*, 172, 'by convention' (*bil-waḍʿ*).

His rational arguments thus amount to two points, which I shall state and comment on. (1) The existence of objective values is a self-evident truth. This does not seem conclusive to modern minds, indeed it is hardly acceptable as an argument at all when so many people deny it. But Plato, Aristotle and their philosophic successors often resorted to such assertions, and philosophers in the West too could not discover the way to reason about the nature of value until modern times when so much attention has been paid to philosophical method and theory of knowledge. (2) He shows the absurd consequences of subjectivism, clearly choosing as examples the most sacred duties of Islam such as belief in one God and worship of Him, and showing that according to subjectivism these duties would have only a conventional and not an intrinsic value. The unspoken completion of the argument is: 'But in fact, as all Muslims know, these duties are intrinsically right; therefore the subjectivist theory must be false.' Such an argument makes a point which was hard for Muslims to answer.

Apart from argument, Ibn Rushd shows some feeling on this question and uses emotive language to discredit his Ashʿarite opponents. He calls their views 'extremely disgraceful' (*fī ghāyat ash-shanāʿa, Manāhij*, 113.15).[5] He likes to name them 'sophistical', by which he means 'fallacious and specious' in a general way, but also intends a comparison with the doctrines of the Greek sophists on value. For in one of his attacks on the Ashʿarite position he concludes with the remark, 'All these are views like those of Protagoras' (*Jāmiʿ*, 172). Here he refers to the 'social subjectivism' of those sophists who had defined 'justice' in terms of the conventions of society or the laws imposed by governments. In this remark he displays his usual acute intelligence,[6] for he has seen the generic relation between two species of subjectivism which are different in detail and which were separated by a wide gap of history and geography. Another ardent and memorable attack occurs in *Faṣl al-maqāl* (22–3), where he compares the Ashʿarite theologian to an unqualified doctor of the soul who injures people by teaching them false allegorical interpretations of scripture; and he adds:

> ...if he expresses to them false allegories,...this will lead them to think that there are no such things as health which ought to be preserved and disease which ought to

[5] Cf. *Jāmiʿ*, p. 172, *shanāʿa*; Comm. Pl. Rep., I, xi, 3 (Heb. *meghūn*).

[6] Possible sources for Ibn Rushd's attribution of a subjectivist theory of value to Protagoras: (1) Plato, *Theaetetus*, 167c, 172a, etc., if this dialogue was available to Ibn Rushd. (2) Fārābī, *Falsafat Aflāṭūn*, ed. F. Rosenthal and R. Walzer, in *Plato Arabus*, II (London, 1943), 4–5 (Arabic). This contains an allusion to Protagoras' theory of knowledge: 'Man is the measure of all things', but no application to values. (3) Aristotle, *Metaphysics*, 1062b, 13ff., where Aristotle infers the application to values. Ibn Rushd's comments on the passage are lacking in *Tafsīr mā baʿd aṭ-ṭabīʿa*, III. What Protagoras really thought on the subject is uncertain. See especially A. Capizzi, *Protagora* (Florence, 1955), pp. 40–50, 61–6, 70–1, 247–61.

be cured – let alone that there are things which preserve health and cure disease (22.20–23.1).

Ibn Rushd as a Muslim *qāḍī* naturally used scriptural arguments to support his position, especially in *Manāhij* where he was expounding the doctrines of the Qurʾān as he thought they should be taught to the public. After the rational arguments quoted above from that book, he goes on:

As for [the conclusions to be drawn from] authority (*al-masmūʿ*), God has described Himself in His Book as righteous (*bil-qasṭ*) and denied that he is a wrongdoer (113.20–1).

Then he gives three quotations from the Qurʾān, none of which quite proves his case. It is sufficient to quote one as an illustration:

inna llāha lā yaẓlimu n-nāsa shayʾan walākinna n-nāsa anfusahum yaẓlimūn (x, 45 Flügel/44 Cairo).

Surely God does not injure men in any way, but they injure themselves.[7]

The point of this quotation, as of the others (iii, 18/16 and iii, 182/178) is to show that God is characterized as 'just', though He is not under obligation of the Law; so justice has an objective meaning. The verse quoted, however, could quite easily be interpreted by Shafiʿites and Ashʿarites in their sense: God does not wrong men, because He is above right and wrong.

So much for Ibn Rushd's arguments. We now have to consider the principal objection which he faced, the theological problem of evil. How is it that a perfect God has created evil in His world?[7] The Ashʿarites avoided this problem by their definition of value. Since for them evil as a quality of persons consists of disobeying God's commands, and since God of course never does this, it follows that He is never evil. He creates the evil in the world without thereby becoming evil Himself. This logic did not appeal to Ibn Rushd, nor was it open to him to accept it, on his definition of evil. For him, any person is evil when he does certain types of acts or creates certain things having in themselves a real character of evil; thus the qualification of 'evil' does seem to apply to God if He creates evil, and it makes no difference that He is not disobeying anyone's command in so doing. The problem is how to avoid this consequence of making God really evil, while at the same time upholding His creative power over everything.

The problem takes two forms, a general and a special:

(1) In its general form it concerns all kinds of evil in the world: both natural evil, i.e. pain, and moral evil, i.e. wrongdoing. Why did a perfect God create

[7] See chapters 3 and 4 above on the meaning of *ẓulm an-nafs*.

any kind of evil whatever? Ibn Rushd considers the solution of Zoroastrian dualism, that evil is caused not by God but by other persons, a devil or demons; but he rejects this. The only explanation he gives for his rejection is a very brief remark that dualism implies a shortcoming (*taqṣīr*) in the supreme Agent (*Tafsīr*, 1715). Evidently dualism was ruled out of court for all Muslims, because it was polytheism. In principle he also rejects the opposite solution, that God is the cause of evil as well as good. In a passage of his *Commentary on Plato's Republic* in which he endorses Plato's doctrine (*Republic* iii, 379), he writes: 'He is the absolute Good and does not do evil at any time, and is not the cause of it' (I, xi, 3). But it will be shown how this position is qualified in Ibn Rushd's more detailed theory.

His solution is to attribute evil to an impersonal force other than God, namely matter.

As for [natural] evils (*ash-shurūr*) such as decay, age, etc., their existence is due to the necessity of matter. That is so because this existence [i.e. presumably the existence of earthly beings] is only possible on one of two conditions, either that these things to whose existence some evil is attached should not exist, or that they should exist in this condition, since more than that is not possible in their existence. An example of that is that fire is of evident use in the world, and it happens incidentally (*bil-ʿaraḍ*) that it ruins many animals and plants. But look at providence (*al-ʿināya*) for an animal, how it has given it the sense of touch, but that could not be in its nature without bringing it near to sensible things damaging to it (*Jāmiʿ*, 170).

The view that evil is due to matter goes back to later Platonism, and is derived from suggestions of Plato in his *Timaeus* (147ff.) and *Statesman* (268–74), though Plato's doctrine of the cause of evil is less simple.[8] This view had a long history in later Greek philosophy. For a Muslim philosopher it presented a new difficulty which did not disturb a Greek too much: it implied that God's omnipotence is limited, that He could not have created a world completely free of evil. Ibn Rushd faced the difficulty bravely, by admitting that some things are impossible for God.

...as for those evils which necessarily befall the individual, it is not possible to say that that does not come from God...

...As for the fact that not all things are possible [for God], it is very evident, for it is not possible for the corruptible to be eternal or the eternal corruptible, just as it is not possible for the angles of a triangle to equal four right angles or for colour to be audible; and whoever says such a thing is harming human wisdom greatly (*Jāmiʿ*, 171).

[8] See R. Demos, *The philosophy of Plato* (New York, 1939), pp. 116–19; F. M. Cornford, *Plato's cosmology* (London, 1937), pp. 159–88; A. E. Taylor, *Plato: the Sophist and the Statesman* (London, 1961), 209–10.

In this passage, which is the only one which explains his position, we see that he has chosen examples of logical impossibilities. But these are beside the point, because in his previous examples he has pointed to evils – in fire and sensation – which are not due to any logical impossibility. Granted, then, that God cannot do what is logically impossible, the question still remains whether He has done His best within the limits of the possible. To take his own examples: why could God not have provided man with something as useful as fire but which does not hurt when it touches flesh? Or provided animals with a sense of touch but also with greater alertness to what might injure them? In other words, he should have shown how matter limits providence by a necessity which is not merely the logical one of non-contradiction. This question certainly needs clarification if such a view as Ibn Rushd's is to justify itself.[9]

(2) The special form of the problem of evil in Islam concerns divine justice and human injustice. God's justice is on the surface inconsistent with His creation of men who would do injustice and then suffer for it. To be more exact, He could not be just in any familiar sense if (*a*) man suffers for his unjust acts, yet (*b*) God is Himself the ultimate cause of all man's acts. For in that case God would be making man suffer for acts for which man was not ultimately responsible. Since Ibn Rushd believed firmly in the justice of God in an objective sense, he could only avoid the contradiction by modifying the traditional view of either (*a*) man's suffering or (*b*) God's responsibility. I shall examine next what he thought on each.

(*a*) Man's suffering for his own injustice takes a different form in Ibn Rushd's view from that of the Muʿtazilites, so that the problem of divine justice looks different as well. For the Muʿtazilites, the question concerned the everlasting torment of the wicked in the next life. But Ibn Rushd almost certainly did not believe in the survival of the individual, body or soul, as an individual. If then, as he probably held, the surviving parts of the soul are united in the world soul, they cannot have personal happiness or misery in the next life. He did believe, however, that the soul in the present life produces its own happiness or misery by its acts, not as a reward or punishment sent

[9] A similar problem arises about Plato's teleological explanations of human anatomy in *Timaeus*, 73ff., especially 74 a–c. See Cornford, *Plato's cosmology*, pp. 175–6. For instance, the usefulness of bone in the body is due to its hardness, but this involves disadvantages because 'the constitution of bone was unduly brittle and inflexible' (74 a–b). We may ask why. Plato's conception of the 'necessary accident' (*sunebainen ex anangkēs*, 77a) would reveal a logical difficulty all too sharply, if we understood 'necessity' in a modern sense. But see Cornford, pp. 162ff., on the meaning of *anangkē*. If it is a name for the disorderly, uncontrollable forces of nature, an accident can be 'necessary' in this sense. The fact that God cannot altogether control nature raised no theological difficulty for Plato, but it does for a Muslim faced with divine omnipotence.

by God but as a natural effect (*Comm. Pl. Rep.*, I, xi, 5–7). Thus he writes, 'Man is just in order to gain in his soul by justice, and if he were not just that good would not exist' (*Manāhij*, 117.4–5). This is Platonism. And though such a view alleviates the problem of divine justice, since it no longer concerns eternity, it does not solve it. There is still a problem of how a just God can create men with diseased souls.[10] Thus, since Ibn Rushd's answer on (*a*) does not solve the problem of divine justice, the weight of his solution must fall on (*b*), if anywhere.

(*b*) Does God cause human injustice? The answer depends on Ibn Rushd's theory of the human will (*al-irāda*), in its relation to the divine will. This is found mainly in a passage of *Manāhij* (104–13) where he discusses the problem of predestination. His starting-point is the well known principle of jurisprudence that choice (*al-ikhtiyār*) is a condition of human obligation (*Faṣl*, 13.21). Since we are certainly under obligation we must therefore have choice. This means that we will our own acts. A willed act can be contrasted with a compelled movement in at least this respect: that a willed act comes about through an operation of the agent's mind, while a compelled act comes about through outside forces bringing about the act directly. The Jabarites, he says, were wrong in assimilating willed acts to compelled acts, and the Ashᶜarites held what amounted to the same thing, 'for if the acquisition (*al-iktisāb*) and the acquired act are created by God the Exalted then the servant is unavoidably compelled to his acquisition' (*Manāhij*, 105.20–1). So far it looks as though Ibn Rushd is an advocate of free will, like the Muᶜtazilites. Such a view provides a solution of the problem of evil, by making man responsible for it. But Ibn Rushd rejects the Muᶜtazilite view as undermining God's power, because it does not allow for the fact that God creates all acts. He therefore proposes what he claims is a middle solution which allows for both man's obligation and God's creation. This is, ostensibly, a theory of cooperation between human and divine will.

But when we study the details we find that in reality he gives the ultimate decision to God, through a theory of complete determination of human acts. They are determined by God in three ways.

(i) He has made the 'secondary causes' in the world, the forces of nature which react on each other in a regular way, and it is through their operation that an act of ours becomes effective. Thus, for example, I can only hit a target with an arrow because God has determined that the flight of the arrow must

[10] There is also a problem arising from the suffering of the *victims* of injustice: how is this suffering compatible with God's justice, when there is no personal survival in which the balance of happiness would be adjusted in their favour? Ibn Rushd does not mention this problem; we can well understand that he was reluctant to draw attention to his impersonal view of the future life.

correspond in a certain way to the force and direction of the bow. God has made the laws of nature. (*Manāhij* 107.4–8).

(ii) Secondary causes also determine immediately the decision of the will itself.

And these external causes that God has subdued not only complete or hinder the acts which we wish to do, but they are also the cause of our willing one of the two opposites; for the will is only a desire which is produced in us by some imagination (*takhayyul*) or judgement (*taṣdīq*) of something, and this judgement is not due to our choice, but is something which happens to us from external events (107.8–12).[11]

For instance, we necessarily (*biḍ-ḍarūra*) desire and move towards what is desirable, and hate and shun what is repulsive (107.12–15). That this is Ibn Rushd's view can easily be confirmed from his debate with Ghazālī in *Tahāfut at-tahāfut* on the possibility of choosing between equals. Ibn Rushd denies this possibility, because for him the will always requires a sufficient cause to move it, the existence of a stronger desire, which in turn is caused by a stronger stimulus (34ff.).

(iii) But God's determination of our wills penetrates even further, into the internal background of our acts of willing. For if we desire certain things, that is due not only to the nature of the objects but also to our own predispositions; and these are created by God who has made the human species with a certain nature, with individual members varying within definite limits (114.15–17).

Thus from all sides the will of man is determined: God is the ultimate cause of the effects of our acts, of our stimuli and of our very natures. This means that He is the ultimate cause of our unjust as well as our just acts. Consequently the problem of God's justice still remains to be solved.

Ibn Rushd presents his solution in the course of a discussion on the correct interpretation of the predestinarian verses of the Qurʾān. For example,

yuḍillu man yashā'u wa yahdī man yashā'u (xvi, 95/93, etc.)

He leads astray
whom He will, and guides whom He will (tr. Arberry).

He denies that this sentence should be taken in its most obvious senses, that God leads astray particular men, or creates them with a predisposition to go astray (*Manāhij*, 114.5–14). He says that the verse

refers to the antecedent [divine] Will which required that there should be among the kinds (*ajnās*) of beings creatures who go astray, i.e. predisposed to go astray by their

[11] Cf. *Faṣl*, 13.18–20: 'For assent to a thing as a result of an indication of it arising in the soul is something compulsory, not voluntary: i.e. it is not for us to choose not to assent or to assent, as it is to stand up or not to stand up.'

natures, and impelled to it by causes of misguidance, both internal and external, which surround them (114.15–17).

Now what does this mean, if it does not mean that God creates certain men predisposed to wrongdoing? The key to understanding Ibn Rushd's interpretation of the verse is furnished by his doctrine of providence, which is expounded in several places in his writings.[12] The relevant point is that providence does not extend to particulars but only to species. Therefore God has not decided to make this individual just and that unjust, but only to make a species among whom a certain number of unknown individuals would necessarily be just and a certain number unjust. In this way he removes from God the imputation of directly creating erring individuals.[13]

But this position still does not solve the problem of God's justice, for it suggests one remaining objection:

What need was there to create a class (*ṣinf*) of creatures who by their natures would be predisposed to go astray – the extreme of injustice? (*Manāhij*, 115.6–8).

We can now understand this question in the light of his theory of providence. It means, Why did God create any species of whom *some* would be unjust (even if He did not know which individuals would have this fault)? Why did He not create a human species pure of injustice, with no unjust members at all? Ibn Rushd's answer (115.7–16) to this crucial question is that God chose to create a minority of bad natures for the sake of the majority of good ones; and this was made necessary by 'the natural elements (*aṭ-ṭabīʿa*) from which He created man and the composition (*at-ṭarkīb*) in which man was formed' (115.9). The only alternative would have been not to create man at all, and that would have meant renouncing the greater good.[14]

That is as far as Ibn Rushd goes towards settling the question. Two criticisms may be made. One is that we still wonder why the composite nature of man entails that a certain number should be defective, and why an omnipotent 'Giver of forms' (*wāhib aṣ-ṣuwar*) could not have combined only

[12] *Jāmiʿ*, 171; *Tafsīr*, 1607; *Tahāfut*, 504.

[13] *Jāmiʿ*, 171, shows that he is conscious of this consequence as one of the advantages of his theory of providence: '...he who says this [that providence covers all particulars] necessarily ascribes injustice to divinity, because if it undertakes the direction (*tadbīr*) of each individual, how could evils belong to individuals without divinity directing them?'

[14] Cf. St John of Damascus, *De fide orthodoxa*, ii, 21, for a similar argument about God's omniscience and justice and man's sinfulness: God created people who He knows will sin; but if He had refused to create them, evil would have won a victory in preventing the creation of some people with potentialities for good. In *Nicene and post-Nicene fathers*, IX. St John's argument, however, is based on the idea of human freedom which necessarily carries the risk of sin. Such a solution was not open to Ibn Rushd, when once he had rejected the Muʿtazilite position that man is the free creator of his own acts. Ibn Rushd's doctrine on evil can be traced more clearly to Ibn Sīnā, at this and other points.

good forms. But perhaps we should ask this question of Plato, from whom ultimately Ibn Rushd derived the doctrine that composition is a cause of corruption.[15] The other criticism is that, even if we accept the explanation of the evil in man as due to his composite nature, this still does not solve the problem of divine *justice*, for it merely says that some men must be evil and suffer for the good of the whole. Admitting for the sake of argument that God could not do better than this, we still feel that it is less than perfect justice on His part, and He *is* supposed to be perfectly just, not merely 'as just as He can be, in the circumstances'.

Thus Ibn Rushd does not satisfy us about the problem of evil in its general and special forms. But perhaps no one could have done so, given the premises from which he had to start. At any rate he thought deeply about the problem and made an ingenious attempt at a solution, using all the knowledge and ideas he had acquired from his rich heritage of Greek and Islamic thought.

B.

Philosophical ethics discusses questions concerning value as it is attributed to human life, acts and character. The questions of this order which Ibn Rushd discussed philosophically are primarily those of the Greek philosophers, especially Aristotle. His thought is therefore best understood if we examine at least the primary questions in an Aristotelian order, which will show the logical links between these questions and answers even though Ibn Rushd himself has left only isolated remarks.

(1) What is the good or end for man as an individual? Ibn Rushd's most general answer seems to be that it is happiness (*as-saʿāda*). This is implied in a sentence of the *Commentary on Plato's Republic* (I, x, 8), where he is quoting from Fārābī:

> The kinds of ultimate happiness which are the ends of the acts of human virtue are represented [in allegories] by corresponding goods such as are [commonly] supposed to be the ends.[16]

Here, endorsing Fārābī, he takes 'happiness' and 'good' as equivalent in meaning. Other evidence occurs in *Faṣl*:

[15] See Demos, *The philosophy of Plato*, p. 118.

[16] My translation, direct from Fārābī, *Taḥṣīl as-saʿāda*, in *Rasāʾil al-Fārābī* (Hyderabad, 1926), p. 41. The passage is about allegorical representation of spiritual things by physical ones, in myths or religious books, for the sake of popular understanding: e.g. in accounts of the pleasures of paradise. Rosenthal's translation of the sentence is not altogether clear. The source in Fārābi has been pointed out by J. L. Teicher in his review of Averroes–Rosenthal, *Journal of Semitic Studies*, 5 (1960), 176–95. Teicher (183–4) thinks the whole passage is a gloss by a commentator; if he is right, it cannot be used as evidence for Ibn Rushd.

Right practice consists in performing the acts which bring happiness and avoiding the acts which bring misery (19.1–2).

Since there is little doubt that 'right practice' is also definable as that which brings about the good, the equivalence of happiness and good can be taken as highly probable. It is what we should expect of an Aristotelian and a Muslim.

(2) What does true happiness consist of? First of all we must ask: Did Ibn Rushd think of this present life, or the life of eternity, as that whose happiness is the end of human action? We should expect him as a Muslim to give priority to the future life. In fact he does so verbally in several statements of *Faṣl* and *Manāhij*,[17] such as the following in *Faṣl* which immediately precedes the sentence just quoted above:

True science is knowledge of God, Blessed and Exalted, and the other beings as they really are, and especially of noble beings, and knowledge of happiness and misery in the next life (*as-saʿāda al-ukhrāwīya wash-shaqāʾ al-ukhrāwī*) (18.21–19.1).

But it is hard to believe that Ibn Rushd really thought of this happiness as an end which could be brought about by individual action, because his commentaries on Aristotle's *De animā* lead us to conclude that he did not believe in the *individual* survival of any part of a man's soul. So it may be that in the passages referred to he is only paying lip service to the public belief, in two exoteric works, whereas his real views are shown in his commentaries.

Here it may be objected that a commentary is in the first place an exposition of someone else's thought, not necessarily shared by the commentator. But in Ibn Rushd's case the difficulty is less than might be supposed since all his work shows him as a faithful Aristotelian. The *prima facie* assumption, then, must be that Aristotelian assertions by him in the commentaries represent his own opinions. With this in mind, let us consider some of his statements about man's happiness in his *Commentary on Plato's Republic.* He says in the opening chapter (I, i) that the other human perfections exist 'for the sake of the speculative ones', i.e. the perfect development of man's intellectual powers in their theoretical exercise (I, i, 10). Elsewhere he states that the end of man is the excellent performance of those activities which are peculiar to him, i.e. those of the rational soul (II, viii, 9–ix, 1). He proceeds in the following chapters (II, ix–xiii) to specify the kinds of end, corresponding to the functions of the rational soul, and states that the excellence of the theoretical part is the supreme end, to which that of the practical part is subordinate, at least in part. All this is Aristotelian,[18] and the fact that it comes in a commentary

[17] Cf. *Faṣl*, 14.20ff., 22.7; *Manāhij*, 122.6

[18] See especially *Eth. Nic.*, i. 7 and x, 7.

on Plato should reassure us that it is Ibn Rushd's own view. But confirmation is found in *Manāhij*, which is not a commentary. Here it is said that all creatures are made to attain their end in acts peculiar to them, and the peculiar acts of man are those of the rational soul. This has two functions, cognitive (*ʿilmī*) and practical (*ʿamalī*), so it is required of man (as his end) that he should perfect himself in both functions through acquiring theoretical and practical excellence (119.11–18). This again is nothing but a statement of Aristotle's doctrine.

Now all these statements on man's happiness refer to the present life: We can therefore conclude at least this much: that even if Ibn Rushd believed in some kind of happiness for the individual in another life, he had little to say about it; and that whenever he refers to human happiness as a specific kind of life and an end to be achieved by action he always writes in terms of this life. We have seen how he thinks of the happy life: as the perfect activity of the rational soul, and especially of its purely intellectual functions.

(3) What is the relation of right action and practical virtue to the supreme end? Ibn Rushd appears to take a straight teleological position, defining right action as that which leads to the end.

> everything that leads to (*she-yābhī al*) the end is good and beautiful, whereas everything that impedes it is evil and ugly (*Comm. Pl. Rep.*, II, vi, 5).

> Right practice consists in performing the acts which bring (*tufīd*) happiness and avoiding the acts which bring misery (*Faṣl*, 19.2–3).

In these sentences, the words 'leads to' and 'brings' naturally suggest to us means to ends, which are exterior to ends themselves. This interpretation would exclude the supreme activities mentioned previously from being called 'good' and 'beautiful' and 'right practice', and that would not be in accord with Ibn Rushd's outlook in general. We must understand him in Aristotelian terms. Aristotle was aware of the distinction between the intrinsic value of acts, in so far as they constitute ends in themselves, and their instrumental value as means towards these ends; but his language often fails to make the distinction where it is needed. Thus he speaks of 'means' where he refers to or includes 'constituents' of the end. Among constituents of the end Aristotle gives primacy to theoretical activity, but he also includes practical or moral activity in the case of most people for whom this is the highest attainable end (*Eth. Nic.*, x, 8). It is safe to assume that Ibn Rushd follows his master.

Now the immediate means to the perfection of these final activities are the intellectual and moral virtues, settled dispositions of good character. Of these two, Ibn Rushd emphasizes the moral or practical virtues in a passage of *Tahāfut* (581.5–8); but this emphasis may be due to the context.

He goes on to say that these practical virtues can best be strengthened by religious beliefs and practices (581.8–11). Here he has added a religious, Islamic element to what is in Aristotle, but the principle is the same, that sound moral beliefs and acts build up the virtues. Besides, there is much in Plato's *Republic* and *Laws* that supports his view of religion as a means of moral education.

Here we are in the realm of means in the proper sense.

> the acts which gain for (*tukassib*) the soul these virtues [theoretical and practical] are the good and beautiful ones (*al-khayrāt wal-ḥasanāt*), while those which hinder it are the bad and evil ones (*ash-shurūr was-sayyiʾāt*) (*Manāhij*, 119.19–20).

In the light of the two quotations given above it is best to understand this statement as a *definition* of good and evil acts.

In all this Ibn Rushd affirms the dependence of the rightness of actions on the happiness *of the agent*. This strikes a modern person as queer and mistaken; we look for a social criterion of rightness.

(4) How does man know what is right in particular situations? So far we have drawn our understanding of Ibn Rushd from one side of his work, the philosophical and theological. For the present question we shall have to compare what he wrote on that side with his words as a jurist; and this will raise some problems of harmonization.

As a philosopher, he takes the Aristotelian position that man can know the right by practical wisdom (Greek *phronēsis*). In commenting on Plato's doctrines of the state and the soul (*Comm. Pl. Rep.*, I, iii), he says with Plato that moral virtue exists in a man when the rational element of his soul rules over the other elements.

> This means that he will be impelled towards things which are worthy of impulse, in such measure and time as the intellect judges right (I, iii, 3).

How practical wisdom proceeds in making moral judgements is mentioned in his commentary on the *Nicomachean Ethics*, but he merely paraphrases Aristotle and there is no need to describe Aristotle's doctrine. The important points for our survey are that Ibn Rushd believed that reason can find out at least a part of what is right, and that this belief presupposes the objective character of the right, which he actually upheld strenuously as we have seen.

As a jurist, Ibn Rushd writes a different language. In *Bidāyat al-mujtahid* (1–5) he expounds briefly the classical theory of jurisprudence, making clear its basic principle that all judgements of what is lawful have to be derived, directly or ultimately, from the texts of the Qurʾān and Traditions. Practical morality is known from the *sharīʿa*. In *Faṣl*, instead of stating the problem of the book directly in moral terms – 'is it right for Muslims to study philosophy?' – he prefers to state it in the language of *fiqh*, deriving the law (i.e. the practically right) from scripture:

The purpose of this treatise is to examine, from the standpoint of the study of the Law, whether the study of philosophy and logic is allowed by the Law, or prohibited, or commanded – either by way of recommendation or as obligatory (1.7–9).

Such language at first glance suggests an acceptance of the Shafiᶜite-Ashᶜarite 'command' theory of value, referred to above as 'theistic subjectivism', which Ibn Rushd vigorously opposed as a philosopher and theologian. But in fact his use of this language does not carry such an implication. Like the Muᶜtazilites in an earlier period, he thought of the *sharīᶜa* as a source of law, of divine origin, which reveals and commands to man *what is objectively right*. Thus there is no incompatibility between the assertions of Ibn Rushd the philosopher and Ibn Rushd the jurist. His own reconciliation of the two is made clear in the *Commentary on Plato's Republic* (II, vi, 4–5). After stating that the *sharīᶜa* of Islam prescribes for religious knowledge and practice, he says:

Its intention as regards this purpose is essentially the same as that of philosophy in respect of class and purpose.
Therefore some people are of opinion that these religious laws only follow ancient wisdom. It is obvious that Good and Evil, beneficial and harmful, beautiful and ugly are in the opinion of all these men something that exists by nature, not by convention. This means that everything that leads to the end is good and beautiful, whereas everything that impedes it is evil and ugly. This is evident from the nature of these laws and in particular our own law. Many people of our region hold this opinion about our own law.

It is clear enough that Ibn Rushd shares the opinion of these people.

(5) But why is it ever necessary to proceed through the *sharīᶜa* if man can have direct access to knowledge of the right through his reason? The need for the *sharīᶜa* is at least partly explained in the parable of the doctor and the Legislator in *Faṣl*. The doctor's aim is

to preserve the health and cure the diseases of all the people, by prescribing for them rules which can be commonly accepted...He is unable to make them all doctors, because a doctor is one who knows by demonstrative methods the things which preserve health and cure disease (22.9–13).

This view is stated again very clearly in *Tahāfut*:

In short, the religions are, according to the philosophers, obligatory, since they lead towards wisdom in a way universal to all human beings, for philosophy only leads a certain number of intelligent people to the knowledge of happiness[19] and they therefore have to learn wisdom, whereas religions seek the instruction of the masses generally (582.7–11).

So practical wisdom can be used effectively only by the wise; it is too weak in most people, who have to follow laws and rules given by a religion. Ibn Rushd adds that this majority includes the wise themselves when they are young, and that throughout their lives they should show respect for the teachings of their religion.

Does he go still further in justifying religion as a guide to morality? Do the Legislators, the prophets who found religions, have knowledge of moral truths not attainable even by the wise in their maturity who use practical reason? To give a full answer to this question would require a far-reaching study of Ibn Rushd's doctrine of prophecy, as well as of the Aristotelian doctrine of practical reason; this would take us beyond the scope of this article, and I shall content myself here with a few provisional remarks. One of the most significant passages for this question ocurs in the last section of *Tahāfut* where Ibn Rushd writes:

And never has wisdom (*al-ḥikma*) ceased among the inspired, i.e. the prophets, and therefore it is the truest of all sayings that every prophet is a sage (*ḥakīm*), but not every sage a prophet; the learned (*al-ʿulamāʾ*), however, are those of whom it is said that they are the heirs of the prophets (583.12–584.1).

This sentence asserts that prophets have wisdom, which must certainly include practical wisdom; but they have something more. What this is is stated soon afterwards:

Every religion exists through inspiration and is blended with reason. And he who holds that it is possible that there should exist a natural religion based on reason alone must admit that this religion must be less perfect than those which spring from reason and inspiration (584.3–6).

What, then, is the distinctive contribution of inspiration to moral knowledge, over and above what could be supplied by the practical reason of an intelligent and educated person? A part of the answer is found in *Faṣl* where Ibn Rushd lists three unique and miraculous properties of the more 'popular' religious *dicta* of the Qurʾān:

There exist none more completely persuasive and convincing to everyone than they (25.14–15).

[19] *taʿrif saʿādat baʿd an-nās al-ʿaqliyya* 'leads a certain number of people to the knowledge of intellectual happiness'?

This emphasizes their imaginative quality of expression and does not indicate any difference in content from what practical reason would provide.[20]

But a passage in *Manāhij* (100–1) seems to go much further, and to attribute to prophets a knowledge of the content of morality which is unattainable by ordinary intellectual methods. Ibn Rushd is discussing how the Qurʾān proves its miraculous and prophetic character, and he argues that the most fundamental way is that

The Laws (*ash-sharāʾiʿ*) which it includes on doctrine and practice are such as could not be acquired by learning (*bit-taʿallum*) but [only] by inspiration (*bil-waḥy*) (100.8–9).

For the knowledge of the right legislation can only be attained when the Lawgiver has acquired knowledge of God (on a basis of knowledge of the universe), of human happiness in the next life, the nature of the soul, and the actions and virtues which procure happiness, in their right proportions; and on top of all this he must know how much the masses should be told for their own happiness, and how they should be told it.

Thus we find all this determined in the scriptures. And all or most of this only becomes clear through inspiration, or else [in the remainder] its explanation through inspiration is superior [to a purely rational explanation] (101.3–5).

And all this, or most of it, cannot be grasped by learning (*taʿallum*), art (*ṣināʿa*) or rational wisdom (*ḥikma*). This [truth] can be understood for sure by whoever has practised the sciences – especially [with respect to] the making of divine Laws and the drafting of statutes (*waḍʿ ash-sharāʾiʿ wa taqrīr al-qawānīn*), and the indications of conditions in the next life (101.8–10).

Then he concludes that since the Qurʾān contains the whole of this knowledge in the most perfect form possible, it must be divinely inspired. As the final proof he adduces the supposed illiteracy of Muḥammad. What are we to make of this passage? Taken in isolation, it would have to be regarded as Ibn Rushd's real and final conviction. But in the light of the rest of his work there is reason for doubt, because it seems to say too much. For nearly all the subjects which he says can be known only through inspiration had in fact been studied thoroughly in his own philosophic and scientific works as well as those of the Greeks and other Muslim philosophers. Take psychology, for instance, which he describes here as 'the knowledge of what the soul is and of its substance' (100.20): it is hard indeed to believe that Ibn Rushd

[20] The other two properties are connected with the allegorical art of scripture, but this is only found in its doctrinal or homiletic passages. Its practical precepts are always made plain to everyone (*Faṣl*, 9.15–16).

thought this was better known or better explained through scripture than through philosophy. Bearing in mind, then, that *Manāhij* is an exoteric work, I shall have to leave this question in suspense. But enough reasons have been given previously to justify the usefulness of scripture to morality, in teaching morality effectively to the majority of people.

(6) What, in Ibn Rushd's view, was the function of the Islamic lawyer in the moral order? He wrote little on this question, either because he had no occasion to discuss it in his philosophical or legal works, or because he held views on it which if stated too plainly might have offended the *faqīhs*, who were his professional colleagues, and endangered his own career. But the *Commentary on Plato's Republic* contains a discussion which is very revealing (III, i, 6–9). First he declares that the true king of an ideal state must combine wisdom, intelligence, rhetoric, imagination and the military ability to conduct *jihād*, and must be free of physical defects. Here Ibn Rushd has combined the qualities of Plato's philosopher king with some of the traditional qualifications of a caliph, following Fārābi's idea of the identification of the philosopher, king, lawgiver and *imām*.[21] The wisdom of this ruler must clearly include practical reason if he is to fulfil his functions. Then he goes on:

> It also happens sometimes that the prince of this State will be one who does not attain this status, that is, the dignity of king, yet he is expert in the laws which the first [lawgiver] laid down, and possesses a [power of] good conjecture so as to deduce from them what the first did not expound for every single legal decision and every single lawcase. To this category of knowledge belongs the science called among us the art of jurisprudence.

He who can do this is 'the legal expert' (Heb. *dayān*, Ar. *faqīh*). This passage goes beyond interpretation of Plato, and should be understood as expressing Ibn Rushd's own opinion. It shows that he thought of *fiqh* as on a lower level than the wisdom of a philosopher king. It also indicates what the activity of the *faqīh* is: it is not the direct exercise of moral judgement (practical wisdom), but deduction of moral decisions from scripture. This is legal reasoning or legal analogy (*qiyās fiqhī*) (*Faṣl*, 3). It is justified at *Bidāyat al-mujtahid*, as against Zahirite condemnation of it, by the ordinary argument of classical Islamic jurisprudence, neatly stated as follows:

> But the indication of intellect supports its correctness, because occurrences [in the relations] between people are infinite [in variety], whereas texts, acts and decisions [of the Legislator] are finite, and it is impossible for something finite to correspond to something infinite (2–3).[22]

[21] Cf. also II, i, 6. But Teicher regards this paragraph as part of a gloss (Review of Rosenthal, p. 191).

[22] Cf. Shahrastānī, *Kitāb al-milal wa n-niḥal*, ed. M. Badran (Cairo, 1954), I, 180.

To perform this operation expertly is, of course, a respectable profession. Yet for Ibn Rushd it must be no more than an employment of dialectical, not demonstrative reasoning, in the Aristotelian senses; for it works from commonly accepted premises, not from principles of reason.

He himself could work sincerely as a *qāḍī*, because he believed in the worth of the *sharīʿa* as a guide to practice for most people and most cases. If ever he thought that in his work he was employing practical reason, not mediated by the *sharīʿa*, he did not proclaim this operation which would have appeared to most Muslims as an arrogation of the right to free opinion (*ijtihād ar-raʾy*), such as had long ago been condemned by all schools of law. To announce it would have aroused hostility on the part of his fellow lawyers and discredited philosophers in Andalus. And apart from considerations of prudence it would also have been morally wrong, in his eyes, because it would have set a dangerous example and encouraged other lawyers to follow one who did not have the necessary 'demonstrative' education and abilities. We do not hear of attacks on Ibn Rushd's legal career, but only on his opinions on matters of religious doctrine. It is therefore safe to assume that he kept to himself his views on practical wisdom in law, or hinted at them quietly in commentaries, where they would be read only by earnest students of Plato and Aristotle.

An indication of how he may have thought practical reason could be used in legal decisions is found in the *Commentary on Aristotle's Nicomachean Ethics*, 248r (on Book v, ch. 10). He quotes Aristotle's definition of the equitable as 'a correction of law where it is defective owing to its generality', and illustrates this from the Islamic law of *jihād*. It is stated as a general injunction to make war on all non-Muslim nations at all times. But the Muslims have suffered much harm from taking it thus generally. 'This happened from their ignorance of the intention of the Legislator, and for this reason it should be stated that peace is preferable [as a rule], and war only sometimes.' Such correction of positive law by equity implies the existence of a natural right, to which the Legislator conformed, and by our direct knowledge of which we may interpret his intentions.[23] This operation would be equivalent to the

[23] L. Strauss, *Natural right and history* (Chicago, 1953), attributes to Ibn Rushd (243v.) an interpretation of Aristotle, *Eth. Nic.*, v, 7, which 'implies the denial of natural right proper' (p. 159). According to Averroes, Aristotle understands by natural right 'legal natural right' (p. 158). Cf. also Strauss's *Persecution and the art of writing* (Glencoe, Illinois, 1952), 97, n. 5. But the chapter in Aristotle is about *political* right or justice (*politikou dikaiou*), i.e. justice as embodied in the laws of states. See H. H. Joachim, *Commentary on the Nicomachean Ethics* (Oxford, 1951), pp. 153–6. Ibn Rushd therefore merely makes the sound observation that in spite of its relative invariability even the 'natural' (*phusikon*) kind of political justice is only quasi-natural because it is still man-made. '*lex autem non naturalis, genere quidem quasi naturalis est, et non est in ea diversitas*' (243v). The question is about a *jus gentium*. Natural right, in

'judgement of public interest' (*istiṣlāh*) which was printed in the Malikite legal traditions. But as far as I know Ibn Rushd never made this equation, which would have been theoretically most enlightening, if he had attempted in writing to harmonize Islamic law with philosophical ethics, as he harmonized Islamic doctrine with natural philosophy, psychology and metaphysics.[24]

the sense of objective moral right independent of laws, is not discussed here at all, either by Aristotle or by Ibn Rushd.

The interpretation of Aristotle as a conventionalist would indeed be surprising in Ibn Rushd (1) because he must have known from other passages, such as the accounts of the other virtues, that Aristotle believed in natural right, and (2) because Ibn Rushd himself believed in it, as shown above, and would have been much agitated at finding a contrary view in Aristotle.

[24] See R. Brunschvig, 'Averroes juriste', *Études d'orientalisme dediées à la memoire de Lévi-Provençal* (Paris, 1962), I, 35–68. This review of Ibn Rushd's jurisprudence, based on *Bidāyat al-mujtahid*, shows him as conservative in his principles, with a preference for basing Islamic law on Traditions. It does not reveal any interest in applying the principle of *istiṣlāh* to the solution of legal problems, but merely allows a modest freedom of choice between different schools in arriving at sensible and often liberal conclusions.

16

COMBINATIONS OF REASON AND TRADITION IN ISLAMIC ETHICS

Standards of conduct and character in any society are derived from several sources: from religious prescription, custom, model individuals such as prophets, parents and friends; from literature; finally from the value decisions of everyone in judging his own behaviour and that of others in the past and present, and in prescribing for himself and others in the future. Amid this variety, no accurate answer can be given to the question: to what extent were the ideals of classical Islamic society derived from specifically Islamic sources – the Qurʾān and Traditions as interpreted by Muslim scholars? But at least it is certain that these sources were of predominant importance in all Muslim countries until the nineteenth century and still prevail in the more conservative countries and in all rural areas. This was and is inevitable wherever the basic education of children is the study of the Qurʾān, with its well defined ethical precepts and attitudes to life on earth.

So it will be worth our while to review briefly the norms emphasized by the scripture of Islam, as a prelude to the main topic of this paper, which will be the methods by which norms have been thought to be properly learned by the Muslim community; in other words the methods of ethics according to Muslim thinkers.

The main virtues taught by the Qurʾān were: piety, i.e. humble obedience and fear of God; honesty in dealings; justice and avoidance of all wrongdoing; benevolence; gratitude to God and to human benefactors; and chastity. Love of God and fellow men is rarely mentioned explicitly, but is really implied by the other virtues. Performance of the ritual duties and legal obligations mentioned in the Qurʾān is required of every individual, with exceptions made for circumstances of hardship. These duties include payment of alms at 10 per cent of income (*zakat*), which is practically a tax for welfare purposes of the community. Then there is a collective duty of the community to defend itself when it is attacked, by 'holy war; (*jihād*). Non-Muslim subjects are to be governed according to certain principles; the main group are Christians and Jews, the 'People of the Book', who should be protected and tolerated in the practice of their religions, but subjected to discrimination in taxation, armed service and the highest government positions.

The Qurʾān's prescriptions were supplemented by the far more extensive Traditions (*ḥadīth*), recording the sayings and way of life (*sunna*) of Muḥammad and to a smaller extent of his Companions. These Traditions were recorded and criticized diligently. With a few exceptions they conform to the norms of the Qurʾān.

But even the Qurʾān and Traditions together could not easily cover every situation that might arise, especially after the Muslim empire extended beyond Arabia and required rules for urban life, commerce and government in the advanced countries of the former Sassanid empire of Iran and the former Byzantine provinces of Syria and Egypt.

The primary question for ethical theology was therefore: what methods is man authorized to use (if he is *ever* authorized) to decide issues that appear to go beyond anything mentioned in revelation or Traditions? This question first arose among *qāḍīs* and provincial governors, who were faced with a practical necessity to make justifiable legal verdicts, which could be defended against accusations of making arbitrary decisions. Notice that the question as I have put it is already within the framework of religious thought, since it refers to *authorization* of decisions, and authorization implies an authority, which in Sunnite Islam can only be the Qurʾān of God and the Traditions of His prophet, Muḥammad. Thus even rationalist theologians (the Muʿtazilites) were obliged to justify their advocacy of reason as derived from religion, or at least not contradicting it. (This last condition was binding on all ethical theories, including those of philosophers.)

So I have formulated the question of *the relation of ethics to religion* in Islamic terms. In Arabic, the debate concerned the use of *naql* (transmitted knowledge, from revelation and Traditions) and *ʿaql* (reason). Five positions can be distinguished.

(1) Revelation and independent reason. This position may be subdivided into two, with different emphases.

(*a*) Revelation supplemented by independent reason. From an early date, lawyers relied on the Qurʾān and Traditions whenever they gave clear guidance. When these sources failed, however, they felt free to use judgements of equity. This practice was followed in ʿIrāq, and later formulated by the jurists Abū Ḥanīfa and Mālik, whose authority gave legitimacy in their schools to the use of independent opinion (*ijtihād ar-raʾy*) under certain conditions.

(*b*) Independent reason supplemented by revelation. Muʿtazilite theologians looked at the broader field of ethical judgements and concluded that any sane person knows by reason that it is evil to harm another person (except as deserved punishment), to lie, murder, steal, etc., and he knows his obligations in general in the same way. An obligatory act is defined as one for which an agent deserves blame for not doing it. An evil act is one for which an agent deserves blame for doing it. Since everyone rational can know the rules of right action, everyone is responsible and therefore justly rewarded and punished by God in the next life, even if he lived before Islam or otherwise has had no access to scripture.

God has delegated to men the power to choose their acts and to do what they have chosen. This is also necessary if God's rewards and punishment are to be just.

Rational knowledge of ethical principles is supplemented in detail by the *sharīʿa*.

(2) Revelation supplemented by dependent reason. This became the majority opinion of the Sunnites; it is indicated by the name they adopted for themselves, 'the party of custom' (of the Prophet) (*ahl as-sunna*). We may call them 'conservatives'. In the field of law, this view was elaborated thoroughly in the writings of the great jurist Shāfiʿī (d. 820). The impetus came from a rejection of human opinion in making legal decisions, as being an arbitrary lack of method and a failure to make the law fully Islamic, fully a *sharīʿa* system of law. What Shāfiʿi did was in the first place to make more use of the Traditions as a valid source of law, because these Traditions were the record of the *sunna*. Then he extended the range of coverage of scripture and Traditions by supporting the method of analogy, which could apply a prescription mentioned in scripture or Traditions for one kind of case to similar cases with the same relevant characteristics. This was a method of reason in the service of scripture, thus 'dependent'. (He was lukewarm towards the fourth principle of the *sharīʿa*, consensus of the jurists.)

Shāfiʿī's theory of Islamic jurisprudence was generally accepted by Sunnite lawyers, except for the Hanbalites and another school to be mentioned under the next heading.

Moreover, his theory was backed by theologians of similar outlook, who later created a kind of orthodoxy in Sunnite theology. There were predecessors of Ashʿarī (870–915) but it was he who put together conservative ideas in a wide-ranging theological system. The core of Ashʿarī's creed was that Muslims must follow the guidance of scripture closely in all matters of religious relevance. Ethical guidance in every sphere of life would have to remain within the limits set by Shāfiʿī for legal decisions. This is necessary because the Qurʾān stresses its own rôle as the supreme guide to human conduct, declaring that without guidance by God man gets lost and wanders in a maze of fancies and desires. But Ashʿarī added an ontological support for this ethical epistemology, when he argued that right conduct has no meaning beyond conduct commanded or recommended by God. This ethical voluntarism served another purpose, as we shall soon see. But the immediate purpose was to remove any limits on divine omnipotence which would be set by objective standards of value.

Ashʿarī also followed the Qurʾān in its emphasis on predestination, although he made an effort to reconcile it with man's power to choose his own acts, a fact which is also made clear in the Qurʾān. Ultimately, however, he gave the last word to predestination, when he wrote that men become believers by the grace of God and unbelievers due to His withholding of grace from them. This position of course raises the problem of theodicy in an acute form, since God's justice is called into question by His assigning to Hell people whom He had preordained to be sinners. To this challenge Ashʿarī answered by arguing that since injustice means nothing but disobedience to a divine law, and since God is not subject to any law, therefore He can never be unjust.

The proper answer to this piece of sophistry had to be to insist that 'injustice' has an objective meaning in every human language, to work out what this meaning is and then to apply it to the acts of God. The Muʿtazilites tried to define the terms of ethics in objective senses, and to allow man freedom of choice, thus solving the problem of theodicy in a straightforward manner. But the Ashʿarites won the battle for recognition by rulers and the learned class, for reasons not based on intellectual merit, in my opinion. The turning point came in the early eleventh century, when a Sunnite caliph at Baghdād issued a creed which every scholar had to accept, if he was to continue in his profession. The Muʿtazilites could not accept this creed and had to stop teaching in public.

(3) Revelation alone. This was the most conservative position, adopted by Ibn Ḥanbal (d. 855) and his school, also by the Zahirites (believers in the apparent meaning of the Qurʾān, the *ẓāhir*). Ibn Ḥanbal made a very large collection of Traditions to supplement revelation. Another interesting method of covering more ground without the use of analogy was the doctrine of 'permission to do anything not prohibited', which revealed a liberal side of Hanbalism. Both Hanbalites and Zahirites rejected allegorical interpretations of scripture. But even they had to resort to a doctrine of 'implications' of scripture (*mafhūm*). Ibn Ḥazm of Córdoba (994–1064), worked out the doctrine in the sphere of theology in a polemical spirit. But the Zahirite school faded out soon after his time. The Hanbalite school survived and produced some notable thinkers such as Ibn Taymiyya of Damascus (1263–1328). But they too declined, until the eighteenth century when they were revived in Arabia by the Wahhābī revolution, backed by the Saʿūdī dynasty which still rules Arabia. Such a conservative movement of thought and practice was

natural for Arabians, who until recently lived in conditions closest to those of Muḥammad's time. There are some strains in their present circumstances of great wealth, high technology and international trade and diplomacy. But they, like the Japanese and Chinese peoples, have their own ideas about how their assets should be channelled, and it will be interesting to see how they develop their society.

(4) Revelation extended by *imāms*. This was the Shiʿite position, that there were seven (or twelve) *imāms* descended from ʿAlī, who were infallible and developed the divine law in a catholic style. Unfortunately they went into hiding after the seventh (or the twelfth), but they are due to re-emerge before the end of the world. And their teachings are being developed by later scholars or *mujtahids*, who to this day have far more prestige and authority in Iran than Sunnite lawyers and scholars in other countries. Shiʿism has an intense emotional power for believers, going back to the martyrdom of Ḥusayn b. ʿAlī, the third *imām*. This emotion helps to explain the force of the recent Islamic revolution in Iran, which took the West by surprise, as well as many Iranians with western education and life-styles.

(5) Reason is prior to revelation. This description fits the position of the few but influential Muslim philosophers, with some qualification. It was most boldly expressed by Fārābī (*c.* 870–950), who argued that philosophy is prior to religion both temporally and logically: temporally prior, because he takes the beginning of philosophy back to ancient Egypt and Babylon, before the prophets Abraham and Moses; and logically prior, because all the truths of religion had first to be understood and declared in a rational way, before they could be taken up by prophets. The function of prophets is to express these truths in imaginative language which could appeal to ordinary people. Thus he set up two classes of people: an intellectual élite capable of understanding the demonstrative philosophies of Plato and Aristotle, which he took to be scientific, and the mass of ordinary people who could only be persuaded of the truths of the universe by prophets, who would have understood philosophy but would find it useless and even harmful to try to teach it to the masses.

These ideas were adopted by Ibn Sīnā (980–1035) with differences in emphasis, and by Ibn Rushd (1126–98), who softened them somewhat by asserting that religion should be a part of everyone's moral education and that only after it should anyone study philosophy, if he is capable of understanding it. Religion and philosophy teach the same truths in different ways; there is no 'double truth' in Ibn Rushd's thought. He expresses admiration for the unique way in which the Qurʾān appeals simultaneously to people with different levels of understanding. He takes more pains than Fārābī and Ibn Sīnā to emphasize his belief in Islam, partly because he was himself an Islamic qāḍī and jurist and partly because he lived later than

Ghazālī (1058–1111), who had made powerful attacks on the earlier Muslim philosophers for their supposed heretical and infidel metaphysics.

In ethics the philosophers followed the main line of Plato and Aristotle in upholding the objectivity of values. It was Ibn Rushd who treated ethics most seriously. With great perception he grasped the common subjectivism of the ancient Greek sophists and the Ashʿarites, with all the difference in the subjects who were said to decree values – in one case the rulers of cities, in the other case God. He exclaims 'All these are views like those of Protagoras!' His bold attacks finally put him in trouble with the lawyers and theologians of Córdoba, and even his Almohad patron 'the Prince of the Muslims' could not save him from a trial (1195) in which he and other scientists were condemned to exile for a few years as heretics and even infidels.

Soon after the life of Ibn Rushd philosophy faded away in the western half of Islam, except for Ibn Khaldūn of Tunis (1332–1406), who was more of a social scientist in quite a modern sense and did not develop a distinctive theory of ethics. In the east, philosophy survived in Shiʿite Iran as a kind of mystical wisdom; this tradition is still alive. It produced some discriminating metaphysics, such as that of Mullā Ṣadrā (1571–1640) on the well worn problem of essence and existence.

So, with the diminution of the other theories of ethics, the one that held the field in the later centuries of classical Sunnite Islam was the second described above, revelation supplemented by dependent reason, which was the mainline tradition of Shafiʿism and Ashʿarism and was supported by the powerful and continually influential writings of Ghazālī.

Now we may ask a final question: Did the predominance of this ethical voluntarism make any difference to the practical attitudes of Muslims in all those past centuries? It is hard to answer with confidence such a broad question of fact, but I shall venture an answer. Ethical voluntarism puts the determination of ethical questions firmly in the hands of experts in the interpretation of the *sharīʿa*, which was supposed to give guidance in every sphere of practical life. These experts were the *ʿulamāʾ*, the professional Islamic scholars who included the staffs of the *madrasas*, mosque preachers, qāḍīs, muftīs and theoretical jurists. Private lay people were discouraged by these tendencies as well as by autocratic sultans from proposing reforms in a state or organizing secular groups such as our labour unions, charitable organizations and especially political parties.

Thus all *peaceful* changes in society had to be initiated from the top, by the heads of state, who most times were satisfied with the way things were. The only other path to change was through revolutionary movements. But the only forces strong enough to gather supporters were religious leaders, claiming to be *mahdīs* bringing in a golden age. A weak head of a dynasty would be overthrown by one of these leaders, such as the Safavids in Iran or Ibn Tümart in the Maghrib with the help of the Almohad dynasty. But before long the dynasty would become an autocratic régime lacking any genuine religious inspiration, and nothing would have changed in the life of the people. The pattern can be observed today in the recent political upheaval in Iran, with disastrous effects for its suffering people, who backed Imām Khomeini in the hope of a better life on earth, not for martyrdom in a religious war.

But in spite of the resurgence of fundamentalism in several Muslim countries, I believe it is bound to fail, in competition with the many good things offered by modern life in a more relaxed society: freedom above all – for women to choose their husbands and their dress, to be able to drive cars and go out without veils, for minorities not to suffer discrimination or persecution, for boys and girls to attend the same schools and colleges, for everyone to listen to the music they like best, to be able to criticize the government and religious leaders without fear of reprisals, unlawful detention or torture; freedom to lend and borrow money with interest without having to resort to legal fictions (*ḥiyal*) – and so I could prolong this sentence endlessly.

There are still strong forces of liberalism in many Muslim countries: Egypt, Turkey, Jordan, Tunisia, Kuwait, probably in Malaysia. But they lack a firm theoretical grounding in Islamic thought. A few Muslim thinkers such as Fazlur Rahman are urging their co-religionists to understand the spirit of the Qurʾān as a whole before trying to interpret isolated passages. If this revelation was meant to endure as guidance for man as long as he remains on this earth, then it must be adaptable to changing conditions of life and the rethinking of many values. Otherwise it will become more and more obsolete, and will eventually cease to inspire belief in the religion. Fundamentalism and even Sunnite conservatism are attempts to cling to the safety of the past, which can have only temporary success. If I had a choice of what intellectual path Muslims should follow – a choice which I do not have, looking at Islam from outside – I would start over again at the points where the early jurists and the Muʿtazilites left off, and work to develop a system of Islamic law which would openly make use of judgements of equity and public interest, and a system of ethical theology which would encourage judgements of right and wrong by the human mind, without having to look to scripture at every step. The Muʿtazilites were correct in their doctrine that we can make objective value judgements, even if their particular theory of ethics had weaknesses, which would have to be revised by modern ethical philosophers and theologians. So I think this is the best way for Muslims to revive Islam, and I wish them success in a formidable task.

SELECT BIBLIOGRAPHY OF SOURCES ON CLASSICAL ISLAMIC ETHICS, IN ARABIC AND MODERN TRANSLATIONS

ᶜAbd al-Jabbār:

al-Mughnī fī abwāb at-tawḥīd wa l-ᶜadl, ed. I. Madkour et al. (Cairo, 1962ff.), especially vols. VI, i and ii, XI–XIV and XVII.

al-Uṣūl al-khamsa, ed. D. Gimaret in 'Les *Uṣūl al-Ḫamsa* du qāḍī ᶜAbd al-Gabbār et leurs commentaires', *Annales Islamologiques*, 15 (1979), 79–96. (See also 'Mānkdīm'.)

Āmidī, al-, Sayf ad-Dīn:

al-Iḥkām fī uṣūl al-aḥkām, 3 vols. (Cairo, 1347 h./1928).

Ashᶜarī, al-:

al Ibāna ᶜan uṣūl ad-diyāna (Cairo, 1348 h./1929). Eng. trans. W. C. Klein (New Haven, 1940).

al-Lumaᶜ fī r-radd ᶜalā ahl az-zaygh wa l-bidaᶜ, ed. and Eng. trans. R. J. McCarthy, *The Theology of al-Ashᶜarī* (Beirut, 1953).

Maqālāt al-Islāmiyyīn wa ikhtilāf al-muṣullīn, ed. H. Ritter, 2 vols. (Istanbul, 1929–30) and ed. A. A. ᶜAbd al-Hamid, 2 vols. (Cairo, 1369–73 h./1950–4).

Fārābī, al:

Fī mabādiᵓ arā ahl al-madīna al-fāḍila, ed. and English trans. R. Walzer, *Al-Farabi on the perfect state: Abu Nasr al-Farabi's 'The Principles of the views of the citizens of the best state'* (Oxford, 1981). French trans. R. P. Jaussen, Y. Karam and J. Chlala, *Al-Fārābī: Les idées des habitants de la cité vertueuse* (Cairo, 1949). Spanish trans. M. Alonso, '"Al-Madīna al-fāḍila" de Abū Naṣr al-Fārābī', *Al-Andalus*, 26 (1961), 337–88 and 27 (1962), 181–227. German trans. F. Dieterici, *Der Musterstaat von Alfārābī* (Leiden, 1900).

Ghazālī, al-:

Iḥyāᵓ ᶜulūm ad-dīn, ᶜIrāqī edition, 16 vols. (Cairo, 1356–7 h./1937–9). Book i, English trans. N. Faris, *The Book of knowledge* (Lahore, 1962). Book ii, trans. Faris, *The Foundations of the articles of faith* (Lahore, 1963). German translations of Books ii, xii, xiv, xxxvii, L. Bauer (Halle, 1912–22). Book xix, French L. Bercher, *L'obligation d'ordonner le bien et d'interdire le mal* (Tunis, 1961). Other partial translations in English, French and German.

(Incorporated into *Iḥyāᵓ*, Book ii): *ar-Risāla al-Qudsiyya*, ed. and Eng. trans. A. L. Tibawi, *Al-Ghazālī's tract on dogmatic theology* (London, 1965).

al-Iqtiṣād fī l-iᶜtiqād, ed. I. A. Çubukçu and H. Atay (Ankara, 1962). Spanish trans. M. Asín Palacios, *El justo medio en la creencia* (Madrid, 1929).

Mīzān al-ʿamal, ed. M. S. Kurdī and M. S. Nuʿaymī (Cairo, 1328 h./1909–10). French trans. H. Hachem, *Critère de l'action* (Paris, 1945).

al-Munqidh min aḍ-ḍalāl, ed. J. Saliba and K. ʿAyyad, 7th printing (Beirut, 1967); ed. ʿA. H. Mahmud, 6th printing (Cairo, 1388 h./1968). Ed. and French trans. F. Jabre, *Erreur et déliverance* (Beirut, 1939). Eng. trans. R. J. McCarthy, *Freedom and fulfillment* (Boston, 1980): based on Istanbul, Sehid Ali Paşa MS. 1712, dated 509 h./1115–16.

al-Mustaṣfā min 'ilm al-Uṣūl (Cairo: Tijariyya Press, 1356 h./1937).

Ḥillī, al-:

al-Bāb al-hādī ʿashar (Meshed?, 1320 h./1902). Eng. trans. W. McE. Miller, with commentary by Miqdād-i-Fādil al-Ḥillī (London, 1958).

Ibn Abi d-Dunyā:

Makārim al akhlāq, ed. J. A. Bellamy, *The noble qualities of character* (Wiesbaden, 1973).

Ibn Ḥazm:

al-Fiṣal fi l-milal wa l-ahwāʾ wa n-niḥal, with Shahrastānī, *al-Milal wa n-niḥal* in the margin, 5 vols. (Cairo, 1308–21 h./1890–1903); re-edition, 5 vols. in 2 (Baghdād, 1960). Spanish trans., almost complete, M. Asín Palacios, *Abenházam de Córdoba y su historia critica de las ideas religiosas*, 5 vols. (Madrid, 1927–32).

al-Iḥkām fī uṣūl al-aḥkām, ed. A. M. Shakir, 8 parts in 2 vols. (Cairo, 1346–7 h./1927–8).

Mudāwāt an-nufūs or *Kitāb al-akhlāq wa s-siyar*, ed. and French trans. N. Tomiche (Beirut, 1961). Spanish trans. M. Asín Palacios, *Los caracteres y la conducta, tratado de moral práctica por Abenházam de Córdoba* (Madrid, 1916).

Mulakhkhaṣ Ibṭāl al-qiyās wa l-istiḥsān wa t-taqlīd wa t-taʿlīl, ed. S. al-Afghānī (Damascus, 1960).

Ṭawq al-ḥamāma, ed. and French trans. L. Bercher, *Le Collier du pigeon: ou de l'amour et des amants* (Algiers, 1949). Ed. H. K. Sayrafi (Cairo, 1950). Ed. F. Saʿd (Beirut, 1972). English trans. A. J. Arberry, *The Ring of the dove* (London, 1953). German trans. W. Weisweiler (Leiden, 1941). Italian trans. F. Gabrieli (Bari, 1949). Spanish trans. E. García Gómez, *El Collar de la paloma* (Madrid, 1952). Russian trans. A. Salie (Moscow–Leningrad, 1933).

Ibn al-Murtaḍā:

Ṭabaqāt al-Muʿtazila, ed. S. Diwald-Wilzer, *Die Klassen der Muʿtaziliten* (Wiesbaden, 1961).

Ibn Rushd:

Kitāb al-kashf ʿan manāhij al-adilla fī ʿaqā'id al-milla, ed. M. J. Müller, in *Philosophie und Theologie von Averroes: thalāth rasāʾil* (Munich, 1859). German trans. M. J. Müller, in *Die Philosophie und Theologie von Averroes* (Munich, 1875). Ed. M. Qasim (Cairo, 1955). Spanish trans. M. Alonso in *Teología de Averroes* (Madrid–Granada, 1947).

Ibn Sīnā:

ash-Shifā': Ilāhiyyāt, II, ed. I. Madkour, M. Y. Musa, S. Dunya and S. Zayed (Cairo, 1960), book ix.

al-Ishārāt wa t-tanbīhāt, ed. J. Forget (Leiden, 1892). Ed. S. Dunya, with commentary by Naṣīr ad-Dīn aṭ-Ṭūsī (Cairo, 1379 h./1960). French trans. A.-M. Goichon, *Livre des Directives et remarques* (Beirut–Paris, 1951). English trans. S. Inati *Remarks and Admonitions* (Toronto, 1984).

Risāla fī sirr al-qadar, ed. and English trans. G. F. Hourani, 'Ibn Sīnā's "Essay on the secret of destiny"', *Bulletin of the School of Oriental and African Studies*, 39 (1966), 25–48.

Ibn Taymiyya:

Maʿārij al-wuṣūl ilā maʿrifat anna uṣūl ad-dīn wa furūʾahu qad bayyanahā r-rasūl (Cairo, 1318 h./1900). French trans. H. Laoust, *Contribution à une étude de la méthodologie canonique de Taḳī-d-dīn Aḥmad b. Taimīya* (Cairo, 1939).

Juwaynī, al-:

al-Irshād ilā qawāṭiʿ al-adilla fī uṣūl al-iʿtiqād, ed. M. Y. Musa and ʿA. ʿA. ʿAbd al-Hamid (Cairo, 1369 h./1950). Ed. and partial French trans. J. D. Luciani (Paris, 1938).

Mānkdīm:

Taʿlīq sharḥ al-uṣūl al-khamsa li qāḍi l-quḍāt ʿAbd al-Jabbār, ed. ʿA. K. ʿUthman (Cairo, 1384 h./1965), entitled *Sharḥ al-uṣūl al-khamsa li-qāḍi l-quḍāt 'Abd al-Jabbār b. Aḥmad*. (See the article of D. Gimaret mentioned under 'ʿAbd al-Jabbār'.)

Miskawayh:

Tahdhīb al-akhlāq, ed. C. Zurayk (Beirut, 1966). English trans. C. Zurayk, *The Refinement of character* (Beirut, 1968).

Qurʾān, al-:

al-Qurʾān al-karīm (Cairo, 1344 h./1924). Ed. G. Flügel, *Corani textus arabicus* (Leipzig, 1834). English trans. A. J. Arberry, *The Koran interpreted*, 2 vols. (London and New York, 1955). English trans. M. M. Pickthall, *The Meaning of the glorious Koran* (London and New York, 1930); with Arabic text opposite, *The glorious Koran* (London and Albany, 1976). French trans. R. Blachère, *Le Coran*, vols. II and III (Paris, 1949–51). German trans. R. Paret, *Der Koran: Übersetzung* (Stuttgart, 1962).

Rāzī, al-, Abū Bakr Muḥammad b. Zakariyya:

Rhagensis (Razis) Opera philosophica, fragmentaque quae supersunt, vol. I, ed. P. Kraus (Cairo, 1939), containing *aṭ-Ṭibb ar-rūḥānī*, pp. 1–96. English trans. A. J. Arberry, *The Spiritual physick of Rhazes* (London, 1950).

Shāfiʿī, ash-:

ar-Risāla, ed. A. M. Shakir (Cairo, 1359 h./1940). English trans. M. Khadduri, *Islamic jurisprudence: Shāfiʿī's Risāla* (Baltimore, Md., 1961).

Kitāb al-Umm, 7 vols. (Bulaq, 1321–25 h./1903–7): Treatise vii, *Kitāb Ibṭāl al-istiḥsān*.

Shahrastānī, ash-:

al-Milal wa n-niḥal, 2 vols., ed. M. F. Badran (Cairo, 1375 h./1956), I, 51. German trans. T. Haarbrücker, *Schahrastani's Religionspartheien und Philosophen-Schulen* (Halle, 1850–1).

Nihāyat al-aqdām fī ʿilm al-kalām, ed. and English summary A. Guillaume, *The Summa Philosophiae of al-Shahrastānī* (London, 1934).

Traditions:

Bukhāri, al-: *al-Jāmi' aṣ-ṣaḥīḥ*, ed. M. L. Krehl and T. W. Juynboll, *Le Recueil des traditions mahométanes*, 4 vols. (Leiden, 1862–1908). French trans. A. Houdas and W. Marçais, *El-Bokhari, Les Traditions islamiques*, 4 vols. (Paris, 1903–14). M. Ali, *A Manual of hadith* (Lahore; M. Dost Mohammad, no date). (Select Traditions in Arabic and facing English.)

Ṭūsī, aṭ:

Akhlāq-i Nāṣirī (Persian) (Lahore: University of Punjab, 1952). English trans. G. M. Wickens, *The Nasirean Ethics by Naṣīr ad-Dīn Ṭūsī* (London, 1964).

INDEX

References which occur very frequently (e.g. to Islam, philosophy, the Qurʾān, etc.) have not been included here.